EARLY C

LOUDOUN COUNTY, VIRGINIA

1745-1800

Marty Hiatt

Willow Bend Books
Westminster, Maryland
2000

Willow Bend Books
65 East Main Street
Westminster, Maryland 21157-5026
1-800-876-6103

Source books, early maps, CDs—Worldwide

For our listing of thousands of titles offered
by hundreds of publishers see our website
<www.WillowBend.net>

Visit our retail store

Reprinted: 2000 by Willow Bend Books

International Standard Book Number: 1-58549-368-6

Printed in the United States of America

CONTENTS

INTRODUCTION

Religious congregations began meeting in this area long before Loudoun County was established. The earliest denominations were Anglican, Reformed, Society of Friends, Lutheran, Baptist, Methodist and Presbyterian.

The Anglican church was established as the state church of Virginia during colonial times. When Loudoun County was formed, in 1757, all residents were under the jurisdiction of Cameron Parish. As the population increased, Shelburne Parish was formed from Cameron in 1770. People living north and west of Goose Creek were then cared for by the Shelburne Parish vestry.

Unfortunately, there are no known extant records for Cameron Parish. Neither is the Shelburne Parish register extant. However, the minutes of the vestry exist from 1771-1805. The minutes discuss church business, selection of ministers, construction of buildings, care of the sick and poor, and other concerns of the members.

The Society of Friends was an early religious group in the region. Fairfax Monthly Meeting was established in 1745, made up of Monocacy Preparative Meeting of Frederick County, Maryland and Fairfax Preparative Meeting. The monthly meeting met at alternately at the two sites, Fairfax (Waterford) and Monocacy. At that time the Waterford region was a part of Fairfax County, hence the name Fairfax Monthly Meeting. Later meetings at the middle branch of Goose Creek (winter season), another at the house of Jacob Janney, Jr. and another at William Mead's. In 1759 the meeting house at Monocacy burned down, never to be rebuilt. Pipe Creek, near Union Bridge, Maryland, and Bush Creek, near New Market, Maryland were formed as additional meetings of Fairfax Monthly Meeting. Pipe Creek and Bush Creek formed as Pipe Creek Monthly Meeting in 1776. Potts Meeting at the Gap was settled in 1759 with Goose Creek coming into being as a winter meeting in 1746 and South Fork Meeting formed a few years later, all as a part of Fairfax Monthly Meeting. Goose Creek was established as a monthly meeting in 1785 with subordinate meetings at South Fork and Goose Creek. South Fork was discontinued in 1868. Fairfax Monthly Meeting was discontinued in 1929.

At the same time Quakers were moving into this fertile area, German Protestants were crossing over the Potomac River from Frederick County, Maryland. They began migrating in the 1730s and came in such numbers that the northern section of Loudoun County became known as "The German Settlement." The New Jerusalem congregation was organized in 1765. A log church and a schoolhouse were built. A stone church was build in 1802. The register begins in 1784 and contains baptisms, communicants, marriages and deaths (beginning in 1785). Lutheran pastors included Samuel Schwerdtfeger (1765-1768) and Andrew Krug (1771 - 1790s). There are many others who served.

Although some contend that German Reformed congregations may have been organized as early as 1733 the first reliable evidence of an organized congregation in Loudoun County appears in 1764. Only the records from 1789 are extant. Reformed ministers include Charles Lange, Frederick Henop and Henry Giese. It should be noted, that during the earliest years, neither of these German congregations had a full-time minister, so you will notice a cross-over of family names between the Lutheran and Reformed churches.

The author wishes to thank Margaret Myers, of Frederick, Maryland, for sharing her translation of the Reformed baptisms. Three translations of German records for both churches were compared to compile information for this publication.

Several Baptist congregations began meeting during the days of colonial Virginia. Records remain for the Ketoctin, Frying Pan, or Frying Pan Spring, and North Fork Baptist churches. A fire destroyed the early records of Little River Baptist Church, and the minutes from New Valley church have not been found. Ketoctin Baptist Church was constituted October 8, 1751. The minute book covers the period, 1776-1890. The minute books for North Fork Primitive Baptist Church begin in 1784. Frying Pan Baptist Church was constituted May 15, 1791. It was aligned with the Old School Baptists. The surviving minute book covers 1791 - 1828.

The author extends appreciation to Elsie Payne, of Hamilton, Virginia, for allowing access to her copy of the North Fork records.

The first Methodist Church in Virginia was built in Leesburg, shortly after 1766 when land was conveyed for a meeting house and graveyard. Today, the only records of its members come from headstones in the graveyard. Sadly, the same is true of the earliest Presbyterian congregation. Written records for the Leesburg Presbyterian church date from 1804, even though it was known to have been established prior to 1800.

This book is a compilation of abstracts of the records, not ver batim transcriptions, from church records of Loudoun County, known to have survived through 1800.

Marty Hiatt, C.G.R.S.
Lovettsville, Virginia
1995

Fairfax Monthly Meeting. Register (1722), marriages (1751), removals (1783), minutes (1746) and women's minutes (1745). Originals at Friends Historical Library, Swarthmore College, Swarthmore, PA. Microfilm copies available through inter-library loan from Maryland State Archives, Annapolis.

Goose Creek Monthly Meeting. Register (1732), marriages (1786), removals (1786), minutes (1786), minutes - rough (1789), women's minutes (1785). Originals at Maryland State Archives (special collections). Microfilm copies available through inter-library loan from Maryland State Archives, Annapolis.

New Jerusalem Luther Church. Baptisms (1784), marriages (1784) and burials (1785). Microfilm copies may be borrowed through LDS Family History Centers.

Reformed Church of Loudoun (now St. James U.C.C.). Baptisms (1789). Originals are held at the Evangelical and Reformed Historical Society, Lancaster, PA. Microfilm may be borrowed through LDS Family History Centers.

Frying Pan Baptist Church. Minutes (1791). Originals are held at the Virginia State Library. Microfilm copies are available on loan through the Virginia State Library and through LDS Family History Centers. They may also be view at the Thomas Balch Library, Leesburg, Virginia.

North Fork Baptist Church - minutes (1784) and Ketoctin Baptist Church - minutes (1776). Originals are held at the Baptist Historical Society, Richmond, Virginia. You may view these records in Richmond; however the Baptist Historical Society does not lend or sell copies.

FAIRFAX MONTHLY MEETING

MARRIAGE CERTIFICATES

Most of the within named people resided in Loudoun County, and were married at the Fairfax Meeting House in Waterford, Virginia. When other locations were indicated they have been included in these abstracts. If there is no location, Loudoun County, and Fairfax Meeting House can be assumed.

William Pidgion, son of Charles Pidgion of Menallen Twp., York Co., Pennsylvania, married Rachel Everitt, daughter of John Everett of Hamilton's ___, York Co., Pennsylvania, 9th day of October 1760, at Pipe Creek Meeting House in Frederick Co., Maryland. Witnesses: John Everett, Isaac Everett, Barbary Everett, Ann Ererett, Martha Everett, Joseph Everett, Benjamin Everett, Joseph Right, Mary Miller, Sarah Uncles, Mary Michel, Sophia Hanes, Mary Ridgway, Sarah Forqher, Ann Orr, Mary Young, Jr., Susanah Forqher, Rachel Forqher, Ann Forqher, Sarah Braselton, Sarah Conner, Hannah Uncles, Samuel Forqher, Richard Plummer, Wm. Forqher, Thomas Willson, Alan Forqher, Jr., John England, Alen Forqher, Wm. Forqher Jr., William Braselton, Solomon Miller, Robert Miller, Saml Miller, Solomon Shepard.

William Ballenger, son of Henry Ballenger of Frederick Co., Maryland, married Casander Plummer, daughter of Samuel Plummer of Prince George Co., Maryland, 3rd day 8th mo 1751, at Monoquesy Meeting House. Witnesses: Ruth Holland, Mary Ballinger, Thos Plummer, Oliver Matthews, Thos. Palmer, Thos. Taylor, Hannah Matthews, Hannah Hersey, Eliz. Matthews, Sarah Peirpoint, J. Peirpoint, Call Taylor, Mary Matthews, Wm. Matthews, Edward Matthews, Aquilla Massey, Alexr. Tanzey, Humphrey William, Edward Tanzey, Alexr. Tanzey, Jr.

James Brooke of Frederick Co., Maryland married Hannah Janney, 13th day of 10th mo 1759. Witnesses: Mary Janney, Ann Janney, Elizabeth Brooke, Richard Brooke, Mahlon Janney, Sarah Janney, Mary Brooke, Jane Hague, Ann Matthews, Richard Thomas, Richd. Richardson, Thos. Brooke, Francis Hague, Edward Thompson, Mary Janney Jr., Rebeckhah Hague, Mary Hague, Hannah Hague, John Hague, Robert Bell, John Hough, Jos. Janney, Mary Williams, Abel Janney, Jacob Janney, Thos. Plummer, Sarah Richardson, Mary Parker, Hannah Janney, Eliz. Norton,

Eliza. Janney, Elener Poultney, Rachel Hollingsworth, Martha Mead, Mary Rhodes, Ann Thompson, Elia. Hough, Alice Yates, Jr., Ann Richardson, Sarah Janney, Magrett Williams, David Cadwallader, Thos. Dodd, John Ball, Eliz. Walker, Margrett Norton, Edward Norton, William Norton, Levy Wells, Midser Brown, Prisylla Wms., Jos. Yates, Alice Yates.

William Stanley of Hanover Co., VA married Elizabeth Walker, daughter of William Walker, deceased, and Sarah his wife, 28th day of 11th mo 1758. Witnesses: Sarah Walker, Isaac Walker, Elener Poultney, Barbary Walker, Martha Standly, John Poultney, Hannah Janney, John Hough, Wm. Kirk, George Gregg, Israel Thompson, Edward Norton, Samuel Harris Jr., Mr. Farling Ball, Mahlon Janney, Mary Janney, Jane Hague, Rachel Hollingsworth, Sarah Janney, Rebeckah Hague, Ann Thompson, Hannah Janney, Sarah Hague, Rebeckah Janney, John Steer, Hannah Spencer, Ann Matthews, Alice Yates, Margrett Williams, Martha Mead, Mary Harris, Mary Parker, Mary Janney Jr., Elizabeth Hough, Ruth Janney, Mary Hardin, Elizabeth Norton, Hannah Roach, Mary Norton, John Hague, James Hatcher, John Ball, Mary Hatcher, Ann Janney, Mary Janney.

Benjamin Burson, son of Joseph Burson married Ann Roberts, 23rd day of 10th mo 1760. Witnesses: Joseph Burson, Owen Robert, Jane Robert, Catherine Robert, William Robert, Owen Williams, William Williams, Margrett Williams, Feby? West, Elizabeth Potts, Prisylla Williams, Elizabeth Hough, Samuel Potts, Jonas Potts, Mary Kirk, Margret Norton, Elener Poultney, Alice Yates, Elizabeth Norton, Jane Cunard, James Burson, Mary Burson, Jonas Potts (smith), David Potts, Elizabeth Potts, Mary Potts, Martha Hatfield, Sarah Potts, Jos. Burson (mason), James Cunard, Shadrick Lewelin, Levy Wells, John Hough, Francis Hague, Wm. Grant, James Carter, Edward Norton, Jos. Yates, Thos Lewillin, Isaac Williams, Mercer Brown, Robert Yates, Andrew Adam, Ann Carr.

Mahlon Janney, married Sarah Plummer of Frederick Co., Maryland, daughter of Samuel and Sarah Plummer of Prince George Co., Maryland, 29th day 8th mo 1758. Witnesses: Ruth Holland, Rachel Plummer, Cassinder Plummer, Elizabeth Plummer, Ann Janney, Hannah Janney, Jane Hague, Ann Matthews, Sarah Plummer, Mary Brooke, Elizabeth Walker, Rachel Ballenger, Thomas Plummer, Jos. Plummer, Saml. Plummer Jr., Abram Plummer, Wm. Ballenger, Richard Holland, John Hague, Isaac Hague, John Hough, Wm. Matthews, Israel Thompson,

Boger Brooke, Samuel Price, Kessah Plummer, Elizabeth Fout, Hannah Richardson, Margret Richardson, Mary Peirpoint, Rachel Moore, Ann Naylor, Margrett Turner, Catherine Scott, Mary Sollers, Nutte Turner, George Tinkle.

Thomas Plummer of Frederick Co, Maryland, married Elener Poultney 29th day 4th mo 1761. Witnesses: Sarah Walker, Rebeckah Teirhorn, Isaac Walker, Barbary Walker, Mahlon Janney, Sarah Janney, Rachel Hollingsworth, Elizabeth Cadwallader, Rehoboth Williams, Mary Janney, Isaac Hague, Abraham Davison, Elizabeth Norton, Sarah Hough, Ann Thompson, Margery Nichols, Elizabeth Hough, Mary Barrott, Ann Janney, Ann Richardson, Joseph Janney, Hannah Cadwallader, Sarah Hutten, James Stere, John Stere, Mary Kirk, Micajah Standley, Jos. Yates, William Kirk, Elizabeth Everitt, Sarah Dodd, William Hough, John Cadwallader, Rachel Synum, William Brooks, Thomas Dodd, David Brown, Jo. Hough, Farling Ball, Mary Janney, Ruth Janney.

John Conard, son of Sarah Conard married Elizabeth Potts, daughter of David Potts 16th day December 1762. Witnesses: David Potts Jr., David Potts Senr., Jonathan Potts, Samuel Pearson, Jonas Potts, Thos. Hatfield, James Conard, Jonathan Conard, Samuel Potts, Nathan Potts, Jos. Burson, Benjamin Burson, Jos. Burson (mason), Shadrick Lewellin, Elizabeth Potts, Mahlon Janney, Margrett Osburn, Sarah Potts, Susannah Martin, Ann Burson, Jane Potts, Mary Potts, Mary Janney, Rachel Hollingsworth, Deborah Lewellin, Mary Pearson, Ann Vestill, Sarah Janney.

Richard Richardson, son of Richard Richardson, married Mary Pierpoint, daughter of Francis Pierpoint, both of Frederick Co., Maryland, 13 Sept. 1762, at Monococy in Frederick Co. Witnesses: Francis Peirpoint, Sarah Peirpoint, Obed Peirpoint, Francis Peirpoint Jr., Thos. Richardson, Chas. Devir, Thos. Taylor, Bazil Devir, Hannah Richardson, Margret Peticoat, Charles Peirpoint, Ann Richardson, Jos. Richardson, Elizabeth Pooley, Wm. Kirk, Mary Janney, Mary Kirk, Mary Mcgredor, Ann Janney, Elizabeth Hough, Mary Janney Jr., Susannah Scott, Sarah Davis, Rebeckah Towmhill, Matthias Pooley, Maridith Davis, Wm Peticoat, Saml Plummer, Alexr. Magruda, Robert Bell, Jo. Hough, Thos. Plummer.

James Megrew of Menallen, York Co., Pennsylvania, married Mary Ridgeway of Pipe Creek, Frederick Co., Maryland, 11th day 12th mo 1760 at Pipe Creek. Witnesses: Mary Younger, John England, John England, Sarah England, Nathan Megrew, John Cox, John Megrew, Alexander Megrew, Samuel England, Sarah Forqheir, Sarah Miller, Ann Forqheir, Susannah Forqheir, Mary Copelin, Elizb. Forqhier, Rachel Forqhier, Mary Forqhier, Sophia Hanes, Jane Shepheard, Martha Everitt, Hannah Uncles, Charity Polston, Charity Polston, Isaac Everitt, Wm. Forqhier, Wm. Forqhier Jr., Allin Forqhier, John Willson, Allen Forqhier Jr., Samuel Forqhier, Nathan Haines, John Sheppeard, Wm. Plummer, Solomon Miller, John Norton, Wm. Braselton, Richard Plummer.

Joseph Wright, son of John and Elizabeth Wright of Manallin, York Co., Pennsylvania, married Mary Forqhar, daughter of William and Ann Forqhar of Pipe Creek, Frederick Co., Maryland, 9th day 4th mo 1761 at Pipe Creek. Witnesses: William Forqhar, John Wright, Ann Forqhar, Wm. Forqhar Jr., Samuel Wright, Sarah Miller, Allen Forqhar, Samuel Forqhar, Rachel Forqhar, John Wright Jr., Christopher Willson, Solomon Miller, Robert Miller, Charles Pidgion, Samuel Miller, Nathan Haines, Isaac Everitt, Martha Everitt, Ann Price, Robert Price, Sophia Simpson, Sophia Haines, Mary Price, Ann Orr, Jane Mickle, Elizabeth Forqhar, Susannah Forqhar, John Pope, Alexr. Thompson, Wm. Brazelton, Daniel Rawlings Senr., John Brazilton, Charles Pidgion Jr., John Michle, William Delap, George Dewilbiss, Richard Simpson, John England, John Shepherd, Jos. Lawrance, Rebeckah Blackburn, Mary Meckle, Margret Blackburn, Mary Norris, John England, Saml England, Isaac Brazelton, Moses Forqhar, Sarah Forqhar, Sarah Forqhar Jr., Hannah Uncles, Barbary Everitt.

Thomas Dodd married Sarah Sample, 29th day 7th mo 1760. Witnesses: William Dodd, George Norman, Margrett Norman, John Dodd, Jane Gore, Lydia Dodd, Margrett Caslett, Francis Hague, Mahlon Janney, Edmund Sands, Jos. Yates, Edward Norton, Isaac Hague, John Ball, Thomas Lamb, Levy Wells, Isaac Sands, James Steere, Daniel McIlheney, Elizabeth Norton, Mary Kirk, Mary Janney, Sarah Janney, Ann Matthews, Alice Lam, Martha Hawkins, Elener Poultney, Sarah Janney, Sarah Hutten, Mary Roach, Hannah Cadwallader, Mary Janney, Sarah Sands, Mary Janney, Sarah Hague, Elizabeth Hough, Ann Roberts, Barbary Walker, Mary Cadwallader, Ann Janney, Mary Schooley.

Thomas Gregg, of Kennet, Chester Co., Pennsylvania, married Rebeckah Janney, daughter of Jacob Janney, 7th day 10th mo 1762 at Goose Creek.

Witnesses: Jacob Janney, Hannah Janney, Martha Parker, John Gregg, Ruth Gregg, Margery Nichols, Elizabeth Janney, Abel Janney, Joseph Janney, John Hakker, Naomy Smith, Rebeckah Trehern, Elizabeth Hough, Ann Janney, Sarah Hatcher, Benjamin Pool, Margret Mead, Sarah Morlan, Mary Parker, Martha Wilks, Sarah Hutten, Mary Hatcher, Prissilla Gregg, Mary Nichols, George Gregg, Samuel Mead, Elizabeth Gore, Naomy Whitacre, James Sanders, John Ethell, Martha Marks, Sarah Hutoon, Hannah Austell, Jane West, Tacy West, William Brown, Elizabeth Brown, Jo. Hough, Mary Janney Jr., Isaac Hague, Samuel Janney, Rebeckah Pool, Samuel Smith, Thomas Gregg, Rebeckah Wilks, James Hatcher, Joseph Parker, Hannah Spencer, Isaac Walker, Saml. Mead, Nathan Spencer, Thomas Gore, Sarah Gore, Ann Hogue, Hannah Clovis, Solomon Hogue, Christian Clovis, Edward Thompson, Ann Janney.

Joseph Hutten married Sarah Janney, 16th day 9th mo 1761. Witnesses: Sarah Janney, Sarah Hutten, John Hutten, Abel Janney, Mary Janney, Joseph Janney, Rachel Janney, Ann Janney, John Hough, Mahlon Janney, Nathan Baker, Enuch Williams, Thomas Hutten, Mary Hutton, Sarah Janney Jr., Ann Janney, Elizabeth Hough, Mary Janney, Ann Richardson, Rachel Hollingsworth, Hannah Cadwallader, Margrett Williams, Elizabeth Cadwallader, Mary Cadwallader, Mary Barrett, Sarah Treebe, Pressylla Gregg, William Williams, William Baker, Jo. Hough, Jos. Richardson, Robert Bell, Samuel Janney, William Hough, John Cadwallader, Jos Parker, Abel Janney Jr., Thos. Gregg.

Samuel Plummer, of Frederick Co., son of Samuel and Sarah Plummer of Prince George Co., married Mary Tucker, daughter of Robert and Lydia Tucker of Bucks Co., Pennsylvania, 18th day 2nd mo 1764 at Bush Creek Meeting House in Frederick Co., Maryland. Witnesses: Thomas Plummer, Joseph Plummer, Ruth Holland, Cassandra Ballenger, Ursula Plummer, Elener Plummer, Sarah Plummer, Richard Holland, William Ballenger, Richard Roberts, Gideon Gibson, Anthony Bull, Joseph Plummer Jr., Richard Watts, Mary Roberts, Sarah Ballenger, Susannah Plummer, Sarah Poultney, Mary Poultney.

Micajah Handley, of Roann Co., North Carolina, married Barbara Walker 10th day 10th mo 1765 at Bush Creek in Maryland. Witnesses: Ellen Plummer, Thomas Plummer, Sarah Poultney, Ruth Holland, Sarah Ballinger, Susannah Plummer, Ann Plummer, Mary Ballenger, Richard

Holland, William Ballenger, Joseph Plummer, Richard Roberts, Richard Watts, Joseph Plummer, John Gabsoll?

Thomas Gregg married Amey Gregg, both , 3rd day 12th mo 1766. Witnesses: Amos Gregg, Prisila Gregg, Blakestone Janney, Ezekiel Potts, Rachel Hollingsworth, Ann Hollingsworth, Francis Hague, Aaron Hackney, Mary Janney, Mary Hoge, Elizabeth Hough, Ruth Janney, Hanah Gregg, Hanah Hague, Sarah Janney, Fredrick Greder Jr., Elizabeth Baker, Mary Gregg, Ruse Cadwaleder, Wm. Hoge, Thomas Hague, Samuel Hague, Wm. Williams, John Ball, Wm. Baker, Abel Janney, William Gregg, Thos. McIlheney, Joseph Whitekar, David Willson, Thomas Jones, Isaac Hague, John Hanby, Rebecah Gregg, Nathan Baker, Rebeckah Janney, Ruth Janney, Thomas McGeach.

Obed Peirpoint of Frederick Co., Maryland, married Esther Myres, 7th day 4th mo 1773. Witnesses: Francis Peirpoint, Jonathan Myres, Mary Myres, Sarah Peirpoint, Wm. Richardson, Isaiah Myres, Pheby Myres, Ely Peirpoint, Sarah Schooley, Saml. Schooley, John Richardson, John Schooley, Charles Peirpoint, Elijah Myres, Thomas Taylor, Mary Taylor, Rachel Taylor, Ann Schooley, Sarah Janney, Mary Baker, Ruth Janney, Rachel Janney, Hanah Brooke, Joseph Janney, Abel Janney, Isaac Steer, George Grigg, John Smith, Margret Davis, Wm. Schooley, Elizabeth Canby, Elizabeth Cadwaleder, Rachel Holingsworth, Mary Cadwaleder, Sarah Schooley, Francis Hague, Moses Cadwaleder, Mahlon Janney, Jas Myres Jr., Wm. Williams, Phebe Holingsworth, Elisha Schooley, Wm. Myres, Wm. Schooley, Robert Smith.

Samuel Waters of Frederick Co., Maryland, son of Samuel and Artrage Waters of Prince George Co., married Susanah Plummer, daughter of Joseph and Sarah Plummer of Frederick Co., Maryland, 31st day 12th mo 1772 at Bush Creek. Witnesses: Joseph Plummer, Sarah Plummer, Anne Plummer, Joseph Plummer Jr., Ruth Holand, Thos. Plummer, Sumucb [Tunnis?] Plummer, Richard Holand, Ellener Plumer, Mary Plumer, Mary Balanger, Sarah Poultney, Sarah Balanger, Hanah Gibson, Mary Moses, Mary Poultney, Debra Plummer, Wm. Balanger, Joseph Janney, Joseph Wright, Richard Roberts, Mary Roberts, Gideon Gibson, Anthony Poultney, Wm. Morsell, Samuel Plummer.

Lewis Neal, son of Lewis Neale, both of Frederick Co., Maryland, married Rachel Janney, daughter of Abel Janney, 15th day 6th mo 1774.

Witnesses: Sarah Janney, Abel Janney, John Neale, Ann Neale, Ann Reese, Mary Baker, Mahlon Willson, Hannah Janney, Rachel Hollingsworth, Jonah Hollingsworth, Jacob Janney, Jacob Janney Jr., Abel Janney Jr., John Janney, Thomas Neale, Samuel Janney, Sarah Janney, Mary Leaver, Mary Gilbert, Hanah Brooke, Mahlon Janney, John Hough, Ann Schooley, Mary Myres, Ruth Janney, Joseph Hough, Moses Cadwaleder, John Hough Jr., Reese Cadwaleder, John Smith, Sarah Hutton, Rebekah Janney, Sarah Woodard, Ruth Cadwaleder, Arlee Yates, Jonathan Myres, James Tompkins, Israel Thompson, William Williams, Mary Ball, Elener Mead, Ann Mead, John Jackson, Farling Ball, John Gregg Jr., Joseph Cogwell, John Nickson, Thomas Matthews, Amos Janney, Sarah Baker, Sarah Hough Jr., Israel Janney, John Gregg, Mahlon Hough, Pheby Hollingsworth, Mary Hollingsworth, Mary Myers, Jr.

Jonathan Connard, yeoman, son of Sarah Connard, married Jane Potts, daughter of David Potts, 18th day of 4th mo 1764 at Gap Meeting House. Witnesses: David Potts, John Connard, Jonas Potts, James Connard, Ezekiel Potts, Samuel Potts, David Potts, Nathan Potts, Ann Vestal, Samuel Pearson, John Vastal, Issac J., Abraham Smith, Mary Pearson, And. Hatfield, David Williams, Affinity Cadwalader, Jane Hague, Mary Jenkin, Alice Yates, Francis Hague, Nicholas Osborn, Jonathan Myers, Thomas Pursel, Mary Pursel, Mary Potts, Jane Todd, Ann Burson.

William Baker married Mary Janney, 17th day 4th mo 1765. Witnesses: Abel Janney, Sarah Hutton, Samuel Janney, Abel Janney Jr., Joseph Hutton, Nathan Baker, Rachel Janney, Joseph Parker, Elizah. Eblen, Amos Hough, Elizabeth Hough, Ruth Janney, John Hutton, Mary Janney, Sarah Janney, Mary Kirk, Ann Schooley, Mary Myers, Mary Ball, Jo. Hough, Mary Parker, Hannah Pancoast, Mary Eblin, Mary Janney Jr., Ann Janney, Ann Richardson, Mary Barrell [Barrett], William Hough, Francis Hague, Jane Hague, Ann Thompson, Affinity Cadwalader, Sarah Trebbe, Blackstone Janney, Rees Cadwalader, Wm. Hanks, Robert Akers, Israel Thompson, William Mead, John Eblen, Mary Hoge, William Hoge, Thomas Hague, Jonathan Myers, Ruth Akers, Rachel Hanks, Sarah Hutton Jr., Hannah Clowes, Ann Hollingsworth, Nich. Minor, Stephen Donaldson, Jo. Richardson.

Joseph Parker, son of Nicholas Parker, deceased, and Martha his widow, married Elisah Eblen, daughter of John and Mary Eblin, 23rd day 4th mo 1765. Witnesses: Martha Parker, John Eblen, Sarah Hough, Mary Parker,

Rebekah Poole, Elizabeth Janney, Jane Hague, Mary Myers, Ellen Mead, Mary Lemon, Mary Janney, Mary Baker, William Baker, Joseph Richardson, John Hough, Ann Janney, James Hatcher, William Hatcher, Joseph Clowes, Mary Hatcher, William Mead Jr., Owen Williams, Benjamin Poole, Thomas Gregg, Ann Janney Jr., Petir Eblen, Ruth Janney, Joseph Elgar, Jo. Hough, Elizabeth Hough, William Hough, Ann Richardson, Samuel Janney, Mary Janney Jr., Rachel Janney, Sarah Hague, Hannah Pancast, Ann Ross, Sarah Seward, Elizabeth Mead, Sarah Mead, Mersey Shrieve, Ruth Clowes, Elizabeth Ross, Jesse Dodd, Benjamin Mead, Jas. Buckalew, William Mead, Samuel Smith, Jesse Davis, Stacy Janney, Mahlon Janney Jr., George Hatcher, William Hayhurst, Isaac Sinkler, Mary Cadwallader, John Dodd, Henry Lewis, John Pyott, William Hatcher Jr., George Tavenier.

John Smith married Sarah Myers, 14th day 5th mo 1766. Witnesses: Samuel Smith, Naomi Smith, Joseph Myers, Mary Myers, Thomas Smith, Abraham Smith, Jonathan Myers, Joseph Whitacre, George Whitacre, Joseph Myers Jr., William Myers, Esther Whitacre, Mary Hoge, Mary Kirk, Rachel Hollingsworth, Ruth Janney, Elizabeth Hough, Mary Janney Jr., Sarah Hague, Elizabeth Everitt, Elizabeth Mead, Mary Harris, Pleasant Hague, Mary Cadwalader, Hannah Cadwalader, Mary Lamb, Elinor Harris, Hannah Hague, Elizabeth Cadwalader, Jean Williams, Robert Beall, John Whitacre, William Williams, Moses Cadwalader, Francis Hague, John Hough, William Baker, Edmund Sands, Jno Cadwalader.

William Gregg married Rebekah Gregg, 4th day 11th mo 1767. Witnesses: George Gregg, Thomas Gregg, Mary Gregg, Mary Gregg, Mary Harden, John Hanby, Pleasant Hague, Sarah Janney, Rachel Hollingsworth, Elizabeth Cadwalader, Elizabeth Everitt, Mary Harris, Mary Trebbe, Jane Hague, Alice Yates, Elizabeth Hough, Mary Janney, Lydia Hollingsworth, Mary Wildman, Thomas Hague, Joseph Hackney, Thomas Matthews, James McGeach, James Nixon, Levi Wells, To. Hough, Samuel Hague, Rees Cadwalader, Ruth Cadwalader, Jonathan Bis_oe, Rachel Johnson, Francis Hague, Samuel Harris, Mahlon Janney, Joseph Janney, ___ Hackney, George Dunnington, William Keyes, Abel Janney, Elizabeth Nixon, Elizabeth Trebbe, Ann McIlhany, Abigail Johnson, Isaac Hague.

Isaac Nickols married Rebekah Gibson, 10th day 12th mo 1767 at Goose Creek. Witnesses: Alice Gibson, Joseph Gibson, Thomas Gibson, John

Gibson, James Gibson, Moses Gibson, Ann Gibson, Mary Nickols, Mary Parker, Ginnet Donaldson, Hannah Janney, Mary Hatcher, Mary Nickols, Isaac Nickols Senr., Margery Nickols, Solomon Hoge, Benjamin Poole, George Hatcher, Jesper Sybold, Isaac Hatcher, William Nickols, Thomas Nickols, William Hatcher, Robert Donaldson, Henry Philips, Evan Philips, Joseph Clowes, John Clark, Phebe Gibson, Ann Clark, Martha McNabb.

Aaron Hackney of Frederick Co., Maryland, married Hannah Gregg of Loudoun, 31st day of 3rd mo 1768. Witnesses: Mary Gregg, Joseph Hackney, William Gregg, Thomas Gregg, Emey Gregg, George Gregg, John Hanby, John Gregg, John Gregg Jr., George Gregg, Elizabeth Gregg, Amos Gregg, Elijah Harlan, John Harlan, Aaron Davice, Francis Hague, William Hoge, Sarah Janney Jr., Mary Kirk, Mahlon Janney, Thomas Hague, Elizabeth Hough, Mary Janney, Ruth Janney, Amos Hough, Farling Ball, Ann Schooley, Lydia Hollingsworth, William Kirk, Thomas McGeach, Samuel Harriss, Mary Roach, Mary Hoge, Hannah Raoch, Hannah Brown, Mary Brown, Pleasant Hague, Eunise Howell, Rachel Howell, Mary Ball, Hannah Howell, Samuel Hague, Mary Harris, Lydia Hough, Hannah Boone, Jacob Sands, James McGeach, Sarah Sands, Adam Carnahan, Joseph Sands, John Brown, David Howell, Isaac Hague, Benjamin Sands, Richard Roach, William Walton, William Cavins, Thomas Hanes, John Walton, Levi Wells, Isaiah Boone, David Wilson.

James Gibson married Mary Hatcher, 11th day 1st mo 1768 at Goose Creek. Witnesses: William Hatcher, Ann Hatcher, Alice Gibson, Joseph Gibson, John Bison, Thomas Gibson, John Clark, Moses Gibson, James Hatcher, Blackstone Janney, Sarah Hatcher, Abel Janney, Jacob Janney, Benjamin Pool, Nathan Spencer, Phebe Gibson, Francis Hague, Isaac Nickols, Joseph Janney, George Hatcher, Samuel Russel, Hannah Spencer, Sarah Russel, Rebekah Nickols, Hannah Janney, Rebekah Pool, Jonas Janney, Ruth Clowes, Hannah Clowes, Ruth Fairhurst, Ann Russel, Phebe Janney.

William Williams married Elizabeth Everitt, 6th day 9th mo 1769. Witnesses: Rehoboth Williams, Hannah Cadwalader, Hannah Brooke, Margaret Davies, Hannah Janney, Mary Myers, Ruth Janney, Mary Janney, Mahlon Janney, Francis Hague, William Hoge, Jonathan Myers, Abel Janney, John Hough, Joseph Janney, Moses Cadwalader, Israel Thompson, Abel Janney Jr., Joseph Hough, Jane Hague, Rachel Hollingsworth, Elizabeth Cadwalader, Ann Thompson, Elizabeth Hough, Ann

Hollingsworth, Pleasant Hague, Lydia Hollingsworth, Elizabeth Mead, Sarah Hague, Levi Wells, Isaac Baker, Amos Hough, Isaac Hague, Jonah Hollingsworth, Deborah Brooke, Elizabeth Brooke, Sarah Janney.

Samuel Canby married Elizabeth Hough, 28th day of 2nd mo 1770. Witnesses: John Hough, Sarah Hough, William Hough, Amos Hough, Joseph Hough, Samuel Hough, Francis Hague, Mahlon Janney, Joseph Janney, Samuel Janney, Jas. Hamilton, Stephen Donaldson, William Neilson, William Lawder, William Mead, Jonathan Myers, William Matthews, Abel Janney Jr., William Baker, Rees Cadwalader, Nathan Baker, Sarah Janney, Mary Baker, Ruth Janney, Hannah Janney, Ann Thompson, Rebekah Janney, Ann Mead, Jane Hamilton, Hannah Hough, Sarah Thompson, Elizabeth Wilson, Jane Hague, Hannah Thompson, Rachal Hollingsworth, Ruth Cadwallader, Mary Janney, Hannah Hague, Alice Yates, Mary Cadwalader, Mary Myers, Ann Burson, Lydia Hanks, John Gibson, Isaac Hague, Thomas Hague, John Cadwalader, Jonah Hollingsworth, Mary Pordom, Alice Ross, Sarah Hague, Ann Hollingsworth, Eliner Hough, William Keyes, Catharine Keyes, Rachel Janney, Jonah Thompson, Samuel Hague, Lydia Hough.

James Ball married Mary Brown, 8th day 8th mo 1770. Witnesses: Henry Brown, William Brown, John Brown, Farling Ball, William Ball, Mercer Brown, William Kirk, Mary Kirk, Hannah Brown, Mary Ball, Mary Ball, Sarah Brown, Elizabeth Brown, Martha Ball, Samuel Harris, Mary Harris, Pleasant Hague, Rachel Janney, Ann Schooley, Sarah Janney, George Gregg, Ann Dawson, Sarah Hague, John Gregg, Hezekiah Boone, Adam Carnahan, John Smith, Benjamin Sands, Richard Roach, Francis Hague, Mahlon Janney, Richard Roach, Hannah Roach, Jonathan Myers, Mary Myers, William Williams, Joseph Hough, James McGeach, Isaac Hague, Jacob Sands, Isaac Sands, Joseph Sands, Thomas Harris, John Hough, James Roach, Abraham Dawson, Joseph McGeach, Elisha Gregg, Elizabeth McGeach, Sarah Gregg, Sarah Hough, Mary Williams, Hannah Hough, Elizabeth Holmes, Margaret Holmes.

Jonathann Nutt married Elizabeth Trebbe, 28th day 11th mo 1770. Witnesses: Mary Trebbe, William Trebbe, John Morris, Amos Janney, George Gregg, John Hough, Francis Hague, William Baker, Mahlon Janney, Samuel Canby, William Williams, Elizabeth Williams, William Brown, Elizabeth Janney, Ruth Janney, Rachel Hollingsworth, Sarah Janney, Hannah Brooke, Elizabeth Canby, Hannah Roach, Elizabeth

Baker, Ann Schooley, John Smith, Samuel Hague, Lydia Hollingsworth, Ann Hollingsworth, Rachel Janney, Ann Janney, Sarah Wiatt, Martha Lovett, Lydia Gregg, Joseph Neale, Mahlon Janney, Isaac Hague, Joseph Janney.

Gideon Gipson of Linganore, Frederick Co., Maryland, married Hannah Unkles of Pipe Creek, 12th day 12 mo 1770 at Pipe Creek, Maryland. Witnesses: William Farquhar, Ann Farquhar, Sarah Unkles, Allen Farquhar Jr., Sarah Farquhar, Mary Wright, Elizabeth Farquhar, Susanna Farquhar, Joseph Wright, Moses Farquhar, William Farquhar Jr., Samuel Farquhar, Rachel Farquhar, Thos. Farquhar, Ruth Holland, William Farquhar, Solomon Miller, Sarah Miller, Ruth Miller, Sarah Poultney, Anne Plummer, Jarre [Jane] Wilson, Benjamin Vanhorn, Richard Roberts, William Pigeon, Norris Ellis, Rachel Miller, Sophia Haines, Mary Haines, Anna Plummer.

Abel Janney married Mary Janney, 3rd day 4th mo 1771. Witnesses: Abel Janney, Sarah Janney, Hannah Brooke, Ruth Janney, Sarah Janney, Mary Baker, Samuel Janney, Jane Hague, Francis Hague, Ann Thompson, Hannah Janney, Elizabeth Canby, Rachel Janney, John Hough, Alice Yates, William Baker, Rees Cadwalader, Phebe Myers, Mary Myers, Go. Johnston, James Ball, Elizabeth Williams, Samuel Canby, Israel Thompson, Jonah Thompson, Jonah Hough, John Collins, William Mead, Isaac Steere, William Williams, Hannah Hough, Pleasant Hague, Ruth Janney, Mahlon Taylor, Amos Hough, Nathan Baker, John Hough Jr., Samuel Hague, Hannah Hague, Sarah Hague, Ann Hollingsworth, Ruth Cadwalader, Joel Wright.

Amos Hough married Elizabeth Wilson, 10th day 4th mo 1771. Witnesses: Sarah Hough, David Wilson, John Hough Senr., Ruth Janney, Samuel Hough, Elizabeth Baker, Mary Janney, Jane Hague, Sarah Janney, Hannah Brooke, Sarah Hague, Francis Hague, Thomas Hague, Samuel Janney, Rachel Hollingsworth, Ann Hollingsworth, Ruth Cadwalader, William Williams, Elizabeth Williams, Joel Wright, William Mead, Jonah Hollingsworth, William Hoge, Samuel Hague, Ruth Janney, Sarah Hutton, Stephen Morlan.

Benjamin Burson, yeoman, son of George Burson and Sarah his wife, married Hannah Young, daughter of Hercules Young and Sarah his wife, 8th day 1st mo 1772 at South Fork. Witnesses: George Burson, Sarah

Burson, Hercules Young, Sarah Young, James Young, James Burson, Sarah Dixon, Solomon Dixon, Evan Philips, Elizabeth Pryor, Benjamin Overfield, Ruth Remine, Peter Remine [Romine], John Gregg, John Garrett, Isaac Brown, George Jones, George Brown, Jehu Brown, Joshua Dunkin, John Williams, William Warford, Henry Philips, Joseph James, Thos. Garrett Jr., Isaac Brown, Martha Brown, Elizabeth Russel, Rachel Smith, Rebekah Cowgill, Sarah Millar, Tamar Warford, Sidney Dunkin, Margaret Young, Elizabeth Brown, Rebekah Trahern, Mary Overfield, Elizabeth Dunkin Jr., Sarah Trahern, James Trahern, Thomas Smith, William Hough, Isaac Cowgill, Henry Smith, John Votaw, Joseph Hoge, Thos. Llewellen, John Gibson, Joseph Brown, John Dunkin, Isaac Walker.

John Hough Jr., married Lydia Hollingsworth, 29th day 4th mo 1772. Witnesses: John Hough, Sarah Hough, Rachel Hollingsworth, Amos Hough, Samuel Canby, Mary Ball, Sarah Janney, Ruth Janney, Sarah Janney Jr., Hannah Brooke, Phebe Hollingsworth, Joseph Hough, Lewis Neill, Samuel Hough, Joseph Janney, Eleanor Hough, Thomas Hague, Samuel Janney, John Neill, Sarah Hough Jr., Leah Ball, Hannah Hough, Amos Janney, Rebekah Janney, Francis Hague, Mahlon Janney, Abel Janney Jr., Ann Thompson, Mahlon Taylor, Wm. Johnston, Thos. Matthews, Farling Ball, Joseph Hough, Eliza. Cadwalader, Eliza. Williams, William Mead, Wm. Williams, Isaac Hague.

William Harris married Elizabeth Holmes, 22nd day 10th mo 1772 at Goose Creek. Witnesses: William Holmes, Margaret Holmes, Sarah Hoge, Samuel Coombs, John Brown, William Brown, Elizabeth Brown, Thomas Carleton, Jno Churchman, Jonathan Myers, Thomas Brown, William Kirk, William Hoge, Jacob Janney, Blackstone Janney, Mary Hoge, Solomon Hoge, William Hays, Tho. Gore, Mary Myers, Rebekah Gregg, Rachel Hollingsworth, Margery Nickols, Hannah Janney, Eliza. Cadwalader.

Joel Wright, son of John and Elizabeth Wright of Menallen Township, York Co., Pennsylvania, married Elizabeth Farquhar, daughter of William and Ann Farquhar of Pipe Creek, Frederick Co., Maryland, 1st day 7th mo 1772 at Pipe Creek. Witnesses: William Farquhar, Ann Farquhar, Wm. Farquhar Jr., Rachel Farquhar, Mary Wright, Allen Farquhar Jr., Samuel Farquhar, Moses Farquhar, Samuel Wright, Joseph Wright, John Wright Jr., Jonathan Wright, Susanna Farquhar, Sarah Miller, Phebe Farquhar, Sarah Farquhar, Thomas Farquhar, Sarah Unkles, Wm. Ballinger, Morris Ellis, Joseph Janney, David Scholfield, Anthony

Poultney, William Farquhar 3, Benjamin Vanhorn, Sarah Ellis, William Ellis, Thomas Ellis, William Gilmore, Morris Ellis Jr., Rachel Miller, Mary Cookson, Ruth Miller, Anna Everitt, Joseph Plummer, William Pigeon, Rachel Pigeon, Samuel Cookson, Elizabeth Farquhar, William Robison, William Kenworthy.

James Hatcher married Rebekah Nichols, 14th day 4th mo 1773 at Goose Creek. Witnesses: William Hatcher, Isaac Nichols, Ann Hatcher, James Hatcher, Mary Nichols, Catharine Hatcher, William Nickols, Margery Nickols, Lydia Nickols, Hannah Janney, Ann James, George Hatcher, Isaac Brown, Jacob Janney, Sarah Russel, Sarah Nickols, William Hatcher Jr., Samuel Nickols, Jacob Nickols, John Gregg, Joshua Nickols, Richard James, Israel Janney, Rebekah Russel, Jehu Brown, John Nickols, George Nickols, Ann Russel, Rebekah Gregg, Mary McCullah, Mary Gregg, Ann Fred, Joseph Fred, Rachel Dillon, John Gregg, Jr., Solomon Hoge, Benjamin Barton, Robert Russel, Elisha Gregg, Jonas Janney, Sarah Gregg, Jane Shuard, Mary Fred, Sarah Hoge, Elizabeth Janney, Samuel Gregg, Stacy Janney, Jonathan Milbourn, Henry VanOver, William Janney, Joseph McKee, Thomas Gregg, Samuel Russel, John Russell.

Israel Janney, son of Jacob and Hannah Janney, married Pleasant Hague daughter of Francis Hague, 5 May 1773. Witnesses: Francis Hague, Ann Schooley, Isaac Hague, Hannah Hague, Blackstone Janney, Jonas Janney, Samuel Hague, Joseph Janney, Hannah Brooke, Mary Janney, Sarah Janney, Eleoner Mead, Elizabeth Cadwalader, Elizabeth Janney, Samuel Janney, Jacob Janney, Jonathan Myers, Mercy Shrieve, John Hough Jr., Sarah Woodward, Alice Yates, Thomas Hague, Thomas Matthews, William Janney, William Drish, Elizabeth Janney, William Mead, Israel Thompson, Abel Janey Jr., John Janney, Lydia Hough, Rachel Hollingsworth, Elizabeth Brooke, Moses Cadwalader, Wm Williams, Thomas Woodford, Wm. Baker, Jonah Thompson, Amos Hough, Jonah Hollingsworth, Caleb Shrieve, Joshua Daniel, Hannah Shrieve, Elizabeth Williams, Benjamin Vanhorn, Amos Janney, Mary Hollingsworth, Deborah Brooke, Rachel Janney, Rebekah Janney, Jonah Hough, Sarah Hague, James Shrieve.

Stephen Morlan, son of William Morlan, married Mary Rhodes, daughter of Mary Rhodes, 20 October 1773. Witnesses: Sarah Morlan, William Mead Senr., Elenor Mead, Jasoni? Morlan, Ann Morlan, Richard Morlan, Abigail Rhodes, William Rhodes, Ann Mead, Martha Wright, Martha Thomas, Rachel Hollingsworth, Mary Rhodes, Sarah Janney Senr., Sarah

Janey, Mary Myers, Phebe Myers, Hannah Janney, Mary Baker, Mahlon Janney, Israel Thompson, Abel Janney, William Hoge, Nathan Spencer, Anthony Wright, Edward Conner, Ezekiel Potts, Elizabeth Potts, William Morlan, Michael Weasly, Jonas Potts.

Solomon Hoge married Mary Nickols, 11th day 11th mo 1773 at Goose Creek. Witnesses: William Hoge, Isaac Nickols, Margery Nickols, Mary Hoge, Rebekah Hatcher, Margery Nichols, Sarah Hoge, Rebekah Nickols, Hannah Janney, James Dillon, Jacob Janney, Nathan Spencer, Thomas Hatcher, Sarah Nickols, Edith Nickols, Isaac Nickols, Samuel Russel, Israel Janney, Pleasant Janney, Joseph Janney, Joseph Hoge, Isaac Nickols, Richard James, Blackstone Janney, Elizabeth Janney, William Nickols, Jonas Janney, Sarah Russel, Hannah Spencer, Rebekah Dillon, Rebekah Pool, Benjamin Davis, Hannah Davis.

Samuel Hague married Jane Shuard, 23rd day 12th mo 1773. Witnesses: Francis Hague, Pleasant Janney, Hannah Hague, Israel Janney, Mahlon Janney, Sarah Janney Jr., Hannah Brooke, Abel Janney, Margaret Trebbe, Thomas Hague, Jacob Janney, Sarah Janney, Amos Hough, Joseph Janney, Marcy Shrieve, Jonathan Nutt, Elizabeth Hough, Jonas Janney, Thomas Smith, Andrew Brown, Martha Thompson, James Shrieve, Job Cooper.

Benjamin Steer married Anna Everitt, 7th day 9th mo 1774. Witnesses: Ann Steer, Hannah Steer, Elizabeth Williams, John Steer, Isaac Steer, Joel Lewis, Hannah Lewis, Mary Steer, Ann Steer, William Williams, George Gregg, Abel Janney, Ann Schooley, Alice Yates, Sarah Janney, Hannah Brooke, Lydia Hough, Elizabeth Cadwalader, Mary Baker, Mary Schooley, Moses Cadwalader, Joseph Janney, Abel Janney Jr., Samuel Berry, Israel Thompson, George Hatcher, John Smith, Mahlon Janney, Susanna Hill, Isaac Siddall, John Schooley, Joseph Scott, James Tomkins, Jonathan Myers, Mary Myers, Abraham Hill, Daniel Hill, Sarah Overfield.

Joseph West Plummer, son of Joseph and Sarah Plummer, married Mary Taylor, daughter of Thomas and Caleb (sic) Taylor, both of Frederick Co., 4th day 1st mo 1775 at the house of Thomas Taylor at Monocacy. Witnesses: Thomas Taylor, Caleb Taylor, Sarah Plummer, Rachel Taylor, Susanna Waters, Anne Plummer, Thomas Taylor Jr., Joseph Taylor, Jesse Taylor, Fras. Peirpoint, Samuel Waters, Mahlon Janney, Thos. Plummer, Sarah Janney, Mary Richardson, Sarah Peirpoint, Sarah Peirpoint, Rachel

Peirpoint, Obed Peirpoint, Richard Richardson, Joseph Peirpoint, Eliza Pierpoint, Charles Pierpoint, Sarah Taylor, Henry Taylor, Ann Taylor, Mary Poultney, Francis Hague, Morris Birkbeck, John Hough, Hancock Nevill, Alice Yates, Hannah Brooke, Joseph Janney, Francis Matthews, Thomas Lewis, Anthony Poultney, Michael Wilkes.

Moses Gibson married Lydia Leonard, 15th day 2nd mo 1775 at South Fork. Witnesses: Alice Gibson, Esther Gibson, Rachel Neal, Ann Gibson, Phebe Gibson, Suckey Drummond, Rebekah Seybold, Rachel Long, Polley Ship, Mary Clark, Alice Clark, Isaac Gibson, John Gibson, William Neal, Jasper Seybold, Joseph Bigson, Thomas Gibson, James Gibson, Stephen McPherson Senr., Stephen McPherson Jr., Joseph McPherson, Joseph Parks, John Long, Sarah Dixon, Isaac Walker, George Burson, Elizabeth Pryor, James Burson, Joseph Brown, Elizabeth Brown, Jas. Sinkler, Edward Rees, Ricd. Wiatt Shipp, Laban Ship, Isaac Nickols, Rebekah Nickols, Rebekah Trahern, John Seybold.

John Brown married Mary Rhodes, widow, 8th day 2nd mo 1775. Witnesses: John Brown, Stephen Morlan, Isaac Brown, Ezekiel Potts, George Brown, William Brown, William Brown, Joseph Rhodes, Thos. Rhodes, Sarah Hague, Jane Hague, Ann Mead, Sarah Morlan, Martha Wright, Martha Thomas, Mary Thomas, Abigail Rhodes, Mary Rhodes, Catharine Brown, Rachel Hollingsworth, Hannah Janney, Sarah Janney, Ann Schooley, Ruth Janney, Mary Myers, Mary Baker, Lydia Hough, Ann Morlan, Mary Lasley, Elizabeth Williams, Francis Hague, Jonathan Nixon, Margaret Nixon, Sarah Nixon, Eliza. Cadwalader, John Hough, Jonathan Myers, Wm. Williams, Samuel Hague, Mahlon Janney, Moses Cadwalader, James Ball, Richard Morlan.

Elisha Gregg, son of George and Elizabeth Gregg married Martha Lovett, daughter of Daniel Lovett, 1st day 3rd mo 1775. Witnesses: George Gregg, Elizabeth Gregg, Sarah Lovett, William Gregg, Joseph Lovett, John Hanby, George Gregg Jr., John Gregg, Ann Gregg, Sarah Janney, Hannah Janney, Rachel Hollingsworth, Lydia Hough, Hannah Janney, Phebe Myers, Hannah Brooke, Jane Hague, Joseph Janney, William Wildman Jr., Anna Wildman, Rebekah Trebbe, John Hough, Jonathan Myers, Mahlon Janney, Wm. Williams, Moses Cadwallader, Samuel Hague, John Hough Jr., Francis Hague, William Beans, Isaac Hughes, Jonathan Nutt, John Wildman, Sarah Marks, Isaac Nickols, John Megeath, Ralph McKindly, Adam Carnahan, Thomas Haines, Elisha

Marks, Thos. Woodford, Benjamin Howel, Hannah Beans, Thos. Williams, Saml. Borland, William Trebbe.

Thomas Hague, son of Francis Hague married Sarah Wilkinson, daughter of Joseph and Barbara Wilkinson, 2nd day 5th mo 1775. Witnesses: Francis Hague, Joseph Wilkinson, Barbara Wilkinson, Ann Schooley, Isaac Hague, Sarah Hague, Samuel Hague, Jane Hague, William Schooley, Benjamin Lacey, Jacob Hibbs, Thomas Higgs, Mary Hibbs, Sarah Janney, Mahlon Janney, Samuel Canby, Sarah Janney Jr., Susanna Plummer, Martha Ball, John Hough Jr., Strainge Backhouse, William Hough, Farling Ball, Joseph Hough, Benjamin Purdum, Hannah Brooke, John Schooley, Mahlon Hough, Anthony Wright, Amos Hough, William Richardson, Jonah Thompson, Martha Wright, Rachel Hollingsworth, Mary Ball, Fras Hague Jr., Ann Sheane, Alice Yates, Mary Hollingsworth, Sarah Hough, Sarah Hough Jr., Martha Hough, Phebe Hollingsworth, Hannah Schooley.

John Gregg married Hannah Steer, 7th day 9th mo 1775 at Goose Creek. Witnesses: Thomas Gregg, Mary Gregg, Benjamin Steer, Ann Steer, Samuel Gregg, Anna Steer, Thomas Gregg, Alice Lewis, Joel Lewis, Hannah Lewis, William Daniel, Isaac Brown, Isaac Nickols, James Hatcher, William Hoge, Jacob Janney, James Daniel, John Hirst, Mary Hirst, Mary Hoge, Mary Brown, Sarah Morlan, Esther Daniel, Catharine Hatcher, Rebekah Gregg, Thomas Hatcher, Rebekah Hatcher, Rebekah Poole, George Hatcher, Solomon Hoge, Mary Hoge Jr., James Sinkler, Mary Sinkler, Ruth Steer, Mary McCullah, Israel Jennings, George Fox, Robert McCullah, Joseph McKee, Sidney McKee, Samuel Nickols, John Iden, Solomon Hoge Jr., Margery Nickols Jr., Ann Steer Jr.

John Gibson married Ruth Janney, 22nd day 2nd mo 1776. Witnesses: Alice Gibson, Mary Janney, Joseph Gibson, Mahlon Janney, James Gibson, Moses Gibson, Sarah Janney, Rebekah Nickols, Abel Janney, Deborah Brooke, Hannah Schooley, Francis Hague, Ann Schooley, Hannah Janney, Mary Baker, John Hough, Jonathan Myers, Thomas Hague, Isaac Nickols, Alice Yates, Joseph Janney, Thos. Matthews, Mahlon Hough, Samuel Hough, John Janney.

James Daniel, son of William, married Hannah Seybold, daughter of Jasper Seybod, 15th day 4th mo 1778 at South Fork. Witnesses: Jasper Seybold, William Daniel, Rebekah Seybold, Esther Daniel, William Daniel Jr., John Seybold, Mary Smith, Sarah Daniel, Jane Daniel, Samuel Smith,

Jasper Seybold Jr., Robert Seybold, John Gibson, Alice Gibson, Benjamin Burson, Mahlon Janney, Isaac Walker, Ann Votaw, Jacob Janney, Nathan Spencer, Thomas Gregg, William Smith, Ann Smith, Hannah Spencer, Rebekah Gregg, Margaret Spencer, Sarah Janney, Hannah Janney, John Hirst, Mary Spencer, Rebekah Hirst, Mary Fred, Elizabeth Philips, Elizabeth Philips, Sarah Smith, Ezekiel Smith, Jacob Oldaker, Jane Butcher, Jane West, Jesse Gauf?, Joseph West, Solomon Philips, Joseph Fred, Solomon Dixon.

Stacy Janney married Hannah Brown, 10th day 4th mo 1776, Witnesses: Henry Brown, Elizabeth Janney, Mahlon Janney, Elizabeth Janney, Sarah Brown, Mary Ball, Mary Ball, James Ball, Samuel Janney, Hannah Janney, Joseph Janney, Elizabeth Booke, Ann Schooley, Francis Hague, John Hough, ___ Janney, Jonathan Myers, Jonathan Nutt, Thomas Hague, John Hough Jr., Sarah Hague, Sarah Janney, Jane Hague, Samuel Hague, Wm. Williams, Mary Baker, Marg. Myers, John Smith, Jonah Hollingsworth, Thos. Matthews, Leah Ball, Jonah Hough, John Janney, James Roach, Joseph Sands, Edmund Roach, Thomas Harris, Micaiah Roach, Farling Ball, Letitia James, Ruth Brown, Henry Brown, John Brown, Martha Brown, Sarah Roach, William Janney, Levi Janney, Mary Roach, Richard Brown.

John Brown, son of Henry and Esther Brown, married Martha Ball, 10th day 4th mo [1776]. Witnesses: Henry Brown, James Ball, Farling Ball, Sarah Brown, Mary Ball, Mary Ball, Margaret Todhunter, Leah Ball, Mahlon Janney, William Janney, Alice Janney, Hannah Janney, Ann S___, Francis Hague, John Hough, Mahlon Janney, Jonathan Myers, Jonathan Nutt, Thomas Hague, John Hough Jr., John Hollingsworth, Sarah Hague?, Samuel Hague, Sarah Janney, Jane Hague, Mary Baker, Marg. Myers, John Smith, Elizabeth Nutt, Emos Janney, Joseph Janney,Samuel Janney, Thomas Matthews, Jonah Hough, Elizabeth Brooke, John ___, Wm. Williams, ___ Roach, Joseph Sands, Edmund Roach, Thos. Harris, Elizabeth Janney, Micajah Roach, Jacob Janney, Mary Roach, ___ Myers, ___ Brown, Henry Brown Jr.

Samuel Smith married Mary Daniel, 11th day 4th mo 1776 at Goose Creek. Witnesses: Henry Smith, William Daniel, Esther Daniel, Alice Smith, Sarah Daniel, Hannah Daniel, Jane Smith, George Smith, John Smith, Wm. Daniel Jr., John Smith, Sarah Smith, Thomas Smith, Rachel Smith, Sarah Smith, Hannah Smith, Mary Harris, Elizabeth ____, James

Daniel, Mahlon Smith, Sarah Nickols, Samuel Canby, Elizabeth Cadwalader, Ruth Cadwalader, Hannah Janney, Rebekah Gregg, Jacob Janney, William Smith, Mary How[ell], Hannah Spencer, Sarah Cadwalader, Sarah Smith, Margaret Spencer, Martha Pool, Nathan Spencer, Israel Nickols, Samuel Harris, John Hirst, Thomas Gregg, Moses Cadwalader, Timothy Howell, John Grigg, Mary Gray.

Caleb Whitacre married Phebe Gore, 31st day 10th mo 1776 at Goose Creek. Witnesses: Alice Whitacre, Christian Carruthers, Robert Whitacre, Naomi Smith, Joshua Whitacre, George Whitacre, Joseph Whitacre, Samuel Smith, William Daniel, Catherine Hatcher, Jonas Janney, Benjamin Whitacre, Abigail Rhodes, James Dillon, John Fairhurst, Jacob Janney, John Hirst, William Smith, Solomon Hoge, Rachel Dillon, Rebekah Fairhurst, Rachel Dillon Jr., Wm. Dillon, Ruth Smith, Hannah Smith, Esther Whitacre, Anna Whitacre, Mary Holmes, Jacob Janney Jr., Moses Cadwalader, Nathan Spencer, Solomon Hoge, Aquila Janney, Ruth Janney, George Brown, Catharine Brown, Ruth Whitacre, Daniel Hixon, Joseph Janney, George Fairhurst, John Bon__, Elisha Janney, Jonathan Milburn, William Hoge, James Hatcher.

George Hatcher married Prudence Woodward, 28th day 5th mo 1778. Witnesses: Prudence Woodward, Mary Gibson, Jane James, Sarah Thompson, William Hatcher, John Hatcher, Joshua Hatcher, Sarah Russel, James Hatcher, Thomas Hatcher, Ann Hatcher, Hannah Thompson, Nathan Spencer, ___, Solomon Hoge, Mary Hoge, John Brown, William Daniel, William Hoge, William Smith, Ann Smith, James Daniel, John Hirst, Mary Hirst, Joel Lewis, Hannah Lewis, Ruth Steer, Isaac Nickols, James Gibson, Ann Steer, Joseph Pool, Moses Cadwalader, Eliz. Cadwalader, Ruth Cadwalader, Ruth Cadwalader, Richard Pool, George Fairhurst, John Fairhurst, Rachel Fairhurst, Ann Pool, Esther Daniel, Rufus Updike, Mary Fairhurst, Phebe Fairhurst, Sarah Hirst, Rebekah Fairhurst, Elizabeth Updike, Phebe Updike, Jane Fairhurst.

Joseph Janney Jr., married Mary Holmes, 4th day 6th mo 1778 at Goose Creek. Witnesses: Hannah Janney, Thomas Gregg, Rebekah Gregg, Blackston Janney, Mary Janney, Israel Janney, Jonas Janney, Pleasant Janney, Phebe Bennett, Ruth Janney, Cornelia Janney, Mary Hirst, Hannah Gregg, Hannah Janney, Moses Cadwalader, William Smith, Ann Smith, Esther Daniel, William Daniel, James Hatcher, Elizabeth Cadwalader, Mary Smith, Sarah Smith, Thomas Cadwallader, Solomon Hoge, John

Hirst, Nathan Spencer, Hannah Spencer, William Harris, Elizabeth Harris, Margaret Holmes, Mary Hoge, ___ Holmes, ___ Holmes, ___ Spencer, ___ Spencer, ___ Spencer.

Israel Thompson married Sarah Hague, daughter of Francis Hague, 2nd day 7th mo 1778. Witnesses: Francis Hague, Ann Schooley, Isaac Hague, Rebekah Howell, Hannah Hague, Samuel Hague, Ann Hague, Sarah Hague, Israel Janney, Pleasant Janney, Mahlon Janney, John Hough, Joseph Janney, Mary Janney, Thos. Matthews, Timothy Howell, Jonah Hough, Jonah Thompson, Thomas Howell?, Mary Schooley, Elizabeth Williams, John Schooley, Rachel Baker, Sarah Hough, Ann Sheane, Hannah Schooley.

Thomas Hughes, son of Matthew and Elizabeth Hughes, married Sarah Schooley, daughter of John and Mary Schooley, 13th day 1st mo. [rest is unreadable].

John Nickols married Margaret Spencer, 18th day 2nd mo 1779 at Goose Creek. Witnesses: James Nickols, Nathan Spencer, Hannah Spencer, Ann James?, George Nickols, J___ Nickols, Ruth Nickols, Samuel Spencer, Eli Nickols, Richard James, George Brown, Catherine Brown, Thomas Nickols, Dinah Walters, Keterah Hatcher, John Hirst, Margery Nickols, Isaac Nickols, Mahlen Janney, Moses Cadwalader, Elizabeth Cadwallader, Cornelius Janney, Rebekah Gregg, Esther Daniel, William Daniel, Solomon Hoge, Thomas Hatcher, Isaiah Nickols, Marcus Baldwin, [rest is unreadable].

William Hatcher Jr. married Mary Myers 29th day 5th mo 1779. [First witnesses are unreadable, last ones are] Stephen Gregg, Ruth Janney, John Gregg, Solomon Hoge, William Dillon.

James Roach, married Elizabeth Gregg, 4th mo 1779 [per women's minutes, full date and witnesses unreadable].

Samuel Canby married Ann Shene 1st day 9th mo 1779. Witnesses: John Hough, Israel Thompson, Isaac Thompson, John Hough Jr., Amos Hough, Lydia Hough, Samuel Hague, Jane Hague, Francis Hague, Mahlon Janney, John Hough, Samuel Thompson, Sarah Janney, Sarah Janney Jr., Ann Schooley, Hannah Janney, Sarah Roach, Anne Wildman, Margaret Leyton, Sarah Hough, Sarah Hurst, Jonah Thompson, Mary Myers,

Mahlon Hough, Samuel Hough, Jonah Hough, Henry McCabe Jr., Thos. Roper, Abel Janney, James Tomkins, Isaac Thompson Jr., Joseph Janney, George Gregg, Mary Baker, William Williams, Jonathan Myers, Benjamin Purdom, Thomas Hague, Sarah Hague, John Welch, Joseph Thompson, John Wildman, Thos. Matthews, Sarah Thompson Jr., Ann Wildman, Francis Hague Jr.

John Pancoast, of Montgomery Co., Maryland married Ruth Nickols, 26th day 10th mo 1779 at Goose Creek. Witnesses: William Hoge, Isaac Nickols, Mary Hoge, Margery Nickols, Solomon Hoge, Mary Hoge, Abigail Pancoast, Samuel Nickols, Ann James, William Nickols, Isaac Nickols Jr., William Pancoast, James Nickols, George Walters, Richard James, Elizabeth Nickols, Thos. Hatcher, Mary Brown, Sarah Nickols, Elizabeth Boone, Mary Janney, Dinah Walters, Rebecah Pool, Mary Hatcher, William Hatcher, Isaac Walker, William Dillon, Thomas Gregg, Hannah Janney, James Hatcher, Joseph Pool, George Fairhurst, James Trahern, John Fairhurst, Rachel Fairhurst.

Elisha Schooley, son of John and Mary Schooley, married Rachel Holmes, daughter of William and Mary Holmes, deceased, 17th day 12th mo 1779 at Goose Creek. Witnesses: John Schooley, Eliz. Cadwalader, Elizabeth Harris, Mary Janney, Mary Myers, Margaret Holmes, Thomas Hughes, Sarah Hughes, Reuben Schooley, Richard Brown, Thomas Gregg, John Hirst, Moses Cadwalader, James Hatcher, William Smith, George Hatcher, Jonas Janney, Israel Janney, John Brown, Joel Lewis, Nathan Spencer, Jacob Janney, Solomon Hoge, Mary Hirst, Mary Hirst, Mary Hatcher, William Holmes, Samuel Hague, Jesse Myers, William Schooley, Deborah Holmes.

Abner Gregg, son of John Gregg, married Sarah Smith daughter of Wm. Smith, 30th day 12th mo 1779 at Goose Creek. Witnesses: John Gregg, William Smith, Ann Smith, Ruth Gregg, Rebekah Gregg, Ezekiel Smith, Mary Smith, Samuel Spencer, George Nickols, Ann Nickols, John Nickols, Margaret Nickols, William Brown, Joshua Smith, James Moore, Thomas Gregg, Alice Spencer, Mahlon Smith, William Smith, Thomas Gregg, John Hirst, Solomon Hoge, Mary Hirst, Israel Janney, Jane Hague, James Nickols, James Hatcher, William Daniel, Timothy Howell, Rebekah Howell, Rachel Scholefield, Hannah Spencer, Catharine Hatcher, John Howell, William Beans, David Scholefield, Hannah Beans, Elizabeth Howell, Elizabeth Nickols, Ruth Gregg, Hannah Gregg, Edith Smith,

Thomas Smith, Mary Janney, Samuel Gregg, John Gregg, Ann Pool, Sarah Reeder, Joseph Pool, George Brown, Robert Whitacre, Isaiah Nickols.

Thomas Brown, son of Isaac Brown and Martha his wife, married Ann Beck, daughter of Edwd. Beck and Ann his wife, the former deceased, 26th day 1st mo 1780 at South Fork. Witnesses: Isaac Brown, Martha Brown, Ann Beck, Joseph Brown, Preston Beck, Hannah Brown, Abigail Wells, Susanna Burson, Sarah Richards, Ruth Smith, Ann Russel, Hannah Smith, George Smith, Benja. Cummings, Joseph Burson, Sarah Fred, Priscilla Cumming, Samuel Guy, John Hirst, William Neal, Rachel Neal, Isaac Walker, James Burson, William Wells, Rebecca Trahern, Ben. Burson, Hannah Burson, James Trahern, William Trahern, William Goff, Constantine Hughes, Sarah Hirst, Rebekah Hirst, Jasper Seybold.

Isaiah Myers married Alice Yates Jr., 15th day 10th mo at South Fork. Witnesses: Alice Yates, Jonathan Myers, Mary Myers, Benjamin Yates, Esther Pierpoint, Elijah Myers, Sarah Schooley, Phebe Myers, Phebe Yates, William Schooley, Elisha Schooley, Ann Overfield, John Seybold, Ruth Gibson, Sarah Dixon, James Burson, Isaac Votaw, Ann Votaw, Benjamin Burson, Lewis Lemert, Isaac Walker, Sarah Fred, James Sinkler, Jesper Seybold, Ben. Overfield, Rebekah Seybold, William Neal, Samuel Smith, Solomon Dixon, Abraham Cowgill, Hannah Philips, Hannah Smith, Hannah Seybold.

George Gregg Jr., married Mary Gregg, 14th day 9th mo 1780 at Goose Creek. Witnesses: John Gregg, Samuel Gregg, Thomas Gregg, William Gregg, Ruth Gregg, Aaron Hackney, Wm. Mcgeath, Micajah Roach, Edmund Roach, Moses Calwell, Sarah Roach, Janney Patterson, William Daniel, Ann James, Moses Cadwalader, Ruth Cadwalader, Sarah Hirst, Rebekah Hatcher, Mary Mccullah, Owen Thomas, Devannah Bennett, Richard James, Jas. Mcfarlin, Thos. Hatcher, William Smith, Solomon Hoge, James Hatcher, Mercy Hatcher Jr., Catharine Hatcher.

William Schooley married Hannah Brown, 15th day 11th mo 1780. Witnesses: John Schooley, Mary Schooley, Wm. Brown, Phebe Myres, Richard Brown, Thomas Hughes, Reuben Schooley, James Ball, Mary Ball, Jonathan Myers, John Smith, Joshua Knowles, Elisha Schooley, Mary Myers, Elizabeth Ball, Mary Myers, Elizabeth Myers, Mercer Brown, Sarah Brown, Henry Brown, Mary Baker, Esther Brown, Mary Purdom,

Sarah Overfield, Ann Overfield, Stacy Janney, Rachel Schooley, David Caston, Jesse Myers, Benjamin Purdum, Jacob Scott, Benjamin Brady, William Scott, Edward Potts, John Eblin, Mary Dodd, Samuel Hague, George Gregg, Ann Scott, Elizabeth Brooke, Sarah Hough, Leah Ball, Sarah Baker, Eleanor Hough, Samuel Janney, John Eblin, Joel Lewis, Isaac Reeder, Rebekah Scott.

Owen Rogers of Hampshire Co., Virginia, married Mary Roach, daughter of Richard and Hannah Roach, 29th day 11th mo 1780. Witnesses: Owen Rodgers, Mary Rodgers, [many of the witnesses' names are unreadable]. Richd ___, Hannah ___, ..., Mary Baker, Hannah Janney, Eleanor Hough, Alice Myers, Israel Pidgeon, Mary Schooley, Catherine Brown, Ann Myers, Isaac Reeder, Joseph Janney, Isaac Thompson, William Pidgeon, John Schooley, George Gregg, William Brown, Thos. Matthews, John Hough, Mahlon Janney.

George Gregg married Margaret Todhunter, 27th day 12th mo 1780. Witnesses: William Gregg, John Todhunter, Aaron Hackney, Joseph Burgoyne, Ruth Gregg, Mary Gregg, Richard Roach, George Nixon, Mary Nixon, Hannah Roach, Jacob Todhunter, Joseph Todhunter, Hannah Janney, Elizabeth Janney, Sarah Brown, Mary Brown, Susannah Brown, Mary Baker, John Smith, Thomas Matthews, John Hough, Saml. Murrey, Mahlon Janney, Samuel Hough, Mahlon Hough, John Janney, William Mcgeath, Henry Brown, Isaac Hague, Abel Janney, Jonathan Myers, John Hough Jr., Elizabeth Ball, Ruth Ball, Sarah Hough, Sarah Baker, Lydia Hough, Eleanor Hough, Ann Scott, Mary Myers, Phebe Myres, Elisha Schooley, Jonah Hough, Sarah Roach, Ann Ball, Esther Brown, Joseph Janney.

James Moore, son of Thomas and Elizabeth Moore, married Phebe Myers, daughter of Joseph and Phebe Myers, 9th day 1st mo 1782. Witnesses: Joseph Myers, Elizabeth Moore, Phebe Myers, William Myers, Ann Smith, William Smith, Jonathan Myers, Mary Myers, Thomas Moore Jr., Asa Moore, Evan Taylor, Amy Taylor, Elizabeth Moore, Mary Myers, John Smith, Hannah Thompson, Rachel Pidgeon, Sarah Janney, Mary Baker, Lydia Hough, Deborah Brooke, Ann Stabler, Sarah Hough, Mary Stabler, Elizabeth Williams, Marah Cadwalader, Sarah Janney Jr., Ann Wildman, John Schooley, Sarah Overfield, Ann Overfield, Mary Myers Jr., Sarah Myers, Jonas Potts, Jonah Hough, John Janney, John Wildman, James Ball, Isaac Reeder, Edward Potts, Wm. Wildman, Joshua Knowles, Jacob Scott, John Neilson, Rebekah Scott, Hannah Janney, Mary Purdum, Sarah Roach, Elizabeth Myers, Mary Scott, Martha Scott, Mahlon Janney,

Benjamin Steer, Abel Janney, William Brown, William Pidgeion, Jos. Cadwalader, Mary Schooley, Rachel Schooley, Isaac Siddall, John Hough, Joseph Janney.

Constantine Hughes, son of Matthew Hughes and Elizabeth his wife of Bucks Co., Pennsylvania, married Elizabeth Nickols, widow of Thomas Nickols, deceased, daughter of William Janney and Elizabeth his wife, 10th day 1st mo 1782. Witnesses: Elizabeth Janney, Thomas Hughes, Sarah Hughes, Jacob Janney, Hannah Janney, Israel Janney, Saml. Canby, Rebekah Nickols, Letitia Wildman, Isaac Nickols, Joseph Pool, Jonas Janney, Ruth Janney, Jacob Janney Jr., Stacy Janney, [other names are unreadable].

Mahlon Hough, son of John Hough, married Mary Stabler, daughter of Edward Stabler of Dinwiddie Co., Virginia, 6th day 3rd mo 1782. Witnesses: John Hough, Sarah Hough, Edward Stabler, Sarah Janney, Ann Stabler, Sarah Hough Jr., Eleaner Hough, John Hough, Jr., Lydia Hough, William Hough, Samuel Hough, Jonah Hough, Samuel Canby, Ann Canby, Deborah Brooke, Mary Janney, Hannah Janney, Mary Baker, Sarah Hague, Mahlon Janney, Sarah Baker, Sarah Janney Jr., Margaret Thompson, Phebe Moore, Rachel Pidgeon, Ann Steere, Hannah Hague, Samuel Janney, Elizabeth Janney, William Pidgeon, Joseph Janney, James Moore, Israel Thompson, Jonah Thompson, John Janney, Jonas Potts, Thos. Matthews, John Pidgeon, Isaac Hague, Samuel Harris, Jr., Mary Myers Jr., Richard Roach, Mercer Brown, Jonathan Myers, Mary Myers, Mary Scott, Sarah Roach.

John Long married Mary Clark of Fauquier, 13th day 10th mo 1782 at South Fork. Witnesses: John Clark, Ann Clark, Daniel Clark, Alice Clark, John Clark Jr., Rebecka Clark, Thos. Gibson, Ann Gibson, William Gibson, Moses Gibson, David Gibson, Sarah Gibson, Isaac Votaw, Ann Votaw, Benjamin Borson, John Hirst, Mary Hirst, James Trahern, William Neal, John Gibson, Benjamin Sulkerson, Josiah Clawson, Robert Donaldson, James Sinkler, Mary Sinkler, Sarah Fred, James Ball, Rebekah Fairhurst, Sarah Overfield, Sarah Trahern, Rachel Neal, Sarah Roach, Ann Ball, John Coffee, Jonas Potts, George Fairhurst, Ann Sinkler, Isaac Nichols, Rebeka Nichols, Isaac Gibson, James Gibson, Richard Bird, Jesper Seybold, Solomon Dixon.

Samuel Hough, son of John? Hough, married Ann Stabler, daughter of Edward Stabler of Dinwiddie Co., Virginia, 13th day 4th mo 1783. [Witnesses are unreadable].

Robert Whitacre, son of John and Naomi Whitacre, married Sarah Roach, daughter of Richard and Hannah Roach, 28th day 5th mo 1783. Witnesses: Richard Roach, Joseph Whitacre, Phebe Whitacre, Alice Whitacre, Elizabeth Roach, James Roach, Benjamin Whitacre, Caleb Whitacre, Sarah Roach, Tabitha Tavener, Deborah Harris, Richard Roach, Jean Whitacre, Jacob Sands, Thomas Harris, Nathan Roach, Edmund Roach, Sarah Janney, Mary Baker, Eleanor Hough, Hannah Janney, Sarah Hough, Mary Myers, Elizabeth Williams, Sarah Baker, Mary Myers, Ann Ball, Mary Williams, Dewanner Bennet, Margaret Gregg, Ruth Gregg, Phebe Myers, Esther Brown, Permelia Johnston, Thos. Moore Jr., Benjamin Scott, John Smith, Jonah Hough, Jonas Potts, John Janney, John Coffee, Joseph Pool, David Hoge, Mahlon Janney, William Hough, Abel Janney, Joseph Janney, William Pedgeon, George Gregg, Aquila Janney.

George Chandlee of Frederick Co., Maryland, married Deborah Brooke, 27th day 8th mo 1783. Witnesses: Mahlon Janney, Sarah Janney, Betsey Brooke, Sarah Hough, Susannah Chandlee, James Brooke, Thomas Hague, Abel Janney, Jonas Potts, Hannah Janney, Mary Baker, Mary Myres, Margaret Gregg, Eleanor Hough, Rachel Pidgeon, Ann Steer, Ann Steer, Jr., Mary Poultney, Sarah Brown, Sarah Baker, Lydia Hough, Sarah Janney Jr., Mary Smith, Jean Griffith, Elizabeth Janney, Rachel Baker, Mary Scott, John Hough, Jesse Plummer, Thomas Moore Jr., Israel Thompson, Wm. Hough, Thomas Matthews, Benjamin Purdum, Wm. Pidgeon, Wm. Betts, Joseph Jonney, John Smith, John Pidgeon, Solomon Whitson, Mercer Brown.

Simeon Haines married Elizabeth Randall, 27th day 11th mo 1783 at Goose Creek. Witnesses: Joseph Randall, Rachel Randall, John Randall, Elisabeth Pancoast, James Dillon, Jacob Janney, James Hatcher, David Lacey, Sarah Lacey, Sarah Randall, Hannah Randall, Catharine Hatcher, Henry Nichols, Susanna Nichols, William Nichols, Sarah Nichols, Mary Pancoast, Simeon Pancoast, William Smith, Anne Smith, Moses Dillon, John Janney, Sarah Cox, Rachel Pidgeon Jr., Mary Hatcher, John Hirst, Moses Cadwalader, Mahlon Smith, Solomon Hoge, George Fairhurst, Joel Lewis, Elisabeth Fairhurst, Isaiah Hatcher.

John Smith married Sarah Hirst, 6th day 5th mo 1784 at Goose Creek. Witnesses: Henry Smith, Alice Smith, John Hirst, Mary Hirst, Judith Connard, Thomas Smith, Rachel Smith, Samuel Smith, Mary Smith, Thomas Smith, Rebekah Hirst, Hannah Janney, William Smith, Israel Janney, Mary Hoge, Mary Finniken, William Daniel, Jacob Janney, John Gregg, Solomon Hoge, James Hatcher, Catharine Hatcher, Anne Janney, Rebekah Gregg, Joseph Smith, William Smith, Thomas Cadwalader, Joel Lewis, William Hatcher, Mary Hatcher, William Patten, Lawrence Craft, John Hays, Jesse Hirst, David Hirst, Patterson Ingledew, Sarah Smith, Moses Cadwalader, Thomas Gregg, Stephen Gregg.

Isaac Hoge, son of Solomon Hoge and Amelia his wife, married Elisabeth Nichols, daughter of James Nichols and Elisabeth his wife, 29th day 4th mo 1784 at Goose Creek. Witnesses: Solomon Hoge, James Nichols, Mary Hoge, Isaac Nichols, Mary Hoge Jr., Blackston Janney, Thomas Gregg, William Nichols, George Nichols, Ann Nichols, Joshua Gore, Jonathan Lovett, Isaiah Nichols, Charity Nichols, Jacob Janney, John Hirst, Mary Hirst, Moses Cadwalader, Benjn. Mead, Hannah Janney, William Daniel, Sarah Hirst, Sarah Cadwalader, Ruth Cadwalader, Mary Hatcher, Rebekah Hirst, Israel Janney, Susannah Gregg, Ann Smith, Sarah Gregg, Sarah Nichols, Mary Janney, Ruth Gregg, Edith Smith, John Gregg, Stepehn Gregg, William Smith, Sarah Lemon, Margaret Nichols, Ruth? Gregg.

Isaac Brown, Jr., married Sarah Burson, 26th day 5th mo 1784 at South Fork. Witnesses: Isaac Brown, Martha Brown, James Burson, Jonathan Burson, Rebekah Burson, Benjamin Burson, Jessper Sybold, Thomas Brown, Ann Brown, Thos. Russell, Mary Russell, Hannah Burson, Joseph Burson, Henry Plaister, Susannah Plaster, Edward Whitacre, Martha Whitacre, Hannah Brown, Mary Brown, William Treyhorn, Anne Burson, Isaac Votaw, Ann Votaw, Thos. Reeder, Jacob Janney, Thos. Gregg, Solomon Dixon, John Preston, Israel Janney, Rebekah Preston, Rachel Neal, Sarah Hibbs, Sarah Treyhorn, William Neal, Rachel Burson, John Plaster.

John Seybold, son of Jesper Seybold married Hannah Cranmer, daughter of Andrew Cranmer, 30th day 6th mo 1784 at South Fork. Witnesses: Jesper Seybold, Andrew Cranmenr, Rebekah Seybold, Rebekah Trayhorn, Solomon Dixon, William Clayton, James Daniel, Alice Seybold, Joshua Fred, Sarah Fred, Rebekah Preston, Phebe Sinkler, Jas. Sinkler, John

Preston, Isaac Votaw, Ann Votaw, Hannah Daniel, Isaac Cowgill, Sarah Fred, Elisabeth Dixon, Isaac Brown, Wm. Neal, Rachel Neal, Benjamin Yeats, Ann Clark, Elisabeth Russell, Hannah Dillon, Sarah Brown, Thos. Russell, Mary Russell.

John Coffee married Rachel Pidgeon Jr., 8th day 12th mo 1784. Witnesses: William Pidgeon, John Pidgeon, Ruth Pidgeon, Elizabeth Williams, Benjamin Steer, Anna Steer, William Pidgeon Jr., Isaac Pidgeon, John Cleaver, Susannah Cleaver, William Kenworthy, William Kenworthy Jr., Rebekah Scott, Martha Scott, Elizabeth Scott, Mary Kenworthy Jr., Robert Miller, John Williams, Mary Betts, Ruth Taylor, Ann Hough, Sarah Hough Jr., Ann Ball, Elizabeth Hains, Eleanor Hough, Mary Purdom, Rachel Baker, Barbarah Wilkenson, Abigail Wood, Ruth Wood, Ruth Steer, Sarah Janney, Mary Janney, Mary Miers, Sarah Thompson, Ann Moore, John Hough, Richard Roach, Jonathan Myers, William Brown, Benjamin Purdom, George Gregg, William Betts, Jonathan Nutt, Ruth Gregg, Benjamin Scott, Amos Janney, Joseph Scott, Solomon Haines, Isaac Hague, Abel Janney, Israel Thompson, John Hayward, Elizabeth Moore Jr., Isaac Jacobs, Hough Judge, Thomas Matthews, Joseph Janney, William Hough, Samuel Hough, Humpry (sic) Baugham, Obed Pierpoint, Joseph Wood, Jonah Hough, Jonas Potts, Sarah Randle.

Samuel Gover married Sarah Janney, 16th day 12th mo 1782 at Goose Creek. Witnesses: Jacob Janney, Hannah Janney, Maragret Ingledue, Thomas Gregg, Rebekah Gregg, Hannah Janney, Ursula Plumer?, Mary Poultney, Sarah Trahern, Jonas Potts, Elisha Janney, Sarah Janney, Mary Hatcher, James Hatcher, Catharine Hatcher, William Smith William Hatcher, Jeseph Randal, Thomas Smith, Rachel Smith, Solomon Hoge, Mary Hoge, Moses Cadwalader, Mahlon Janney, Isaac Lane, Ezekiel Cleaver, John Hirst, Mary Hirst, Lydia Miller, John Smith, Sarah Smith, Elizabeth Williams, Mary Hatcher Jr., Benjamin Mead.

Thomas Cadwalader married Jane Daniel, 31st day 3rd mo 1785 at Goose Creek. Witnesses: William Daniel, Hester Daniel, Moses Cadwalader, Samuel Smith, Mary Smith, Sarah Cadwalader, Ruth Cadwalader, Sarah Daniel, Hester Daniel Jr., Martha Daniel, Moses Cadwalader Jr., Jesse Cadwalader, Joseph Daniel, Benjamin Daniel, Isaac Miller, Joel Lewis, James Dillon Jr., Ann Hatcher, Jane Howel, Deborah Howel, Mary White, Sarah White, William Smith, Elizabeth Smith, Sarah Smith, Thomas Smith Jr., Hannah Gregg, Thomas Gregg, John Gregg, William Smith,

Ann Smith, James Dillon, Nathan Spencer, Hannah Spencer, Solomon Whitson, Phebe Withson, Alice Smith, Ruth Gregg, Sarah Nichols, George Fairhirst, Israel Janney, Hannah Janney, John Smith, Anne Mead, Sarah Smith, Alice Lewis, Joseph Pool, Rebekah Pool, James Hatcher, William Beans, John Hirst, Rebekah Gregg, Solomon Hoge, Thomas Smith, Thomas Hatcher, Rebekah Hatcher, Margery Nichols, Benjamin Mead.

Benjamin Mead married Ann Patterson 31st day 3rd mo 1785 at Goose Creek. Witnesses: Joseph Clowes, Joseph Gore, Nancy Clowes, Rebekah Pool, Hannah Janney, Sarah Gore, Hannah Janney Jr., Dinah Gregg, Sarah Nichols, George Fairhirst, Thomas Welch, Rebekah Gregg, Elizabeth Smith, Ruth Gregg, Rachel Patterson, Israel Janney, Solomon Hoge, Wm. Kenworthy Jr., Elisha Janney, Thomas Gore, Samuel Gregg, James Trahern, Bleackstone Janney, William Nichols, Joseph Pool, Ann Smith, John Gregg, William Smith, William Daniel, James Dillon Jr., Joel Lewis, Alice Lewis, Thomas Hatcher, Stephen Gregg, Thomas Smith, Solomon Whitson, James Dillon, James Hatcher, Jonas Janney, Joseph Janney, Thomas Smith, Joseph Randal, John Hirst, William Hatcher, Thos. Gregg.

James Dillon married Ann Hatcher, 7th day 4th mo 1785 at Goose Creek. Witnesses: William Dillon, John Hatcher, Rachel Dillon, Sarah Hatcher, James Dillon, Rebekah Dillon, George Fairhirst, Agness Dillon, Rebekah Beans, Eliza Fairhirst, Joshua Hatcher, Jane Hatcher, Josiah Dillon, William Hatcher, Sarah Dillon, Thomas Smith, Elizabeth Smith, Thomas Cadwalader, Jane Cadwalader, William Smith, Anna Smith, Samuel Goodin, Martha Goodin, Rebeca Hirst, David Goodin, Timothy Beans, Sarah Goodin, John Hirst, Mary Hirst, Benjamin Mead, Joel Lewis, Wm. Kenworthy, Rebekah Gregg, Hannah Janney, Moses Cadwalader, John Smith, Mary Hatcher, James Hatcher, Esther Daniel, Ann Mead, Joseph Smith, Martha Daniel, William Daniel, William Daniel, William Beans, Hannah Beans, Hestor Daniel.

Samuel Gregg, son of Thomas and Rebekah Gregg, married Ann Sinclear, daughter of James and Mary Sinclear, 15th day 6th mo 1785 at South Fork. Witnesses: Thomas Gregg, James Sinclare, Benjamin Mead, Joshua Swayne, Hannah Janney, Phebe Sinclar, George Sinclear, Albinah Gregg, Elisha Janney, Jacob Gregg, Dinah Gregg, Isaac Votaw, Ann Votaw, Isaac Brown, James Burson, William Neal, Hannah Burson, Hannah Dillon, Mary Burson, Elizabeth Russel, Mary Reeder, Esther Gibson, Phebe

Gibson, John Brown, Sarah Brown, John Clark, Ann Clark, Sarah Clark, Benjamin Burson, Rebekah Burson, John Sinclear, Margaret McVickers, Euphany Lacey, Tacey Lacey, James McNabb, Archibald McVickers, David Gibson, Sarah Gibson, Letty McVickers, Thomas Gibson, Ann Gibson, Jesse Lewis, Jane McVickers, Joel Lewis, George Lewis, Esther Gibson, John Preston, Rebekah Paeston (sic), Elisabeth Pryor, Gasper Sebold, Solomon Dixon, Wm. Kenworthy Jr., Rebekah Gibson, James Hagaman.

Samuel Hutton married Sarah Cadwalader, 8th day 9th mo 1785 at Goose Creek. Witnesses: Moses Cadwalader, Moses Cadwalder Jr., Jesse Cadwalder, Ruth Cadwalader, Benjamin Hutton, Thomas White, Wm. Malin, Wm. Daniel, Esther Daniel, Thos. Cadwalader, Jane Cadwalader, Isaac White, Esther Daniel Jr., Sarah White, Elizabeth Updike, Sarah Updike, Thomas Hutton, Benjamin Mead, Anne Mead, William Kirk, Judith Cunnard, Ann Hirst, Wm. Kenworthy Jr., Wm. Pidgeon, John Coffee, Rachel Coffee, Rebekah Gregg, Thomas Malin, Sarah Malin, Thomas Hatcher, Rebekah Hatcher, John Pidgeon, Ruth Pidgeon, Samuel Massey, John Hirst, James Hatcher, Rachel Randal, William Smith, Solomon Hoge, Israel Janney, William Brown, John Smith, Margery Nichols, Rebekah Pool, Mary Hatcher, Stephen Gregg, Anne Janney, Rebekah Hirst.

Francis Hague of Leesburg, son of John Hague deceased, and Ann his wife, married Ruth Rattikin, daughter of James Rattikin and Susannah his wife, 4th day 1st mo 1786. Witnesses: Jane Rattikin, Susannah Rattikin, Jane Rattikin, Susannah Rattikin Jr., Sarah Rattikin, Samuel Hague, Ann Wildman, Wm. Wildman Jr., John Schooley, Jonathan Myers, Mary Myers, Edward Potts, Jonas Potts, Caleb Bentley, Rachel Paxon, Thomas Matthews, Thos. Moore Jr., Joseph Wood, Isaac Pidgeon, Wm. Pidgeon, Rachel Pidgeon, Ann Jones, Jane Griffith, John Campbell, Mahlon Janney, Wm. Hough, Ann Hough, Lydia Hough, Sally Hough, Mary Betts, Wm. Betts, Elizabeth Moore, Sarah Baker.

Richard Brown, son of William Brown and Elizabeth his wife, married Sarah Cox, daughter of Joseph Cox and Sarah his wife, 11th day 1st mo 1786. Witnesses: William Brown, Joseph Cox, Sarah Cox, Elizabeth Brown, William Brown Jr., John Brown, Elizabeth Hains, Semion Hains, Mary Pancoast, Samuel Hague, Reuben Schooley, Esther Schooley, Ephraim Lacey, Joel Lewis, Stacy Hains, Elisabeth Moore Jr., Hannah Pancoast, Samuel McFarling, John Hawkins, Mary McFarling, Mahlon

Janney, Henry Brown, John Brown, John Hirst, Israel Thompson, William Hough, Sarah Janney, Susannah Rattikin, Rachel Coffee, Elizabeth Williams, Ann Hough, Sally Hough, Elisabeth Jolliffe, Samuel Hough, James Rattikin, Mary Betts, Sarah Lacey, Elisabeth Moore, John Schooley, Benjamin Steer, William Pidgeon, John Coffee, Rachel Pidgeon, [Jona]than Myers.

Edward Reece married Sarah Smith, 18th day 1st mo 1786 at South Fork. Witnesses: Ralph Cowgill, Sarah Cowgill, Abraham Cowgill, Isaac Cowgill, Hannah Cowgill, Tamer Cowgill, Sarah Smith, Dorithy Cowgill, Mary Smith, Elisabeth Smith, Joseph Smith, Sarah Gibson, David Gibson, Solomon Dixon, Isaac Brown, Martha Brown, Lydia Gibson, William Neal, Benjamin Yeats, Rebekah Burson, Simon Hancock, Mary Hancock, William Jones, John Gibson, Stephen Willson, William Gibson, Isaac Votaw, Ann Votaw, Mary Votaw, Mary Leonard, Hester Gibson, Mariam Gibson, Benjamin Burson.

Benjamin Scott, son of Joseph and Ann Scott, married Sarah Randall, daughter of Joseph and Rachel Randall, 6th day 9th mo 1786. Witnesses: Joseph Scott, Ann Scott, Joseph Randall, Rachel Randall, Jacob Scott, Elisabeth Scott, Rebekah Scott, Mary Scott, Ruth Randall, Rachel Randall Jr., Martha Scott, Sarah Janney, Eleanor Hough, Elisabeth Williams, Elisabeth Moore, Rachel Pidgeon, Mary Betts, Elisabeth Janney, Sarah Janney, Ann Steer, Elisabeth Brown, Mary Schooley, Mahlon Janney, John Hough, Jonathan Myers, Mary Myers, Benjamin Purdum, Wm. Pidgeon, John Coffee, Wm. Brown, Thos. Moore Jr., Joseph Wood, Mary Wood, Stephen Scott, Obed Perpoint, James Moore, James Burson, Hamilton Rogers, Jonas Scott, John Schooley, Joseph Randall Jr., Joseph Scott Jr., John Randall, Thomas Green, Isaac Siddall, Asa Moore.

John Roberts, son of Richard and Mary Roberts of Frederick Co., Maryland, married Rebekah Scott, daughter of Jacob and Elizabeth Scott (the former deceased), 2nd day 1st mo 1788. Witnesses: Elizabeth Scott, Richard Roberts, Henry Roberts, Joseph Scott, Sarah Janney, Hannah Janney Jr., Miriam Roberts, Wm. Hayward, Martha Scott, Sally Roberts, Rachel Paxson, Ann Ball, Ruth Pidgeon, Eliza Gregg, Mary Jolliffe, Eliza Moore, Ann Talbott,Sally Taylor, Mary Myres, Elizabeth Williams, Mary Betts, Hannah Janney, Lydia Hough, Anna Steer, Hannah Lewis, Elizabeth Bennett, Winifred Bennett, Phebe Moore, Eliza. Richardson, Sarah Richardson, Nancy Taylor, Rachel Coffee, Eliza. Janney, Joseph

Wood, John Schooley, Jesse Hughes, Stephen Wilson, Wm. Betts, Thos. Moore Jr., Rachel Taylor, Nancy Moore, Rachel Scott, Jonas Potts, Joseph Roberts, John Pidgeon, Christopher Hussey, Jas. McCormick, Mary Scott, John Hough, Mahlon Janney, Joseph Janney, Jas. Rattiken, Benjn. Steer, Wm. Hough, Benjn. Purdom, Wm. Pidgeon, James Moore, John Coffee, Fielder Richardson, Wm. Paxson, Benjn. Scott, Sarah Scott, Joseph Taylor, Hezekiah Ford, Asa Moore.

Joseph Wilkinson, son of Joseph and Barbary Wilkinson, married Elizabeth Gregg, daughter of William and Rebekah Gregg, 26th day 11th mo 1788. Witnesses: William Gregg, Samuel Gregg, Ruth Gregg, James Roach, Esther Gregg, Aaron Gregg, Rachel Scott, Hannah Janney, Hannah Janney Jr., Betsy Bennett, Ann Schooley, Elizabeth Moore Jr., Sarah Janney Jr., Elizabeth Scott, Martha Scott, Winifred Bennett, Joseph Taylor, Jonathan Myers, Wm. Hough, Samuel Baker, Charles Bennett Jr., Jonas Potts, Wm. Paxson, Mahlon Janney, Wm. Hough, Benjamin Steer, Joseph Talbott, James Rattikin, Richard Richardson, Benjamin Scott, Joseph Scott, Joseph Janney.

Abraham Griffith, son of Isaac Griffith of Baltimore, married Rachel Taylor, daughter of Thomas Taylor, 30th day 12th mo 1788. Witnesses: Thomas Taylor Senr., Caleb Taylor, Jesse Taylor, Ruth Taylor, John Griffith, Joseph Burson, Mordicai Price, Ann Griffith, Sally Taylor, Nancy Taylor, Joseph Taylor, John Schooley Jr., Stephen Wilson, Rachel Scott, Elizabeth Scott, Jane Griffith, Sarah Janney Jr., Elizabeth Bennett, Hannah Janney, Rebekah Gregg, Elizabeth Moore, John Matthews, Charity Comety, Wm. Gregg, Mary Jolliffe, Elizabeth Richardson, Elizabeth Moore Jr., Hannah Janney Jr., Martha Scott, Susanah Bennett, James Moreley, Thomas Moore Jr., Jonah Hough, Samuel Pierpoint, Joseph Wilkinson, Jonas Potts, Elizabeth Wilkinson, Sarah Richardson, Winifred Bennett, Henry Taylor, Joseph Talbott, Joseph Janney, Joseph Scott, Charles Bennett, Sydnor Bennett, Wm. Paxson, Edward Potts, Charles Bennett Jr., Baulis Comes, James Moore.

Richard Larue married Hannah Lewis, daughter of John and Alice Lewis, late of Loudoun, 8th day 4th mo 1789. Witnesses: Benjamin Steer, Ann Steer Senr., Anna Steer, Hannah Siddall, Ruth Steer, Sarah Janney, Eleanor Hough, Hannah Janney, Elizabeth Moore, Ann Scott, Elizabeth Baugham, Phebe Moore, Lydia Hough, Ann Talbott, Eliza. Moore Jr., Sarah Janney Jr., Sarah Overfield, Jane Erwin, Magdalen Erwin, John

Hough, Israel Thompson, John Schooley Jr., Thomas Siddall, Samuel Erwin, Isaac Siddall, Mary Schooley, Elizabeth Myers, Hannah Williams, Elizabeth Williams, Mary Bynns, Joseph Janney, Wm. Hough, Jonathan Myers, Joseph Talbott, James Rattiken, Thos. Moore Jr., Jonas Potts, James Moore, John Schooley, James Erwin.

Stephen Wilson, son of Samuel and Sarah Wilson, married Martha Scott, daughter of Jacob Scott, deceased, and Elisabeth Scott his wife, 13th day 5th mo 1789. Witnesses: Samuel Wilson, Sarah Wilson, Elizabeth Scott, Rebekah Roberts, Ann Scott, John Roberts, Saml. Wilson Jr., Rachel Scott, Sarah Roberts, Mary Wilson, Stephen Scott, Anne Talbott, Sarah Janney, Isaac Siddall, Elisabeth Williams, Hannah Siddall, Rebekah Siddall, Jane Whitacre, Anna Wildman, Ann Ballinger, Hannah Scott, Mahlon Janney, Chas. Bennett, Lydia Hough, Eleanor Hourgh, Sarah Rogers, Jane Erwin, Jane Rattiken, Mary Myers, Joseph Wilson Joseph Whitacre, Joseph Talbott, Jonathan Myers, Isaac Garretson, Thos. Siddall, Wm. Hayward.

Benjamin Purdum married Elizabeth Williams, 9th day 12th mo 1789. Jeremiah Purdum, John Williams, Abner Williams, Hannah Williams, Benjamin Steer, Anna Steer, Elizabeth Steer, Eleanor Hough, Lydia Hough, Anna Talbott, Joseph Talbott, John Hough, Sarah Janney, Mary Myers, Elizabeth Moore Jr., Sarah Janney Jr., Anna Wildman, Hannah Janney, Ann Scott, Elizabeth Moore, Samuel Erwin, Thomas Siddal, Joseph Wilson, John Schooley Jr., Thos. Moore Jr., Jonas Potts, Jonah Hough, James Moore, Isaac Siddall, John Martain Senr., Jane Erwin, Hannah Siddall, Mary Erwin, Joseph Janney, Thomas Vickers, Israel Thompson, William Hough, Sarah Thompson, Mary Nicklin.

John Scott Pleasants, son of Jacob Pleasants, deceased, and Sarah Pleasants his wife, of Henrico Co., married Sarah Lownes, daughter of James and Sarah Lownes of Alexandria, 29th day 4th mo 1790 at Alexandria. Witnesses: James Lownes, Sarah Lownes, Hyatt Lownes, John Lownes, Debby Lownes, Sarah Pancoast, Aaron Hewes, Mary Saunders, Lydia Greene, John Saunders, Rebekah Shrieve, Sarah Hewes, Elichal? Dick, Thomas Erwin, A. Brown, Robert Donaldson, John Porter, H. Dick, O. Winsor?, Joshua Maryman, Joseph Dalenty, Caleb Green, Mary Harris, Mary Sykes, Mary Paton, John Butcher, Wm. Hartshorne, Sarah Hartshorne, Rachel Hartshorne, Rebekah Hartshorne, Ann Butcher, Susa. Hartshorne.

Thomas Irwin of Alexandria, son of Thomas and Abigail Irwin, married Elizabeth Janney, daughter of Joseph and Hannah Janney, 31st day 8th mo 1791. Witnesses: Joseph Janney, Hannah Janney, Mary Baker, Hannah Janney Jr., John Janney Jr., Sarah Janney Jr., Sarah Baker, Rebecca Janney, Susan Janney, Sarah Janney, John Janney, Lydia Hough, John Hough, Benja. Rice, Anne Steer, Mahlon Janney, Elizabeth Moore Jr., Sarah Taylor, Anne Taylor, Elizabeth Moore, Eleanor Hough, Mahlon Janney Jr., Margert Gregg, Susannah Rattikin, Winifred Bennett, Anne Ball, Elizabeth Bennett, Joseph Taylor, Samuel Talbott, Chas. Bennett, Joseph Hough, Edward Potts, Elizabeth S. Hough, Sarah Talbott, Benjn. Purdum, Sarah Paxton, James Paxson, Ruth Taylor, Rachel Peirpoint, Lucy Acton, Benj. Willett, Wm. Jackson, Henry Burkitt, Charles Bennett, Wm. Hough, Joseph Talbott, Wm. Gregg, Thomas Harris, Asa Moore.

Charles Harper of Fairfax Co. married Sarah Janney 28th day 12th mo 1791. Witnesses: Jos. Janney, Hannah Janney, Eliza. Erwin, Hannah Janney Jr., Rebekah Janney, Susan Janney, John Hough, Mahlon Janney, Sarah Janney, Elizabeth Moore, Elizabeth Purdum, Sarah Matthews, Lydia Hough, Thos. Matthews, Jonah Hough, Jos. Talbott, Sarah Mason, Charles Douglas, Wm. Gregg, John Schooley, Benjamin Purdum, John Schooley Jr., Anne Ball, Sarah Paxson, James Paxson, Wm. Jackson, Eliza. Moore Jr., Benjamin Steer, Anna Steer.

Philip Wanton, of Alexandria, son of Phillip Wanton, deceased, of Newport, Rhode Island, and Sarah his wife, married Mary Saunders, daughter of David Pancoast, deceased, and Sarah his wife, of Alexandria, 31st day 5th mo 1792 at Alexandria. Witnesses: Sarah Pancoast, R. Prescott, John Lownes, Aaron Hewes, Mary Hewes, Susanna Shrieve, Lydia Greene, Sarah Hewes, Mary Davis, Mary Patton, Sarah Saunders, Wm. Hartshorne, Susa. Hartshorne, Rebekah Hartshorne, Deby Lownes, Benjn. Shrieve, Elisha C. Dick, Job Greene, Ann Butcher, John Hornor, Ann Patton, Mary Shrieve, Henry Stanton Earl, Phebe Earl, Eliz. Dulany, Margaret Murry, Thos. Patton, Wm. Newton, Leml. Bent, John Taylor, Amy Budd, Hannah Dick, John Jefferson, Robt. Hartshorne, Wm. Hartshorne Jr.

Samuel Hopkins, son of John and Elizabeth Hopkins, of Ann (sic) Arundel Co., Maryland, married Hannah Janney, daughter of Jos. and Hannah Janney of Loudoun, 29th day of 8th mo 1792. Witnesses: Joseph Janney,

Hannah Janney, Rebekah Janney, Elia. Hopkins, Susanna Janney, John Janney, Gerard Hopkins, John Cowman Jr., John Hough, Mahlon Janney, Sarah Janney, Sarah Matthews, Eleanor Hough,, Ann Hough, Sarah Maison, Farling Ball, Alice Myers, Ruth Hague, Sarah Hough, Nancy Thompson, Wm Hough, Elizabeth Hough, Charles Douglass, Sarah Paxson, Ann Steer, Martha Wilson, Anna Ball, Ruth Taylor, Hannah Williams, Elizabeth Moore Jr., Asa Moore, Elizabeth Moore, Sarah Hough, James Paxson, John Schooley Jr., John Hollingsworth, Joseph Talbott, Jonah Hough, Benjn. Steer, Thos. Gillingham, Wm. Stabler, Thomas Hough, Samuel Hough, Samuel Gregg, Benjn. Purdum.

Bernard Taylor, son of Timothy Taylor late of New Town in Bucks Co., Pennsylvania, deceased, married Sarah Smith, daughter of Henry Smith, late of Loudoun, deceased, 15th day 11th mo 1792. Witnesses: Alice Smith, Esther Penquite, Stacy Taylor, Fanny Taylor, Mahlon Taylor, Mary Taylor, Timothy Taylor, Achsah Taylor, Jonathan Taylor, Ann Taylor, David Taylor, Catherine Taylor, Wm. Smith, Thos. Smith, Sarah Smith, Ann Fisher, Thos. Smith, Hannah Smith, Ann Smith, David Smith, Anne Potts, Mary Potts, John Stokes, Eliza. Stokes, Joseph Beale, Mahlon Baldwin, Mercy Baldwin, Hannah Beale, Theophilous Hoff, John Janney, Thos. Gore, Joseph Fisher, Benjamin Purdum, Rachel Daniel, Sarah Love, Rebekah Dillon, Eliza. Love, Abelon? Dillon, Mary Hough, Susanna Nut, Grace Beale, Eliza. Nut, Thos. Beale, John Harfeld, Samuel Russel, Wm. Thopson (sic), James Dillon, Wm. Daniel, Jesse Hirsh, Thos. Love, Wm. Stallcup, Thos. Gregg, Wm. Beale, Joseph Pool, James Love, Nathan ___, Abel Keys.

Mordecai Miller of Alexandria, son of Warwick and Elizabeth Miller, deceased, of Chester Co., Pennsylvania, married Rebecca Hartshorne, daughter of William and Susanna Hartshorne of Fairfax Co., VA, 8th day 11th mo 1792. Witnesses: Rachel Saunders, Hannah Lewis Jr., Wm. Hartshorne Jr., Robt. Hartshorne, Mary Hartshorne, Jos. Hartshorne, Peter S. Hartshorne, Lydia Greene, Sarah Hewes, Nancy Patton, Susanna Shrieve, John Horner, Jas. Lownes, Phillip Wanth[on], Jos. Lewis, A. Moore, Wm. Hartshorne, Susanna Hartshorne, Ann Butcher, Mary Patton, Rebecca Shrieve, Deborah Lownes, Abram Hewes, Mary Wanton, Sarah Pancoast, Mary Davis, Rachel Miller, Betty Donaldson, Anna H. Chapin, Eliza. Burr, Wm. Mendinall, Benjn. Dulanny, John Lownes?, Robt. Donaldson, John Foster, ___ Hanson, S. Hanson of Saml., John Taylor, Edward Harper, ___ Deulele, Ebenezer Stark?, Ezra Kinsey, Saml.

Thompson, Gurden Chapin, Edward Stabler, Cornelious Hinson, Benjn. Shrieve Jr., Mahlon Janney, Samuel Lownes, John Butcher, Eliza. Dulany, Mary Ann Hartman, Ann Peyton, T. Thompson, John Hough, Eliza. Dulany Jr., Mary Robertson, Nancy Peyton, Ann H. Hanson, Margaret Millnor, Martha Mendinhall, Maria Hanson, Mordecai Lewis, Aaron Hewes, Benjn. Shrieve, Job Greene.

Edward Potts, son of Jonas Potts and Mary his wife, deceased, married Mary Backhouse, daughter of John Backhouse and Mary his wife, of Newcastle, Delaware, 12th day 12th mo 1792. Witnesses: Jno. Hollingsworth, Levi Hollingsworth, Thos. Backhouse, Lydia Hough, Jonas Potts, Betsy Hough, Eleanor Hough, Eliza. Bennett, Anna Ball, Eliza. Moore Jr., Martha Wilson, Sarah Hough, Dinah Rion, Stephen [Wilson?], Betsy Hough, Sarah Janney, Sarah Thompson, George Gregg, Wm. Gregg, Hannah Brooke, Thos. Moore Jr., Jos. Wilkinson, Mary Holingsworth, Mary Moore, Sarah Paxson, Nancy McCormick, Charles Bennett, Mahlon Janney, James Rattiken, Benjn. Scott, Obed Peirpoint, Elizabeth Purdum, Sarah Gover, Elizabeth Scott, Mary Schooley, Susanna Rattiken, Samuel Gover, Asa Moore, Wm. Hough, Jno Scooley Jr., Wm. Hough the 3rd, Jonah Hough, Ben. H. Canby, Samuel Hough Jr., Richard Griffith, Jno. Schooley, Mahlon Janney Jr., Isaac Siddall, Jas. Heaton.

Benjamin Hough Canby, son of Samuel and Elizabeth Canby, deceased, married Sarah Taylor, daughter of Thomas Taylor and Caleb his wife, 26th day 12th mo 1792. Witnesses: Thos. Taylor, Caleb Taylor, John Hough, Richd. Richardson, Obed Peirpoint, Jesse Taylor, Wm. Richardson, Joseph Taylor, Nancy Taylor, Henry Taylor, Margaretta Gaunt, Thos. Gillingham, Richd. Richardson Jr., A. Southerland, J. Sm. H. Canby, Joseph Hough, Eleanor Hough, Lydia Hough, Rebekah Janney, Susanna Janney, Wm. Hough, Mary Moore, Phebe Moore, Elizabeth Purdum, Eliza. Moore Jr., Martha Wilson, Elizabeth Scott, Sarah Paxson, Joseph Talbott, John Schooley Jr., Joseph Janey, Thos. Moore Jr., Robert Braden, John Williams, Elizabeth Hough, Mary Peirpoint, Sarah Richardson, Sarah Hough, Jonah Hough, Benjn. Purdum, John Hollingsworth.

Jacob Sands, married Esther Brown, 8th day 1st mo 1794. Witnesses: H__ Brown, S__ Sands, Hanah Brown, Eleanor Hough, Ann Ball, Hannah Janney, M__ Sylbott (sic), Martha Burgoin, Hannah Ball, James Ball, John Hough, Wm. Hough, Sarah James, Elizabeth Purdum, Elia. Moore

Jr., Mahlon Janney, Dorothy Schooley, Jos. Wood, Wm. Gregg, Sarah Paxson, Jos. Talbott, Thos. Matthews, Henry Burkitt, John Williams, Wm. Paxson, Asa Moore, Isaac Siddal, Benn. Steer, A.B. Thompson Mason, Richard Griffith.

Joseph Bond, of Frederick Co., Virginia, son of Samuel and Thomzin Bond, both deceased, married Elizabeth Moore Jr., daughter of Thomas and Elizabeth Moore, 1st day 12th mo 1794. Witnesses: Thomas Moore, Elizabeth Moore, James Moore, Hannah Bond, Thos. Moore Jr., Ann Moore, Jas. McCormick, Anne McCormick, Jane McPherson, Samuel Bond, Rachel Taylor, Eleanor Hough, Elizabeth Scott, Elizabeth Purdum, Rebecca Janney, Isaac Janney, Ann Steer, Sarah Janney, Eliza. Hough, Sarah Hough, Jos. Talbott, Sarah Smith, Ann Steer, John Williams, Abner Williams, Hannah Williams, Rebecah Talbott, Eliza. Plumer, John Hough, Wm. Hough, Abel Walker, Mahlon Janney, Thos. Matthews, Benjn. Purdum, Benjn. Steer, Charles Rogers, Jas. Rattiken, Obed Peirpoint, Jonah Hough, Richard Griffith, Isaac Siddal, Jas. Wood, John Hollingsworth.

John Brown, son of Isaac Brown and Margaret his wife, deceased, of Frederick Co., Virginia, married Elizabeth Richardson, daughter of Richard Richardson and Mary his wife, of Frederick Co., Maryland, 29th day 1st mo 1795 at Richard Richardson's house. Witnesses: John Brown, Elizabeth Brown, Richard Richardson, Mary Richardson, Sally Richardson, ___ Richardson, Fielder Richardson, Saml. Richardson, William Richardson, Eliza. Purdom, Thos. Taylor, Ann Taylor, Wm. Hough, Mahlon Janney, Joseph Tolbot, Joseph Hough, Obed Pierpoint, Sarah Taylor, F. Gaunt, James Marshall, Baylis Combs, Ann Richardson, Elizabeth Hough, Sarah Hough, Joseph Taylor, Saml Hough, Anna Steer, Susanna Gaunt, Ursley Richardson, Jane Pancoast, Lucey Anderson, Margeretta Gant, Rebecca Beale, Charles Rogers, Christn. Kemp, Jenny Brisk.

George Drinker of Alexandria, son of Joseph and Hannah Drinker of Philadelphia, married Ruth Miller, daughter of Warwick and Elizabeth Miller, deceased, of Chester Co., Pennsylvania, 9th day 7th mo 1795. Witnesses: Susa. Hartshorne, Rebecca Miller, Robert Hartshorne, Rachel Miller, Hannah Coats, William Hartshorne, Mordica Miller, John Butcher, Lydia Greene, Mary Shrieve, Sarah Pancoast, Ann Butcher, Mary Shrieve, Ann Hewes, Philip Wanton, Jonathan Butcher, R.P. Richardson, Isaac Shrieve, William Poultney?, Betsey Voteh, Margaret Thompson, R.

Greenway, Elisa Hannah, Amos Love, Peggy Triplet, Sus. Janney, Eliz. Hough, Rachel Baker, Mary Hartshorne, Ann Patton.

Daniel Hirst, son of John and Mary Hirst, married Ann Smith, daughter of Thomas and Rachel Smith, 6th day 4th mo 1796. Witnesses: John Hirst, Mary Hirst, Thomas Smith, Joseph Tolbot, Rebecca Tolbot, Jesse Hirst, Hannah Smith, Mary Hatcher, Sarah Tolbot, Sarah Janney, Jane Raticane, Sarah Raticans, Lydiah Hough, Elizabeth Scott, Doroty Schooley, John Smith, Saml. Thompson, Mahlon Janney, James Raticans, Joseph Wood, Elenor Hough, Susan Janney, John Brown, Ann Brown, Mary Tolbot, James Paxton, Sarah Paxton, Benjamin Purdom, Isaac Siddall, Elisabeth Purdom, Sarah Thompson, John [Willis/Williams?], Wm. Hough, Abner Williams, Elisabeth Beal, Mercy Beal, Mary Myars, Rebecca Janney, Dun. McLean, Benjamin Steer, Anna Steer, Ann Steer, Hannah Williams, Polly Clandennen, Joseph Tolbot, Evan Griffith.

John McClun, of Loudoun, son of Thomas and Hannah McClun, of Fredrick, Virginia, married Elizabeth Beal, daughter of Joseph and Hannah Beal, 1st day 6th mo 1797, at the Gap [Hillsboro]. Witnesses: Joseph Beale, Hannah Beale, Thomas Beale, Mary McClun, Sarah Beale, Samuel Beale, Hannah Beale Jr., Rachel Beale, Robert Russel, Wm. Cambell, Mahlon Janney, Wm. Stalcup, Rebekah Stalcup, Jonas Potts, John Russell, Wm. Smith, John Hollingsworth, James Thompson, Nancy Beale, Sarah Love, Thomas Beale, Maragrett Russell, Lydia Purssell, Nancy Russell, Polly Blake, Benjn. Purdom, John Hirst, Mary Hirst, Sarah Janney, Sarah Smith, Elizabeth Purdom, Jamima Hollingsworth, Martha Beale, Hannah Russell, Saml. Smith, James Love, Joseph Tribbee, Josiah White Jr., Thomas Keys, Ruth Tribbe, Elisabeth Smith, Wm. Thompson, Elizabeth Morris, Asa Moore, Sarah Moore, Danl. Stone, Anna Potts, David Potts, Jane Potts, Mercy Beale, Elisabeth Russell, Saml Russell, John Love, Jane Thompson, Susannah Potts, Sarah Roach, Sally Ogdon, Wm. Russell Jr.

Abram Hewes, of Alexandria, son of James and Ursula Hewes of Middlesex, New Jersey, married Rachel Miller, daughter of Warwick and Elizabeth [Miller], of Chester Co., Pennsylvania, deceased, 14th day 7th mo 1796 at Alexandria. Witnesses: Mordica Miller, Rebekah Miller, Ruth Drinker, Wm. Hartshorne, Susa. Hartshorne, George Drinker, Aaron Hewes, Mary Hewes, Lydia Green, Saml. Davis, David Hewes, Peter S. Hartshorne, Sarah Hewes, Eliza. Brown, Philip Wanton, Wm. Patton Jr.,

Mary Wanton, Saml. Stansbury, Benjamin Shrieve Jr., Wm. Hartshorne Jr., Elizabeth Browne, Hannah Robertson, Ann M. Patton, Peggy Sanford, Mary Hartshorne, Sarah Hartshorne, Ann Butcher, Ann Coast, Sarah Saunders, Mattw. J. Bowen, John Janney, Caleb Shrieve, John M. Rea, Wm. Mendenhall, Jesse Pugh, Thomas Shrieve, Stephen Aby, Isaac Shrieve, John Butcher, Robt Hartshorn, Pattison Hartshorne, Edward Stabler, Jonathan Butcher, James H. Hamilton, J.[I.] Hartshorne.

Abner Williams, son of Wm. Williams, deceased, and Elizabeth his wife, married Mary Wood, daughter of Joseph and Abigail Wood, 30th day 11th mo 1796. Witnesses: Benjamin Purdom, Joseph Wood, Elizabeth Purdom, Abigal Wood, John Williams, James Ball, Ruth Ball, Naomi Wood, Anna Steer, Isaac Steer, Wm. Steer, John Wood, Jesse Wood, Ann Steer, Josesph Wood Jr., John Hough, Mahlon Janney, Sarah Janney, Susanna Ratikin, James Siddall, Elisha Talbott, Thomas Poulton, Wm. Hough, Elenor Hough, Joseph Talbott, Rebekah Tolbott, Mary Schooley, Isaac Siddall, John Purdom, John Schooley, Asa Moore, Sarah Moore, Obed Pierpoint, John Hollingsworth, Sarah Talbott, Ann Cunnard, Sarah Cunnard, Moses Givin, Danl. Stone, Joseph Tolbot Jr., John McClun, Richard Roberts, Cornelia Janney, Sarah Raticane, Jane Raticane, Mary Talbott.

Jesse Hirst, son of John and Mary Hirst, married Mary Peirpoint, daughter of Obed and Esther Peirpoint, 27th day 12th mo 1797. Witnesses: John Hirst, Mary Hirst, Obed Peirpoint, Esther Peirpoint, Edward Cunnard, Richard P. Richardson, Samuel Peirpoint, Joseph Peirpoint, Rebekah Talbott, Ann Mason, Sarah Brown, Mary Talbott, Jane Rattikin, Sarah Rattikin, Susannah Rattikin, Mary Scott, Ann Hirst, Pamela Myars, Ann Cunnard, Edward Cunnard Jr., Jacob Brown, John Hirst Jr., Richard Hirst?, Mahlon Myars, Sarah Thompson, Sarah Janney, Elenor Hough, Elizabeth Purdom, Lydia Hough, Sarah Moore, Joseph Talbott, Thomas Hirst, David Hirst, Eleanor? Piggott, Francis Pierpoint, Sarah Cunnard, Abijah Janney, John Williams, Daniel Stone, Abner Williams, Anna Steer? Jr., Hannah Williams, Nancey Griffith, Joseph Wood, Pleasant Thompson, Sarah Thompson, Benjamin Steer, Rebekah Janney, Israel Myars, John Hollingsworth, Benjami Purdom, Mary Schooley, Cephus? Fox.

John Schooley (Jr.), son of William and Anna Schooley, married Elisabeth Hough, daughter of William Hough, 1st day 6th mo 1796. Witnesses:

William Hough, Elenor Hough, Ann Schooley, Joseph Hough, John Canby, John Hough, Sarah Mason, Ann Hough, Sarah Canby, Sarah Matthews, Duvannis Binns, Dorothy Schooley, Samuel Hough, Samuel Hough Jr., Thomas Hough, B. Hough, A. B. Mason, Nancy Hough, Sally Hough, Sarah Moxley, Mahlon Janney, Mary Schooley, B. Ball, Francis Ball, Nancy McIlhaney, Ann Spachman, Mildred Ball, Rosannah McIlhaney, Uriah Williams, Susann Janney, William Moxley, Jonas Potts, Danl Stone, Phebe Potts, Jonah Hough, Benjamin Purdom, Elizabeth Purdom, James Ratticane, Joseph Wood, Mary Myars, Ruth Taylor, Stephen Wilson, Abner Williams, Thomas Hirst, Sarah Janney, Rebekah Janney, Lydia Hough, Rachel Hough, Anna Ball, Betsey Thompson, James Paxson, Sarah Paxson, Elizabeth Moore, Asa Moore, Cornelia Janney, Thomas Hough, Rachel Baker, Thomas Lewis, R. P. Richardson, J. Willis?

Parmonas Lamburn, son of Thomas and Dinah Lamburn of Chester Co., Pennsylvania, married Hannah Williams, daughter of Williams Williams, deceased, and Elizabeth his wife, since married to Benjamin Purdom, 2nd day 5th mo 1798. Witnesses: Elizabeth Purdom, Anna Steer, Benjamin Steer, John Wildman, Abner Williams, Joseph Wood Senr., Anna Steer Jr., Elizabeth Steer, Isaac Steer, Mary Williams, Elinor Hough, Lydia Hough, Sarah Talbott, Dewanmer Binns, Amy Taylor, Rebeckah Talbott, Mary Talbott, Rebekah Janney, Susan Janney, Mahlon Janney, Sarah Janney, Sarah Thompson, Joseph Talbott, Sally Hough, Pleasant Thompson, Hannah Evans, Elizabeth Morris, Evnah? Purdom, Elizabeth Scott, Asa Moore, Sarah Moore, James Rattikin, James Moore, Abigal Wood, Samuel Evans, Isaac Siddall, Wm. Siddall, Joseph Wood.

Daniel Stone, son of Thomas Stone, and Jamimah his wife, deceased, of Westmoreland Co., Virginia, married Sarah Hough, daughter of William and Eleanor, 30th day 5th mo 1798. Witnesses: Elenor Hough, Elizabeth Schooley, Nancy Hough, Ann Schooley, Arulah? Hough, Joseph Hough, Thomas Hough, Saml Hough, Saml. Hough Jr., William Hough Jr., Elizabeth Moore, Rachel Taylor, Phebe Potts, Lydia Hough, Ann Steer, Elisabeth Scott, Abner Williams, Wm. S. Neale, Parmenas Lamborn, Mary Myars, Anna Ball, Elizabeth Myars, Mahlon Janney, Mary Broomhall, Susan Janney, Benjn. Purdom, Elizabeth Purdom, James Moore, Phebe Moore, Sarah Janney, Benjamin Steer, Anna Steer, Hannah Lamborn, Anna Steer Jr., Mary Talbott, Sarah Tallbott, Joseph Wood, James Ratticane, R .P. Richardson, Thomas Phillips, J. W. T___, Wm. Hamilton, J. Talbott, Asa Moore.

Stephen Scott, son of Jacob Scott, deceased, and Elizabeth his wife, married Sarah Talbott, daughter of Joseph and Anna Talbott, 30th day 1st mo 1799. [Most witnesses are unreadble, others are:] Elizabeth Scott, Rebekah Talbott, Stephen Wilson, A__ Wilson, __rab [Jacob] Scott, Hannah Scott, Thomas Poltney, Anthony Gover, Samuel Gover, Phebe Moore, Joseph Wood Jr., Eleanor Hough, Charles Binns?, Abner Williams, Benjamin Steer, Benjamin Purdom, Danl Stone, Sarah Moore, Isaac Siddall, Hannah Lamburn, Joseph Nicklin, Anna Steer Jr., Sarah Pierpoint, Jacob Sands, Anna Steer.

Arthur Paxton, son of Jacob Paxton deceased, of Hunderton Co., New Jersey, and Mary his wife, married Pamelia Myers, daughter of Elijah and Mary Myers, 29th day 10th mo 1800. Witnesses: Elijah Myers, Wm. Paxton, Anne Ball, Rachel Wright, Jane Paxton, Mary Schooley, James Paxton, Sarah Paxton, John Schooley, Mary Myers, ___ Peirpoint, Mahlon Janney, Elenor Hough, Ann Spachman, Lydia Hough, Rachel Taylor, Susan Janney, Sarah Stone, Mary Pancoast, Ann Talbott, Wm. Schooley, Sarah Moore, Robt. Wright, Benjamin Purdom, Sarah Janney, Ann Schooley, Sarah Thompson, Elizabeth Scott, James ___, Phebe Moore, Sarah Peirpoint, Jesse Taylor, Ruth Taylor, Mary Taylor, Hannah Ball, Betsey Pierpoint, Ann Pierpoint, Wm. Hough, Danl. Stone, Asa Moore, Joseph Wood, Lightfoot Janney, Francis Pierpoint, Jess Hirst, Obed Peirpoint, Mahlon Meyers, Mary Hirst, Nancey Peirpoint, Jacob Sands, Benjn. Steer.

John Pancoast, of Frederick Co., Maryland, son of William and Sarah Pancoast, the latter deceased, married Mary Talbott, daughter of Joseph and Ann Talbott, both deceased, 1st day 5th mo 1799. Witnesses: Mary Poultney, Sarah Janney, Stephen Scott, Sarah Scott, Robt. Pancoast, Joseph Talbott, Mahlon Janney, Sarah Poultney, Jesse Talbott, Thos. Poulton, Joseph Wood, William P. Thompson, John Hirst, Polly Gover, Ann Schooley, Benjn. Steer, Mary Janney, Nancy Hough, Elizabeth Scott, Sarah Paxton, Abel Janney, Mirib Scott, Hannah Scott, Elizabeth Gover, Isaac Vandevanter, Naomy Wood, Anne Ball, Stephen Henry, Benjamin Purdome, Elizabeth Purdom, John Williams, Nancy Griffith, Ann Jones, Abner Williams, Rachel Taylor, Jesse Talbott, Jesse Wood, Amasa Hague, Sam. Poultney, Asa Moore, Sarah Moore, Danl. Stone, Hannah Janney, James Paxton, Saml Gover, James Moore, Phebe Moore.

Williams Williams m. 9th mo 6th, 1769, Elizabeth Everett. Their children: John Williams, b. 28th day of 9th mo 1771, d. 28th day, 2nd mo 1840; Abner Williams b. 24 day of 9th mo 1773, d. 20th day, 7th mo 1851; Hannah Williams b. 8th day of 1st mo 1776, m. [Parmenus] Lamborn, removed to Ohio; Isaac E. Williams b. 14th day of 12th mo 1777, d. young; Elizabeth b. 20th day of 3rd mo 1779, d. young; William Williams d. 1782. Elizabeth afterwards m. Benjamin Purdom and d. 8th of 9th mo 1800.

Abner Williams m. 30th day 11 mo 1796, Mary Wood. Their children: Elizabeth Williams, b. 27th day, 7th mo 1798, d. young; Abigail Williams, b. 7th day, 10 mo 1801, d. young; [name not readable] d. 11th day 3rd mo 1873; Abner was disowned. Mary d. 4th day, 8th mo 1823.

Isaac Steer, b. 6th day of 12th mo 1757, Center MM, m. 21st day of 4th mo 1779, Phebe Hollingsworth, b. 20th day of 3rd mo 1757. Their children: Mary Steer, b. 17th day of 7 mo 1780, m. Samuel McPherson 15th day of 4th mo 1801; Joseph Steer, b. 2nd day of 7th mo 1783, m.(1) Sarah Moore, b. 30th day 5th of mo 1786, m.(2) Beula Wright, m.(3) Mary Clevenger, b. 18th day of 9th mo 1791; Ann Steer, b. 11th day of 5th mo 1786, m. William H. Hough (son of Wm. and Eleanor) 29th day of 2nd mo 1805; Jonah Steer, b. 10th day of 6th mo 1788, disowned, m. Ruth Steer contrary to discipline; Ruth Steer, b. 9th day of 7th mo 1790; Lydia Steer, b. 9th day of 12th mo 1791, m. Richard Wood (son of Wm. and Mary) 17th day of 6th mo 1815; William B. Steer, b. 29th day of 8th mo 1794, m. Louisa Brown; Rachel Steer, b. 10th day of 6th mo 1796, m. Joshua Russell and removed to Bush Creek, MD; Phebe Steer, b. 11 day of 2nd mo 1799, m. Lewis Coale; Isaac Steer d. 24th day of 8th mo 1844. Phebe Hollingsworth Steer d. 25th day of 11th mon 1822. Elizabeth Bond was the 2nd wife of Isaac Steer. They m. 25th day of 8th mo 1824.

Benjamin Steer m. 7th day of 9th mo 1774, Anna Everett at Fairfax. Their children: Elizabeth Steer, b. 5th day of 7th mo 1775; Ann Steer, b. 20th day of 7th mo 1777, m. Jonathen Peirpont and removed to Ohio (27th day of 4th mo 1799); Isaac E. Steer, b. 19th day of 7th mo 1779, [more information - unreadable]; William Steer, b. 13th day of 7th mo 1786, either resigned his right or was disowned for non-attendance of meetings; Hannah Steer, b. 1786, m. William Birdsall and removed to Ohio.

Elisha Janney m. Albina Gregg 19th day of 4th mo 1786. She d. 2nd day of 9th mo 1787. Their issue: Sarah Janney, m. Anthony P. Goser? of Alexandria Monthly Meeting.

Elisha Janney m.(2) 4th day of 3rd mo 1795, Mary Gibson. She d. 15th day of 7th mo 1846. Their children: Ruth Janney, b. 1st day of 12th mo 1795, d. 24th day of 8th mo; Albina Janney, b. 12th day of 1st mo 1797, m. William Summers, 9th day of 11th mo ---; John Janney, b. 8th day of 11th mo 1798, m. a non-member and disowned [bride's name unclear]; Mary Janney, b. 28th day of 10th mo 1801, d. 1857; Anna Janney, 25th day of 9th mo 1802, m. Robert H. Miller of Alexandria, 28th day of 4th mo 1823; James C. Janney, b. 20th day of 11th mo 1804, d. 25th day of 2nd mo 1878, m. Rebecca Jane Walker, 20th day of 6th mo 1838, removed to Philadelphia; Aquilla Janney, b. 9th day of 9th mo 1806, removed to Goose Creek MM; Cornelia Janney, b. 23rd day of 11th mo 1808, d. 3rd day 12th mo 1831; Nathaniel E. Janney, b. 6th day of 5th mo 1813, d. 8th day 10th mo 1848; Elisah Janney, b. 9th day of 3rd mo 1816, d. 29th day of 3rd mo 1838; Charles P. Janney, b. 19th day of 10th mo 1818, d. 17th day 6 mo 1839.

Reuben Schooley and Esther Lacey, of Gunpowder MM, m. 1st day of 11th mo 1785 at Little Falls MM, Harford Co., MD. Their issue: Ephraim Schooley, b. 27th day 9th mo 1786; Mahlon Schooley, b. 23rd day 6th mo 1788; Daniel Schooley, b. 31st day 5th mo 1790; Enoch Schooley, b. 28th day 11th mo 1792; Thomas Schooley, b. 11th day 8th mo 1795; John Schooley, b. 21st day 3rd mo 1797; Eli L. Schooley, b. 16th day 8th mo 1799. Reuben Schooley d. 10th day of 3rd mo 1825; Esther Lacey Schooley d. 1st day of 1st mo 1817.

John Schooley and Elizabeth Hough m. 1st day of 6th mo 1796. Their issue: Jonas P. Schooley, b. 11th day of 12th mo 1797, married out; Phebe P. Schooley, b. 17th day of 1st mo 1801, married out; Sarah Stone Schooley, b. 26th day of 2nd mo 1805, married out; Emma Schooley, b. 6th day of 11th mo 1808; William H. Schooley, b. 11th day of 11th mo 1810; Eliza M. Schooley, b. 29th day of 7th mo 1814; Mary C. Schooley, b. 20th day of 4th mo 1817. John Schooley d. 5th day of 1st mo 1854. Elizabeth Hough Schooley d. 22nd day of 1848.

Samuel Gover (son of Robert) and Sarah Janney (widow of Jacob) m. [16th 12th mo 1784]. Their issue: Mary Gover, b. 18th day of 8th mo

1785; Elizabeth Gover, twin, b. 18th day of 8th mo 1785; Anthony P. Gover, b. 14th day of 5th mo 1787; Sarah Gover. b. 1788; Robert Gover, b. 14th day of 4th mo 1790; Jesse Gover, b. 11th day of 7th mo 1792; Jonathen Gover, b. 13th day of 12th mo 1793; Samuel Gover, b. 11th day of 6th mo 1795; Ann Gover, b. 2nd day of 5th mo 1797; Hannah Gover, b. 19th day of 3rd mo 1799; Rachel Gover, b. 9th mo 1803; Thomasin Gover, b. 19th day of 4th mo 1802; Albina Gover, b. 8th day of 9th mo 1806; William Gover, twin, b. 8th day of 9th mo 1806.

Joseph Talbott and Ann Plummer m. 3rd day of 3rd mo 1771. Their children: Samuel Talbott, b. 18th day of 12th mo 1772; Joseph Talbott, b. 12th day of 5th mo 1774; Sarah Talbott, b. 8th day of 1st mo 1776; Mary Talbott, b. 18th day of 3rd mo 1778; Rachel Talbott, b. 3rd day of 3rd mo 1780; Elisha Talbott, b. 21st day of 1st mo 1782; Jesse Talbott, b. 26th day of 8th mo 1783; Anna Talbott, b. 31st day of 1st mo 1786; Elizabeth Talbott, b. 29th day of 8th mo 1788.
Joseph Talbott m.(2) Rebecca Hirst, 1st day of 11th mo 1792, at Goose Creek MM. Their children: Susan Talbott, b. 15th day of 12th mo 1793; John H. Talbott, b. 24th day of 12th mo 1795; Rebecca Talbott, b. 2nd day of 10th mo 1797. Joseph Talbott d. 15th day of 11th mo 1798.

William Hough (son of John) b. 11th mo 1746, m. Eleanor Hite, b. 5th day of 11th mo 1749. [Marriage date not given]. Their children: Joseph Hough; John Hough; Samuel Hough; Elizabeth Hough; Thomas Hough; Sarah Hough; William Hough; b. 23rd day of 12th mo 1783; Eleanor Hough; Nancy Hough; Benjamin Hough; Amasa Hough.
William Hough d. 2nd mo 1815. Eleanor Hite Hough d. 5th mo 1823.

Obed Peirpoint, b. 3rd day of 9th mo 1740, son of Francis and Sarah Peirpoint, m. Esther Myers, dau of Jonathan and Mary Myers, 7th day of 4th mo 1773. Their issue: Jonathan Peirpoint, b. 1st day of 3rd mo 1774; Sarah Peirpoint, b. 16th day of 9th mo 1775; Mary Peirpoint, b. 7th day of 2nd mo 1777; David Peirpoint, b. 23rd day of 11th mo 1778, d. 19th day of 5th mo 1784; Francis Peirpoint, b. 8th day of 9th mo 1780; Elizabeth Peirpoint, b. 16th day of 1st mo 1783; Ann Peirpoint, b. 13th day of 7th mo 1785; Obed Peirpoint, b. 7th day of 10th mo 1787, died 8th day of 5th mo 1794; Samuel Peirpoint, b. 27th day of 12th mo 1789; Eli Peirpoint, b. 18th day of 11th mo 1791; Rebecca Peirpoint, b. 6th day of 7th mo 1793, d. 12th day of 7th mo 1796; Joseph Peirpoint, b. 27th day of 12th mo 1795; John R. Peirpoint, b. 15th day of 11th mo 1798.

Daniel Stone and Sarah Hough m. 30th day of 5th mo 1798. Their children: William H. Stone, b. 5th day of 3rd mo 1799; Eleanor H. Stone, b. 5th day of 5th mo 1801; Elizabeth S. Stone, b. 21st day of 11th mo 1804; Thomas P. Stone, b. 6th day of 3rd mo 1807; Joseph H. Stone, b. 14th day of 11th mo 1808; Samuel S. Stone, b. 25th day of 2nd mo 1811; James H. Stone, b. 24th day of 6th mo 1813; Sarah Ann Stone, b. 11th day of 6th mo 1816; Rachel Jane Stone, b. 10th day of 11th mo 1818.

Children of John Poultney and Ellen [Walker]: Anthony Poultney, b. 31st day of 3rd mo 1752; Sarah Poultney, b. 22nd day of 10th mo 1753; Mary Poultney b. 13th day of 6th mo 1756; John Poultney d. 31st day of 3rd mo 1759.
Thomas Plummer m. the widow Poultney. Names and births of children of Thomas Plummer and Ellen his wife: Isaac Plummer b. 15th day of 2nd mo 1762; Jesse Plummer b. 28th day of 10th mo 1763.

Children of John Hough and Sarah his wife: Joseph Hough b. 19th day of 1st mo 1742/3; d. 7th day of 2nd mo 1769; William Hough b. 24th day of 9th mo 1744; Elizabeth Hough b. 24th day of 7th mo 1746; Elizabeth Canby d. 21st day of 1st mo 1774; Amos Hough b. 27th day of 12th mo 1748; John Hough b. 23rd day of 9th mo 1751; Samuel Hough b. 20th day of 11th mo 1753; Mahlon Hough b. 8th day of 6th mo 1756; Jonah Hough b. 27th day of 10th mo 1758; Sarah Hough b. 5th day of 4th mo 1763.

Children of Edmund Sands and Rachel his wife, and Mary his former wife: Hannah Sands (now Roach) b. 28th day of 8th mo 1721; Sarah Sands b. 25th day of 9th mo 1740; Isaac Sands b. 1st day of 11th mo 1742; Jacob Sands b. 30th day of 11 mo 1744; Joseph Sands b. 16th day of 12th mo 1746; Benjamin Sands b. 16th day of 12th mo 1748.

Children of William Brown and Elizabeth his wife: Ruth Brown b. 12th day of 5th mo 1759; Richard Brown b. 8th day of 12th mo 1760; Hannah Brown b. 2nd day of 5th mo 1762.

Children of Richard Brown and Mary his wife (who after the decease of Richard Brown, m. William Kirk): Richard Brown b. 1st day of 7th mo 1734, d. 4th day of 7th mo 1738; Joseph Brown b. 1st day of 2nd mo 1736, d. 19th day of 3rd mo 1754; Mercer Brown b. 7th day of 5th mo 1740. Richard Brown [Sr.] d. 10th day of 2nd mo 1745.

William Kirk m. the widow Brown but had no issue by her. Mary Kirk d. 11th day of 8th mo 1772. William Kirk d. 29th day of 3rd mo 1774.

Children of William Balanger and Cassandra his wife. Said William b. 11th of 7th mo 1730. Cassandra b. 3rd of 5th mo 17___. Their children: Sarah Balanger b. 8th day of 11 mo 1752; Mary Balanger b. 16th day of 6th mo 1754; Daniel Balanger b. 25th day of 6th mo 1756; William Balanger b. 22nd day of 7th mo 1758; Hannah Ballanger b. 7th day of 10th mo 1761; Rachael Ballanger b. 28th day of 9th mo 1763.

Children of Daniel Matthews and Ann his wife: Thomas Matthews b. 3rd day of 2nd mo 1749; Francis Matthews b. 18th day of 7th mo 1750; Daniel Matthews b. 15th day of 8th mo 1751; Samuel Matthews b. 31st day of 1st mo 1753; Ann Matthews b. 1st day of 3rd mo 1756; Gideon Matthews b. 6th day of 5th mo 1754.

Children of Jonathan Mires and Mary his wife: Isaiah Mires b. 16th day of 3rd mo 1751; Esther Mires b. 23rd day of 8th mo 1752; Elijah Mires b. 9th day of 2nd mo 1755.

Children of Casper Seybald and Rebekah his wife: James Seybald b. 4th day of 3rd mo 1749; John Seybald b. 30th day of 6th mo 1752; Hannah Seybald b. 12th day of 5th mo 1755; Jesper Seybald b. 20th day of 12th mo 1757; Robert Seybald b. 12th day of 3rd mo 1760; Jesse Seybald b. 28th day of 2nd mo 1762; Isaac Seybald b. 27th day of 4th mo 1764; Silas Seybald b. 28th day of 11th mo 1765; Fredrick Seybald b. 17th day of 5th mo 1768; Alice Seybald b. 17th day of 5th mo 1770.

Children of Amos and Mary Janney: Mahlon b. 31st day of 11th mo 1731; Ann b. 25th day of 12th mo 1734; Hannah b. 28th day of 11th mo 1736; d. 1st day of 3rd mo 1776; Abel b. 16th day of 1st mo 1738; Thomas b. 19th day of 5th mo 1741; d. 21st day of 3rd mo 1743; Mary and Ruth (twins) their daughters were b. 15th of 6th mo 1744.

Children of James and Hannah Brooke: Debroah b. 25th day of 11th mo 1760; Elizabeth b. 25th day of 6th mo 1762; James b. 8th day of 6th mo 1765, d. 15th of 8th mo 1767; Amos b. 8th day of 5th mo 1767, d. 15th of 9th mo 1767.

Children of Samuel Canby and Elizabeth his wife: Benjamin Canby b. 16th of 2nd mo 1771; John Hough Canby b. 27th of 4th mo 1772. Elizabeth Canby d. 21st day of 1st mo 1774.

Children of Isaac and Rachel Hollingsworth. Isaac Hollingsworth himself b. 22nd of 2nd mo 1722, d. 4th day of 9th mo 1759. Rachel his wife b. 3rd day of 5th mo 1724. Their children: Abraham b. 9th of 5th mo 1749; Ann b. 6th of 12th mo 1751; Lydia b. 27th of 20th mo 1752; Jonah b. 24th of 2nd mo 1755; Phebe b. 20th of 3rd mo 1757; Mary b. 3rd of 12th mo 1758.

Children of Mercer Brown and Sarah his wife: Mary Brown b. 14th of 8th mo 1765; Richard Brown b. 2nd of 10th mo 1767; Sarah Brown b. 22nd of 12th mo 1769; Ann Brown b. 13th of 3rd mo 1772; Elizabeth Brown b. 15th of 5th mo 1774; Margaret Brown b. 16th of 11th mo 1776.

Children of Richard Roach and Hannah his wife: Mary Roach b. 16th of 5th mo 1743; Tabitha Roach b. 1st of 1st mo 1747; Hannah Roach b. 15th of 11th mo 1748; Richard Roach b. 15th of 8th mo 1750; James Roach b. 27th of 5th mo 1752; Edmund Roach b. 25th of 11th mo 1754; Deborah Roach b. 19th of 10th mo 1756; Sarah Roach b. 22nd of 4th mo 1760; Micajah Raoch b. 27th of 9th mo 1761.

Children of Israel Janney and Plasant, his wife: Jane Janney b. 25th of 2nd mo 1774; Abiyah Janney b. 30th of 5th mo 1773[5]; Sarah Janney b. 4th of 10th mo 1776; Phineas Janney b. 5th of 5th mo 1778. Plasant Janney d, 4th of 3rd mo 1779.

Children of Abel and Mary Janney: Amos Janney b. 24th of 1st mo 1772; Mahlon Janney b. 10th of 10th mo 1773; Richard Janney b. 25th of 7th mo 1776.

Children of Moses Cadwalader and Elizabeth, his wife: Sarah Cadwalader b. 23 of 10th mo 1756; Ruth Cadwalader b. 29th of 10th mo 1759; Moses Cadwalader b. 22nd of 2nd mo 1763; Thomas Cadwalader b. 1st of 1st mo 1765; Joseph Cadwalader b. 23rd of 5th mo 1767, d. 20th of 7th mo 1777; Jesse Cadwalader b. 31st of 8th mo 1770. Elizabeth Cadwalader d. 15th of 11th mo 1780.

Children of Thomas Smith and Rachel his wife: Elizabeth Smith b. 22nd of 12th mo 1768; Mary Smith b. 7th of 1st mo 1771; Hannah Smith b. 27th of 9th mo 1772; Ann Smith b. 11th of 10th mo 1774; Joseph Smith b. 22nd of 12th mo 1776; Jesse Smith b. 2nd of 6th mo 1779; Rachel Smith b. [blank]; Jesse Smith b. 9th of 2nd mo 1784; Thomas Smith b. 6th day of 8th mo 1786; Phebe Smith b. 29 day of 7th mo 1789; Sarah Smith b. 22nd day of 1st mo 1792.

Child of James Daniel and Hannah his wife: Rebekah Daniel b. 20th of 2nd mo 1778.

Children of John Smith and Sarah his wife: Joseph Smith b. 18th of 9th mo 1768; Jonas Smith b. 3rd of 9th mo 1769; Samuel Smith b. 17th of 7th mo 1772; Phebe Smith b. 10th of 7th mo 1774; Aaron Smith b. 18th of 4th mo 1776; Ann Smith b. 23rd of 2nd mo 1777; Sarah Smith b. 19th of 8th mo 1778.

Children of Isaac Votaw and Ann his wife: Mary Votaw b. 12th of 10th mo 1768; John Votaw b. 1st of 1st mo 1770; Moses Votaw b. 5th of 1st mo 1772; Sarah Votaw b. 24th of 2nd 1774; Isaac Votaw b. 5th of 2nd mo 1776; Joseph Votaw b. 9th of 5th mo 1779; Thomas Votaw b. 30th of 5th mo 1781.

Children of Joseph Janney and Hannah his wife: John Janney b. 14th of 7th mo 1765; Sarah Janney b. 14th of 5th mo 1768; Elizabeth Janney b. 12th of 4th mo 1770; Thomas Janney b. 20th of 4th mo 1772; Joseph Janney b. 18th (sic) of 5th mo 1774, d. 30th of 8th mo 1775; Hannah Janney b. 19th of 5th mo 1774; Rebekah Janney b. 14th of 8th mo 1776; Susannah Janney b. 20th of 7th mo 1778; Joseph Janney b. 21st of 7th mo 1780.

Joshua Nickols b. 20th day of 5th mo 1760, d. 30th day of 9th mo 1770. Margery Nichols b. 14th day of 6 mo 1763, d. 10th day of 3rd mo 1770.

Children of Stephen Gregg and Susanna his wife (married after decease of her former husband John Dixon): Sarah Dixon, daughter of John Dixon and Susanna his wife, b. 30th day of 12 mo [no year]; Thomas son of Stephen Gregg and Susannah his wife b. 15th of 1st mo 176__; Samuel Gregg b. 1770; Joshua Gregg b. 1772; Nathan Gregg b. 1774; Susanna Gregg b. 11th of 1st mo 1776.

Children of James Burson and Mary his wife: Susannah Burson b. 19th of 12th mo 1757; Joseph Burson b. 22nd of 2nd mo 1761; Sarah Burson b. 7th of 6th mo 1763; Ann Burson b. 15th of 4th mo 1765; Ruth Burson b. 22nd of 4th mo 1767; Rebekah Burson b. 11th of 4th mo 1769; Lydia Burson b. 18th of 2nd mo 1771; Aaron Burson b. 23rd of 1st mo 1773; John Burson b. 3rd of 4th mo 1775; Isaiah Burson b. 27th of 9th mo 1777.

Children of Benjamin Steer and Anna his wife: Elisabeth Steer b. 5th of 7th mo 1775; Ann Steer b. 20th of 8th mo 1777; Isaac Steer b. 19th of 7th mo 1779; William Steer b. 13th of 7th mo 1781.

Children of James Wood and Phebe, his wife: Abner b. 2nd of 12th mo 1782; Joseph and Thomas their sons were b. 27th of 1st mo 1784.

Children of William Gregg and Rebekah, his wife: George b. 20th of 6th mo 1770, d. 28th of 4th mo 1771; Elizabeth b. 15th of 2nd mo 1772; Samuel b. 28th of 4th mo 1774; George b. 4th of 5th mo 1776; William b. 11th of 7th mo 1778; William d. 18th of 12th mo 1786; Aaron b. 9th of 1st mo 1781; Rebekah b. 9th of 8th mo 1783; Mahlon b. 18th of 2nd mo 1786, d. 23rd of 12th mo 1786; Sarah b. 18th of 2nd mo 1791; Ruth b. 20th of 5th mo 1793.

Children of Benjamin Burson and Hannah, his wife: Sarah Burson b. 29th of 9th mo 1772; George Burson b. 11th of 4th mo 1774; Esther Burson b. 13th of 6th mo 1778.

Children of Samuel Smith and Mary his wife: Susannah b. 29th of 1st mo 1777, d. 16th of 8th mo 1781; Henry b. 26th of 10th mo 1778; Alice b. 9th of 5th mo 1781.

Children of James Moore and Phebe, his wife: Abner b. 2nd day of 12th mo 1782; Joseph and Thomas [twins] b. 27th day of 1st mo 1784.

CERTIFICATES OF REMOVAL OF FAIRFAX MONTHLY MEETING

To Kingwood meeting in New Jersey: Application having been made to us for a certificate for Isaac Reeder who sometime ago removed from these parts and settled within the verge of your Meeting. We therefore inform you that upon inquiry made, it appears that his life and conversation hath been in some designe orderly, frequently attended our meetings whilst here, is clear of debt and marriage engagements as far as we know. As a member of our society we recommend him to your religious care. {10th mo 1783}. Signed in and on behalf of our said meeting, by Thomas Matthews, Clerk.

To Pipe Creek Monthly Meeting: The occasion of our writing to you at this time is on account of Deborah Chandlee, who has removed to settle with her husband within the verge of your meeting and requests a few lines by way of Certificate to be joined in membership with you, and after the needful inquiry made we don't find but her life and conversation has been in a good degree orderly, a frequent attender of our religious meetings and has settled her outward affairs to satisfaction as far as known, therefore as a member of our Society we recommend her to divine protection and your Christian care and remain, your Brethern and Sisters. Signed in and on behalf of Fairfax Monthly Meeting, the 22 of the 11 mo 1783, by Thomas Matthews, Clerk; Lydia Hough, Clerk.

To Wilmington MM: Sarah Hurst who removed some time ago from our parts, is not married, a member of our Society, and recommended to your care, 22nd of 11th mo 1783.

To Pipe Creek MM: William Smith, Jr. hath for some time removed within the verge of your meeting, 27th of 12th mo 1783.

To Hopewell MM: Phebe Moris, wife of Joseph Moris, about to remove with her husband to the west of the Allehany Mountain is a member, 22nd of 5th mo 1784.

To Crooked Run MM: Mahlan Smith, on behalf of himself, Mary his wife, and stepson Nathaniel White, having removed from us and settled within the verge of your meeting, 26th day of 6th mo 1784.

To Crooked Run MM: John Scofield, an apprentice with Mahlon Smith, he being a member of our Society, 26th of 6th mo 1784.

To Hopewell MM: Thomas Greeg, Jr. not married, a member of our society, 24th of 7th mo 1784.

To Hopewell MM: Joseph Cadwalader and Mary his wife, about to remove from amongst us, Mary being subjected to bodily weakness and infirmity, 28th of 9th mo 1774 (sic).

To Bush River MM in South Carolina: Mercer Brown, Sarah his wife and children Richard, Sarah, Ann, Margareta, Phebe, and Mercer, about settle within the verge of your meeting, 25th of 9th mo 1784.

To Crooked Run MM: James Moore and Phebe his wife, and children Abner, Joseph, and Thomas Moore, 27th of 11th mo 1784.

To Richland MM: Sarah Thompson, some time ago removed and settled within the verge of your meeting, 22nd of 1st mo 1785.

To Gun Powder MM: William Scott, having settled within the verge of your meeting, not married, 26th of 2nd mo 1785.

To Bush River MM in South Carolina: David Harris, having removed and settled within the verge of your meeting, years past he was disowned for misconduct which he has lately condemned, 7th of 2nd mo 1785.

To South River MM in Virginia: Joseph Rhodes, is about to remove and settle within the verge of your meeting, not married, 23 of 4th mo 1785.

To Bush River MM in South Carolina or elsewhere: Phebe Whitson, wife of Soloman Whitson, and their children Ann, David, Mary, Willis, Jourdan, Samuel, Phebe, and Solomon, are about to remove and settle within the verge of your meeting. Their daughter Ann is clear of marriage engagements, 23rd of 4th mo 1785.

To Crooked Run MM: Samuel Hage, for himself and his children Ruth, John, and Pleasant (being in their minority), clear of marriage engagements, 23rd of 4th mo 1785.

To Hopewell MM: Samuel Willson, removed some time ago and settled within the verge of your meeting, is clear of marriage engagements, 23rd of 4th mo 1785.

To Crooked Run MM: Jonah Hague, who has removed with Abel Janney as an apprentice within the verge of your meeting, 28th of 5th mo 1785.

To Crooked Run MM: Abel Janney, for himself, Mary his wife, and four of their children, namely Amos, Richard, Lightfoot, and Sarah (also their niece Mary Gibson) being all in their minority, are recommended to your care, 28th of 5th mo 1785.

To Crooked Run MM: Mariah Cadwalader, is clear of marriage engagements, 28th of 7th mo 1785.

To Hopewell MM: Margaret Lewellin is about to remove and settle west of the Allegania Mountains, is clear of marriage engagements, 27th of 8th mo 1785.

To Hopewell MM: Ann Lewellin, hath removed sometime ago over the Allegania Mountain, is clear of marriage engagements, 27th of 8th mo 1785.

To Cain Creek or Center MM in North Carolina: John Clark, Jr. and his parents are about to remove and settle within the verge of your meeting, is clear of marriage engagements, 27th of 8th mo 1785.

To Cain Creek or Center MM in North Carolina: John Clark, Ann his wife, and two daughters Ann and Sarah who are about to remove and settle within the verge of your meeting. The young women are clear of marriage engagements, 27th of 8th mo 1785.

To Westland MM in Pennsylvania: Joseph Hutton and Sarah his wife, children, Abel, Sarah, Elisabeth, Amos, John, and Asael, 24th of 12th mo 1785.

To Westland MM: Isaac Lewellin, recently removed and settled within the verge of your meeting, is clear of marriage engagements, 24th of 12th mo 1785.

To Westland MM: Deborah Lewellin and her 5 children Deborah, Mary, Hannah, Shadrack, and Sarah, the clear of marriage engagements. Signed Thos Matthews, Elisabeth Williams, clerks, 24th of 12th mo 1785.

To Westland MM: John Wildman, is clear of marriage engagements, 25th of 3rd mo 1786.

To Friends in Cork, or elsewhere in Ireland: {William} Abbott about to return to Ireland, clear of marriage engagements, 22nd of 7th mo 1786.

To Hopewell MM: Amos Jolliff, is clear of marriage engagements. 22nd of 7th mo 1786.

To West Land MM: Mary Smith, daughter of John Smith, who is removed from here is clear of marriage engagements, 22nd of 7th mo 1786.

To Westland MM in Pennsylvania: John Smith and Sarah his wife, also seven of their children: Joseph, Jonah, Samuel, Phebe, Aaron, Ann, and Sarah, 22nd of 7th mo 1786.

To Goose Creek MM: Ruth Steer is clear of marriage engagements. 23rd of 12th mo 1786.

To Crooked Run MM: George Watters, Dinah his wife and children Sarah, Thomas, James, Lydia, Judith, and Issac, 24th of 2nd mo 1787.

To Goose Creek MM: Samuel Gover, Sarah his wife, and children Moses, Jacob Janney, Elizabeth, and Mary Gover, 24th of 3rd mo 1787.

To South River in Campbell Co: Sarah Hutton (a widow with her child Jonah Hutton), hath removed with her father Moses Cadwalader, 26th of 5th mo 1787.

To Gun Powder MM in Maryland: Joseph Scott Junr., 22nd of 7th mo 1787.

To Hopewell MM: Elizabeth Jolliffe, 25th of 8th mo 1787.

To Goose Creek MM: Edith Smith, 24th of 11th mo 1787.

To South River MM: Elisha Schooley, Rachel his wife, and children John, Mary, Sarah, Deborah, 24th of 11th mo 1787.

To Bush River MM in South Carolina: Margaret Norman, many years past removed from amongst us, 24th of 11th mo 1787.

To the Philadelphia MM: Joseph Hough, a minor lately placed as apprentice to Thomas Scattergood, a member of your meeting, 24th of 11th mo 1787.

To South River MM: Regarding Latitia Wildman, we have accepted her acknowledgement as satisfaction. 23rd of 2nd mo 1787.

To Pipe Creek MM: Rebekah Roberts (wife of John Roberts), 23rd of the 2nd mo 1788.

To South River MM: John Coffee, about to remove with his family and settle within the verge of your meeting, (wife Rachel, two small sons William and John) 22nd of 3rd mo 1788.

To South River MM in Campbell Co: William Betts and Mary his wife, with 6 children John and Rachel Paxon (by a former husband, and clear of marriage engagements), Hezekiah, William, Aaron, and Susannah Betts. 22nd of 3rd mo 1788.

To South River MM: John Pidgeon recently removed with his parents, is clear of marriage engagements, 26th of 4th mo 1788.

To South River MM in Campbell Co: William Pidgeon, wife Rachel, and children William, Isaac, Charles, Ruth, Hannah, and Sarah, 22nd of 3rd mo 1788.

To Goose Creek MM: Jonas Janney and Ruth his wife, having made satisfactory acknowledgment to our meeting for their outgoing in marriage, 26th of 4th mo 1788.

To Falls MM in Pennsylvania: Joseph Burgess, Sarah his wife, and children Aneas, Lydia, Daniel, 24th of 5th mo 1788.

To Westland MM: Rachel Hatfield, 25th of 10th mo 1788.

To Indian Springs MM: Christopher Hussy, is clear of marriage engagements, 23rd of 8th mo 1788.

To Gunpowder MM: Mary Scott, is clear of marriage engagements. 25th of 10th mo 1788.

To Pipe Creek MM: John and Abner Williams, sons of Elizabeth Williams, whom she had placed as apprentices within the verge of your meeting, they being of tender age, 17th of 9th mo 1788.

To Goose Creek MM: Robert Whitacre and his child Jonas, is clear of marriage engagements, 28th of 2nd mo 1789.

To Goose Creek MM: Simeon Haines, Elizabeth his wife, and children Daniel and Joseph, 28th of 2nd mo 1789.

To South River MM: Benjamin Paxton, who some time ago removed from amongst us, is clear of marriage engagements. 28th of 3rd mo 1789.

To Pipe Creek MM: John Pidgeon is recommended to your care. 28th of 3rd mo 1789.

To Gunpowder MM in Maryland: Rachel Griffith, who settled with her husband in the limits of your meeting, 23rd of 5th mo 1789.

To Goose Creek MM: Samuel Cary, Rachel his wife, also children Jonathan, John, Samuel, Cinthia, Sarah, and Rachel, 23 or 5th mo 1789.

To Goose Creek MM: Benjamin Scott, 27th of 6th mo 1789.

To New Garden MM: Thomas Janney, son of Joseph Janney, who has lately been placed as an apprentice to a Friend within the verge of your meeting. 26th of 9th mo 1789.

To Hopewell MM: Mary Jolliffe, being returned again to you, is clear of debt and marriage engagements, 24th of 10th mo 1789.

To Concord MM in Pennsylvania: Joseph Palmer intending to remove from here, is clear of debt and marriage engagements, 24th of 4th mo 1790.

To South River MM: Elizabeth Oliphant, has for some time past resided within your area, 22nd of 5th mo 1790.

To Westland MM: Amos Hough, his wife {Elizabeth} and children Sarah, Benjamin, Thomas, Elizabeth, Ann, John, Joseph, Ruth, and Mary, (Amos, having regained his right of membership), 24th of 7th mo 1790.

To Goose Creek MM: James Curl, recently removed and settled within the verge of your meeting, 25th of 9th mo 1790.

To Goose Creek MM: James Moore, Phebe his wife, and children Abner, Thomas, Joseph, Sarah, and Elizabeth, 25th of 9th mo 1790.

To South River MM: Sarah Homes, is clear of debt and marriage engagements, 27th of 11th mo 1790.

To South River MM: Richard Larrowe, and Hannah his wife, 25th of 12th mo 1790. (Re-signed Waterford, 3rd mo 2nd 1828).

To South River MM: Samuel Erwirne, who has removed and settled within the verge of your meeting, 27th of 11th mo 1790.

To South River MM: Mary Erwine (wife of James) and their children Jane, Magdelin, Susannah, who are settled within the verge of your meeting. The children are clear of marriage engagements, 27th of 11th mo 1790.

To Indian Springs MM: Ann Scott {wife of Joseph} and children Rachel, Isaac, Jacob, Sarah, and Ann, has moved with her husband and settled within the verge of your meeting, 25th of 12th mo 1791.

To Westland MM: Margret Dunkin, we have accepted her acknowledgement as satisfaction, 22nd of 1st mo 1791.

To South River MM: Elias Fisher, is clear of marriage engagements. 26th of 2nd mo 1791.

To South River MM: Josabed Lodge, Jr. is clear of marriage engagements. 26th of 3rd mo 1791.

To South River MM: Joseph Curl, Rachel {Rebecca in women's minutes} his wife, and children Hannah, Emma, Charles, Rebekah, Elizabeth, Susannah, and Samuel, 26th of 3rd mo 1791.

To Gunpowder MM: Thomas Packney [Poultney]. 25th of 6th mo 1791.

To Goose Creek MM: John Brown, son of Wm. 25th of 6th mo 1791.

To York MM: Isaac Garretson, is clear of marriage engagements. 25th of 6th mo 1791.

To Hopewell MM: Esther Counard, wife of James, having condemned her outgoing in marriage to the satisfaction of this meeting, 27th of 8th mo 1791.

A copy of an Endorsement made on a certificate brought by Mary Tucker from Gunpowder MM: Mary Tucker, having brought the within certificate from your meeting and intended to settle amongst us, but being dissatisfied after her arrival intends to remove back again.

To South River MM: Robert Fisher, son of Jos Fisher, is about to remove and settle within the verge of your meeting, is clear of marriage engagements, 24th of 9th mo 1791.

To Oak Swamp MM in Henrico Co: John Scott Pleasants and Sarrah his wife, 27th of 8th mo 1791.

To South River MM: Joseph Fisher, Jr. is clear of marriage engagements. 24th of 9th mo 1791.

To South River MM: Betty Fisher, being about to remove {with her brothers} and settle within the verge of your meeting, is clear of marriage engagements, 24th of 9th mo 1791.

To Hopewell MM: Martha McPherson, with her infant daughter Jane Beesone McPherson, 24th of 12th mo 1791.

To the Creek MM at Nine Partners in the State of New York: Thomas Harris, is clear debt and of marriage engagements, 24th of 12th mo 1791.

To Goose Creek MM: Thomas Moore, Jr. 28th of 1st mo 1792.

To Buckingham MM: Samuel Reader, 25th of 2nd mo 1792.

To Goose Creek: Joseph Randal and Rachel his wife, 23rd of 6th mo 1792.

To New Garden MM in Pennsylvania: William Jackson, Jr. is clear of marriage engagements, 23rd of 6th mo 1792.

To Gunpowder MM in Maryland: Caleb Floyed, is clear of debt and marriage engagements, 22nd of 9th mo 1792.

To Hopewell MM: Ann Neale, many years past had a right of membership among us, but departed from the Rules of Society in her marriage. Lately applied to be reinstated, condemned her offence, and has been received into membership, 27th of 10th mo 1792.

To Exeter MM in Pennsylvania: Robert Wood, has settled within the verge of your meeting, is clear of marriage engagements, 24th of 11 mo 1792.

To Oak Swamp in Virginia: James Lownes, and his son Joseph, is clear of marriage engagements, 26th of 1st mo 1793.

To Chesterfield MM in New Jersey, John Woodward, went from here about 22 months ago, and resides within the verge of your meeting is clear of marriage engagements, 24th of 11th mo 1793.

To White Oak Swamp MM in Philadelphia: James Lownes requested a certificate for his two sons James and Caleb, they have a birthright among us, 22 of 12th mo 1792.

To Goose Creek MM: Sarah Taylor, wife of Bernard Taylor, recently removed and settled within the verge of your meeting, 23rd of 2nd mo 1793.

To Kensington ? MM in Pennsylvania: Charles Shoemaker is about to remove and settle within the verge of your meeting, is clear of debts and marriage engagements, 23rd of 2nd mo 1793.

To South River MM in Campbell Co: Joseph Fisher, brother Charles Fisher, is recommended to your care. [date not clear].

To Rahway and Plainfield MM in East New Jersey: Rachel Hartshorne, is clear of marriage engagements, 1st day of 5th mo 1793.

To Rahway and Plainfield MM in East New Jersey: Sarah Hartshorne, is clear of marriage engagements, 1st day of 5th mo 1793.

To Indian Spring MM: Hannah Hopkins, who has settled with her husband Samuel Hopkins, within the limits of your meeting, 1st day of 5th mo 1793.

To Goose Creek MM: Levy Hollingsworth and Mary his wife, with their children Thomas and David 1st of 5th mo 1793.

To Kennett MM in Pennsylvania: Err? Hollingsworth, is clear of marriage engagements, 1st of 5th mo 1793.

To Indian Spring MM: Wm. Stabler, Deborah his wife, and Thomas ? Goose Creek, settlement of his father's estate, 22nd of 6th mo 1793.

To South River MM: Mary Harris, 22nd of 6th mo 1793.

To Pipe Creek MM: Thomas Taylor and Sarah his wife, with children Thos, Joseph, Wm., and Caleb, 23rd of 11th mo 1793.

To Wilmington MM: John Phillips, recently removed and settled within the verge of your meeting, is clear of marriage engagements, 25th of 1st mo 1794.

To Goose Creek MM: Pheltie [Phebe] Yates, hath lately made satisfaction to this meeting for the offence for which she was disowned, and has for sometime lived within the verge of your meeting, 22nd of 3rd mo 1794.

To South River MM: Joseph Fisher and his wife Ann, are about to remove and settle within the verge of your meeting, with children John, Hannah, and Ann, 26th of 4th mo 1794.

To South River MM: Sarah Fisher, daughter of Joseph Fisher, is clear of marriage engagements, 26th of 4th mo 1794.

To Goose Creek MM: Josabed Lodge and Catharine his wife, 24th of 5th mo 1794.

To Goose Creek MM: Samuel Talbott, is clear of marriage engagements, 28th of 6th mo 1794.

To Goose Creek MM: Stephen Wilson, and Martha his wife, 28th of 6th mo 1794.

To Indian Spring MM: Caleb Bin [Bentley] and Sarah his wife, 28th of 6th mo 1794.

To White Oak Swamp MM: James Lownes has requested a certificate for his son William, now living within the limits of your MM, 23rd of 3rd mo 1794.

To White Oak Swamp MM: Deborah Lownes, having settled within your MM, is clear of marriage engagements, 23rd of 8th mo 1794.

To Redstone MM: Josiah Wood, 27th of 9th mo 1794.

To Redstone MM: Jane ___ {Joice Warton} is clear of debt and marriage engagements, 25th of 10th mo 1794.

To Redstone MM: Mary Wharton, about to remove and settle within the verge of your meeting with her husband {John} and 7 children, namely Abner, Sarah, Mahlon, Phebe, John, Margery, and Jonathan. Children are in their minority, are recommended with their mother, to your care, 25th of 10th mo 1794.

To Monalen MM: Mary Shrieve, wife of James Shrieve, 22nd of 11th mo 1794.

To Salem MM in Massachusetts: Isaac Shreve, son of Benjamin Shrieve of Alexandria, is placed as an apprentice within the limits of your meeting, and he being in his minority, 22nd of 11th mo 1794.

To Goose Creek MM: [too faint to read]

To Crooked Run MM: Martha [probably Smith] with her husband Thos., two children Rachel and John are recommended to your care {11th mo 1794}

To Westland MM: Sarah Hough, {daughter of Amos Hough} is clear of marriage engagements, 24th of 1st mo 1795.

To Westland MM: Hannah James, who resides within your meeting, hath lately made satisfactory acknowledgement to us for the offence for which she was disowned, 28th of 3rd mo 1795.

To Hopewell MM: Elizabeth Bond, 25th of 4th mo 1795.

To Exeter MM: Abigael Pancoast has made a request to Aden Pancoast, his wife Abigael and daughter Diedamise was delivered to our meeting, the 10th mo of 1769. Their daughter Deidamia now lives in this neighborhood and has married out of unity. Their daughter Sarah sometime ago applied to Goose Creek MM and was received into membership by them. 25th of 4th mo 1795.

To ______MM, London: John Sutton, left us clear of debt and marriage engagements is recommended to your care, 23rd of 5th mo 1795.

To ______MM, London: Danniel Isaac Sutton, son of John, is a minor under his father's care is recommended to your care, 23rd of 5th mo 1795.

To Crooked Run MM: Elizabeth Brown, 22nd of 8th mo 1795.

Thomas Smith, requested a certificate for his son Joseph, who is placed as an apprentice within the verge of your meeting, 26th of 9th mo 1795.

To Southern District of Philadelphia: Joseph Kirkbride, Mary his wife, and three children Frances Maria, John Paul, and Mary Ann, 24th of 10 mo 1795.

To Indian Spring MM: Samuel Barber, Ann his wife, and 3 small children Sarah, Cornelius, and Abraham, 28th of 11th mo 1795.

To South River MM: Hannah Bradfield, hath lately made satisfaction, 26th of 12th mo 1795.

To Goose Creek MM: Peter Blaker, Sarah his wife, and two of his children, Amos, and David, 26th of 12th mo 1795.

To Goose Creek MM: J___ Blaker, residing within the verge of your meeting, is clear of marriage engagements, 26th of 12th mo 1795.

To Westland MM: Thomas Smith, Rachel his wife, and 6 children Jesse, Rachel, Samuel, Thomas, Phebe, and Sarah, 26th of 3rd mo 1796.

To Westland MM: Hannah Smith, is clear of debt and marriage engagements, 26th of 3rd mo 1796.

To Hopewell MM: William Beale, Rachel his wife, and children Philip, Sarah, Joseph, William and Hannah, are recommended to your care. 26th of 3rd mo 1796.

To Baltimore MM: Joseph Scott, 28th of 5th mo 1796.

To New Garden MM, Chester Co. Pennsylvania: Parminius Lamborne, has moved within the verge of your meeting where he formerly resided, is clear of debt and marriage engagements, 23rd of 7th mo 1796.

To New Garden MM: Hannah Williams is clear of marriage engagements, 28th of 1st mo 1797.

To Indian Springs MM: William Morgan, 28th of 1st mo 1797.

To Goose Creek MM: Solomon Nicholas, Hannah his wife, have made satisfaction for the offense for which they were disowned, 28th of 1st mo 1797.

To South River MM: Sarah Milburn hath made satisfaction for the offense for which she was disowned, 25th of 2nd mo 1797.

To: {Westland MM: Isaiah Myers} Alice his wife, and children David, William, and Elizabeth, 25th of 3rd mo 1797.

To Cedar Creek MM: Alban Gilbin {Albian Gilpin} is clear of marriage engagements, 5th of 2nd mo 1797.

To South River MM: Lacy Nickols, hath lately made satisfaction for the offense for which she was disowned, 25th of 3rd mo 1797.

To Goose Creek MM, Bedford Co: James Erwin, hath lately made satisfaction, prevented his having a ? 22nd of 4th mo 1797.

To Crooked Run, John Ball, is clear of marriage engagements, 18th of 10th mo 1797.

To Crooked Run MM: John Bishop is clear of marriage engagements, 25th of 1st mo 1727.

To Redstone MM: Moses Plummer, Elizabeth his wife, 25th of 11th mo 1797.

To Gunpowder MM: Ann Griffith, has condemned her outgoing of marriage, 23rd of 12th mo 1797.

To Goose Creek MM: Abraham Blaker, a minor living with his father, 23rd of 2nd mo 1797.

To Goose Creek MM: Mary Hurt and Jesse Hurt, 21st of 5th mo 1798.

To Purchase MM in New York: Elisabeth Boun and her son Sidney, 26th of 5th mo 1798.

To Westland MM: Children of George Gregg and Mary his wife, who have settled near Middle Island; children have a birth right and are recommended to your care.

To Pipe Creek MM: Henry Ballinger is clear of marriage engagements, 28th of 7th mo 1798.

To Goose Creek MM: Sarah Scott, wife of Benjamin Scott, 25th of 8th mo 1798.

To Concord MM: Israel Thompson, a minor child in school within the verge of your meeting, 23rd of 2nd mo 1799.

To Chesterfield MM in New Jersey: Reubin Shrieve and Mary his wife, with infant daughter Elin? {Eliza}, 25th of 5th mo 1799.

To Chesterfield MM in New Jersey: Thomas Shrieve, about to settle within the verge of your meeting, clear of marriage engagements, 25th of 5th mo 1799.

To Hopewell MM: Thomas [Parmenus] Lamburn and Hannah his wife, 25th of 5th mo 1799.

To Baltimore MM: Thomas Elliott {Ellicot}, is clear of debt and marriage engagements, 22nd of 6th mo 1799.

To Pipe Creek MM: Mary Pancoast, hath removed with her husband John Pancoast, 27th of 7th mo 1799.

To Baltimore MM: Jacob Janney ...

To Goose Creek MM in Bedford Co: William Wildman, 26th of 10th mo 1799.

To Baltimore MM: John D. Sutton, lately resided in Alexandria, 25th of 1st mo 1800.

To Hopewell MM: David Smith, Ruth his wife, and daughter Rachel, 22nd of 2nd mo 1800.

To Pipe Creek MM: Henry Ballinger...

To New Garden MM: Martha Mendenhall, and infant son William, is clear of marriage engagements, 23rd of ? mo 1800.

To Baltimore MM: Amos Alley, clear of marriage engagements, 27th of 9th mo 1800.

To Goose Creek MM: Jacob Brown...

To Redstone MM: Abraham Davis {and wife Hannah, 3 youngest children, Edward, Ellis, Rachel}, 22nd of 11th mo 1800.

To Westland MM: James Young, and Dinah his wife, lately made satisfaction for their outgoing in marriage, 27th of 12th mo 1800.

To Pipe Creek MM: Hannah Scott, clear of marriage engagements, 24th of 12th mo 1800.

MEN'S MINUTES OF FAIRFAX MONTHLY MEETING

6th mo 1746: Abel Janney and wife, presented certificate from Middletown MM. William Williams, accepted from Gwynedd MM. Mary Goodwin and children given certificate to Hopewell MM. Oliver Matthews and Hannah John married. Joseph Hollingsworth, from Newark, born in unity, accepted as member.

7th mo 1746: Ann Moore and children, from Middletown, Bucks Co. are accepted as members.[unreadable date]: Richard Williams and Prudence Beals intend to marry. Edward Thompson Jr. presented certificate from ? meeting in Chester Co.

3rd mo 1745: Friends settled near Goose Creek request a first day meeting amongst them.

4th mo 1745: Thomas Bourn and wife produced certificate from Bradford MM. Ann Janney received from Falls MM.

5th mo 1745: Henry Brown and Esther Harriss Jr. intend to marry. William ___ and family received from Calvert Co. MD. William Leasey received into membership. Amos Janney appointed Elder of Fairfax Preparative Meeting and clerk of MM until further notice. Henry Mayner and John Wright appointed overseers of Monocacy meeting. Monthly meeting should be held alternately at Monocacy and Hopewell.

6th mo 1745: Samuel Harriss and Jacob Janney appointed overseers of Fairfax Preparatory meeting. Testimony prepared against James Shrieve. James Conard Jr. has left these parts. Alexander Tanzey charged Geo. Matthews with being a lyar. Friends say the charge is false, and Alexander ought to acknowledge his fault. Monocacy preparatory meeting complains of Alexander Tanzey for being frequently guilty of great disorder in his family, it also being confirmed by the testimony of Samuel Lacy, and also by the confession of the said Tanzey to Jonathan Williams and Charles Davis, that if the said Tracy had not hindered him he should have whipped his wife most cruelly, and at the same time treated the said Tracy with very abusive language.

1st mo 1747: Jacob Miller and wife presented certificate from Merion MM in Chester Co., PA. John Poultney accepted on certificate from Horse Cydown in Southwork, Old England. Eleazer Hunt received into membership.

2nd mo 1747: Joseph Hollingsworth condemned his disorderly practice of drinking to excess. John Crumpton and wife {Elizabeth Compton} request certificate to Nottingham MM.

6th mo 1747: William Dodd guilty of drinking strong liquor to excess, also has encouraged the visits of a man not of our society in courtship to his daughter Ann.

8th mo 1747: Edward Lamb received from Cecil Co. Md. Richard Roach received into membership.

11th mo 1747: Jacob Mellon, marked some young swine that appeared to be none of his own. Ordered to make satisfaction.

12th mo 1747: Walter Moore received into membership. Alexander Underwood and Sarah Beale intend to marry. She is a widow. Allen Farquer, Benjamin Poole, Matthias Cooley, George Hyatt, Joseph Walls, and Jeremiah Fairhust received into membership. Abel Janney and wife request certificate to Middletown MM in Bucks Co. PA. Matthias Cooley ... Jacob Janney and Elizabeth Norton are recommended as ministers.

1748: Jonathan Williams requests certificate to NC. Edmund Sands presented certificate from Burlington MM.

7th mo 1748: John Rose? and Ellen Walters intend to marry. Friends condemned the affairs of Edmund Sands. There is still an affair between him and Ellen Wishat?, widow ... David, Jonas and Jonathan Potts, received into membership.

1st mo 1749. William Kersey having had carnal knowledge of Hannah Hunt who is also a member of this meeting, went to a priest to be married. George Hyatt acted contrary to discipline by contracting beyond his ability.

2nd mo 1749: Friends appointed to draw a testimony against William Henery, and Hannah his wife, for their disorderly actions. Thomas and Joseph Plummer received on certificate from West River MM. Joseph Wells and wife, John Wright, Anthony Chamness and wife, Thomas Beales and wife, Richard Williams and wife, Richard Kemp and wife, request certificates to Cane Creek in NC.

2nd mo 1749: Edward Sands had made satisfaction to widow___?

5th mo 1749. Complaint against Joseph Janney for endeavoring to violate the chastity of Margaret Ingledue. William and Hannah Kersey condemned their out going of marriage. Thomas and Joseph Plummer produced certificate from West River MM.

6th mo 1749: Thomas Hunt and Robert Sommers request membership. Martha Parks {Parker} produced certificate from Falls MM. Her son Joseph Parks {Parker} to be taken under care of Friends. Thomas Gore requests membership.

8th mo 1749: Thomas Wilson and wife accepted from Warrington MM in York Co., PA. Edward Dodd received into membership.

9th mo 1749: Humphrey Williams received in membership. Charles Davis requests to be excused from place of overseer; Oliver Matthews appointed in his stead. Joseph Plummer married by a priest.

10th mo 1749: Friends at Goose Creek request to hold first day meeting at Isaac Nichols. William Kirk and Henry Brown, executors of Richard Brown, dec'd, request Friends to assist with the division of land between son Moses Brown and other sons.

11th mo 1749: Jacob Janney and John Hough to prepare certificate for Joshua Shrieve, and produce it at next meeting.

12th mo 1749: George Hyatt, who came on certificate from Hopewell, now returns there.

2nd mo 1750: Complaint against William Dodd for drinking strong liquor to excess and using unsavory expressions. Daniel Matthews recommended to quarterly meeting of ministers and elders. Walter Moore and wife request certificate to Abington MM.

3rd mo 1750: Henry Maynes [Maynard], also Charles Davis and wife, request certificates to Carvers Creek MM.

5th mo 1750: Joseph Plummer produced a paper condemning his outgoings. Marriage of Joseph Wells Jr. and Charity Carrentine [Carrington] was accomplished (with parents' consent). Edward Everet accepted into membership. Thomas Hunt and wife, also Joseph Wells Jr. and wife request certificates to Carvers Creek MM. Thomas Gore used unsavory expressions and offered to fight. Samuel Harris Senr. has given way to a light and airy disposition of mind which led him to dance after musick in a public company which is very disagreeable to the discipline of Friends. Ordered to appear next meeting and make satisfaction. Stephen Scott and William Moore, on a religious visit from NC, need certificates to prove their service.

28th of 7th mo 1750. William Farquar appointed to read Joseph Plummer's paper of condemnation. John Hough and Edward Norton to read Samuel Harris' paper condemning his outgoings. If Thomas Gore does not appear to read his paper of condemnation then John Hough or Edward Norton will do so in his place. Testimony against William Laskey and his scandalous actions was read. 5 mo 1750: Joseph Plummer condemned his marriage.

8th mo 1750: Samuel Harris read paper condemning his actions (dancing). [Signed with a mark]. Testimony against Thomas Gore for dancing and other unseemingly behavior, was read. Testimony against William Leakey and his scandalous actions (proceeding to defraud his creditors) was read. He is no longer a member of the society, until he produces satisfaction.

11th mo 1750: Francis Pierpont and wife produced certificate from Baltimore Co. MM.

1st mo 1751: Jacob Miller appears in an abusive railing manner to the great disturbance of Friends; at divers times has been treated with to no avail.

2nd mo 1751: William Dodd condemned his misconduct. Daniel Matthews requests certificate to visit West River yearly meeting.

3rd mo 1751: William Dodd read condemnation of his behaviour (being disguised with strong liquor). Testimony against Jacob Miller. He hath a contentious disposition and hath become very troublesome ....Therefore, deny Miller membership until his repentance.

4th mo 1751: Henry Ballinger and wife, and such of his family as are going, request certificate to Carvers Creek MM. John Hough excused from overseer, William Mead to replace him. Elizabeth Louis produced certificate from Newark MM.

5th mo 1751. George M__'s certificate produced, approved, and signed. Solomon Miller, produced certificate from Bradford MM.

31st of 6th mo 1751. Richard Holland and wife, produced certificate from quarterly meeting of West River.

7th mo 1751: Eleazor Hunt, removed to NC, sent for a certificate. Testimony was read against Charles Mellor [son of Jacob Meller], who erred in vain conversation and abusive behavior towards his mother.

8th mo 1751. Thomas Palmer and Francis Peirpoint appointed to attend the marriage of William Ballinger and Cassandra Plummer. Peirpoint was sick, but still reported that it was accomplished. Thomas John formerly made a complaint against Rachel Steer for refusing to comply with a contract her husband in his life time made with him concerning some lands. Appoint Joseph Yates, William Mead, and John Janney Jr. to hear the allegations on both sides.

1st mo 1752: William Hallsey guilty of drinking strong liquor to excess. 2 mo 1752: Thomas Wilson condemned his behavior. Jonas Potts requests replacement as clerk of the meeting. John Hough appointed in his stead.

3rd mo 1752: Jonas Potts received certificate to marry Mary Stroud, a member of Hopewell MM. Jacob Janney and wife received certificate to Newark MM.

4th mo 1752. Richard ___?, wife and children produced certificate from Baltimore Co. MM.

5th mo 1751, Alexander Tansey accepted into membership.

6th mo 1752: Bocker Beals request certificate to Cane Creek MM in NC.

7th mo 1752: John Peirpoint produced certificate from ___ [Baltimore?] Co. MM, He and children accepted as members. William Forker appointed overseer of this meeting.

8th mo 1752: Oliver Matthews excused from overseer; Thomas Palmer appointed in his place. Abel Janney and wife produced certificate from Falls MM.

9th mo 1752: Edward Matthews received certificate to Cane Creek, NC.

10th mo 1752. William Matthews received certificate to Cane Creek, NC.

4th mo 1753: Joseph Haywood accepted into membership. Thomas Palmer being indisposed of body requests to be replaced as overseer; Oliver Matthews appointed in his stead.

7th mo 1753: Edward Harmon Cox and wife request certificate to Cane Creek MM in NC.

8th mo 1753: Joseph Burson Senr. produced certificate from Buckingham MM for self and children, Rachel, Benjamin and Deborah. Joseph Burson Jr. accepted into membership. Hannah Ballinger visited us.

9th mo 1753. Edward Dodd requests certificate to Hopewell MM in order to marry.

10th mo 1753: Jacob Janney desires to be excused as overseer; Joseph Yates appointed in his room.

1st mo 1754: Aquilla Massey requests certificate to West River MM.

2nd mo 1754: Certificate for Aquilla and Israel Thompson approved and signed.

5th? mo 1754. Thomas Palmer, wife and children request certificate to NY.

6th mo 1754. Thomas Lamb, wife and children, produced certificate from Middleton MM. Jonathan Potts, ___, William ___ [not clear] and his younger children request membership.

7th mo 1754. Richard Holland appointed overseer at Monocacy Preparative Meeting. Jonathan Potts' paper of condemnation was read.

8th mo 1754: George Burson produced certificate from Gwynedd MM. Edward and William Matthews produced certificates from Cane Creek MM. William Mead excused as overseer; William Williams appointed in his place. George Hyatt requests another certificate to New Garden MM in NC, but his affairs are not in order.

9th mo 1754: Edward Lamb, wife and children received as members. Rachel Wright, Mary Jackson, and Jeremiah Piggot received certificates for service on their visit here from NC.

2nd mo 1755: Children of John Peirpoint have removed to Gunpowder MM. James Butcher received as a member. Susannah Mankin hath been remiss in attending worship and not using plain language and apparel. William Matthews appointed to draw up testimony against her. Edward Dodd has been charged with the ... of young women.

4th mo 1755: Oliver Matthews, wife and children, also Joseph Haywood request certificates to Gunpowder MM.

5th mo 1755: Testimony against Edward Dodd will be delivered by Joseph Yates to Hopewell, where Dodd now resides. William Ballinger appointed Elder for Monocacy particular meeting.

6th mo 1755. Daniel Bayley produced certificate from Newark MM. Casper Sibbolt produced certificate for self, wife and younger children from New Garden MM. George Matthews requests certificate for wife and children to Cane Creek MM. William Mead requests to have a meeting at his house every second first day in each month for his family and neighbors. Approved. Daniel Matthews appointed to read the Book of Discipline in every preparative meeting preceding the Quarterly meeting.

8th mo 1755: Umphrey Williams requests certificate for self, wife and children to Cane Creek MM. Joseph Haywood's affairs not yet settled, therefore his request is discontinued. Certificate for George Matthews and children approved and signed. Friends living above the Short Hills request a meeting kept at David Potts' house. Approved for every first and third first day. Thomas Burson produced certificate from Gwynedd MM.

9th mo 1755: Friends at Bush Creek request permission to have meeting on first day preparative.

10th mo 1755: Jonathan Massey requests certificate to Nottingham MM. Edward Tansey requests certificate to Cane Creek MM. William Dodd charged with drinking to excess and playing cards. He is disowned until he makes satisfaction to meeting. Thomas Dodd charged with disorderly behavior and using scandalous and vile language. Forest Thompson and Edward Norton to draw up testimony. Thomas John for several years guilty of drinking strong liquor to excess both at home and abroad. Francis Hague and John Hough to draw testimony against him. Thomas Wilson made request of overseers to be disowned from amongst us.

2nd mo 1756: Testimony to be drawn against Jeremiah Plummer, William Dodd, Thomas Dodd, Thomas John, Thomas Willson, and George Plummer.

3rd mo 1756: Nathan Haines produced a certificate for himself and wife from Gunpowder MM.

5th mo 1756: Edmond Sands requests membership. Joseph Burson Jr. married a non-member.

6th mo 1756: Jonas Potts guilty of quarreling and fighting with one of his neighbors. William Williams excused as overseer; John Poultney appointed in his place.

9th mo 1756: Samuel Plummer Jr. produced a certificate from West River MM.

10th mo 1756: Jonas Potts acknowledged sorrow for his misconduct. John Hatcher requests membership.

11th mo 1756: Thomas Lewis, late of Pennsylvania, settled within the verge of Monocacy, appears as a Friend, but has not produced any certificate. Alexander Tanzey has removed privately, without settling his affairs nor paying his debts.

12th mo 1756: Joseph Yates requested to be removed as overseer; Isaac Nichols was appointed in his room.

1st mo 1757: Evan Rogers and wife, Owen Rogers and wife, also Henry Lewis produced certificates from Hopewell MM. William Farquier appointed Elder.

2nd mo 1757: James Cunnard and wife produced certificates from Gwynedd MM.

3rd mo 1757: Edward Lamb guilty of irregularities in transacting affairs with Thomas Logston. William Matthews excused from overseer; Richard Richardson appointed.

4th mo 1757: Ann Farquar appointed elder for Monocacy, and Mary Janney for Fairfax. Joseph Thompson requests certificate to Hopewell MM. John Coleman requests membership. William Williams complains against Edward Thompson and Levy Wells not agreeing in their judgements. Testimony against Keziah Plummer was approved. Question whether Alice Yates, formerly Carter, had a birthright among Friends by her mother was agreed to.

5th mo 1757: Mary Lightfoot and Grace Fisher are on a religious visit. George Matthews from Carolina is on a religious visit.

6th mo 1757: Certificate for Joseph Thompson was produced. Edward Thompson agreed with the judgement of committee in his affair with William Williams. John Woolman is on a religious visit.

7th mo 1757: John Peirpoint produced a certificate from Gunpowder MM. John England requests membership. Martha Harris appointed to meeting of ministers.

8th mo 1757: Abraham and Edward Tanzey are not following the principles of Friends. Edward Everett requests a certificate to Warrington MM in order to marry Jane Hodge. Richard Holland excused as overseer; William Ballinger appointed in his place.

9th mo 1757: Daniel Baley offered a paper of condemnation.

10th mo 1757: William Holms accepted as a member.

11th mo 1757: Oliver Matthews complains about William Matthews, administrator of Daniel Matthews' estate.

12th mo 1757: Isaac Hollingsworth produced a certificate from Hopewell MM. Daniel Matthews' Estate falls short of discharging debts, so the friends will raise money for his wife and children. John Peirpoint requests certificate to Gunpowder MM. William Hatcher guilty of several attempts to violate the chastity of Rachel Tanner. Mr. Farling Ball requests membership.

1st mo 1758: Thomas Taylor has a difference with Abraham Tanzey.

2nd mo 1758: Frederick Lamb requests certificate to New Garden MM in NC.

3rd mo 1758: Owen Rogers requests certificate for self and wife to Hopewell MM. William Brazelton received as a member. James Burson married a non-member.

4th mo 1758: Daniel Bailey requests a certificate to New Garden MM in North Carolina. Evan Rogers requests a certificate for self, wife {Sarah} and children to Hopewell MM. [very fuzzy copy follows, not all was abstracted]. William Kersey? [Hersey?] requests certificate for self, wife and children to New Garden MM in North Carolina. Samuel Harriss Senr. guilty of drinking strong liquor to excess. John Hough appointed Elder for Fairfax preparative meeting. Friends Mary Ballenger and Mary Kirk have visited Fairfax families. Thomas Dodd produced a paper condemning his former misconduct.

7th mo 1758: Oliver Matthews complains against Ann Matthews, admx. of her deceased husband Daniel Matthews for a considerable sum of money. Nathan Harris appointed overseer for Pipe Creek.

8th mo 1758: James Burson condemned his outgoing in marriage. This meeting received an answer from Philadelphia relating to assistance for Ann Matthews. Thomas Dodd condemned his former misconduct. Israel Thompson to deliver testimonies against Elizabet (sic) Wils, and Sarah Mekenney. Samuel Potts is guilty of fornication and marrying a non-member. Joseph Burson appointed overseer. William Brazleton requests a certificate to Warrington MM in order to marry a member of that meeting.

10th mo 1758: Morriss Reece produced certificate from Hopewell for himself, wife and children. Francis Hague appointed overseer. Israel Thompson and John Hough to visit Falls MM concerning Samuel Mead.

11th mo 1758: Richard Ridgway produced a certificate from Burlington MM. William Matthews excused from serving as overseer at Monocacy.

12th mo 1758: William Matthews removed to Carolina and left considerable debts. Friends living near Back Creek in Maryland request to hold a meeting during winter. Thomas Lewis ...[too fuzzy to read].

2nd mo 1759: Isaac Hollingsworth returned his certificate with endorsements from Eastern Shore in Maryland. Jonathan Potts' conduct has been reproachful. William Hatcher guilty of fornication. Henry Carting has removed to Hopewell MM.

3rd mo 1759: James Hawkins produced certificate for self and wife {Martha} from Abington MM. Israel Thompson appointed overseer in room of John Poultney, deceased.

4th mo 1759: The meeting house at Monocacy some months ago was burnt down. Has not yet been rebuilt.

6th mo 1759: James Wright produced a certificate from Hopewell MM for himself, wife and children. John Tribbe produced a certificate from New Garden MM for himself, wife and children. Henry Lewis and Morris Reece request certificates for themselves, wives and children to Hopewell MM. Monocacy will meet at Fairfax until further orders, signed John Churchman, Samuel England, John Mickle, James Hammell.

7th mo 1759: David Cadwalleter produced a certificate from Goshen MM for himself, wife and children. Certificate produced for Morris Reece. William Halsey condemned his misconduct of drinking to excess.

8th mo 1759: William Farquhar Jr. requests certificate to Warrington MM in order to marry Rachel Wright. William Matthews produced a paper condemning his behavior.

10th mo 1759: Solomon Hogue produced a certificate from Richland MM for himself and wife. Isaac Everett requests certificate to Warrington MM to marry a Friend of that meeting.

11th mo 1759: William Williams produced a certificate from Goshen MM. William Brooks produced a certificate from Hopewell MM.

1st mo 1760: William Ballenger excused as overseer; Richard Holland appointed. Daniel Brown and Thomas Lightfoot Jr. have visited several branches of our monthly meeting.

4th mo 1760: Robert Millar of Pipe Creek produced a certificate from Newark MM for himself, wife, and seven children. Testimony against Margaret Richardson for her misconduct.

5th mo 1760: John and Joseph Hullen [Hutton] produced certificates from Goshen MM for themselves and wives. Ann Moore produced a certificate from Gunpowder MM. Farling Ball, married a non-member, cannot produce satisfaction, so requests to be disowned.

6th mo 1760: William Hallsey, a member of Monocacy, is frequently guilty of drinking strong liquor to excess.

7th mo 1760: William Schooley produced a recommendation from Friends of Kingwood MM in New Jersey ... [not clear].

8th mo 1760: William Pegion of Warrington MM, intends to marry Rachel Everet, daughter of John Everett of Pipe Creek.

9th mo 1760: Moses Cadwaladar, and Elizabeth his wife, produced certificate from Goshen MM. Mahlon Janney appointed overseer at Fairfax. Nathan Dicks and William Beason visited from New Garden in North Carolina.

10th mo 1760: Joseph Hoge produced a certificate from Hopewell. Thomas Goodwin visited from Goshen. William Harris requests certificate for himself, wife and children to Hopewell.

11th mo 1760: Susannah Hatton visited from Waterford MM, Ireland, and several other places. Phebe Way visited from Flushing, Long Island. Sarah Dungan was her companion from Wrightstown.

12th mo 1760: William Matthews requests a certificate to Sadsbury MM. William Norton is guilty of uncleanness with the young woman who he hath since married by a priest.

2nd mo 1761: Thomas Steer requests a certificate to Sadsbury MM in order to marry.

3rd mo 1761: Joseph Wright, his wife and family removed some time ago. Now request a certificate be sent after them. [location can't be read]. William Schooley has gone out in marriage with Ann Matthews, both members amongst us. It is believed they had carnal knowledge of each other before marriage.

4th mo 1761: Thomas Clowes excused as overseer; Isaac Walker appointed. Nathan Harris excused as overseer at Pipe Creek; William Farquar Jr. appointed.

5th mo 1761: Samuel Schooley Senr. produced a certificate from Kingwood MM, for himself, wife Sarah, and daughters Ann Schooley and Phebe Myers. Jonathan Myers produced a certificate from same place. Isaac Everett requests a certificate for himself and wife Martha to

Warrington MM. James Hawkins has been guilty of drinking to excess much to the abuse of himself and others.

6th mo 1761: Friends appointed to treat with John England have done so. William Hunt is on a religious visit from New Garden in NC.

7th mo 1761: Francis Hague excused as overseer; William Mead appointed.

9th mo 1761: Micajah Standley produced a certificate from Caroline MM in Virginia. Joseph Hoge guilty of drinking to excess and other questionable behavior.

10th mo 1761: John Whiteacre produced a certificate from Kingwood MM for himself, wife {Naomi} and children George, Joseph, Benjamin, Joshua, Caleb, and Robert. John Gregg produced a certificate from Kennett MM for himself, his wife Ruth, and children James Sherward?, Abner George, and Thomas Gregg. Thomas Gregg, a single man, produced a certificate from Kennett MM. Sarah Lewis requests certificates for two of her sons who are removed to Philadelphia. Thomas Hatfield requests membership for himself and children John, ___, Tabitha, Elizabeth and Thomas. Israel Thompson excused as overseer; Moses Cadwalader appointed.

11th mo 1761: Nathan Spencer produced certificate from Abington MM. Certificates were drawn for Thomas and Giles Lewis, sons of widow Sarah Lewis. William Hatcher requests certificate for his son Joseph Hatcher whom he hath bound as apprentice to a Friend in Derby, PA.

12th mo 1761: Testimony against Catherine Popkins and Joseph Janney is to be read at close of some first day meeting. Joseph Hoge has left these parts with some of his debts unpaid.

1st mo 1762: Complaint against John Dodd for dancing and other libertine behavior. He also keeps company in order for marriage with one not of our society. Richard Holland excused as overseer; Thomas Plummer appointed. John Hough is desired to bring William Brooke's certificate to next meeting in order to endorse it to Hopewell MM.

2nd mo 1762: John Beeson, son of Richard Beason, being bound apprentice to David Brown a member of Nottingham MM.

3rd mo 1762: Marriage of John Hague and Ann Schooley was orderly accomplished. Jacob Lewis, son of Thomas Lewis, deceased, is about to remove to Philadelphia and requests a certificate. Jacob Janney appointed overseer at Goose Creek.

5th mo 1762: William Norton proposes to condemn his outgoings in order to receive a certificate to Carolina. John Scarborough visited from Buckingham MM. Jonathan Maris visited from Chester MM.

6th mo 1762: Thomas Taylor has lately purchased a Negro. Rachel Hollingsworth is appointed an elder. William Williams being about to remove to North Carolina with his family requests certificate for himself, wife {Margaret}, and 9 children to Cane Creek MM.

7th mo 1762: Joseph Wright and Mary his wife produced a certificate from Warrington MM. Edward Norton requests certificate for himself to Cane Creek MM.

8th mo 1762: Joseph Burson excused as overseer; David Potts appointed.

9th mo 1762: John and Jonathan Conard produced certificates from Gwynedd MM.

10th mo 1762: David Williams requests membership. Samuel Smith and Isaac Nichols have had a considerable difference in their affairs which they cannot settle between themselves.

11th mo 1762: Robert Miller of Pipe Creek requests certificate for his son Samuel Miller who has been placed as an apprentice in Sadsbury MM. Two of John Everett's sons, Joseph and Benjamin, have removed from their habitation and have not been heard from for several months, ...

2nd mo 1763: John Jackson's affair is continued, as is William Mead's. The care of Sophiah Matthews and Hannah Richardson is continued. Isaac Walker excused as overseer; James Hatcher appointed.

3rd mo 1763: Robert Andrews produced a certificate from New Garden ... [illegible]. William Tate produced a certificate from Kennett MM and has suddenly removed.

4th mo 1763: The Friends appointed to endorse Robert Andrews and wife's certificate have done so, and directed it to Warrington MM. James Hawkins has fallen again into the ill practice of drinking to excess. Complaint has been made by John Warford, not a member, against Isaac Nichols for refusing to make ... [illegible].

5th mo 1763: Certificate produced from Philadelphia MM on behalf of William Baker, hatter, was not accepted at this time. His conduct has been reproachful and he uses vain conversation. A certificate was sent from Warrington MM on behalf of Joseph Jones, apprentice to a person now settled in Frederick town, MD. This meeting, having under consideration his dangerous situation respecting his place of abode, concluded not to receive the certificate till later. The Friends appointed to treat with Isaac Nichols report they had a full opportunity and that the affair between him and John Warford was likely to be settled, it being submitted to judges bond. But the affair of John Grant was not so happily accommodated, said Isaac refusing to submit that case.

Children of Edward Lamb and wife, of PA, have for a number of years quite neglected attending meeting, ... They are denied membership.

7th mo 1763: The Friends appointed in the affair of Isaac Nichols and John Grant report they had an opportunity with them and the parties seem likely to agree between themselves.

10th mo 1763: Matthias Pooley of Monocacy purchased a Negroe. Complaint against David Potts Jr. for fighting, which he confesses.

11th mo 1763: William Baker produced a paper condemning his past conduct, which was accepted as satisfaction. David Burson produced a certificate from Philadelphia. William Jackson, from Abington MM two years past, has neglected attendance at meetings. His son William has life and conversation of the most base and libertine cursing, and swearing. Jesse Dodd, son of William Dodd, appears to be of a loose and libertine conduct. Micajah Stanley requests a certificate to Cedar Creek MM. John Hough excused as overseer; Jonathan Myers appointed.

12th mo 1763: Jesse Davis produced a certificate from Radnor MM for himself, wife Martha and child Mary. James Nichols has taken liquor to excess as plainly appears in public. Robert Yates, of late has conducted himself in a loose and base manner. He is also guilty of fighting. Israel Thompson [something about hireling priest and his collectors]. Thomas Dodd some years past, for his base conduct and ill conversation, was disowned by Friends, after which he condemned the same. He was accepted back into membership, but now is guilty of crimes, especially keeping company with a young woman who is said to be with child by him. He has treated his wife cruelly and left her following the woman aforesaid.

1st mo 1764: Mercer Brown has lately been carried away with insincere temptations of the wicked ones. He hath committed fornication with a woman not of our society. Complaint against William Hatcher for abuse of himself and reproachful conduct in frequenting taverns and public places. Richard Richardson of Monocacy lately purchased a Negroe contrary to the advice of Friends.

2nd mo 1764: John Schooly requests membership.

3rd mo 1764: Jesse Dodd accused of bad conduct in several respects, as swearing and other evils. Jeremiah Fairhurst charged with drinking. William Hoge appointed an elder of this meeting.

4th mo 1764: William Pegion produced certificate from Warrington MM for himself, Rachel his wife, and two children. Complaint from Pipe Creek against Allen Farquhar Senr. for complying with the payment of the Priest's demand. Complaint against Matthias Pooley for drinking to excess which he did not deny. James Nichols appeared and condemned his conduct.

6th mo 1764: Joseph Janney requests a certificate to Abington MM in order to marry Hannah Jones.

8th mo 1764: Jacob and Edward Beason request certificates to Hopewell MM.

9th mo 1764: William Baker has beat and abused a man and has been treated with on that subject. James Hatcher excused as overseer; Solomon Hoge appointed.

10th mo 1764: William Hanks produced a certificate from West River MM. David Harris married a non-member.

11th mo 17164: Nathan Potts and Jonathan Hawkins, both Friends, have quarreled and fought in a public place.

12th mo 1764: William Baker verbally condemned his misconduct.

2nd mo 1765: Allen Forquhar Jr. requests a certificate to Goshen MM in order to marry Phebe Hibberd. Complaint against Ezekiel Potts for fighting. David Brown married a non-member.

3rd mo 1765: Thomas Lamb Jr. is guilty of fighting. Nathan Spencer and Hannah his wife request that their children Margaret, Samuel, Mary and John be received as members.

4th mo 1765: Isaac Nichols Jr., a single man, produced a certificate from Kennett MM. Nathan Potts presented a paper condemning his past evil conduct. Ezekiel Potts sent a paper condemning his past conduct of fighting. Benjamin Burson contributed to the support of an hireling minister, and attended a shooting match where he shot for a prize.

5th mo 1765: William Pancoast and Simeon Haines produced certificates from Burlington MM. Ezekiel Potts condemned his former misconduct. Sophia Matthews has married a non-member. William Pancoast requests a certificate to West River in order to marry Sarah Gover.

6th mo 1765: James Carter married Hannah Eblin by a priest.

7th mo 1765: A certificate for Isaac Nevit, a youth under the care of James Steer, was received from Warrington MM. Allen Forquhar Senr. made satisfaction.

8th mo 1765: Micajah Stanley produced a certificate from Caroline MM so that he may marry Barbara Walker. Thomas Lamb Jr. condemned his misconduct. Complaint against John Cadwalder for attending a public place of diversion, quarreling and fighting.

9th mo 1765: Benjamin Burson continues to pay the parish demand. Abigail Pike, Elizabeth Norton and Charles Stout are on a religious visit.

Complaint against John Eblin for using bad and unsavory language, and for abusing several of his neighbors.

10th mo 1765: A certificate was received from West River MM for Milcah, William and Lucy Richardson, children of Richard Richardson, deceased. Jacob Nichols produced a certificate from Kennett MM. A Friend, in behalf of Francis Matthews, a minor, requests a certificate for him to Gunpowder MM.

11th mo 1765: John Cadwalader condemned his misconduct. Micajah Stanley requests certificate to New Garden MM in NC.

12th mo 1765: Amos Gregg produced a certificate from Kennett MM. A certificate was produced for Francis Peirpoint Jr. and put into the hands of Obed Peirpoint. Samuel Mead Jr. requests a certificate to Salem MM in the Jerseys. Complaint against Jason Morelan for going out in marriage with Ann Richardson, both members of our society.

1st mo 1766: Testimony drawn against Ann Dawson, formerly Harris. Jacob Janney excused as overseer; Benjaman Pool appointed. William Pancoast married Sarah Gover among Friends at West River, however, it now appears they had carnal knowledge with each other before marriage.

3rd mo 1766: Elizabeth Pryor, about to remove to PA, her former place of residence, requests a certificate. Thomas Lamb Jr. has married a non-member with whom he had carnal knowledge before marriage.

4th mo 1766: Jesse Davis requests certificate to Radford MM for himself, wife, and children.

5th mo 1766: James Hatcher and Catherine Nichols were married by a priest.

6th mo 1766: Certificate from Kennett MM was produced by John Gregg for himself and five youngest children. Caleb Cadwalder's certificate from Exeter confirmed his birthright among friends. He has been under the care of his brother James Cadwalader. Isaiah Boon had a three year old certificate which he did not submit. Now he wants to marry a Friend's daughter [not clear]. Reported by Pipe Creek that John England had left Friends and joined in society with some other persuasion of people. Thomas Lamb requests a certificate to Wateeas [Waterrie?] MM in SC for himself, Alice his wife, and their six youngest children.

8th mo 1766: Peter Beason requests a certificate to Hopewell MM. Tabitha Tavener, formerly Roach, has gone out in marriage with a man not of our society. She is also with child, supposedly by him before their marriage.

10th mo 1766: Isaiah Boon intends to appeal to the quarterly meeting. Thomas Gregg requests membership.

11th mo 1766: Arnel Boon, a single man, produced a certificate from Exeter MM. Complaint against Joseph Richardson, [not clear] and vain practices such as frequenting..., gaming or wagering, and dancing with a woman.

12th mo 1766: William Hough married a non-member. Thomas Smith, son of Samuel, requests a certificate to Buckingham MM. Complaint against John Cadwalader for libertine conduct, quarreling, and stripping to fight.

2nd mo 1767: Robert Willis is here on a religious visit.

3rd mo 1767: Henry Beeson has gone out in marriage by a priest. Francis Matthews' certificate to Gunpowder MM was lost, therefore, another will be produced.

4th mo 1767: Richard Holland and Joseph Plummer "being possessed of a Negro each..."

5th mo 1767: James Cadwalader requests certificate for himself, wife and children to Exeter MM. John and Isaac Hawkins request certificates to Bush Creek MM in SC. Complaint against Abraham Smith for keeping disagreeable company, quarreling and fighting.

6th mo 1767: John Cadwalader condemned his past conduct. John Hawkins certificate is delayed because he paid the sheriff militia fines. Abraham Smith condemned his evil conduct.

7th mo 1767: Isaac Hawkins who obtained a certificate last MM has since married out of the unity of Friends. John Stear married a non-member. Reese Cadwalader requests a certificate to Hopewell MM in order to marry Ruth Perkins. William Forquer Jr. excused from overseer at Pipe Creek; Allen Forquer Jr. appointed.

10th mo 1767: Martha Olden has removed again towards Hopewell MM. The testimony against her will be sent there. Complaint against Allen Farquer Senr. for drinking strong liquors to excess.

11th mo 1767: Joel Wright produced a certificate from Warrington MM. Testimony produced against Milke [Milcah] Richardson for outgoing in marriage as well as for light and airy disposition. Arnal Boon was married out of unity by a priest. William Wildman Jr. charged with fornication, which he did not deny. Joseph Pryor produced a certificate first from Gunpowder, then Kingwood MM for himself, wife and children.

12th mo 1767: The Friend appointed in the case of Mrtha (sic) Haldernd (sic) has performed the service he was appointed to by a former minute. Israel Thompson's case is continued.

1st mo 1768: Complaint against Robert Yeats for loose and libertine conduct for some time past, and lately becoming more obvious to the public. John Cadwalader has been his companion in this matter. Nathan Potts has been guilty of fornication. James Ball charged with fighting in a public manner in the town of Leesburg. Benjamin Pool acted inconsistent with the duty of overseer, so he is set aside from that service.

2nd mo 1768: Israel Thompson condemned his past conduct of supporting a hireling ministry. James Ball condemned his misconduct. John Hough was appointed to attend the quarterly meeting, and did set off one days journey, but indisposition of body rendered him incapable of proceeding.

4th mo 1768: Friends were appointed to correct and deliver a list of the male members of our society above the age of 16 years in Loudoun County to the Chief officer of said county...which was delivered to Nicholas Miner. Nathen Spencer who was complained of some time ago and regularly brought before the meeting for burning his neighbor's fence, but as he then denyed the fact, a suit in law was brought against him. Complaint against Thomas Richardson of Monocacy for showing a light and airy disposition and encouraging dances at his house.

5th mo 1768: William Hoge requests to be excused from serving in the station of an elder.

6th mo 1768: Jonathan Wright, a single man, produced a certificate from Warrington MM. George Whiteacre married a non-member.

7th mo 1768: Francis Peirpoint Jr. some time ago received a certificate to Gunpowder MM which he never delivered to that meeting, and inasmuch as he has proved of a loose life and conversation and gone out in marriage since he received the certificate, and making little or no appearance of a Friend, this meeting appoints Mahlon Janney and John Hough to draw a testimony against him.

8th mo 1768: Testimony produced against Sarah Marris, formerly Tribee, for marring a non-member. John and James Gibson produced certificates from Bradford MM. Three children of Edward Mathews, deceased, namely Sarah, Elizabeth and Richard Mathews have a birth right in our society and are now being removed by the mother and step-father to South Carolina. A certificate will be sent to Bush River MM for them. James Connard complained against Ezekiel Potts' ill usage concerning his daughter. Isaac Walker appointed overseer at Goose Creek. William Schooley condemned his outgoing for which he stands disowned.

9th mo 1768: Certificate from Bradford MM was produced for three of Evan Williams' children, namely Israel, Hester, and William.

10th mo 1768: Abraham Todhunter produced a certificate from Uwchlan MM. James Hatcher, who has condemned his marriage, requests membership, also his daughter Mary, an infant.

11th mo 1768: Samuel Ogdon produced a certificate from Burlington MM. Rachel Wilson is visiting from Great Britain. Benjamin Burson condemned his conduct of frequenting shooting matches and paying the priest. John Hanby married a non-member.

12th mo 1768: Jessey Woodward Jr. produced a certificate from Wilmington MM. John Williams has married a non-member.

1st mo 1769: Samuel Smith was disowned. Joel Wright requests a certificate to Warrington MM. Blexstone Janney requests certificate to Kennett MM to marry Mary Nicholls among her relatives. Joseph Clews has married a non-member.

2nd mo 1769: James Young produced a certificate from Plainfield MM in East Jersey. Ezekiel Potts hath offered another paper condemning his past misconduct of wronging James Conard's daughter. Samuel Ogdon requests a certificate to Burlington MM.

3rd mo 1769: Ianathe [Jonathan] Wright requests certificate to Warrington MM.

5th mo 1769: Isaac Gibson produced a certificate from Bradford MM for himself, Esther his wife and their children William, Joseph and M--- [Moses].

6th mo 1769: Morris Ellis produced a certificate from Exeter MM for himself, Sarah his wife, and their two sons Morris and Thomas; also Adah Yarnal, a young woman under their care.

7th mo 1769: Samuel Canby produced a certificate from Falls MM. John Hatfield, son of Thomas, has married a non-member.

8th mo 1769: Solomon Hague excused as overseer at Goose Creek, Thomas Gregg appointed.

9th mo 1769: Samuel Screves condemned his conduct of quarreling and fighting.

10th mo 1769: Henry Smith produced a certificate from Buckingham MM for himself, wife and children Samuel, George, John, Thomas, William, David and Sarah. Pipe Creek reports Gideon Gibson requests membership. Complaint from Pipe Creek against Joseph Jones, who had the care of Friends extended to him while an apprentice. He now neglects meetings. Joseph Burson, an ancient Friend belonging to Fairfax, is now ...death of his son, ...[not clear]. William Ballenger and Jos. Janney will accompany women Friends on a visit to Ann Orr, who has been under notice for her misconduct.

11th mo 1769: Joseph Jones disowned. George Gregg, son of deaf John, late married a non-member. Isaac Walker excused as overseer at Goose Creek; appointed to same at new meeting called South Fork.

12th mo 1769: Jonathan Nutt produced a certificate from Falls MM. Thomas Plummer excused as overseer at Bush Creek; Richard Holland appointed. James Ball, having lately been off his watch so as to quarrel and fight. Joseph Benjamin Whitaker guilty of quarreling and fighting in a public place. William Nichols requests certificate to Abington MM to marry Sarah Spencer. Jacob Janney appointed overseer at Goose Creek in the room of Isaac Walker, and Casper Sybole appointed at South Fork.

1st mo 1770: Abraham Smith married out of unity, for which this meeting denies him the right of membership.

3rd mo 1770: James Ball's paper of satisfaction was read. A testimony against William Janney from the Falls MM was read. A testimony against John Beasor and Dinah his wife, from Philadelphia MM was read.

4th mo 1770: Certificates were produced for part of the children of Jas. Phillips, deceased, viz, Dinah, Elizabeth, Solomon, and Eli [to Kennett MM].

5th mo 1770: Mahlon Taylor produced a certificate from Falls MM.

6th mo 1770: Jonathan Burson has married a non-member.

7th mo 1770: Benjamin Whitaker condemned his misconduct. The paper Merser Brown submitted to last meeting is now accepted as satisfaction.

8th mo 1770: Isaac Siddal produced a certificate from Middletown MM for himself, Rebekah his wife, and son Thomas. Joseph Steer and Saml. Srieve married non-members.

9th mo 1770: The proposal of having a meeting occasionally at David Williams's coming under consideration, it is concluded and desired that Francis Hague, Jonathan Myres, Israel Thompson, and Jos.. Janney may endeavor to meet with Friends there once in three months. A certificate for Hannah Cadwalader and daughters is directed to Warrington MM. New Garden MM requests information about Thomas Gibson who has requested membership with them.

12th mo 1770: . Benja. Srieve produced a certificate for himself and Hannah his wife from Philadelphia MM.

1st mo 1771: Joseph Brown's certificate indicates he has fallen short in the payment of his debts so he will be under Friends' care for awhile. Joseph Everitt was several years past disowned, now desires to reconcile with Friends, and offered a paper condemning his former bad conduct. Benja. Yates has married a non-member.

2nd mo 1771: James Ball has lately given way to quarrel, fight and lay wagers. Jacob Janney and Benja. Pool complain against Isaac Nichols concerning an old account which they can't settle between themselves, and Isaac refuses to leave it to the judgement of arbitrators.

3rd mo 1771: Israel Thompson and Ann his wife, have under their care a cousin about 11 years old, whom they have brought up from a child, her parents being dead. They ask that she, Ann Stein, {Sheen} be received into membership.

4th mo 1771: Richard Richardson condemned his misconduct in purchasing a negro, whom he promises to set free.

5th mo 1771: The meeting received a few lines from William Kirk and Thomas Lightfoot, from Uwchland MM, respecting Jeremiah Thompson, who has conducted himself disorderly. Allen Farquhar Jr. excused as overseer at Pipe Creek; Jos. Wright appointed. William Roads married a non-member.

6th mo 1771: Isaac Janney, son of William, some time past went to Bucks County. A certificate should be sent after him.

7th mo 1771: David Williams produced a certificate from Uwchland MM. Ann Moore is visiting from Gunpowder MM.

8th mo 1771: Joel Wright produced a certificate from Philadelphia MM with an endorsement from Warrington MM.

10th mo 1771: It appears from good authority that Benja. Sands, since his removal to some back county of this colony has married out of the unity of Friends. Jacob Sands removed to some of the back settlements of this colony (it is said to Augusta county) without giving any previous notice to this meeting. Such conduct is inconsistent with good order among us. Wm. Jackson Jr., some years past, left the parts, and as we are informed, removed to Redstone, or Allegany. As his conduct was but loose before, we have no hopes of his being bettered by removing; nay, the contrary is said of him. Timothy Davis from Sandwick MM in New England, and Benja. Jones from Burlington MM in New Jersey are on a religious visit.

11th mo 1771: Complaint made that John Hough, Joseph's son, has been quarreling and fighting.

12th mo 1771: Isaac Brown produced a certificate from Buckingham MM. The Friends appointed to visit Francis Peirpoint report they had an opportunity with him, and find, by his own confession that he continues to pay these demands called Priests Wages. William Mead Jr. requests a certificate to South River MM in Bedford Co. Complaint against Thomas Harris for quarreling and fighting. Joseph Janney appointed overseer at Fairfax in the room of Jonathan Mires.

1st mo 1772: The affair of Thomas Harris is referred to the consideration of next meeting.

2nd mo 1772: Complaint against Benjamin Mead for outgoing in marriage. Francis Hague named overseer.

4th mo 1772: William Ellis produced a certificate from Exeter MM. [An additional note reads "John Hirst Jr. was born the 5th of the twelfth mo 1761 and deceast the 23rd day of the 8th mo 1778] No opportunity has been had with John Hough, (Joseph's son) as he has not returned from Redstone. Jesse Woodard has privately removed (or concealed himself) leaving several debts unpaid. Abraham Todhunter has behaved badly toward a young woman, daughter of Wm. Woolard.

5th mo 1772: Israel Janney produced a certificate from Falls MM. Testimony against William Jackson Jr. was produced. He has removed a great distance to a remote part. John and Jonathan Conard condemned their misconduct.

6th mo 1772: Richard Roach Jr. requests certificate to Hopewell MM, he being removed within thereof.

7th mo 1772: Richard Griffith produced a certificate from Nottingham MM. Nicholas Tucker produced a certificate from Gunpowder MM. Abraham Todhunder condemned his scandalous conduct toward a young woman. His confession in said paper to an act so highly immodest scarce to be paralleled, and from the general looseness of his conduct and neglect of duty--this meeting has no freedom to receive his offering.

8th mo 1772: William Harris and Elizabeth Holmes voluntarily offered a paper condemning their conduct. "Dear Friends, we the subscribers having too inconsiderately given up our names to a Baptist in order to publish our intentions of marriage with each other contrary to the good order established among Friends. For which we are sorry and do hereby condemn our misconduct ... that Friends may pass it by and suffer us to lay our intentions of marriage before this monthly meeting." Signed, William Harris, Elizabeth Holmes. It now appearing that Thomas Harris has a child, laid to his charge proved by the other (a daughter of Henry Oxley), which he denys. John Schooley requests his children might be entered as members. David Williams requests a certificate to Hopewell MM.

9th mo 1772: Samuel Waters Jr. produced a certificate from West River MM. Benjamin Purdom and Mary his wife, request membership.

10th mo 1772: Margaret Wells, formerly Todhunter, some time ago married out of the unity of Friends, and had a child born a few months after. Samuel Coockson has for some time been under care of Pipe Creek.

11th mo 1772: Margaret Todhunter requests a certificate for herself and child named Evan to Uwchlan MM.

12th mo 1772: Women asked for assistance in drawing testimony against Affinity McGeach, Joanna Sanford, and Ann White for their outgoings in marriage, and other disorders mentioned in the women's minutes.

1st mo 1773: Margaret Todhunter's business is not settled, so a certificate for her cannot be drawn. William Hatcher condemned his past misconduct. Jacob Young married a non-member. Certificate from New Garden MM presented by William Neal, his wife and children George, Sarah and Rachel.

2nd mo 1773: A donation legacy was left by Joseph Neid (as reported in quarterly minutes), to be distributed to various monthly meetings.

3rd mo 1773: Margaret Phillips received as a member. Complaint against James Conard for spreading slanderous reports against Anne Williams. Complaint against William Williams, son of David, for sueing James Conard at law in a suit of scandal.

4th mo 1773: Joseph West visited from Wilmington. Isaac Janney married a non-member.

5th mo 1773: Lewis Lemert requests membership.

6th mo 1773: A certificate was lodged here several years past for Soporah Maneyard from Gunpowder, yet she resides within the verge of Pipe Creek. It is agreed to endorse her certificate to Pipe Creek MM. Complaint against Mahlon Janney Jr. for accompanying his brother to his disorderly marriage. Mahlon Taylor requests a certificate to Kingwood MM in West Jersey.

7th mo 1773: Hannah Brooks is recommended as a minister.

8th mo 1773: John Richards intends to join the Baptists, and has undergone their dipping in water.

9th mo 1773: A proposal of marriage was offered to this meeting by two Friends who are brother and sister by affinity, that is to say the man proposes to marry his former wife's brother's widow, and this meeting is not free at this time to allow the said marriage, but appointed a committee to consider the case. {Issac Griffith, from Gunpowder, wanted to marry Anne Burson}. The case of Abijah Williams is continued.

10th mo 1773: James Conard's offering was received. Complaint against Henry Smith Jr. for sueing Isaac Nichols at law and likewise some other differences between them. David Harris married a non-member.

11th mo 1773: Strange Backhouse produced a certificate from Kennettt MM. Isaac Walker to assist women in preparing testimony against Sarah Reese, alias Brown. Danl. Harris inclines to be Baptist. John Richardson condemned his conduct in joining the Baptists and desires to be continued in Society with Friends.

12th mo 1773: A letter was sent to Gunpowder MM respecting Isaac Griffith's conduct. Jacob Janney visited from Duck Creek MM.

1st mo 1774: Henry Smith Jr.'s offering accepted as satisfaction. Complaint against Saml. Eblen for quarreling and fighting. Susannah Brown (now Miller), daughter of John, married a non-member.

2nd mo 1774: William Hartshorne produced a certificate from Philadelphia MM for himself, wife Susannah, and children Rebeckah and Roberts. Even Phillips married a non-member.

3rd mo 1774: Samuel Eblen condemned his conduct.

4th mo 1774: John Richardson assisted with and was present at a clandestine marriage. Complaint against Wm. Treby for fighting. John Sanders, of Alexandria, produced a certificate from Philadelphia. Benjamin Steer produced a certificate from Warrington MM. John Chamberlin's conduct has not been as reputable as it ought to be, so receiving his certificate is delayed. John Conard condemned his conduct. Margaret Todhunter, a widow, laying under difficulty in settling the business relative to her deceased husband's estate, applies for assistance.

6th mo 1774: Certificate produced from Gunpowder MM for three children of Isaac Griffith, namely Joseph, John, and James. Solomon Phillips, a youth who has a birth right among Friends, is joined with his sister Betty on certificate. William Treby condemned his past conduct.

8th mo 1774: Jesse Neal produced a certificate from New Garden MM in Pennsylvania. James Sypole married a non-member.

9th mo 1774: John Chamberlain is about to remove from these parts, and does not feel it necessary to condemn his conduct of taking an oath. Friends have assisted Margaret Todhunter, but her son could not be seen. David Williams, Jr., having by request of his parents when in his minority, obtained a right of membership, but after growing more to man's estate hath given way to a libertine conduct, making little appearance of a Friend, and now hath so far deviated from our peaceable principles as to join with a martial ... [illegible].

10th mo 1774: [poor copy, unreadable]. William Janney Jr. has not returned home.

11th mo 1774: Thomas Lamb Jr. of South Carolina sent a paper to condemn his disorderly conduct whilst among us. It was accompanied by a recommendation from Friends of Padgett's Creek, a branch of Bush River MM.

12th mo 1774: Complaint against James Roach for attending his sister's marriage.

2nd mo 1775: Complaint against Isaac Sands for marrying a non-member. Complaint against Joseph Sands for accompanying a couple in their marriage before a hireling priest (magistrate). Thomas Gregg excused as overseer; Nathan Spencer appointed in his room.

3rd mo 1775: Isaac Walker and Rebekah Gregg named as Elders. John Gregg requests membership through Goose Creek.

4th mo 1775: Jesse Neal requests certificate to New Garden MM.

5th mo 1775: Joseph Janney will accompany Joshua Thompson and Hannah Reece to Black Water Yearly Meeting.

6th mo 1775: Benjamin Purdom is indisposed with the small pox, so his visit to Margaret Williams, late Triby, has not been performed. Isaac Steer married out of unity. Complaint against Thomas Goodwin for neglecting attendance at meetings. Complaint against Isaac Yates for leading a loose and disorderly life, using unsavory language, quarreling, absenting from his usual place of abode, and leaving several just debts unpaid. Henry Smith requests a certificate to Hopewell.

7th mo 1775: Jehu Brown has taken up arms in a military manner. William Brown, of South Fork, requests a certificate for himself, his wife, and young children Martha and Jean, and his son Stephen, to Hopewell. Children of Rebekah Trehorn, James, Sarah, and William, request membership. Israel Thompson requests certificate for his son Jonah to Philadelphia MM.

8th mo 1775: William Tribbee has been under care for his conduct such as dancing, using profane language, drinking, and assisting his sister in her marriage...Richard Gregg has married out of unity. Jacob Janney excused as overseer; Solomon Hoge appointed in his room at Goose Creek.

9th mo 1775: Arnald Boon offered a paper to condemn his outgoing in marriage. Case of William and Stephen Brown (his son) is continued. Complaint against Caleb Whitacre for fighting. Benjamin Whitacre is again guilty of quarreling and using profane language. Complaint against Henry Philips for being the father of an illegitimate child.

10th mo 1775: Case of Benjamin Shrieve is continued.

11th mo 1775: Mahlon Janney excused as overseer; John Schooley appointed in his room. Complaint against James Young for marrying contrary to discipline and removing from these parts. Samuel Gregg, son of Thomas, requests membership.

12th mo 1775: Jonah Hollingsworth requests certificate to Hopewell MM.

1st mo 1776: Neither Isaiah nor Arnald Boon appeared. Their case is continued. Richard Gregg has neglected attendance. Certificate received from Philadelphia MM for Jacob Lewis, who lives in Frederick Town, Maryland, and asks to have it endorsed to Pipe Creek MM. Complaint against James Shrieve who acted inconsistent with uprightness. Mary Baker named an Elder. John Hough asked to be excused as clerk.

2nd mo 1776: Daniel Matthews requests a certificate for marriage with a Friend of Gunpowder MM. Complaint against Joseph Hough, son of Joseph, for loose conduct and having enlisted as a soldier.

3rd mo 1776: Jacob Lewis condemned his misconduct. Goose Creek complains against Thomas Reeder for disorderly conduct, drinking spirituous liquors to excess, and using unsavory language.

4th mo 1776:

[very bad copy, unreadable until 8th mo; missing 3 months]

8th mo 1776: Shadract Lewellen and children Isaac, Anne, Margaret, Mesheck, Deborah, Mary and Hannah received into membership. William Jackson's case is continued. David Potts' case is continued. Isaac Griffith's certificate was refused. Complaint against William Richardson for bearing arms and enlisting as a soldier, he having gone out of these parts. Joseph Janney excused as overseer; Benjamin Purdom appointed in his room. Robert Smith requests certificate to Hopewell MM. William Williams recommended as a minister. Tho. Gregg Jr. requests membership.

9th mo 1776: No opportunity has been had with Abraham Devere. George Whitacre's case is continued.

10th mo 1776: Jesse Harris married a non-member. William Shepherd requests membership. His mother has a right among us.

11th mo 1776: Jacob Todhunter is about to place himself as apprentice, from among Friends. Strange Backhouse has removed from these parts some time ago and requests our certificate. Complaint against Joshua Whitacre for fighting.

1st mo 1777: Elizabeth Baker, widow, has two small children under her care, Nathan and Betty. She desires them to be received as members.

1st mo 1777: Elizabeth Baker, widow, has two small children under her care, Nathan and Betty. She desires them to be received as members. Complaint against John Fairhurst for unchastity with a young woman, and also for his conduct in many respects.

2nd mo 1777: Sarah Hough, wife of William Hough, produced a certificate for herself and children Stacy and Sarah, from Buckingham MM. Isaac Reeder is received into membership. Ezekiel Smith, son of William Smith, produced a certificate from Buckingham MM.

3rd mo 1777: Testimony against Ruth Neptune was produced. Complaint against Samuel Eblen whose general conduct appears very reproachful. He also accepted money to enlist as a soldier, as appears clearly by his own confession.

4th mo 1777: Daniel Matthews requests a certificate to Gunpowder MM.

5th mo 1777: Certificates have been lodged in the meeting for some time for Thomas Richardson of George Town and John Butcher of Alexandria.

6th mo 1777: Samuel Eblen has left these parts. Isaac Nichols charges Abel Janney, sadler, with taking, wasting, or concealing some ..., and refuses to take Friends advice, which is to leave the case to competent judges.

8th mo 1777: George Churchman visited from Nottingham MM. Complaint against Robert Whitacre for fornication with Alice Britain, she having charged him with being the father of her illegitimate child, which he does not wholly deny. Complaint against Amos Janney for keeping idle company and outgoing in marriage. Complaint against Jason Morelan for selling a Negro woman as a slave.

9th mo 1777: Friends attempted to have an opportunity with Jason Moreland and wife, but were prevented by their being absent from home, intentionally as 'tis supposed to evade the sight of Friends. Thomas Rhodes disowned for enlisting as a soldier and removing from these parts. Solomon Hoge excused as overseer at Goose Creek. Jonas and Ruth Janney offered a paper respecting their outgoing in marriage.

10th mo 1777: Thomas Taylor has been much laboured with on account of slaves, yet he continues in the practice of keeping them in bondage. Complaint against John and Jonathan Conard for hiring men to go to war, also John's neglecting attendance at meetings, and mustering at times. Complaints against George Gregg Jr. for hiring a man to go with the militia in his room. Benjamin Purdom is excused as overseer and Mercer Brown is appointed. Complaint against Amos Hough for meeting at Musters.

attending musters. William Hough Jr. condemned his outgoing in marriage of some years past.

12th mo 1777: John Piggott, Joseph Lovett, and Blackstone Janney condemned their conduct in meeting with others to discourage the county's proceeding in compelling men to go to war. William Hoge acknowledged his weakness in putting off his hat to a court martial in order to gain their favor in an application he was about to make to them. James Conard informs that his business is now settled and requests a certificate to Hopewell MM.

1st mo 1778: Complaint against John Tribbe Jr. for bearing arms and marching out with the militia, and absenting himself from meetings.

2nd mo 1778: Joseph Janney accompanied Friend Isaac Zane on a visit to Thomas Taylor. He proposed releasing his slaves in two years, paying one of them wages, which gives some hope further labour may be useful. Abraham Smith condemned his outgoing in marriage, for which he was disowned some years past.

4th mo 1778: Arnold Boon requests a certificate to Indian Spring MM. Thomas Matthews is appointed to record marriage certificates, births and burials until further orders.

5th mo 1778: Thomas Taylor condemned his former conduct in dealing in slaves. John Tribbe and William Hoge have condemned their former conduct. Thomas Richardson is dismissed from membership due to his military service. Complaint against Nicholas Tucker for outgoing in marriage. Ruth Miller and Mary Cox are on a religious visit to Hopewell.

6th mo 1778: Complaint against Benjamin Williams for hiring a substitute and joining in the war. He has gone out of the reach of Friends. Nathan Spencer excused as overseer; Moses Cadwalader appointed.

7th mo 1778: Certificate for Lydia Hough, widow of Joseph Hough, from Falls MM was read, and considering her situation and circumstances, a committee was appointed to visit her. It may be necessary to obtain manumissions for the slaves in Francis Pierpoint's family, so that they may have liberty sooner than proposed, and also for a slave which Thomas Taylor sold some years ago.

9th mo 1778: Thomas Hughes produced a certificate from Gunpowder MM. Lydia Hough is destitute of a suitable place for a home. Testimony against Benjamin Williams, near the Gap of the Short Hill, [recorded here]. Joseph Rhodes does not think it was wrong to attend his sister's marriage.

10th mo 1778: Testimony against Abigail Brown, late Rhodes [recorded here]. Goose Creek informs that Ezekiel Smith has gone out in marriage {with Mary Spencer} and forged a paper containing the consent of his wife's parents.

11th mo 1778: William Shepherd's place of abode is so remote from the meeting that little is known of his conduct. Testimony against John Connard, also Leticia Wildman [recorded here]. Septimus Cadwalader has gone out in marriage. Francis Hague released as overseer. Jacob Janney, Joseph Janney, and Elizabeth Williams are recommended as ministers and elders. Solomon Hoge Jr. has married a non-member. Solomon and Eli Philips request certificates to Kennettt MM.

1st mo 1779: Joseph Rhodes condemned his misconduct. Testimony against Ezekiel and Mary Smith, also Isaac Nichols [is recorded here]. James Roach condemned his past misconduct.

2nd mo 1779: Certificate was produced from Pipe Creek MM for Rachel, wife of David Scholefield, and their children Samuel, John, Enoch, Benjamin and Jane. Ruth Gibson recommended as a minister and elder. Complaint against Joseph Cox for appearing at a mustering ground and once standing in rank among the militia, likewise suffering dancing, etc., in his house. Complaint against John Tribbee for marrying a non-member. James Reyley requests certificate to Hopewell MM. Elizabeth Baker requests certificate for her son Nathan, whom she hath bound apprentice to a Friend at Pipe Creek MM. John Churchman is deceased. Due to the infirm condition of William Mead, also Joan Williams and daughter, it may be necessary to hold an afternoon meeting at each of their places.

3rd mo 1779: George Gregg's offering is accepted. He claims he was drafted into the militia, but hired a man to go in his place. James Roach condemned his past misconduct. Mary Roach condemned her misconduct, of having an illegitimate child. John Hough Jr. has so far disregarded the advice of our yearly meeting as to take the Test [oath of allegiance]. Several Friends residing in Alexandria, namely John Butcher, John Saunders, and William Hartshorne have taken the Test. George Nichols confesses he is guilty of fornication.

4th mo 1779: Testimony published against Ruth Dixson but she being removed to Redstone and out of our reach to show it to her, James Sinkler is directed to publish the same at South Fork. A memorial was produced for deceased Friend Hannah Brook. Pipe Creek requests assistance in preparing a memorial for Friend William Farquar, deceased. Goose Creek informs that Joseph Griffith has taken a Test, contrary to the advice of our Yearly meeting.

5th mo 1779: Edmond Philips {of Goose Creek} was received as a member. He requests membership for his younger children Mercy, Ruth, Margaret, Hannah, Sarah, and Edmond. William Schooley requests a certificate for his son Samuel? to Nottingham MM. Moses Cadwalader excused as overseer at Goose Creek; Stephen Gregg appointed. Goose Creek informs that John Brown Sr. has taken a Test.

6th mo 1779: Rebekah Jones visited from Philadelphia. Rebekah Chambers visited from New Garden. Francis Hague has paid a tax or fine imposed in lieu of taking a test of allegiance to the present powers. Complaint against Elisha Gregg for taking spirituous liquors to excess, using corrupt and unsavory language, and taking the Test of Allegiance to the present Government. Israel Thompson has taken the Test. Goose Creek informs that Isaac Votaw has taken the Declaration of Allegiance required by the legislature. Certificate was produced for Elizabeth Baker and daughters Rachel and Betty to Middletown MM.

7th mo 1779: Joseph Cox condemned his misconduct. Micajah Roach is much in a spirit of liberty and not likely to return. Complaint against James Paxton Jr. for enlisting as a soldier, leaving his parents while under age, and going out of these parts. William Mead formerly appointed as overseer for Fairfax Preparative Meeting, being unable to attend to the service is now released. Complaint against Samuel Harris for taking the Test. Complaint against William Harris Jr. for marrying a non-member and having carnal knowledge before marriage with her.

8th mo 1779: Thomas Hague has paid a tax or fine imposed in lieu of taking the Test. Isaac Cadwalder married a non-member. Complaint against John Eblen on account of a difference between him and Joseph Sands about the worldly interests. Simon Hains condemned his conduct in laying money in the Sheriff's way for the payment of a tax. Sarah Hutton, widow, needs a home; so the meeting appoints a committee to purchase a lot of ground and build her a house, and proportion the expense on the members of this meeting, or otherwise provide her a suitable home.

9th mo 1779: Isaac Walker released as overseer at Goose Creek; Solomon Dixon appointed. Thomas Brown requests membership.

10th mo 1779: Joseph Griffith has removed to Maryland. Friends appointed to provide a house for Sarah Hutton report they have a house considerably on the way in building on this meeting house land, but it appears that Sarah declines accepting as she has lately removed to Redstone. Therefore, it is thought the house may be useful for some other Friend. Josabed Lodge and Jonah Thompson took the Test.

Complaint against Jacob Lewis for drinking spirituous liquor to excess, neglecting attendance at meetings, selling spirits at public places and taking the Test. Complaint against Joseph Lovett for having carnal knowledge with a young woman, which he does not deny.

11th mo 1779: Complaint against Stacy Hough for his outgoing in marriage. The Friends under whose care John and Elizabeth Potts' case was rested, are directed to attend thereto, particularly with respect to placing Elizabeth among Friends until she arrives at age. Goose Creek informs that Jasper Seybold Jr. is guilty of fighting. He produced a paper condemning his conduct.

12th mo 1779: Samuel and Margaret (Holmes) Harris disowned. The Friends appointed in the case of Elizabeth Potts visited her grandmother, with whom she is at present, where they made choice of a place to put her, but this meeting received information that she hath since declined her proposal, and intends placing her elsewhere. John Nichols is guilty of fornication before marriage with her that is now his wife.

1st mo 1780: Samuel Spencer married a non-member. John Parish and Samuel Hopkins are visiting.

2nd mo 1780: John Hoge requests a certificate for himself, wife, and one child {William} to Hopewell MM.

3rd mo 1780: Elizabeth Potts is a present at Jonathan Connard's, being placed there by her Grandmother. Joseph Whitacre married contrary to good order.

4th mo 1780: James Dillon condemned his conduct some time ago, it is now accepted. Isaac Votaw condemned his misconduct. He will be watched until further notice. John Brown continues to vindicate his conduct. Francis Hague and Thomas Hague are not convinced of having done wrong. Testimony produced against Jacob Lewis.

5th mo 1780: Testimony against John Brown and Francis Hague was produced. Testimony against Jane Whitacre was published. Abner Gregg requests certificate for himself and wife to Hopewell MM.

6th mo 1780: William Pidgeon produced a certificate from Pipe Creek MM for himself, Rachel his wife, and children John, Rachel, William, Isaac, Ruth, Charles, Hannah, and Sarah. James Moore produced a certificate from Uwchlan MM. Rebekah Davis submitted a paper of acknowledgement. Israel Janney requests a certificate to Pipe Creek MM in order to marry Anne Plummer.

7th mo 1780: Complaint against Isaac Nichols Jr. for being guilty of fornication, which he doth not deny.

8th mo 1780: Jozabad Lodge condemned his deviation. Abraham Smith continues his proposal of removing west, beyond Allegheny mountains. Jacob Janney Jr. requests certificate to Pipe Creek MM to marry Sarah Harris.

10th mo 1780: Mahlon Smith requests a certificate to Hopewell MM to marry Mary White. Joseph Brown's certificate for himself and family to Hopewell was produced, but he was not present to accept it. Francis Hague presented a paper condemning his behavior in regards to taking the Test. [full text included]. Stephen Moreland requests a certificate to South River MM for himself and family.

11th mo 1780: Thomas Moore Jr. produced a certificate from Goshen MM. John and Margaret Nichols condemned their behavior. Joseph Brown's outward affairs are not yet settled in Pennsylvania, but nothing was found in these parts to prevent producing a certificate for him, Elizabeth his wife, and children Ann, Sarah, Isaiah, Rachel, Samuel, Leah, Mary, Mahlon and Joseph, to Hopewell MM. Joseph Elgar appointed to meet with Friends who have taken the Test of Allegiance and Abjuration. Isaac Votaw's acknowledgement was received. Testimony was produced against Isaac Nickols, son of Isaac. The case of Francis, Samuel, and Jonah Hague is continued. Benjamin Mead condemned his outgoing in marriage for which he was disowned some years past. David Brooks visited from Deep River.

12th mo 1780: A suitable place has been procured for Samuel Hague, but none yet has been offered for Francis and Jonah. Aaron Hackney requests certificate for himself and family to Hopewell MM. John Reyley requests a certificate to Hopewell MM. Benjamin Pool hath indulged himself in light and airy company, amongst ___ of frolicking, and in dancing and singing which he refuses to condemn. Samuel Emlen and David Offley visited from Philadelphia. Thomas Thornbery and William Robinson visited from NC.

1st mo 1781: Samuel Harris condemned his behaviour in taking the Test. William Hough's children in their minority, John, Joseph, Thomas, Samuel, Elizabeth, and Sarah, are received as members. Isaac White, son of Thomas White, is received on certificate from Goshen MM. Benjamin Mead is sincere in his acknowledgement, and requests that his children may be received a members. They are minors, named Margaret, Christian, Asenath, and Samuel. Joseph Griffith and Isaac Votaw condemned taking the Test. Benjamin Mead condemned his outgoing in marriage. A certificate was produced for John Reyley, Ann Reyley and several of her children, but it appears they are not full members. A certificate was produced for Mary Rogers directed to Hopewell MM. A committee reports that it agreed to raise 5-10 pounds for relief of Joan Williams. Joseph Griffith requests a certificate to Gunpowder MM. Benjamin Purdom is appointed overseer at Fairfax.

2nd mo 1781: Israel Thompson's acknowledgment was accepted. John Hirst and Mary Smith recommended as Ministers. Stephen Gregg recommended as Elder for Goose Creek. Isaac Todhunter has removed to Hopewell. A certificate will be sent after him. Joseph Janney appointed to attend burials at Fairfax in the room of Francis Hague, deceased. Israel Janney is appointed to attend burials at Goose Creek in the room of John Brown.

3rd mo 1781: Joseph Hutton Jr. produced a certificate from Pipe Creek MM. George Smith requests a certificate to Hopewell MM.

4th mo 1781: Constantine Hughs produced a certificate from Buckingham MM. James Shrieve condemned his misconduct for which he was disowned some years past. Septimus and John Cadwalder produced papers condemning their outgoing in marriage, for which they were disowned. Benjamin Whitacre produced a paper... Testimonies were produced against Thomas Hague, also Sarah Hough. A certificate was produced for Abraham Smith to Hopewell MM. [bad copy] Certificates were produced for George Smith and Ruth Smith, children of Saml. Smith, to Hopewell MM. From Buckingham MM, Martha Firestone and Mary Russell...had been disowned...later acknowledged.

5th mo 1781: [bad copy from here until the end of minutes]. Septimas Cadwalader acknowledged his misconduct. Robert Whitacre condemned his conduct. John Eblin has joined in light and airy company, frolicking and dancing, and married a non-member.

6th mo 1781: Benjamin Pool delivered a paper condemning his misconduct. Thomas Matthews proposed as clerk. Gunpowder MM informs that Isaac Griffith wants to be reinstated. Edward Stabler visited from Burleigh MM.

10th mo 1781: Andrew Grammer ...Gwynedd MM. Received lines from Wrightstown regarding James Love. Gunpowder MM inquired about David Lacey. John Schooley released as overseer; William Pidgeon appointed. Complaint against Thomas Gregg Jr. for fornication, which he does not deny. Complaint against Jasper Seybold for outgoing in marriage. John Long requests membership. William and Thomas Brown produced certificates from Nottingham MM. Complaint against Barnett Hough for light and airy conduct, unsavory language, and other deviate behavior [not clear].

12th mo 1781: William Jackson's paper of acknowledgment was accepted. John and Silas Young, sometime past moved west with their parents, now request a certificate to Hopewell MM. Isaac Griffith produced a certificate from Gunpowder MM.

1st mo 1782: Mary Smith, wife of Mahlon Smith, produced a certificate from Hopewell for herself and son Nathaniel White. Thomas Hatfield requests certificate for himself and children to Hopewell.

3rd mo 1782: [very bad copy] Benjamin Yates condemned his outgoing in marriage, for which he stands disowned. Complaint against Isaac Reeder for ... and abusive language, for which he offered a paper condemning the same.

4th mo 1782: Thomas Taylor Jr. requests certificate to Warrington MM to marry Sarah Musgrove. Complaint against Joseph and Isaac Thompson Jr. for keeping light and airy company, dancing, and quarreling and fighting. Complaint against Jonathan Trebbe for fornication, the venereal disease following as the consequence of his unchastity. Complaint against Joshua Hatcher for marrying a non-member. Complaint against Jonathan Lodge for joining in light and airy company, frolicking and dancing and horse racing.

6th mo 1782: George Walters requests membership.

7th mo 1782: Mary Baker is released from being an Elder. Jacob Janney proposed as Elder. Thomas Moore Jr. appointed to keep the record of marriage certificates, births, and burials.

8th mo 1782: Amos Hough condemned his misconduct for which he stands disowned. Samuel Hutton requests certificate for himself and sons Thomas and Levi to Menallen MM. Edward Ries requests membership. George and Dinah Walters request that their children Sarah, Thomas, James, Lydia and Judith, be received as members.

9th mo 1782: John and James Griffeth, have removed with their father Isaac to Gunpowder MM, so certificates should be sent after them.

10th mo 1782: Jonathan and Jacob Lodge's paper of acknowledgement was received, but Jonathan's was not suitably adapted to the nature of his offense.

11th mo 1782: Joseph and Isaac Thompson, and Jacob Lodge presented papers of acknowledgement. Regarding the conduct of Joseph Hibbs' children, it appears that William resides at Redstone, within the limits of Hopewell MM. Therefore it is necessary to inform Wrightstown MM that Joseph and Sarah have married contrary to discipline, with non-members and Mercy has suffered herself to have an illegitimate child. Thomas Roades who was disowned some years ago, offered a paper of acknowledgement. Buckingham MM informs that William Beans has condemned his fornication. Amos Harris married a non-member.

12th mo 1782: John Saunders and John Butcher acknowledged their misconduct. Jonah Hague has been placed with Abel Janney as guardian.

1st mo 1783: Thomas Rich produced a certificate from Nottingham MM. William Hartshorne appeared in person and offered a paper of acknowledgment. In the case of Joseph Hibbs children: Sarah Emery, formerly Hibbs, offered a paper condemning her outgoing in marriage. A testimony was produced against Mercy [Hibbs]. Joseph [Hibbs] expressed a desire of being treated further. Elizabeth Hibbs, daughter of Joseph, is received from Wrightstown MM. Eli Nichols has removed to Kennett MM. Joseph Hutton, son of Samuel, requests a certificate to Pipe Creek MM.

2nd mo 1783: Isaiah Smith Jr. produced a certificate from Buckingham MM. Hannah James, formerly Smith, offered a paper condemning her misconduct in having an illegitimate child. She now resides within Hopewell MM. John Sanders, by a Friend, requests a certificate to Crooked Run MM in order to marry a woman there.

4th mo 1783: Phebe Whitson, wife of Solomon Whitson, produced a certificate from Buckingham MM. Euphemia and Tacy Lacey were received with their younger children Elias and Meshack. Israel [Lacey] will be asked to attend next meeting. Septimus Cadwalader requests a certificate to Hopewell MM. Isaac Brown Jr. requests membership. The children of James Moreland and Ann his wife, Sarah, Rebekah, Ann, Jason, and Joseph Moreland, have a right of membership, and years ago removed with their parents to Redstone.

5th mo 1783: Joseph Wood and William Beans produced certificates from Buckingham MM. Jasper Seybold recommended as Elder. Complaint against Joseph Peirpoint for marrying a non-member.

6th mo 1783: Goose Creek Preparative informs that Solomon Nickols and Hannah Gregg {daughter of Thos. Gregg}, both members of our Society, have married with the assistance of an hireling teacher. Joseph Baldwin requests membership.

8th mo 1783: John Janney, son of Abel Janney, deceased, offered a paper condemning his attendance at a non-Quaker marriage, and joining the company in frolicking and dancing.

9th mo 1783: Robert Seybold acknowledged his misbehavior of fighting. ...Complaint against Moses Cadwalader for attempting bestiality.

10th mo 1783: Asa Harris married a non-member. George Brown is charged with being the father of an illegitimate child, and that he married a non-member, his first cousin.

11th mo 1783: John Coffin sometime ago requested, and is now received as a member. William Smith Jr. requests a certificate to Pipe Creek MM. Goose Creek complains that Isaiah Nichols joined with others in gaming for a wager.

12th mo 1783: Edmond Roach has neglected attendance at meetings. Thomas Rich and Ann Pool, both members of our society have married contrary to discipline.

1st mo 1784: Thomas Russel and his minor children Ann, Hannah, Thomas, William, Elizabeth and Mary are received into membership. Goose Creek complains about Richard Moreland who now resides near Redstone for quarreling and fighting.

2nd mo 1784: William Ballenger Jr. produced a certificate from Pipe Creek MM. George Gregg Jr. has of late addicted himself to the excessive use of spirituous liquors, even to a degree of drunkenness. William Hough recommended as an Elder.

3rd mo 1784: Mercer Brown excused as overseer. Joseph Hutton removed himself and family without notifying this meeting, so it is thought necessary to write to Hopewell and inform them of his conduct.

4th mo 1784: Amos Jolliffe produced a certificate from Hopewell. Edward Walton? produced a certificate from Philadelphia MM. Testimony against Jane Bolin ... William Ballenger Jr. has removed to Pipe Creek.

5th mo 1784: Timothy Beans produced a certificate for himself, wife Rebekah and children Amos and James from Buckingham MM [conditions not clear]. James Love's certificate from Wrightstown MM is now received, he being present. Certificate was produced for Phebe Myers to Hopewell MM. Complaint against Isaac Eblin for fighting and using corrupt language. Complaint against Joseph Thompson for being at a Publick [place] ... with Stacy Drink accomplished marriage contrary to good order. Mahlon Smith requests certificate to Crooked Run MM for himself, Mary his wife, and children Nathaniel White, her son by a former husband, and John Scolfield an apprentice lad. Complaint against Edmond Philips for wholly neglecting attendance at meetings, and marrying a non-member. Stephen Gregg released as overseer; Solomon Hoge proposed in his stead.

6th mo 1784: Certificate was produced for John Schoolfield to Crooked Run. Thomas Moore Jr. proposed as new clerk of the meeting. Jesse Taylor has married a non-member. Thomas Gregg Jr. requests certificate to Hopewell MM. Jesper Seybold released as overseer at Southfork; William Neal appointed in his place. Complaint from Goose Creek against John Eblin Jr. for neglecting attendance at meetings, quarreling and fighting, using profane language, and being disguised with strong drink.

7th mo 1784: There is a problem with Thomas Moore Jr. being appointed clerk. Thomas Matthews requests a certificate to northern district of Philadelphia in order to marry Sarah Johnson. Complaint against William Daniel Jr. for having attempted bestiality?

8th mo 1784: Daniel McPherson produced a certificate from Hopewell MM. Isaac Thompson Jr. married a non-member. John Schooley appointed overseer.

9th mo 1784: Complaint against Jesse Seybold from Goose Creek for using profane language and joining with other ...[not clear]. He appeared and presented a paper condemning the same.

10th mo 1784: Goose Creek informs that Amos S___ in company with others, has been guilty of taking his neighbor's water mellons without leave. David Smith, son of Henry Smith, deceased, had choice of his brother John Smith as guardian.

11th mo 1784: Aaron Plummer made satisfaction. This meeting received a few lines from Bush River MM respecting David Harris.

12th mo 1784: Jesse Taylor condemned his outgoing. Goose Creek informs that Benjamin Pool is charged as being the father of an illegitimate child, which he denies, although she has established her accusation according to law. Goose Creek complains that Samuel Smith had something to do with the death of one of his neighbor's horses. [Many removals were no longer copied, as certificates are recorded].

1st mo 1785: Anthony Connard, son of John Connard, married out of unity of Friends. Goose Creek informs that Isaac Nickols Senr. has entered a complaint against Nathan Spencer, who refuses to pay a debt.

2nd mo 1785: Jesse Taylor's acknowledgement accepted as satisfaction. Certificate produced for William Scott to Gunpowder MM.

3rd mo 1785: Certificate from Pipe Creek MM received for William Kenworthy Jr. Jonathan Burson condemned his former misconduct for which he stands disowned. Aquilla Janney requests a certificate to Hopewell MM in order to marry Ruth McPherson. Samuel Hutton produced a certificate from Menallen MM.

5th mo 1785: Ann Butcher and Rebekah Burson received as members. This meeting received a few lines from Ignatious Davis in Maryland, grandson to Merideth Davis who gave a deed to Friends of Monocacy for five acres of land for a meeting house and graveyard.

6th mo 1785: Testimony against Ann Lewis was published and returned. Goose Creek informs that Thomas Ford is guilty of quarreling and using profane language. He denies part of the charge.

7th mo 1785: Goose Creek complains of David Hoge for quarrelling, and fighting. Isaac Lewallen requests certificate to Hopewell MM. Benjamin Purdom requests to be released from reading testimony and papers of acknowledgment. William Hoge appointed in his place.

8th mo 1785: A certificate was produced from Pipe Creek MM for Edward Stabler Jr. Certificate was produced by David Lacey from Gunpowder MM. Thomas Fred's case is continued. Reuben Schooley requests a certificate to Gunpowder MM in order to marry.

9th mo 1785: William Daniel's acknowledgment was returned to mens meeting. Ann Mead's case is continued. Goose Creek complains against Jacob and Samuel Roades for quarreling, fighting, and joining with light company in dancing. Complaint against Silas Seybold for being intoxicated with strong drink, and ... his neighbor's wife. John Sutton is apprehensive of sustaining ... a Friend in Alexandria, declining to give him security for money due him.

10th mo 1785: William Abbott and Robert Whitacre being ... Complaint against __ Paxon for quarreling and fighting. John Steere? and Thomas Cotty, from old England, visited this meeting.

11th mo 1785: Acknowledgment was accepted from John Long and wife. Testimony against William Holmes was published and returned. {next few pages unreadable].

12th mo 1785: Benjamin Shrieve produced a certificate from Hopewell. William Paxson condemned his behavior [something about John Sutton's debt]. Dorothy Schooley's request is granted. Certificate to Westland MM was produced for Isaac Lewellen.

2nd mo 1786: David Hoge's acknowledgement is accepted. Exeter MM wrote that David Hopkins has a birthright in the society. John Hatcher condemned his misconduct.

4th mo 1786: Joseph Trebe voluntarily condemned his disorderly conduct. [more bad copy]. Caleb Bently produced a certificate from Warrington MM. He has since settled within the verge of Goose Creek. John McClain? produced a certificate from Crooked Run MM. Elizabeth Moore and Lydia Hough appointed as Elders.

6th mo 1786: Ephraim Long produced a certificate from Gunpowder MM.

7th mo 1786: Edward Folwell produced a certificate from Nottingham MM. Mordicai Miller produced a certificate for himself and wife. Jonathan Butcher produced a certificate from Falls MM. David Hopkins certificate was read and received. Thomas Hough condemned his misconduct. Robert Whitacre requests a recommendation to Goose Creek MM in order to marry Hannah Janney, daughter of Jacob Janney.

10th mo 1786: Complaint against Andrew? Scholfield for being guilty of fornication with Sarah Randall, now Scott.

11th mo 1786: Thomas Moore Jr. appointed clerk for the meeting. James Moore produced a certificate for himself, wife and three children from Crooked Run MM. Complaint against Evan Todhunter for not attending meetings, using profane language, and he is charged as being the father of an illegitimate child, on account of which, we suppose, he has left these parts.

12th mo 1786: William Stabler produced a certificate for himself from Black Watch in Surry County. William Long? married a non-member.

1st mo 1787: Complaint against Jacob Lodge for marrying a non-member.

2nd mo 1787: Richard Matthews presented a certificate from New Garden MM in NC. A certificate was produced for Thomas Scattergood.

4th mo 1787: Jonas Janney presented a paper on behalf of himself and wife condemning their misconduct some years past.

5th mo 1787: James Erwin? presented a certificate from Gunpowder MM.

6th mo 1787: Complaint against Richard Matthews for frolicking and dancing and ... [unclear].

7th mo 1787: William Pidgeon released as overseer; Joseph Talbott appointed. John Paxton? produced a certificate from Buckingham MM.

8th mo 1787: John Hough, son of William, produced a few lines condemning his misconduct (dancing). William Paxton produced a paper condemning a similar offense.

9th mo 1787: Menallen MM requests assistance in treating with Benjamin Hutton. Isaac McPherson requests a certificate to Hartford MM in order to marry Elizabeth Roberts.

11th mo 1787: Caleb Floyd presented a certificate from Gunpowder MM. Joseph Janney complains against Jonathan Myers for failing to settle a dispute between them.

12th mo 1787: Stephen Wilson presented a certificate from ___ MM. Meeting received words from ___ Creek? MM in Hanover Co., that they produced a certificate for John Scott Plummer, but it has been lost. Thomas Taylor and John Sutton complain against Joseph Scott for nonpayment of a debt. Thomas Moore Jr. will serve as clerk for the meeting.

1st mo 1788: Testimony against Rebekah Martin is returned. Richard Lewis? requests membership.

2nd mo 1788: Certificate was presented by Joseph Salmor? from Hopewell MM.

3rd mo 1788: Complaint against David Hopkins for neglecting attendance at meetings, and marrying a non-member. Complaint against William Paston, son of James, for neglecting attendance, using spirituous liquor to excess and marrying a non-member. Complaint against Thomas Hough for neglecting attendance and marrying a non-member.

4th mo 1788: A certificate for Richard Childs from Buckingham MM was approved.

5th mo 1788: Complaint against Joseph Burson who has gone out in marriage with his first cousin, and has been guilty of unchastity before marriage.

6th mo 1788: Thomas Matthews and Sarah his wife are recommended as ministers. Discontinue the case of Joseph Baldwin. Moses Cadwalder Jr. some time ago sent a paper condemning his misconduct. It will go to Goose Creek for consideration.

8th mo 1788: Complaint against William Paxson and John Hough, son of William, for joining in light company and dancing.

9th mo 1788: Esther Matthews presented a certificate... it was sent to Goose Creek. Complaint against John Potts for joining with light company in dancing.

10th mo 1788: John Hough has lately accomplished his marriage with a non-member.

12th mo 1788: Thomas Backhouse presented a certificate from Kennettt MM. John Pidgeon presented a certificate from South River MM. Complaint against John Janney for bringing a suit at law against a Friend.

1st mo 1789: Thomas Poutney Jr. presented a certificate from Philadelphia MM. Complaint against William Milner? for not paying a just debt to John Sutton. Benjamin Purdom released as overseer.

3rd mo 1789: William Stabler requests a certificate to Cedar Creek MM in order to marry Deborah Pleasants. Samuel Hague and Ephraim Lacey have married non-members.

4th mo 1789: William Mendenhall presented a certificate from Kennettt MM. Complaint against Joseph Trebee for marrying contrary to good order, with Ruth Gregg, a member of our society; she having previously contracted matrimony with another man. Asa Beans married a non-member. Moses Cadwalader Jr. condemned his misconduct. Committee appointed to write to South River MM respecting his situation.

5th mo 1789: James Curl presented a certificate from Kennettt MM, but he has removed from this meeting. William Paxson has lately married a non-member. James Curle requests certificate to Goose Creek in order to marry Ruth Randle.

6th mo 1789: Certificate was presented by John Scott Pleasants, from Cedar Creek MM, Hanover Co., which was for some time delayed. John Janney's paper was accepted as satisfaction.

7th mo 1789: John Woodard Jr. presented a certificate from Chester MM. ___? Gibbs presented a certificate from Upper Springfield MM. William Michenor agreed to give up his property into the hands of Friends, in order to satisfy his creditors. Joseph Wood's family requests membership.

9th mo 1789: ___? Bennett presented a certificate from Concord MM.

10th mo 1789: Moses Cadwalder condemned his reproachful conduct, for which he stands disowned. Complaint against Samuel Hough for detaining a just debt due to Joseph Janney.

11th mo 1789: Daniel McFerson requests a certificate to Hopewell MM in order to marry Martha Beason.

12th mo 1789: Abigail Wood, and children Josiah, Robert, Mary, Naomy, Abigail, Joseph, John and Jesse, received into membership.

1st mo 1790: Samuel Hague requests a certificate to Crooked Run MM.

2nd mo 1790: Thomas Poultney requests certificate to Indian Springs MM in order to marry Ann Thomas.

3rd mo 1790: Thomas Erwin? presented a certificate from Philadelphia MM. Samuel Hague informed of the objection to his receiving a certificate, for which he seemed displeased.

4th mo 1790: Committee appointed to consider the propriety of paying Ann Steer's debs, although it has been long neglected, is continued. Complaint against James Bunting Jr. for drinking spirituous liquor to excess. Joseph Beck and John Holinsworth appointed overseers.

5th mo 1790: Complaint against Amos Paxton for drinking spirituous liquor to excess and for quarreling and fighting. Complaint against Henry Taylor for neglecting attendance, and for marrying contrary to discipline with a woman in membership with us.

6th mo 1790: Considering the remote and distant situation of Richard Richardson and Thomas Taylor Jr., and their families, it is decided to visit them. John Butcher is recommended as a minister. Elizabeth Purdom released as Elder.

7th mo 1790: John Schooley Jr. presented a certificate from Hopewell MM. Lydia Green's paper accepted as satisfaction. Elizabeth Purdom recommended as a minister. John Sutton writes that he is about to go to Europe, with his sons Daniel and Isaac Sutton, and James America Sutton to settle his affairs there. Complaint against Richard Gregg for neglecting to return here (from Westland MM) and settle his business.

9th mo 1790: Philip Wanton presented a certificate from Newport, RI. The Suttons left without a certificate.

10th mo 1790: Richard Richardson and Thomas Taylor Jr. request certificates for themselves and their families to Pipe Creek MM. Chesterfield MM wrote that James Bunting and family were members of our Society. James Erwin requests a certificate for himself, wife, and children to South River MM. Samuel Hague requests a certificate to Crooked Run MM in order to marry Hannah? Bishop.

11th mo 1790: William Morgan is received into membership. There was some objection to James Erwin receiving a certificate. His wife and children were approved.

12th mo 1790: The meeting received a certificate for John Cadwalder Jr. from Exeter MM, but since he now lives in South River, it was handed to Jesse Lewis, a member of that meeting, to be forwarded. This meeting appoints Mahlon Janney and William Hough to inspect Joseph Scott's conduct before issuing a certificate.

1st mo 1791: Hopewell wrote that Hester Connard appeared ready to condemn her misconduct for which she stands disowned. Complaint against Titus Bennett for keeping company with a woman. William Morgan requests a certificate to Gunpowder MM in order to marry Sarah Price. Charles Harper requests membership.

2nd mo 1791: Lott Trip produced a minute from Creek MM in New York. Calen Bently requests certificate to Indian Spring in order to marry Sarah Brook. Complaint against Isaac Miller for going away and settling remote from Friends, and marrying a non-member.

3rd mo 1791: Joseph Scott is now clear, and may receive a certificate. Ann Steer, and her daughter Ruth, and Rehobeth Williams are in difficult circumstances. Ephraim Lacey condemned his disorderly conduct for which he stands disowned.

4th mo 1791: Charles Shoemaker presented a certificate from Abington MM. Thomas Harris, late from New York, came in company with Lott Trip, a minister of our Society. He now desires to unite with Friends.

5th mo 1791: This meeting received a few lines from Wrightstown MM respecting Elizabeth Wear and her children.

6th mo 1791: Joseph Hough presented a certificate from the northern district of Philadelphia. Joseph Randal produced a certificate for himself, wife Rachel and two youngest daughters Jane and Charity from Goose Creek MM. Friends have visited Elizabeth Wear and her children.

7th mo 1791: Thomas Love presented a certificate from Goose Creek MM. Thomas Moore Jr. requests a certificate to Indian Spring MM in order to marry Mary Brook Jr.

8th mo 1791: Charles Harper received into membership. Samuel Reeder's paper of acknowledgement was read, but not yet accepted.

10th mo 1791: House that Rehoboth Williams lives in requires repairs to render it fit for her accommodation. The treasury to pay the expense of said repairs. Ann Steer and her daughter Ruth have agreed to return to their former habitation on Benjamin Steer's plantation, to which he consents, being paid six shillings toward the support of his weakly sister Ruth. The meeting agrees thereto, and directs the treasurer to pay accordingly. Asa Moore is appointed to record certificates of marriage and removal in the place of Thomas Moore Jr.

12th mo 1791: William Jackson presented a certificate from New Garden MM.

1st mo 1792: This meeting received a few lines from Gunpowder MM on account of Thomas Lacey Jr. and William James. Samuel Reader's paper of acknowledgement was accepted. He requested a certificate to Buckingham MM. Complaint against Samuel Thompson for drinking spirituous liquors to excess, using unsavory language and attending places of diversions. Complaint against John Cunnard Jr. for marrying with the assistance of an hireling teacher.

2nd mo 1792: Samuel Smith's paper condemning his outgoing, for which he stands downed, was accepted. Complaint against Abel Lodge for being the father of an illegitimate child, which Martha Shingley ... according to law. The constable has taken him into custody. A certificate was received some time ago for Major Hunt, from Concord MM, but he did not attend. Now he is charged with attending places of diversion and promoting gaming and horse racing.

3rd mo 1792: Peter Blaker produced certificates for himself, Sarah his wife, and minor children Abraham, Amos and David, from Wrightstown MM. John Hollingsworth released as overseer at the Gap Meeting. Amos Paxson reinstated as a member. Israel Thompson requests liberty of this meeting to sue at law James Dillon, a Friend, for the payment of debt due by note. Meeting does not grant him this privilege until the proper methods have been tried. Joseph Beal is proposed as an Elder.

5th mo 1792: Friends had an opportunity with James Pasxon and feel his certificate should be received. A certificate was handed to this meeting for Jonas McPherson dated at Hopewell MM, but we are informed that he has returned to live with his father, so the certificate will be returned to Hopewell MM.

6th mo 1792: A certificate was received for John Thomas from Indian Spring, but he returned to live with his father, rather than settle in these parts. William Mendenhall requests a certificate to New Garden MM in PA, in order to marry Martha Beason.

7th mo 1792: John Fisher produced a certificate from Bradford MM. Certificate was produced for Joseph Elgar and directed to Menallen MM. Regarding the children of Thomas Lacey Jr., deceased, it is necessary to quickly find a suitable place for his minor sons William, James and Thomas.

8th mo 1792: John Woodard has left these parts without consent or knowledge of Friends.

9th mo 1792: John Williams presented a certificate from Pipe Creek MM. Joseph Talbott requests a certificate to Goose Creek in order to marry Rebekah Hirst.

10th mo 1792: Levi Hollingsworth presented a certificate for himself, Mary his wife, and children Thomas, and David, from Kennett MM. James Lownes requests a certificate to White Oak Swamp MM for himself and four children John, Deborah, Joseph and William. Also for his two sons James and Caleb to the MM of Philadelphia's northern district. Complaint against John Randall for removing from these parts and leaving his affairs unsettled, for using scandalous conversation, with designs to injure the reputation of another person, and neglecting attendance at meetings. A letter will be sent to South Fork regarding John Randall's affairs.

11th mo 1792: Jonathan Cunnard, son of John, married a non-member. William Smith requests a certificate to Goose Creek in order to marry Sarah Gregg.

12th mo 1792: Joshua Wildman offered a paper condemning some misconduct for which he was disowned. Certificate was produced for William Smith, and given to Joseph Beale to forward to him.

3rd mo 1793: Complaint against Francis Hague for marrying a non-member. Complaint against Hyatt Lewis for non-attendance at meetings, and frequently appearing at places of diversions.

3rd mo 1793: Complaint against Francis Hague for marrying a non-member. Complaint against Hyatt Lewis for non-attendance at meetings, and frequently appearing at places of diversions.

4th mo 1793: A certificate was produced for Asa Moore, so that he could marry Sarah Dodd. Benjamin Purdom and Hannah Beale recommended as Elders. William Schooley presented a certificate from Goose Creek for himself, Hannah his wife, and children ___?, Henry, Eliza, Ruth, John, Ann, and Amos.

7th mo 1793: Jonah Thompson offered a paper condemning certain breeches of discipline for which he stands disowned. Complaint against David Lacey for having sued a Friend, and neglecting attendance at meetings.

8th mo 1793: Elisha Janney presented a certificate from Goose Creek MM. Elisha Butler presented a certificate from Uwchlan MM, directed to Goose Creek, but as he now resides within Fairfax MM it is received here. Complaint against Joseph Taylor for the too free and excessive use of spirituous liquors, being often intoxicated.

9th mo 1793: Albion Griffin presented a certificate from Linden Grove MM. Joseph Taylor denies being intoxicated. He is also charged with treating his father with unbecoming and abusive language. Complaint against Amos Paxson for being intoxicated. Complaint against Samuel Hough and Thomas Hough Jr. for assembling with light and airy company at places appointed for public diversion. A letter from Samuel Coats in regard to Charles Pierpoint's expenses in Philadelphia was received.

10th mo 1793: Eleanor Hough recommended as Elder.

12th mo 1793: A certificate was produced for Edward Stabler. Complaint against William Mendenhall for ... and receiving ... of slaves late at night which appears to have been ... [illegible].

2nd mo 1794: Jonas Potts requests a certificate to Crooked Run MM in order to marry Phebe Brown, daughter of David Brown.

3rd mo 1794: Complaint against Isaac Hough for attending places of diversions, being guilty of fornication, being charged by a woman as the father of her illegitimate child, which he does not deny. Isaiah Balderson and John Burson visited from Baltimore.

4th mo 1794: Abraham Hews presented a certificate from Chesterfield MM in New Jersey. Thomas Janney hath for some time been in the practice of visiting place of diversion and using spirituous liquor to excess. As he has retained membership in New Garden MM in PA, a letter will be sent there informing them of his behavior. Elisha Butler

6th mo 1794: Sarah Hough, daughter of Ann, presented a certificate from Westland MM. William Hough, the 3rd, married out of unity. Complaint against Elisabeth Nicklin, formerly Hough, for marrying out of unity.

7th mo 1794: A letter of request for information about Aden Pancoast, wife and family was received from Burlington MM.

9th mo 1794: Abner Williams presented a certificate from Pipe Creek MM. William Lodge offered a paper condemning his outgoing in marriage some years past, for which he was disowned. Phebe Potts presented a certificate from Crooked Run MM.

10th mo 1794: George Drinker presented a certificate from Philadelphia. [what follows is not clear].

11th mo 1794: There is an objection to preparing a certificate for Thomas Smith and family. Complaint against Samuel Gregg [Jr. or Senr?] for being guilty of fornication. A woman charged him as the father of her illegitimate child, and proved it before a magistrate.

12th mo 1794: Ezra Kinsey presented a certificate from Richland MM. He lives in Alexandria. Edward Fawell who now resides in Pittsburgh, married out of unity. Elisha Janney requests a certificate to Goose Creek in order to marry Mary Gibson. Samuel Barber requests membership.

1st mo 1795: Testimonies against Edward Falwell and Edward Watson were produced. William Mendenhall and Mordecai Walker visited from Hopewell.

2nd mo 1795: A certificate was produced for John James. Thomas and Anna Beale presented a certificate from Baltimore. Complaint against Amos Parker for drinking liquors to excess, frequenting places of diversions, gaming, and removing away from here.

4th mo 1795: Parmenas Lamborn presented a certificate from New Garden MM in PA. Complaint against Joseph Hough for being guilty of fornication. Alexandria Friends inform that John Sutton and his son Daniel Isaac Sutton sometime ago removed to London.

5th mo 1795: Benjamin Myers presented a certificate for himself, wife Elizabeth and children Isaac, Elizabeth, Benjamin, Susannah, Hannah, Thomas, John, and Sarah from Goose Creek MM.

6th mo 1795: Thomas Hirst presented a certificate from Hopewell MM.

7th mo 1795: Complaint against James Siddal for marrying a non-member. Alexandria complains against Jesse Jurdon [Jordan] for marrying a non-member.

8th mo 1795: John Bishop presented a certificate from Crooked Run MM.

7th mo 1795: Complaint against James Siddal for marrying a non-member. Alexandria complains against Jesse Jurdon [Jordan] for marrying a non-member.

8th mo 1795: John Bishop presented a certificate from Crooked Run MM.

9th mo 1795: Complaint against John Canby for gaming and attending places of public diversion.

11th mo 1795: Complaint against William Morgan for removing without settling his affairs.

12th mo 1795: Esther Kirk presented a certificate for herself and children Isaiah, Hannah, Rebekah, Benjamin and Ann from Kennettt MM. They now live within the limits of Redstone MM.

1st mo 1796: Complaint against George Gregg Jr. for quarreling and fighting.

2nd mo 1796: Isaac Shreve, son of Benjamin, presented a certificate from Salem MM.

3rd mo 1796: Complaint against Thomas Hirst for joining light company, frolicking and dancing. A complaint of the same nature is forwarded against Mahlon Janney Jr. and Joseph Talbott. William Mitchner paid for repairs made to the roof and galleries of this house.

4th mo 1796: Abner Gibson presented a certificate from Goose Creek. Jonah Hough, appointed in place of Benjamin Purdom, to collect the money for enclosing the grave yard.

5th mo 1796: Samuel Hague sent a letter wherein he complains of being kept out of a dividend from his father's estate. He refuses to execute a deed to William Hough on that account.

8th mo 1796: Complaint against Thomas Backhouse for fornication.

9th mo 1796: Complaint against Richard Richardson Jr. for quarreling and fighting.

11th mo 1796: Thomas Smith is charged by a woman for attempting to have criminal connection with her in her childhood and other abuses....

12th mo 1796: Thomas Shrieve presented a certificate from Upper Springfield. Alexandria reports that Isaac McPherson has married out of unity.

1st mo 1797: Gunpowder MM reported that Ann Taylor {wife of Henry Taylor} condemned her out going in marriage. Joseph Talbott, Susannah Hartshorne, and Sarah Moore proposed as Elders.

2nd mo 1797: Joseph Plummer presented a certificate for himself, Elizabeth his wife, and children Ann and Sarah from Pipe Creek MM. Warrington MM inquires about Milly Fisher, she being charged with fornication. South River wrote that there was no objection to Tacey

3rd mo 1797: A certificate to Westland MM was produced for Isaiah Myers, Alice his wife, and children David, William, and Elizabeth. Complaint against John and William Mitchner Jr. for having joined with others in publicly accom... [illegible] and restoring the dwelling of Savony (a black man). Both offered papers of acknowledgment and condemnation. James Erwin acknowledged his disorderly drinking to excess.

4th mo 1797: Complaint from Alexandria against James America Sutton for taking oaths.

5th mo 1797: Aaron Smith presented a certificate from Redstone MM. Jacob Myers has removed with his family out of this area.

6th mo 1797: James America Sutton condemned his behavior.

7th mo 1797: Mahlon Janney Jr. condemned his misconduct. Ann Jessep and Joel Willis visited from New Garden MM in NC. Complaint from Alexandria against John Fisher and Charles Harper for marrying non-members.

8th mo 1797: Coats Ridgeway presented a certificate from Mount Holly MM. There is an objection to Elizabeth Bown and Jacob Myers receiving certificates.

9th mo 1797: Warrington MM sent a testimony against Mary Fisher. John Ball has removed and now resides within Crooked Run MM.

10th mo 1798(sic): Alexandria informs that John Bishop has removed to Crooked Run MM.

11th mo 1797: John Canby has left Alexandria and is about to settle in Leesburg. His case is not settled.

12th mo 1797: David Brooks visited from Deep River MM in NC. John Creek? is accompanying him. Complaint against Joseph Paxson for being guilty of fornication, as a woman has charged him with being the father of her illegitimate child, and he joined in marriage with another woman, not a member of our society.

1st mo 1798: Daniel Stone requests membership. Thomas Smith denies the charges against him.

3rd mo 1798: Ann Wildman forwarded a paper condemning her outgoing in marriage. Susannah Mathews is here on a religious visit from Third Haven MM in Maryland.

4th mo 1798: A certificate was produced for Elizabeth Bown's children. John Hollingsworth released as overseer.

5th mo 1798: Arthur Paxson presented a certificate from Buckingham MM. William Smith presented a certificate for himself and Ann his wife, from Redstone MM. Mahlon Janney Jr. offered a paper condemning his fighting.

5th mo 1798: Arthur Paxson presented a certificate from Buckingham MM. William Smith presented a certificate for himself and Ann his wife, from Redstone MM. Mahlon Janney Jr. offered a paper condemning his fighting.

6th m 1798: Joseph Mead appointed overseer.

7th mo 1798: Jacob Jenkins presented a certificate from Hopewell MM. Thomas Ellicott presented a certificate from Buckingham MM. Thomas Erwin has parted with his share of the vessel which was the cause of complaint against him. Fielder Richardson requests a certificate to Gunpowder MM in order to marry Miriam Griffith. Jason Moreland and Nancy his wife have forwarded a paper condemning their having sold a ... [man?].

8th mo 1798: Parmenas Lamborn produced a certificate from New Garden MM. David Smith requests a certificate to Hopewell MM in order to marry Ruth Wright.

10th mo 1798: A certificate for Joseph Pursly was received from Sadsbury MM some time ago. He now resides within Goose Creek MM and requests that his certificate be forwarded there. George Churchman is visiting from PA. James Rattikin released as overseer; Jacob Sands appointed. Jonathan Pancoast's certificate from Philadelphia was accepted, even though he has not attended here.

11th mo 1798: A certificate was produced for John Hague [to Goose Creek?]. A letter from Goose Creek in Bedford Co. requested information about Ann Wildman.

12th mo 1798: Amos Ally presented a certificate from New York MM. A paper of condemnation was produced by William Wilman {Wildman} who has for some time lived within Goose Creek. James Moore and Asa Moore are recommended as elders.

1st mo 1799: Complaint against William Mitchner Jr. for quarreling and fighting. Complaint against Jesse Taylor for neglecting attendance, drinking spirituous liquors to excess, using profane language, and frolicking and dancing at his house.

2nd mo 1799: Complaint against Abner Gibson for great deviation, neglect of attendance, and putting his name on a paper associating with military service. Complaint against Isaac Shrieve who is charged as being the father of an illegitimate child, which he does not deny. Request for certificate for Israel Thompson who is placed at school within Concord MM.

Reuben Paxson, a member of this meeting, has married contrary to rules, whilst amongst them.

7th mo 1799: Complaint against Mahlon Janney Jr. for marrying a non-member.

8th mo 1799: William Mitchner presented a paper of acknowledgement. A certificate was requested for Jacob Janney to Baltimore, where he is placed as an apprentice. Alexandria complains against Jonathan Pancoast for entirely neglecting the attendance of their meetings, gambling and making a common practice of laying wagers. Complaint against James America Sutton for joining with military company, use of spirituous liquors, and also declining attendance. John Sutton, who professes to be a Friend, has lately been in the habit of carrying a cane with a sword in it, which he acknowledges is for self-defense and that he once used it in that way.

12th mo 1799: Mahlon Scolfield presented a certificate from Indian Springs MM. Jonathan Scoolfield presented a certificate from Buckingham MM. William Kenworthy and Rebekah his wife, presented a certificate from Pipe Creek MM. John Sutton has removed from Alexandria to Baltimore MM.

4th mo 1800: Phinehas Janney presented a certificate from Pipe Creek MM. Complaint against Isaac McPherson for frequent breeches of his engagements and having used profane language. Ruth Janney, wife of Phinehas, presented a certificate from Hopewell MM.

6th mo 1800: Benjamin Swett visited from Haddenfield MM in NJ. A letter from Devonshire House MM in London indicated that John Sutton left that country without the consent of his creditors and he has unpaid debts.

8th mo 1800: Complaint against Richard Pierpoint Richardson for marrying contrary to the rules of our society. Complaint against Samuel Richardson for marrying a non-member.

9th mo 1800: James Russell presented a certificate from Pipe Creek MM.

10th mo 1800: Informed from New York MM that Elizabeth Harness, late Brown, a member of this meeting, has married out of unity.

11th mo 1800: William Brown requests a certificate to Goose Creek MM in order to marry Hannah Janney. Complaint against Joseph Wood for fighting, which he does not deny. Complaint against Nathan Connard for marrying a non-member.

12th mo 1800: Joseph Wood Jr. condemned his misconduct. [Something about the children of Thomas Fisher. Need to determine if they are members].

WOMEN'S MINUTES OF FAIRFAX MONTHLY MEETING

1745: Mary Janney and Elizabeth Norton appointed overseers. Jane Hague appointed clerk.

5th mo 1745: Frances Harry requests for certificate to ___ MM in Chester Co. Hannah ___ and Rachell Wright appointed overseers.

6th mo 1745: Susannah Piggott produced a certificate from Nottingham MM.

10 mo 1745: Marriage of Harmon Cox and Jane John was orderly accomplished.

11th mo 1745: Marriage of Richard Kemp and Susannah Piggott was orderly accomplished. Margarett Wells requests membership.

4th mo 1746: Catherine Dodd requests membership. Alice Yates produced certificate from Middletown MM. Elizabeth Janney appointed overseer in place of Elizabeth Norton.

4th mo 1746: Marriage of Oliver Matthews and Hannah John was orderly accomplished.

7th mo 1746: Mary Williams requests membership. Ann Moore produced certificate for herself and children from Middletown MM.

9th mo 1746: Hannah Hunt requests membership. Hannah Balanger and Elizabeth Matthew to draw testimony against Phebe Summers for her outgoings.

12th mo 1746: Marriage of Richard Williams and Prudence Bates {Beals} was orderly accomplished.

3rd mo 1747: Marriage of William Kirk and Mary Brown was orderly accomplished. Elizabeth Janney produced a certificate from Falls MM. Elizabeth Compton requests a certificate to Nottingham MM. Martha Hiatt requests a certificate for herself and children [destination not stated].

4th mo 1747: Rebeccah Willson produced a certificate from Wrightstown MM. Mary Kirk and Eliza Norton to treat with Catherine Dodd to know how far she can clear herself of her daughter's going out in marriage.

5th mo 1747: Hannah Ballanger to treat with Susannah Mayner about her daughter's outgoing in marriage.

6th mo 1747: Marriage of Edward Thompson and Rebecca Willson was orderly accomplished. Testimony produced against Ann Richardson, formerly Dodd, for outgoing in marriage.

8th mo 1747: Elizabeth Norton and Jane Hague to treat with Mary Rhodes, formerly Mead, concerning her outgoing in marriage. Margaret Mead produced a certificate from Falls MM. Marriage of Daniel

Matthews and Ann Hague was orderly accomplished. Hannah Roach requests membership.

9th mo 1747: Susannah Palmer and Hannah Davis to treat with Susannah Mankin, formerly Mayner, concerning her outgoing in marriage.

1st mo 1748: Susannah Mankin condemned her outgoing.

2nd mo 1748: Alexander Underhood (sic) and Sarah Bates continue their intentions to marry. Mary Rhodes, not being willing to be disowned desires Friends to bear a little longer to see if her husband will consent that she should give satisfaction. Ann Slaughter requests membership.

3rd mo 1748: Elizabeth Matthews and Sarah Chamneys appointed overseers. Sarah Underhood requests certificate to Warrington MM.

5th mo 1748: Phebe Summers requests membership.

7th mo 1748: Marriage of Jerimiah Fairhurst and Ann Slaughter was orderly accomplished.

8th mo 1748: Marriages of John Poultney and Elenor Walter [Walker], also Humphrey Williams and Mary Tanzey were orderly accomplished.

9th mo 1748: Rebeckah Thompson requests certificate to Wrightstown MM.

10th mo 1748: Ann Potts and Ann Potts Junr. request membership.

11th mo 1748: Marriage of Allen Forqher and Sarah Moore was orderly accomplished. Margrett Wells appointed overseer.

12th mo 1748: Marriage of John Vestill and Ann Potts was orderly accomplished. Martha Harris and Margret Williams request membership.

1st mo 1749: Hannah Ballenger appointed overseer. Susannah Meaner and Hannah Davis appointed to treat with Hannah Kersey, formerly Hunt, concerning her outgoing.

6th mo 1749: Rachel Steer produced certificate for herself and children from Sadsbury MM. Martha Parker produced a certificate from Falls MM. Jane West produced a certificate from Providence MM.

7th mo 1749: Martha Harris requests certificate to Goshen MM. Margret Willson produced certificate, joined with her husband, from Warrington MM.

9th mo 1749: Ann Vestill requests a certificate to Hopewell MM. Mary Hanby having been absent from this meeting for the space of two years now proposes to make satisfaction for her outgoing in marriage.

12th mo 1749: Rachel Cruthers produced an old certificate. Inquiry will be made before acceptance.

1st mo 1750: Elizabeth Plumer requests membership. Christian Carrington's request is granted. Hanah Mead requests a certificate to Falls MM.

5th mo 1750: Elizabeth Pooley, Keziah Plummer, Charity Wells, Elizabeth Everitt, and Barbary Everitt request membership.

6th mo 1750: Testimony produced against Rachel Parker for her outgoing in marriage.

7th mo 1750: Hanah Kersey requests membership. Elizabeth Lakey requests a certificate to Carvers Creek in NC.

12th mo 1750: Alice Yates appointed overseer.

2nd mo 1751: Testimony against Rachel Taylor, formerly Parker and Cruthers was approved, and she thereby disowned.

3rd mo 1751: Caleb Taylor and wife, formerly Pierpont, produced certificate from Baltimore Co.

4th mo 1751: Elizabeth Lewis produced a certificate which was read to satisfaction. Mary Harden, formerly Hanby condemned her outgoing in marriage.

5th mo 1751: Sarah Miller produced a certificate from Gunpowder MM. Hannah Ballanger requests certificate to Cane Creek. Elizabeth Matthews and Susanah Palmer appointed overseers.

6th mo 1751: Casandra Plumer produced certificate from West River MM. Elizabeth Lewis requests certificate to Newark MM.

9th mo 1751: Mary Miller, wife of Jacob Miller, being removed to Philadelphia, requests a certificate.

2nd mo 1752: Margrett Willson requests membership. Elizabeth Janney requests certificate to Newark MM. Sarah Gore, formerly Clowes, paper condemned her outgoing in marriage.

4th mo 1752: Deborah Wildman produced a certificate for herself and children from Middletown MM. Mary Janney appointed overseer. Jane Gore, formerly Dodd, condemned her marriage.

5th mo 1752: Cathrine Tanzey requests membership.

7th mo 1752: Mary Mathews, wife of Walter, requests a certificate [destination not stated].

8th mo 1752: Mary Bucklew requests membership. Mary Matthews Junr. requests certificate to Cane Creek.

9th mo 1752: Rachel and Mary Ballanger request certificates to Cane Creek MM.

11th mo 1752: Ruth Holland appointed overseer.

12th mo 1752: Jane Hague and Sarah Hough appointed to treat with Rachel Steer about her disorderly behaviour.

2nd mo 1753: Jane Gore requests a certificate to Hopewell MM.

4th mo 1753: Marriage of Benjamin Poole and Rebeccah Parker was orderly accomplished. Hannah Janney is appointed overseer.

6th mo 1753: Marriage of William Holmes and Mary Love was orderly accomplished.

7th mo 1753: Jane Cox requests certificate to Cane Creek MM. Mary Matthews Junr. produced a certificate from Cane Creek MM.

4th mo 1754: Sarah Willson produced a certificate from New Garden MM. Alice Yates appointed overseer.

7th mo 1754: Hannah Matthews appointed overseer.

8th mo 1754: Ann Hatcher and daughter Mary, request membership. Hannah Thomas, formerly Mead, condemned her outgoing in marriage.

9th mo 1754: Sarah Plummer, wife of Joseph Plummer, requests membership.

10th mo 1754: Mary Hague condemned her fornication.

1st mo 1755: Marriages of Edward Matthews and Sophia Richardson, also George Hankle and Rebeccah Plummer {George Hinkle and Rachel Plummer} were orderly accomplished.

2nd mo 1755: Sarah Willson was received into membership.

3rd mo 1755: Ann Matthews appointed overseer. Hannah Matthews requests certificate, with her husband, to Gunpowder MM.

6th mo 1755: Elizabeth Matthews, being about to remove with her husband, requests certificate to Cane Creek. Rebecah Sybolt produced certificate from New Garden MM in PA.

7th mo 1755: Mary Williams, with her husband, requests certificate to Cane Creek in NC.

8th mo 1755: Margrett Matthews requests certificate to Cane Creek. Mary Potts produced certificate from [blot].

9th mo 1755: Catherine Tanzey Junr. requests certificate to New Garden MM in NC.

2nd mo 1756: Complaint against Elizabeth Crum, formerly Plumer, for going out in marriage. Complaint against Elizabeth and Dorcas Plumer for not attending meeting.

6th mo 1756: Margrett Norman, formerly Dodd, some time past having gone out in marriage, presented a paper condemning same.

8th mo 1756: Sarah Lewis presented certificate for self and children from Abington MM.

9th mo 1756: Cathrine Tanzey some time past requested certificate to Cane Creek MM, her affairs now being clear, one is produced.

11th mo 1756: Isabel Holland produced a certificate from New Garden MM in PA. Sarah Ingledew produced a certificate from Middletown MM.

12th mo 1756: Rachel Burson condemned her fornication. Elizabeth Farquhar requests membership.

1st mo 1757: Ruth Holland produced a certificate from Westbury on Long Island and ___, from Oblong Hall?

2nd mo 1757: Mary Ballanger produced a certificate from Hopewell MM. Elizabeth Hattfield produced a certificate from Gwynedd MM.

3rd mo 1757: Sophia Matthews appointed overseer. Keziah Plumer frequently neglects attendance.

4th mo 1757: Elizabeth Everitt requests membership. Margrett Williams appointed overseer. Marriage of John Hatcher and Sarah Ingledew was orderly accomplished.

5th mo 1757: Ellenor Lamb acted disorderly and contrary to truth. Sophia Lamb having gone away unknown to Friends and settled within Goshen MM, this meeting thinks it necessary to send a certificate after her.

6th mo 1757: Marriage of Samuel Richardson and Hanah Matthews was orderly accomplished. Mary Holms requests membership.

9th mo 1757: William Brown and Elizabeth Forquer intend to marry. Isabel Holland requests certificate to New Garden MM in PA.

11th mo 1757: Mary Janney and Ann Janney request certificates to Falls MM.

12th mo 1757: Marriage of Samuel Pearson and Christian Potts was orderly accomplished. Mary Potts and Jane Gore produced certificates from Hopewell MM.

2nd mo 1758: Certificate was produced for Christain Pearson to Hopewell MM. Hanah Thomas, formerly Mead, gave satisfaction for her outgoing, now requests membership. Mary Hague requests membership.

3rd mo 1758: Marriage of Roger Brook and Mary Matthews was orderly accomplished. Jane Everitt produced a certificate from Warrington MM. Mary Brook requests a certificate to West River MM. Lydia Rogers, with her husband, requests certificate to Hopewell MM.

4th mo 1758: Elizabeth Everitt requests a certificate to Goshen MM. Charity Beason and Sarah Davis produced certificates from Hopewell MM. Sarah Morlan produced a certificate from Chesterfield in NJ, for self and children. Mary Rohdes [Rhodes] condemned her outgoing in marriage.

5th mo 1758: Martha Harris applied for certificate to Goshen MM. Hanah Kersey requests certificate for herself and children to New Garden MM in NC.

6th mo 1758: Hannah Hooker requests membership. Elizabeth Wilks, formerly Mead, married out of unity. Sarah McCenty [McKenny] formerly Willson married out of unity.

7th mo 1758: Mahlon Janney and Sarah Plumer intend to marry.

8th mo 1758: Rachel Balanger produced a certificate from New Garden MM.

9th mo 1758: Mary Balanger requests certificate to Hopewell MM.

10th mo 1758: William Stanley and Elizabeth Walker intend to marry. Mary and Ann Janney produced certificates from Falls MM. Sarah Russ wife of Marris Russ [Morris Reese], produced a certificate from Hopewell for herself and children. Ann Mead requests certificate to Falls MM. Deborah Burson, daughter of Joseph Burson, having removed to PA, sometime past, is now married to a man not of our society. Testimony against Lydia Dodd for committing fornication. Mary Janney and Elleanor Mead appointed to visit Cathrine Dodd to see if she can clear herself of her daughter's outgoing.

11th mo 1758: Elizabeth Stanley requests certificate to Cedar Creek in Hanover County. Ann Ore requests membership. Sarah Pierpoint appointed overseer.

12th mo 1758: Marriage of William Stanley and Elizabeth Walker was orderly accomplished. Certificate was produced for Elizabeth Stanley. Ann Stroud produced a certificate from Hopewell MM. Margery Nichols is appointed overseer at Goose Creek with Hannah Janney.

2nd mo 1759: Mary Lewis, daughter of Thomas and Sarah Lewis, removed without a certificate. It was decided to send one after her.

3rd mo 1759: Martha Harokins [Hawkins] produced a certificate from Abington MM, joined with her husband and children.

5th mo 1759: Betty Walker produced a certificate from Hopewell MM.

6th mo 1759: Charity Beeson requests certificate to Hopewell MM. Margrett Matthews produced a certificate from New Garden MM in NC. Sarah Brasinton {Brazelton} produced a certificate from Warrington MM. Mary Farquer requests certificate to Newark MM. Mary Lewis, joined with her husband, requests certificate to Hopewell MM. Complaint against Catherine Dodd for her misconduct in several respects, such as quarreling with neighbors and using unsavory language. Sarah Reese requests certificate, joined with husband, to Hopewell MM.

7th mo 1759: Hanah Unkles requests membership. Complaint against Margrett Richardson Junr. She behaves very disorderly, and keeps company with those of other societies.

8th mo 1759: Rachel Balanger requests certificate to New Garden MM in NC. Margrett Osborn produced certificate from Gwynedd MM.

9th mo 1759: Ann Haywood requests membership. Ann Lewis, daughter of Sarah Lewis, has gone out in marriage.

10th mo 1759: Jean Williams and Rehobath Williams produced certificates from Goshen MM. Sarah Bray, formerly Mayner, condemned her past conduct (married out of unity). Ann Griffeth, formerly Lewis, made no satisfaction for her outgoing in marriage. Deborah Lewellen, formerly Burson, produced a paper condemning her outgoing in marriage. Ann Janney, daughter of Wm. Janney, requests certificate to Falls MM.

12th mo 1759: Hannah Hooker requests a certificate to Gunpowder MM.

1st mo 1760: Ann Haywood requests certificate to Nottingham MM.

2nd mo 1760: Rachel Farquer produced a certificate, joined with her husband, from Warrington MM.

4th mo 1760: Mary Ridgwau (sic) requests membership. Lucy Wright being removed to Hopewell, Friends to send certificate after her.

5th mo 1760: Mary Willson produced a certificate from Sadsbury MM. Martha Everitt produced a certificate from Warrington MM. Elizabeth Walker requests a certificate to Hopewell MM.

7th mo 1760: Benjamin Burson and Ann Roberts intend to marry. William Pidgeon and Rachel Everitt intend to marry. Marriage of Thos Dodd and Sarah Sample was orderly accomplished.

9th mo 1760: Mary Farquer produced a certificate from Kennett MM. Sarah Boon produced a certificate from Exeter MM. Ann Vestal removed some time ago to Hopewell MM. A certificate was sent after her.

10th mo 1760: Martha Mead requests a certificate to Falls MM. Hannah Brook formerly Janney, being removed to West River MM, a certificate was sent to said meeting. Margrett Matthews' certificate was also sent to West River MM.

11th mo 1760: Rachel Pidgeon being removed by marriage to Warrington MM, a certificate will be sent to her. Mary Barrett, daughter of William Barrend (sic) produced a certificate from Hopewell MM. Pheby Way visited from Flushing MM on Long Island. Susanah Hatton visited from Waterford in Ireland.

1st mo 1761: Sarah Janney appointed clerk.

2nd mo 1761: Mary McGrue requests certificate to Warrington MM.

3rd mo 1761: Thomas Plummer and Ellenor Poultney intend to marry. Mary Potts appointed overseer at Gap meeting.

4th mo 1761: Marriage of John Ball and Mary Hague, was orderly accomplished.

5th mo 1761: Mary Wright, formerly Farquar, requests certificate to Warrington MM. Mary Baker, wife of Nathan Baker, produced certificate from Middletown MM. Sarah Schooley, joined with husband

and minor daughters Ann and Phebey; also Mary Mires, produced certificates from Kingwood MM. Rebecca Trahorn produced a certificate from Honey Creek in MD. Mary Lam {Lum}, formerly Clowes, married out of unity. Martha Everitt, joining with her husband, requests certificate to Warrington MM.

6th mo 1761: Ann Janney, daughter of William Janney, produced a certificate from Falls MM. Three of the children of Richard and Margrett Richardson of Monocacy, deceased, namely, Melcah, Lucretia, and William, being removed to West River, will receive certificates from this meeting, they being no longer in their minority.

9th mo 1761: Marriage of Joseph Hutton and Sarah Janney was orderly accomplished. Mary Ball, formerly Hague, having committed fornication, then married John Ball. Testimony will be drawn against them. Catherine Popkins, formerly Roberts, married out of unity.

10th mo 1761: Martha Hattfield requests membership. Hannah Jerritt, and Neomi Whitaker produced a certificate, joined with their husbands, from Kingwood MM. Ruth Gregg, joined with her husband, John Gregg, produced a certificate for herself and her daughter, Jane Sherward from Kent {Kennett} MM.

2nd mo 1762: Certificate was produced for Lucy Wright, joined with her husband and children [no destination stated].

3rd mo 1762: Sarah Lewis, widow, requests certificate for herself and son William to Philadelphia MM.

4th mo 1762: Abigail Steer, wife of James Steer, produced a certificate from Sadsbury MM.

5th mo 1762: Elizabeth Norton requests a certificate for self and 5 children to Cane Creek MM in NC. Robert Andrews and Sarah his wife produced a certificate for themselves and 5 children from New Garden MM in PA.

6th mo 1762: Drisila Williams (daughter of William and Margaret Williams) and Margrett Norton (daughter of Elizabeth and Edward Norton) request certificates to Cane Creek MM in NC. Sarah Boon requests certificate for self and daughter Hanah to New Garden MM in NC. Mary Haines, wife of Daniel Haines, produced a certificate from Gunpowder MM.

7th mo 1762: Deborah Lewellin, formerly Burson, did in the 9th mo 1759, condemn her outgoings, which is now accepted. Mary Wright, daughter of Joseph Wright, produced a certificate from Warrington MM. Alice Leach appointed overseer.

9th mo 1762: Elener Plumer is appointed overseer. Mary Brown, wife of John Brown, produced a certificate for themselves and 5 small children, John, George, Susannah, Jacob, and Catherina from Kennett MM. Martha Tate, wife of William Tate, produced a certificate from Kennett MM for themselves and children, Hannah, Mary, Ruth and Lewis.

10th mo 1762: Barbary Everit, daughter of John Everitt requested a certificate to Warrington MM. Ann Orr requests a certificate to Abington MM in PA. Alice Lewis, wife of Jehu Lewis, produced a certificate for herself and 3 small children, namely Joel, Hannah, and Irvin from Chester MM in PA. Ann Williams, wife of David Williams requests membership.

12th mo 1762: Rachel Hollingsworth appointed overseer. Mary Eblen, wife of John Eblen, joined with her husband, produced a certificate for 8 children, Hannah, Elizar, Mary, Rachel, Samuel, Elizabeth, Ann and James from Chester MM.

3rd mo 1763: Chen Dever, wife of Bazel Dever produced a certificate for herself and children, Abraham, Misael, Marget, and Jonas. Sarah Andrew requests certificate, joining with husband and children to Warrington MM.

4th mo 1763: Hannah Spencer, wife of Nathan Spencer, requests membership. Sarah Cox, wife of Joseph Cox, produced certificate with her husband and daughter Sarah, from Burlington MM in the Jersies. William Hoge and Mary his wife produced a certificate for themselves and daughter Hannah Pancost, from Burlington MM. Sarah Miller requests certificate with husband and children to Warrington MM.

5th mo 1763: Richard Roberts and Mary his wife produced a certificate for themselves and child from Buckingham MM. James Dillen and Rebeckah his wife produced certificate for themselves and small son Moses, from Wrightstown MM.

6th mo 1763: Hannah Uncles request certificate to New Garden MM in PA. Certificate {to Warrington MM} was produced for Sarah Miller, with her husband Robert Miller {of Pipe Creek}, and children Mary, Sarah, Hannah, Robert, James, Thomas, and Margrett.

7th mo 1763: James Nichols and Elizabeth his wife produced certificates for themselves and 3 small children, John, George, and Isaiah from Kenet MM in PA. Solomon Dixon and Sarah his wife produced certificates for themselves and small children, Ruth and James, from Kenet MM. James Phillips and Ruth his wife produced certificates for themselves and children, Iven, Harry, Dinah, Betty, and Solomon from Kenet MM. Ann Potts appointed overseer of the Gap particular meeting.

9th mo 1763: Ann and Mary Everitt, daughters of John Everitt request certificates to Warrington MM.

10th mo 1763: Hannah Pryor presented a certificate from New Garden MM in PA.

11th mo 1763: Ann Schooley having committed an unclean act with William Schooley, the consequences of which put them upon marriage by a priest, so testimony was drawn against both of them by the men. Ann is now in suitable disposition to make satisfaction. Neomi Smith produced a certificate from Kingwood MM in the Jerseys, joined with her husband {Samuel} and children, John, Abraham, Thomas, Henry, Robert, Joseph, Ruth, Hannah, and George.

12th mo 1763: Mary Tucker produced a certificate from Bucks Co. Martha Davis produced a certificate, with husband and child Mary, from Radnor MM. A certificate was produced for children of Joseph Cadwaleder, Rease, Affinity, John, Cathrine, Septimus, and Isaac, from Radnor MM.

1st mo 1764: Certificate produced for Hanah Shrieve, wife of Caleb, and 4 children, Samuel, James, Mary, and Mercy, from Darby MM.

2nd mo 1764: Mary Schooley, wife of John, requests membership, also for her daughter Sarah.

3rd mo 1764: Ann Mead, daughter of William Mead, produced a certificate from Falls MM.

4th mo 1764: Marriage of Jonathan Conard and Jane Potts was orderly accomplished. Certificate was presented by Rachel Pidgeon, with husband and children Mary and John, from Warrington MM.

5th mo 1764: Certificate from Kennett MM for Susanah Hollingsworth, wife of Elias, and 4 small children, Aquilla, Mary, Benjamin and Neomy, was received. Stacey West, daughter of Joseph West, being now at mature age requests membership.

6th mo 1764: Mary Lancaster, formerly Willson, hath removed to the back part of PA or MD, remote from Friends. Therefore, testimony is ordered against her. Hannah Richardson, widow of Samuel, requests certificate to Warrington MM.

7th mo 1764: Rachel Dillon produced a certificate with her husband William, and their children, James, Rachel, William and Agness from Wrightstown MM.

8th mo 1764: Mary Sinklar, with husband James and children, {daughter Phebe} produced a certificate from Bradford MM. Hannah Tate, daughter of Wm. Tate produced a certificate from Kennett MM.

9th mo 1764: Elloner Meed is appointed overseer.

11th mo 1764: Deborah Dillen, wife of Josiah, produced a certificate from Wrightstown MM. Rebecckah Howel, formerly Hague, married out of unity. Rachel Mead, daughter of Samuel Mead, having left her father's house in a reproachful and clandestine manner, with a young man her father apprenticed, also took some of her father's effects. A testimony is to be produced against her.

12th mo 1764: Hannah Thompson, wife of Isaac Thompson, produced a certificate from Uwchlan MM for herself and children, Jeremiah, Sarah, Hannah, Isaac, and Joseph. Hannah Janney, wife of Joseph Janney, produced a certificate from Abington MM. Mary Hoge appointed overseer.

2nd mo 1765: Elizabeth Pryor produced a certificate from Kennett MM. Mary Nichols, wife of Thos. Nichols produced a certificate from Kennet MM. Ruth Holland appointed overseer at Bush Creek.

3rd mo 1765: Sophia Matthews is reported as being under necessitous circumstances, a visit to her might be necessary. Prudence Woodard, wife of Jesse Woodard produced a certificate from Wilmington MM for herself and children Sarah, Jane, and Prudence. Hannah Spencer, and husband Nathan, request that their children, Margrett, Samuel, Mary and John, be received as members,. Ann Harris, a single woman being with child, as she confesses, by John Coleman, {a married man}. For such a scandalous act Friends think they are clear in drawing up a testimony. William Brazelton and Sarah his wife request certificates for themselves and children to New Garden MM in NC.

4th mo 1765: Ruth Gregg appointed overseer at Goose Creek. Sophia Matthews married out of unity, and hath for sometime neglected attendance at meetings. Testimony is directed against her.

5th mo 1765: Sarah and Phebe Mires, daughters of Joseph and Phebe Mires, request membership. Sophia Petticoat, formerly Matthews, was presented a copy of testimony against her. Hannah Eblen {wife of James Carter} married out of unity.

8th mo 1765: Sarah Dodd, wife of Thomas Dodd, requests certificate for herself and children, she not being certain in what meeting her husband may settle.

9th mo 1765: Margrett Mead, wife of Samuel Mead, requests certificate for herself and children to Salem MM. Mary Bucklew requests certificate to Waterrie? MM in SC. Hannah Pancoast (now Boon) has gone out in marriage, so right of membership is denied. Elizabeth Norton and Abigail Pike visited from Cane Creek in NC. Sarah Mead, daughter of Samuel Mead, requests a certificate to Salem MM in NJ.

10th mo 1765: Hannah Uncles produced a certificate from New Garden MM in PA. Phebe Farquer produced a certificate from Goshen MM. Sarah Pancoast produced a certificate from West River MM. Mary Barrett requests a certificate to Hopewell MM. Barbaray Stanley requests a certificate to New Garden MM in NC. Ann Stroud requests certificate to Nottingham MM.

11th mo 1765: Ann Harris (now Dawson) daughter of Samuel Harris, married out of unity. Ann Richardson has gone out in marriage with Jason Morlan, a member of our society.

3rd mo 1766: Elizabeth Pryor requests certificate to Kennett MM. Jacob Nichols and Tacey West consummated their marriage before a priest. Martha Hawkins requests a certificate to Waterrie MM in SC for herself and children Benjamin, Nathan, Martha, William, Amos and James. Martha Davis requests a certificate with her husband and children to Hertford MM. Affinity Cadwaleder requests certificate to Hertford MM.

5th mo 1766: The marriage of John Smith and Sarah Mires was orderly accomplished. Susannah Hollingsworth requests a certificate for herself and children to Waterrie MM in SC. James Hatcher and Catherine Nichols have gone out in marriage; the meeting agrees to draw a testimony against them.

6th mo 1766: James Cadwaleder and Mary his wife produced a certificate for themselves and children Sarah, David, and Ruth from Exeter MM.

7th mo 1766: Mary Nichols, daughter of Thos. Nichols produced a certificate from Kennitt MM.

8th mo 1766: A certificate was produced from Kennett MM for Mary Gregg, daughter of John Gregg. Hannah Harris (now Howell), daughter of Samuel Harris, married a man not of our society. Tabitha Tavener (formerly Roach) married out of unity; {appeared with child by him}.

11th mo 1766: Deborah Pyott produced a certificate from Darby MM. A certificate was produced for Elizabeth Yarnal and daughter. Hannah Janney appointed overseer at Goose Creek.

1st mo 1767: Jane Hague appointed overseer at Fairfax.

2nd mo 1767: Certificate from Hopewell MM was produced for Phebe Barrett, daughter of James Barret. Keziah Hattfield, is guilty of fornication, which plainly appears from the birth brought forth.

4th mo 1767: John Todhunter and wife produced a certificate from Uwchlan MM for themselves and children Hanah, Mary, Margrett, Isaac, Jacob, Joseph, and Evan. Hannah Jones, formerly Todhunter, married out of unity, therefore a testimony will be drawn against her. Asseneth

Yarnal, (now Hollingsworth) married out of unity. Rachel Farquer is appointed overseer at Pipe Creek.

6th mo 1767: John Clark produced a certificate for himself and Ann his wife and their children Mary, Daniel, Rebeckah, and John, from Sadsbury MM. Certificate was produced for James Steer and wife Abigal, directed to Hopewell MM.

7th mo 1767: Mary Cadwaleder requests certificate to Uwchlan MM. William Hunt is on a religious visit to New England. Elenor Plummer is appointed overseer at Bush Creek. A memorial was produced by men Friends concerning Elder Mary Janney, deceased.

8th mo 1767: Rebekah Gregg, daughter of Samuel, requests membership.

9th mo 1767: Hannah Prior requests certificate to Concord MM. Hannah Fairhust hath been guilty of fornication. Rebeckah Gibson produced a certificate from Bradford MM.

10th mo 1767: Alice Gibson produced a certificate from Bradford MM for herself and son Moses. Joseph Gibson and Phebe his wife produced a certificate for themselves and daughter Esther.

11th mo 1767: A testimony was produced from Hopewell against Hannah Harris, widow of William Harris. Men Friends acquainted us of the inconsistency of receiving certificates for Friends residing in George Town, MD. Therefore, we should endorse the certificates of Jermaine Grim, Elizabeth Yarrel and Elizabeth Yarral Junr. directed to West River MM.

12th mo 1767: Certificate was produced for Ann Orr from Abington MM. Ruth Cadwaleder produced a certificate from Hopewell MM. Catherine Cadwaleder, daughter of Joseph, is guilty of fornication, as appears by the birth brought forth. Ann Janney, daughter of William, requests certificate to Falls MM in Bucks Co.

1st mo 1768: Friends cannot send certificate for Ann Janney until she condemns her unbecoming behavior.

2nd mo 1768: The Friends appointed in the case of Milcah Tomble, formerly Richardson, have not performed the service. Ann Orr, living remote from meeting, has neglected attending for near two years. Complaint against Hannah Conard and Ruth Burson, guilty of fornication, by each having an illegitimate child. Mary Boggess, formerly Potts, married out of unity.

3rd mo 1768: Elizabeth Pancost, wife of Israel Pancost, produced a certificate from Burlington MM. Mary Davis, wife of Saml. Davis produced a certificate from Merion MM, for herself and children, Abraham, Abiather, Tacy, Benjamin, Ruth, Sarah, and Samuel Davis Jr.

Isaac Votau and Ann his wife, produced a certificate from Buckingham MM. Hannah Hackney requests a certificate to Hopewell MM.

6th mo 1768: John Pickett {Piggott} and Phebe his wife produced a certificate from East Nottingham MM. A certificate from Falls MM in PA was produced for Joseph Hough's children, namely Hannah, John, Sarah, Joseph, Barnard, Thomas, William, and Janney Hough. Complaint against Sarah Morris, formerly Treby for marrying out of unity.

7th mo 1768: Ann Janney requests a certificate to Falls MM.

8th mo 1768: James Hatcher and Catherine, his wife, condemned their out going in marriage.

9th mo 1768: Hannah Brooke produced a certificate from West River MM for herself and children, Deborah and Elizabeth.

10th mo 1768: Thomas Smith and Rachel his wife produced a certificate from Buckingham MM.

11th mo 1768: Alice Yates appointed overseer at Fairfax. Rachel Willson visited from England.

12th mo 1768: Alice Clark, daughter of John and Ann Clark, produced a certificate from Sadsbury MM. Hannah Hayward produced a certificate to this meeting some time ago from Hopewell MM, but some misconduct appearing, it was not received. She now has gone out in marriage.

1st mo 1769: Mary Nickols requests certificate to Center MM in PA. Jean Gore and Margreat Normand some years past produced papers condemning their outgoing in marriage by which they were continued under the care of Friends, but they continue for the most part in a luke warm state, seldom attending any meeting.

4th mo 1769: A certificate from Falls MM was produced for Danl. Lovett's children, Martha and Joseph. A certificate was produced for Hester Gibson joined with her husband and children from Bradford MM. Hannah Dillion, wife of John, produced a certificate from Wrightstown MM. Sarah Young, wife of Herculas Young, produced a certificate from Rawway MM in NJ for herself and 5 children, Jacob, Hannah, John, Margret and Silas.

6th mo 1769: Certificate was produced for Samuel Marris and Sarah Ellis from Exeter MM in PA. Certificate was produced for Sarah Fred, wife of Joseph Fred from New Garden MM. Margrett Davis, wife of Joseph Davis, produced a certificate from Exeter MM.

8th mo 1769: Jean Clayton produced a certificate from Gwynedd MM.

10th mo 1769: A certificate was produced for Judith Shepard, wife of John Shepard, from the Falls MM. Aden Pancost and his wife produced a certificate from Burlington MM for themselves and child Diedamy.

11th mo 1769: Elizabeth Pryor produced a certificate from Concord MM in PA. Mary Willson, late Wildman, having married out of unity, and they having carnal knowledge of each other before marriage as plainly doth appear, testimony ordered against them. Sarah Uncles having been under the care of Pipe Creek, requests membership.

12th mo 1769: Certificate sent to Kennett MM for Mary Nickols. Anne Hoge is appointed overseer at Goose Creek. Mary Gregg, now Howell, married out of unity. Complaint against Elizabeth Mead, now Potts for her disorderly marriage. Complaint against Phebe Janney of Goose Creek for being guilty of fornication, she having an illegitimate child. Hannah Rhodes, now Mead, married out of unity.

1st mo 1770: Sarah Dixon appointed overseer for the new meeting called South Fork. Decided to send certificates to Radnor MM for the children of Samuel Davis.

2nd mo 1770: Elizabeth Pryor requests a certificate to Concord MM.

3rd mo 1770: Phebe Gibson appointed overseer at South Fork. Hannah Tate requests a certificate to Kennett MM. Mary Nickols, wife of Thomas Nickols, having for some time past absented herself from Friends and meetings, and is about to join the Baptists, this meeting does hereby disown her.

4th mo 1770: Hannah Cadwalader requests a certificate to Uwchlan MM for herself and daughter Lydia. Hannah and Abigail Cadwalader, daughters of David and Hannah Cadwalader request certificates to Uwchlan MM. Elizabeth Willson, Daughter of David Willson produced a letter of recommendation from Middletown MM, stating that her right among Friends is so clear as to give her a certificate.

7th mo 1770: Sarah Brown is received in membership with her children Mary, Richard, and Sarah, her husband being also a member. Ellen {Eleanor} Roberts, formerly Williams, has gone out in marriage with William Roberts, her first cousin, they also had carnal knowledge of each other before marriage.

9th mo 1770: William Brown and Martha his wife, produced a certificate from Bradford MM for themselves and 4 small children, Stephen, Sarah, Martha and Jean. Mary Nickols daughter of Isaac Nickols, being returned from PA, produced her certificate with an endorsement thereon. Sarah Sands, daughter of Edmund Sands, hath been guilty of fornication by having an illegitimate child. The meeting at the Gap, or David Williams', is continued.

10th mo 1770: Thomas Goodwin produced a certificate from Goshen MM for himself, Mary his wife, and children, Elizabeth, Ezra, John, Susanna,

George, and Gidion. Elizabeth Brown, wife of Joseph Brown, produced a certificate from Buckingham MM. Affinity Cadwalader produced a certificate from Merion MM. Grace Fisher and Margaret Sidwell visited from Philadelphia and Nottingham MM. Rebeckah Gregg is appointed overseer at Goose Creek meeting. Hannah, Mahlon, Samuel, William, and John Schooly, children of Wm. and Ann Schooley, being born when their parents were not members and still in their minority; their parents now being members request their children be deemed members, which request is granted.

11th mo 1770: Anne Janney produced a certificate from Falls MM. Sarah Nickols produced a certificate from Abington MM. Certificate from Philadelphia MM was produced for children of John and Dinah Bezor {Beaser}, namely Edith, Guialma, Asa, and Elizabeth. Anne Moreland, {and husband Jason} who some time ago was disowned for marrying disorderly, hath lately offered a paper condemning same. The Friends near Monocacy request a first and week day meeting.

12th mo 1770: Sarah Ellis, daughter of Thomas Ellis, produced a certificate from Exeter MM. Benjamin Shrieve and Hannah his wife, produced a certificate from Philadelphia MM. Jason Morland and wife request that their children, Sarah and Rebeckah, may be deemed members of our society. Ruth Clews, alias Potts; Phebe Yates, late Wildman; Hannah Rice, late Roach; also Mary Jones, late Todhunter; and Mary Finikin, late Parker, married out, so this meeting does hereby disown them for such disorderly conduct.

3rd mo 1770: Complaint against Mary Roach, daughter of Richard Roach for having an illegitimate child.

4th mo 1771: Request was made on behalf of Catherine and Mary Williams, daughters of Owen and Mary Williams, deceased, for certificates to Gwynedd MM.

5th mo 1771: Certificate for Jono. and Susanna Wright was produced from Warrington MM. Stephen Gregg and Susanna, his wife produced a certificate from Kennett MM, also for their children Sarah Dixon, Thomas, and Samuel Gregg.

6th mo 1771: Certificate was produced for Sarah Paxton and her children, James, William, and Amos from Buckingham MM. Clew Dever, wife of Basel Dever, requests a certificate to Gunpowder MM, for herself and children Misail, Margret, and Jonah.

7th mo 1771: Anne Neal, late Hollingsworth, married her first cousin.

8th mo 1771: Complaint against Ann Mead, daughter of Wm Mead, for having an illegitimate child. Complaint against Mary Eblen Jr. (now Pyott) for fornication and marrying out of unity.

11th mo 1771: Hannah Foster visited from Evesham MM in West NJ. Anne Everett produced a certificate from Warrington MM. Ruth Cadwalader requests a certificate to Hopewell MM, joined with her husband {Reese} and small children, Asa, Mary, and Edith.

12th mo 1771: A certificate was produced for Ann Reader and her two children, Thomas and Anne, from Buckingham MM in PA. NB: the first mentioned Ann Reader is dead, since she obtained the above certificate. Complaint against Elizabeth Hough for fornication with him who is now her husband {Amos Hough}.

1st mo 1772: Complaint against Elizabeth Poole of Monocacy for drinking strong liquor to excess, also wholly neglecting attendance. Elizabeth Pryor produced a certificate from Concord MM. It is necessary to appoint an overseer in the room of Jean Hague who is removed by death. Mary Baker was appointed. Pipe Creek requests a monthly meeting.

3rd mo 1772: Josebed Lodge, and Catherine his wife with their 7 children, William, Ester, Jacob, Jonathan, Nathan, Josabed, and Abel produced a certificate from Kennett MM. William Kenworthy, Mary his wife, and 2 children, William, and Mary, produced a certificate from Warrington MM. Phebe Barrett requests a certificate to Hopewell MM. Complaint against Hannah Clews, now Mead, for her outgoing in marriage.

4th mo 1772: Elenor Ellis produced a certificate from Exeter MM.

5th mo 1772: Testimony against Elizabeth Pooley, now Bell, {for taking spirituous liquor to excess, and going out in marriage}. Complaint against Mary Treby for having an illegitimate child.

6th mo 1772: Complaint against Margret Todhunter Jr., now Wells, for being guilty of fornication with a man whom she afterwards married, with the assistance of a Baptist teacher.

8th mo 1772: Certificate from Warrington MM was produced by Anne Reiley. Margery Nichols appointed overseer for Goose Creek Particular meeting. Certificate was produced for Ann Lemert, wife of Lewis Lemert, from New Garden MM in PA. Mary Tucker, wife of Thomas Tucker, produced a certificate for herself and children, John, Mary, and David, from Gunpowder MM.

11th mo 1772: John Willits and Rachel his wife produced a certificate from Exeter MM. David Scofield, Rachel his wife, and 4 children, Samuel, John, Enoch, and Benjamin produced a certificate from

Gunpowder MM. A certificate was produced by Sarah Hutton, daughter of Saml. Hutton, from Warrington MM.

12th mo 1772: [Two pages very faint--something about Hannah Sandford, probably married out of unity]. Anne Janney guilty of fornication and marrying out of unity. Affinity Cadwalader (now Megeath) {McGeach} married a man not of the society. Jane West, wife of Joseph West, requests a certificate to Cedar Creek in VA.

1st mo 1773: Rachel Eblen, daughter of John and Mary Eblen, had an illegitimate child.

2nd mo 1773: Rachel Potts, daughter of Anne Potts, guilty of fornication. Hannah Vestal, formerly Potts, has gone out in marriage with a man that is her first cousin. Margret Phillips, wife of Edmund Phillips, having been under the care of Friends some time, yet they feel it necessary to visit before favoring her request.

3rd mo 1773: William Neal produced a certificate for himself, wife and small children, George, Sarah, and Rachel, from New Garden MM in PA. Friends appointed in the case of Anne White have performed that service, and delivered testimony to the men to publish. It is supposed Hanah Vestal has gone out of these parts. Hannah Updike, formerly Harris has gone out in marriage.

4th mo 1773: Susannah Lightfoot and Phebe Trimble visited from Uwchlan and Concord MM.

5th mo 1773: Hannah Beans, wife of Wm. Beans produced a certificate from Buckingham MM.

6th mo 1773: Mary Ball, wife of Mr. Farling Ball, produced a certificate from Hopewell MM. Anne Russell requests membership.

7th mo 1773: Elizabeth Russell produced a certificate from Buckingham MM. Mary Mires is appointed overseer.

9th mo 1773: Ruth Ellis, late Fairhurst, Sarah Reese, formerly Brown, and Sarah Gregg, {daughter of Edward Gregg} have gone out in marriage.

10th mo 1773: Margret Vickers produced a certificate from Buckingham MM. William Boone and wife, with children Mordiacai, Mary, William, George, Thomas, Jeremiah, and Hesekiah produced a certificate from Exeter MM in PA.

11th mo 1773: Anne Griffith, formerly Burson, offered proposal of marriage to this meeting with Isaac Griffith, who being her brother by former marriage, Friends thought them too near of kin, declined their proceeding. Nevertheless, they have since married out of unity with Friends.

3rd mo 1774: Hannah Jones, wife of William Jones, produced a certificate from New Garden MM in PA. Anne Everett, daughter of John Everett, produce a certificate from Pipe Creek MM.

4th mo 1774: William Daniel and Ester his wife produced a certificate from Buckingham MM, with their children: James, Sarah, William, Hannah, Jane, Ester, Martha, Joseph, and Benjamin Daniel. Mary Daniel, daughter of William Daniel produced a certificate from Buckingham MM. Elizabeth Robertson visited from old England. It is necessary to send a certificate to Nottingham MM for Susanna Stroud, daughter of Saml. and Anne Stroud. Complaint against Susanna Neers, formerly Potts, for outgoing in marriage.

6th mo 1774: Mary Leaver, from Old England, visited. John Hirst produced a certificate for himself, Mary his wife, and children, John Rebeckah, Sarah, Jesse, David, Anne and Thomas, from Wrightstown MM in PA. Dinah Phillips and Elizabeth Phillips produced certificates from Kennett MM. Mary McGray produced a certificate from Wrightstown MM. Rachel Neal, wife of Lew Neal, requests a certificate to Hopewell MM. Ruth Janney, daughter of Abel Janney, has gone out in marriage with Jonas Janney, her first cousin.

7th mo 1774: Sarah Gore, formerly Hoge, and Debora Harris, formerly Roach, have gone out in marriage.

8th mo 1774: Hannah Steer, daughter of Nicholas and Ann Steer, produced a certificate from Warrington MM.

9th mo 1774: Sarah Townsend, wife of Thomas Townsend, produced a certificate from Goshen MM, for herself and children Amos, Mary, John, Rebeckah, Sarah and Thomas. Nicholas and Anne Steer produced a certificate from Warrington MM for themselves and daughter Ruth.

11th mo 1774: Sarah Clandennen, [Clendening], alias Woodard, has gone out in marriage. Lidia Leonard produced a certificate from Sadsbury MM. Barbara Wilkinson produced a certificate for herself and children Sarah and Joseph {to Chester MM}.

12th mo 1774: Rebeccah Poole appointed overseer at Goose Creek. Complaint against Mercy Tomkins, alias Shreeve, for outgoing in marriage.

1st mo 1775: Complaint against Jane Woodard, now James, for outgoing in marriage.

2nd mo 1775: Ellenor Hough received as a member.

3rd mo 1775: Elizabeth Proyer {Pryor} requested a certificate to Concord MM. Mary Tucker, wife of Thomas, requests a certificate for herself and children John, Mary and David Tucker, to West River MM. Mary

Plummer, wife of Joseph West Plummer has settled within the verge of Pipe Creek MM and requests a certificate to same.

4th mo 1775: Hannah Reive and Rebekah Wright visited from Salem in West NJ and Chesterfield, East NJ. Sarah Boone has removed with her children to Exeter MM. Friends think it necessary to send a certificate after her and her children Mary, William, George, Thomas, Jeremiah, and Hezekiah Boone.

5th mo 1775: Margaret Tribee (now Williams) and Margaret Young (now Dunkin), daughter of Herculus and Sarah Young, have gone out in marriage.

7th mo 1775: Sarah Treyhern, daughter of Rebekah Treyhern requests membership.

9th mo 1775: William Smith and Ann his wife produced a certificate from Buckingham MM for themselves and children, Mahlon, Sarah, William, Edith, Ann, Jane, and Aaron. Isaiah Boone and Hannah his wife, condemned their outgoing in marriage.

10th mo 1775: Sarah Fred appointed overseer at South Fork.

11th mo 1775: Dinah Young, formerly Philips, has gone out in marriage and moved a considerable distance away.

12th mo 1775: Complaint against Hannah Burson, daughter of George Burson for having an illegitimate child.

3rd mo 1776: Hannah Boone {wife of Isaiah} and children Elizabeth, Mary, Mordecai and Esther received into membership. Rachel Hollingsworth requests a certificate for herself and two daughters Phebe and Mary to Hopewell MM.

4th mo 1776: Ann Gibson, wife of Thomas, requests membership. Jane Conard, wife of James, requests a certificate for herself and daughters Sarah and Elisabeth to Hopewell MM. Hannah Shrieve, wife of Benjamin, requests a certificate to Hopewell MM.

5th mo 1776: Elizabeth Hatfield, an ancient friend, lately removed to Hopewell. It may be best to write to that meeting to inform of her circumstances and know how far they are to receive a certificate for her.

6th mo 1776: Phebe Gore, daughter of Sarah Gore, requests membership. Elizabeth Janney (now Nichols), daughter of William and Elisabeth, has gone out in marriage.

7th mo 1776: Margaret Williams (now Hebron), daughter of David and Ann Williams has gone out in marriage.

8th mo 1776: Complaint against Ann Reader for having an illegitimate child. Certificates were provided by this meeting for Sarah Peirpoint and her children Joseph, Sarah, and Ely; Caleb Taylor and her children

Thomas, Rachel, Joseph, Jesse; Richard Richardson and Mary his wife, with their children Joseph, Fielder, Elisabeth, Sarah, Richard, and Samuel; Obed Peirpoint and Esther his wife with their children Jonathan and Sarah. [No locations given].

9th mo 1776: Ann Schooley appointed overseer.

11th mo 1776: Mary Myers appointed overseer. Elisabeth Cadwalader appointed overseer at Goose Creek.

12th mo 1776: Complaint against Edith Carter, formerly Bezor, for marrying out of unity.

[No minutes for next 4 months.]

5th mo 1777: Complaint against Lucretia Richardson for having an illegitimate child. Complaint against Rebekah Davis, formerly Trebe for outgoing in marriage.

7th mo 1777: Complaint against Lydia Howell, formerly Gregg, for outgoing in marriage.

8th mo 1777: Ann Quaintance produced a certificate for herself and daughter Esther, from Bradford MM. Complaint against Ann Morland, from Goose Creek, for joining with her husband Jason in selling a negro woman.

9th mo 1777: Complaint against Ann Wildman, formerly Hague; and Ann Mcfarson, formerly Fred, for outgoing in marriage. Jonas Janney and Ruth his wife, offered a paper respecting their outgoing in marriage.

10th mo 1777: Marriage of Isaiah Myres and Alice Yates was orderly accomplished. Ann Jones and Rachel Baker have been under the care of Friends for some time, and now request membership.

12th mo 1777: Sarah Hirst produced a certificate from Buckingham MM. Complaint against Rachel Fairhurst, formerly Dillon, for outgoing in marriage.

1st mo 1778: Mary Ball, daughter of William Ball, requests membership.

3rd mo 1778: Ann Beck requests membership. Rebekah Seybold appointed overseer at South Fork.

4th mo 1778: Complaint against Esther Connard, formerly Burson, for outgoing in marriage with a relation. Isaiah Boone, wife {Hannah} and children Elisabeth, Mary, Mordecai and Esther, request certificates to Indian Spring MM.

6th mo 1778: Joseph Scott, and Ann his wife, produced a certificate from Gunpowder MM for themselves and children William, Benjamin, Mary, Joseph, Rachel and Isaac Scott. Jacob Scott and Elisabeth his wife, produced a certificate from Gunpowder MM for themselves and children Rebekah, Martha, Hannah, Stephen, Ann and Elisabeth Scott. Complaint against Abigail Brown, formerly Rhodes, for her outgoing in marriage. Rachel Lane {Lewellen} requests membership.

7th mo 1778: Friends appointed to visit Rachel Lawellin and Ann Beck report is now safe to grant their requests. Certificate was produced for Lydia Hough, widow of Joseph Hough, from Falls MM.

8th mo 1778: A certificate was produced from Hopewell MM for Aaron and Hannah Hackney and children George, Joseph, Lydia and Jehu.

9th mo 1778: Mary Ball is received into membership. Latitia Wildman, formerly Janney, has gone out in marriage.

11th mo 1778: Elizabeth Thomas appointed overseer at Fairfax.

12th mo 1778: Marriage of Elijah Myres and Mary Ball was orderly accomplished. Lydia Hough appointed clerk.

1st mo 1779: Complaint against Hannah Smith, daughter of Samuel Smith, for having an illegitimate child. Certificate was produced from Providence MM for Agness Wilkinson, wife of Jesse Wilkinson. Friends are appointed to visit her before accepting the certificate.

2nd mo 1779: Agness Wilkinson is not altogether clear of the charges against her, being guilty of adultery, therefore, it may be safe to return the certificate from whence it came. Certificate was produced from Hopewell for John Hogue and Mary his wife. Certificate was produced from Wrightstown MM for Sarah Wilson, wife of Saml. Wilson, and children Jane, Samuel, Stephen, Joseph, Rachel, Mary, and Nancy. Mary Roach offered a paper condemning her misconduct. The case of Rachel Baker was revived. Friends appointed to visit her.

3rd mo 1779: Complaint against Ruth Dixon for her outgoing in marriage with her first cousin.

4th mo 1779: Ellisabeth Prior produced a certificate from Concord MM. Lydia Philips, daughter of Edmond Philips, requests membership.

5th mo 1779: Ann Smith is appointed overseer at Goose Creek. Complaint against Elisabeth Rhodes for having an illegitimate child.

6th mo 1779: Men Friends request women to join them in a visit to Joseph Lacy's children. Rebekah Jones visited from northern district of Philadelphia. Rebekah Chambers visited from New Garden MM.

7th mo 1779: Samuel Canby and Anne Shean intend to marry. A certificate was produced from Bradford MM for Elisabeth Sinkler and her husband {Job Sinclair}, and children John, Mary, and Hannah. Complaint against Margarett Harris, formerly Holmes, for outgoing in marriage.

8th mo 1779: Ann Mcferson condemned her outgoing in marriage.

9th mo 1779: Complaint against Rachel Lewellen for having an illegitimate child.

10th mo 1779: Ruth Nichols requests certificate to Indian Spring MM. This meeting received a few lines from Chester MM, regarding Agnes Wilkinson, with a copy of a testimony enclosed.

11th mo 1779: A certificate was produced from Gunpowder MM for our ancient friend, Hannah Scott. A certificate was produced for Mary Burson, wife of James Burson, from Gwynedd MM. A daughter of Jonas and Mary Potts, being left to her grandmother to bring up, and she being now grown to the years of age, and having no learning, this meeting appoints Mary Janney and Mary Myres to take care of that matter. Complaint against Hannah Nichols, formerly Hoge, daughter of Solomon Hoge, for outgoing in marriage. Complaint against Mary Harris, daughter of William Harris, deceased, for going to her brother's marriage, consummated contrary to the rules of our discipline; appearing in an obstinate disposition of mind; and absenting herself from meetings.

12th mo 1779: Lydia Philips, after due consideration, is received into membership. The Friends appointed in the case of Elisabeth Potts reported that they have provided a place for her. Complaint against Gule Besor, now Davis, daughter of John and Dinah Besor {Gulielma Bezor}, for outgoing in marriage. Complaint against Margaret Nichols, formerly Spencer, for her misconduct in giving her company indecently to a man who is now her husband, which she confesses to, and appears by the time the child was born.

2nd mo 1780: Complaint against Jane Wilson for suffering herself to be published with a man by an hireling teacher in order for marriage, and other disorderly conduct.

3rd mo 1780: Elisabeth Potts has been placed with her aunt, Jane Connard, where she is likely to be schooled, but it is so remote from meeting, that Friends are still concerned for the welfare of the child. Sarah and Ann Overfield request membership. Complaint against Mary Nixon, formerly Gregg, for outgoing in marriage.

4th mo 1780: Complaint against Ann Whitacre, formerly Steer, for her outgoing in marriage.

5th mo 1780: Sarah Gregg, joining her husband, requests a certificate to Hopewell. Mary Gregg requests membership. Complaint against Catharine Brown for having an illegitimate child.

7th mo 1780: Complaint against Esther Lodge for having an unlawful child.

8th mo 1780: Ann Patterson produced a certificate from Bradford MM. Complaint against Phebe Fairhurst for having an unlawful child.

9th mo 1780: John Nichols and wife presented a paper condemning their misconduct. Joseph Brown is removed over the Allegany Mountains and requests a certificate for himself and wife to Hopewell. (Also children Ann, Sarah, Isaac, Rachel, Samuel, Leah, Mary, and Mahlon).

10th mo 1780: Stephen Morlan, by a Friend, requests a certificate for himself, wife, and children (Eden, Abigail, and Jonah) to South River MM.

11th mo 1780: Thomas Moore produced a certificate for himself, wife {Elizabeth} and children Asa, Elisabeth, and Ann from Uwchlan MM.

12th mo 1780: Ann Janney produced a certificate from Pipe Creek MM. Mary Rodgers and Ann Ryley request certificates to Hopewell MM. Men Friends think it necessary to appoint someone to visit the widow Williams.

1st mo 1781: Sarah Janney, wife of Jacob; and Sarah Hootten, daughter of Saml Hootten {Hutton}, produced certificates from Pipe Creek. Friends appointed to visit Joan Williams and daughter report that they were not in any want at present. Complaint against Ann Pool for going to places of diversion. Abraham Davis produced a certificate from Goshen MM for himself, Hannah his wife, and their children Phebe, Tacey, and Mary. Certificate was produced for Aaron Hackney, Hannah his wife, and children George, Joseph, Lydia, Jehu, Aaron and Elisabeth to Hopewell.

2nd mo 1781: Susannah Ratiken requests membership. Complaint against Ann Mcpherson, formerly Quaintance, for outgoing in marriage. Complaint against Sarah Hough, daughter of Lydia Hough, widow, for indulging herself in the pernicious practice of card playing and attending places of diversion where dancing is practiced. Lydia Hough, widow, produced a certificate from Falls MM.

3rd mo 1781: Naomi Smith requests a certificate for herself and children Naomi, Benjamin, and Mary, to Hopewell MM. Ann Neal presented a paper condemning her conduct in marrying her first cousin.

4th mo 1781: Report that Lydia Trebbe, daughter of John Trebbee was about to join the Methodists. Complaint against Betty Philips for having an illegitimate child. Mary Russell and Martha Freestone are about to move to Buckingham MM.

5th mo 1781: A certificate from Pipe Creek MM was produced for Samuel Hutton, Mary his wife, and children William, Benjamin, Joel, Jonathan, Thomas, and Lucy. Ann Patterson requests a certificate to Bradford

MM. Elisabeth Nichols condemned her outgoing in marriage, {for which she was disowned some time ago}.

6th mo 1781: A certificate from Burleigh MM was produced by Ann and Mary Stabler, daughters of Edward Stabler. Sarah Reader requests membership. Case of Mary Steer and Ann Whiteacre being revived, Friends appointed to endeavor to know if they are sincere.

8th mo 1781: Mary Nixon, Mary {Mercy} Tomkins, and Elizabeth Nichols offered papers condemning their outgoing in marriage {for which they were disowned some years past}.

10th mo 1781: Ann Whitacre condemned her outgoing in marriage. Hannah Scott requests a certificate to Gunpowder MM.

11th mo 1781: Mary Russel produced a certificate from Buckingham MM. Aimy Taylor {wife of Evan Taylor} produced a certificate from Chester MM. Ann Ball and Mariah Cadwaleder request membership. Certificate {to Hopewell MM} was produced for William and Ann Schooly {and children Mahlon, William, John, and Isaac}.

12th mo 1781: Sarah, the wife of Herrcules Young, being removed to Redstone with her husband, requests a certificate to Hopewell MM. Complaint against Ann Roads for having an illegitimate child.

1st mo 1782: Abner Gregg produced a certificate for himself, wife, and child Ann from Hopewell MM. Sarah Townsend, wife of Thomas Townsend, requests a certificate for herself and children Amos, Mary, John, Rebekah, Sarah, Thomas, Phebe and Hannah to Hopewell. Complaint against Elizabeth Pool for having an illegitimate child.

2nd mo 1782: Ann Pool condemned her misconduct.

3rd mo 1782: Complaint against Sarah Potts, formerly Harris, for her outgoing in marriage. Margaret Cook visited from New Garden in PA. Complaint against Elizabeth Oliphant, formerly Harris, for going out in marriage. Mary Hogue Jr. appointed overseer at Goose Creek. Jonas Janney and Ruth his wife, condemned their outgoing in marriage and the impropriety of connection between persons of their kin. Job Sinclair and Elizabeth his wife request certificates for themselves and children John, Hannah, and Casia? {Mariah} to Wilmington MM.

4th mo 1782: Mary Finikin condemned her outgoing in marriage.

5th mo 1782: Rachel Hanks and Mary Shrieve request membership. Complaint against Hannah Brown {Bromhall} [or Browner, Brownel] formerly Schooly, for her outgoing in marriage. A case reporting a slave being kept in bondage, belonging to Sarah Pierpoint in Maryland, comes now under consideration.

6th mo 1782: Dinah Walter, wife of George Walter, produced a certificate from Chester MM. Alice Whitacre {wife of Benjamin Whitacre} requests membership.

7th mo 1782: Sarah Pierpoint produced a manumission for a two year old slave child. Elizabeth Brook requests a certificate to Indian Springs MM. Mary Purdom is appointed overseer. Complaint against Rachel Hutton for having an unlawful child, and denying it. Complaint against Sarah Gregg, formerly Dixon, for outgoing in marriage.

8th mo 1782: Catharine Burson, being removed with her parents to Gunpowder MM, requests a certificate in order to be joined thereto. Ann Mead condemned her misconduct, being guilty of fornication over years past.

9th mo 1782: A certificate from Hopewell was produced for Hannah Shrieve and children Rebekah, Isaac and Benjamin; also for Aaron Harris? Mary his wife, and children Lydia, Sarah, and David.

10th mo 1782: Complaint against Lydia Spensor, formerly Phillips, for outgoing in marriage. Phebe Sinclair, daughter of Jas. Sinclair requests certificate to Bradford MM. Joseph Hibbs produced a certificate for his children, William, Joseph, Sarah, Marcey, and Elizabeth, from Wrightstown MM.

11th mo 1782: A certificate from Indian Springs was produced for John Pancoast, his wife, and child Lydia. Complaint against Mary Brown for outgoing in marriage with her first cousin. Mary Fread, the daughter of Joseph and Sarah Fread, requests a certificate to Gunpowder MM. The case of Alice Whitaker being now revived, it is agreed to accept her into membership.

12th mo 1782: Sarah Taylor, wife of Thos. Taylor, produced a certificate from Warrington MM. Miriam Plummer produced a certificate from Pipe Creek MM. The Friends appointed to treat with Sarah and Mercy Hibbs report they had an opportunity with them and that Sarah showed a disposition to condemn her outgoing in marriage, but Mercey did not appear capable to condemn her misconduct. Amos Hough, his wife and children, members of this meeting, being removed over the Allegany Mountain, also Thomas Gregg, his wife and children, Sarah Hutton (widow) and Rebecca Gregg, daughter of Jno Gregg; are within the limits of Hopewell MM. All need certificates. Elizabeth Scott appointed overseer. Elizabeth Moore appointed overseer at Goose Creek. Hannah Grammar requests membership.

1st mo 1783: Sarah Emery offered a paper condemning her outgoing in marriage.

2nd mo 1783: Our men Friends inform this meeting that Ruth, the wife of William Hibbs, hath a certificate for herself and children {Sarah, Amos, and Mary} which she hath kept from Friends for several years past. We find it needful to unite with men Friends to inquire into the cause.

3rd mo 1783: Sarah Marlin {Moreland}, wife of William Marlin requests a certificate to Hopewell, she having removed some years past with her husband {to settle near Redstone}. Complaint against Elizabeth Lemmard {now McPherson} for her outgoing in marriage.

4th mo 1783: Mary Cadwallader {wife of Joseph} produced a certificate from Abington MM. Certificates from Buckingham MM were produced by Phebe Whitson for herself and children Ann, David, Mary, Willis, Jordan, Samuel, and Phebe; Susannah Vickers; John Preston for himself, Rebecca his wife, and children Zany, John, Amos, and Moses; John Wilkinson for himself, Elizabeth his wife and children Mary, Sarah, Joseph, and John; for 2 of the children of Abram Vickers, viz, Mary and William. A certificate was produced for Joseph Lacy's children Uphamy and Tacy, on their accounts. Complaint against Martha Pool for fornication, which she doth not deny. A certificate was produced for Willm. Reader's children {Sarah, Jacob, Hannah, Samuel. They have resided in these parts for several years past}.

5th mo 1783: Hannah, Rebecca and Elizabeth Randal produced certificates from Uwchlan MM. Joseph Randel and Rachel his wife, with children John, Rachael, Ruth, Joseph, Mary, Jane and Charity produced certificates from Uwchlan MM. A certificate from Middletown MM was produced for Ruth Hibbs and children Sarah, Amos and Mary. Complaint against Mary Long {wife of John Long}, formerly Clark, for being guilty of unchastity before marriage. Susannah Plaster, formerly Burson, has gone out in marriage.

6th mo 1783: Mary Shrieve requests membership. Complaint against Sarah Reader for fornication, which she doth not deny.

7th mo 1783: A certificate from Buckingham was produced for Wm. Betts, Mary his wife, and children Hezekiah, William, Aaron and Rachel Paxon, she being a daughter of his wife by a former husband. Mary Marsh, a young woman, produced a certificate from Buckingham. Sarah Vickers, having resided a short time amongst us and now about to return home, requests a certificate from this meeting.

8th mo 1783: A certificate from Gunpowder MM was produced by Judith Connard, for herself and children Sarah, Ann, Edward and Parmelia. A certificate from Buckingham was produced by Hannah Reeder. Mary

Saunders, wife of John Saunders, produced a certificate from Crooked Run MM. Complaint against Sarah Pierpoint, now House, also Deborah Holmes, now Craig, for outgoing in marriage. Anne Janney appointed overseer at Goose Creek.

10th mo 1783: Simeon Haines and Elizabeth Randal intend to marry. A certificate from the Gilfast MM, Goldbert, {Cold Beck} Cumberland, England was produced by John Sutton for himself, his wife {Catherine}, and children {John, Daniel, Isaac, James}. A certificate from Buckingham was produced for Samuel Caray, Rachel his wife, and children Cynthia, Sarah, and Jonathan. Phebe Sinclair produced a certificate from Bradford MM. Deborah Chandlee requests a certificate to Pipe Creek MM. Sarah Hirst requests a certificate to Wilmington MM.

11th mo 1783: Ann Gilbert, wife of Joseph Gilbert produced a certificate from Buckingham MM.

12th mo 1783: Complaint against Hannah Nixon, formerly Hague; also Ann Pool, now Rich,; and Susannah Dillquon {Dilwyn}, now Nichols, for outgoing in marriage. Complaint against Mary Nichols, formerly Hogue for outgoing in marriage with Isaiah Nichols.

2nd mo 1784: Mary Nichols has been guilty of unchastity with him that is now her husband.

3rd mo 1784: Complaint against Jane Boling, formerly Fairhurst, for outgoing in marriage and being guilty of unchastity before marriage.

4th mo 1784: Hannah Grammar is received into membership. A certificate from Crooked Run MM was produced by James Lownes for himself, wife and children Sarah, Hyat, John, Deborah, James, Caleb, Jane and Joseph. A certificate was produced for children of John Dillon, viz, Ann, John, Sarah, Hannah and Josiah. Phebe Myres requests a certificate to Hopewell MM. Rebeccah Preston appointed overseer for South Fork particular meeting.

5th mo 1784: Mary and Elizabeth Jolliffe produced a certificate from Hopewell MM. Ann Patterson produced a certificate from Bradford MM. Mary Smith, wife of Mahlon, requests a certificate to Crooked Run MM to be joined with her husband.

6th mo 1784: Marriage of Isaac Brown and Sarah Burson was orderly accomplished. Ann, Sarah, and Hannah Dillon are received in membership. A certificate from Hopewell MM was produced by Joseph Fisher and wife, with children Elizabeth, Joseph, Elias, Robert, John, Sarah, Susannah {Samuel}, Hannah and Ann. Complaint against Rebecca Oram, formerly Fairhurst for going out in marriage. Ann Smith appointed overseer for Goose Creek particular meeting.

7th mo 1784: Rachel Kirk, wife of William Kirk, produced a certificate from Warrington MM. Elizabeth Bangam, wife of Humphrey, produced a certificate from Buckingham MM. Complaint against Rebecca Dilwyn, formerly Randal, for marrying contrary to discipline with a member of our society. Joseph Cadwallader requests a certificate for himself and wife {Mary} to Hopewell MM. Buckingham MM requests information about Mary Reader {who married her first cousin}.

8th mo 1784: William Mitchner and Esther his wife, produced a certificate for themselves and children Rebecca, Sarah, John, William, Esther, Thomas, and Rachel from Bradford MM. Sarah Brown, wife of Moses Brown requests a certificate to be joined with husband and children {Richard, Sarah, Ann, Margaret, Phebe, Moses} to Bush River MM in SC. Complaint against Edith Smith for being guilty of unchastity.

10th mo 1784: Complaint against Sarah Cogal {Cowgill}, formerly Fredd for outgoing in marriage. James Moore requests a certificate for himself, wife, and children to Crooked Run MM.

11th mo 1784: Sarah Matthews, wife of Thomas Matthews, produced a certificate from the northern district in Philadelphia. John and Mary Long have offered a paper condemning their conduct of being guilty of fornication before marriage.

12th mo 1784: Abraham Randal produced a certificate from Wilmington MM for himself, wife Jane, and children Ann, Elizabeth, Mary, Rachel and Abraham. Complaint against Sarah Hough, daughter of William Hough for being guilty of unchastity. Ann Butcher requests membership.

1st mo 1785: Complaint against Hannah Miller, formerly Tomson; also Elizabeth Osburn, formerly Potts, for outgoing in marriage. Complaint against Jane Connard for consenting to the buying of a slave. Ann Smith, daughter of Wm. Smith, requests a certificate to Crooked Run MM.

2nd mo 1785: Edith Sharpless and Sarah Talbot visited from Concord MM. Complaint against Elizabeth Stump, formerly Hibbs, for outgoing in marriage. Miriam Plummer requests certificate to Pipe Creek MM. Complaint against Rebecca Boram {Boum}, formerly Harris, for outgoing in marriage.

3rd mo 1785: Elizabeth Pool offered a paper condemning her misconduct. Phebe Whiston wife of Solomon, requests a certificate for herself and children to Bush River MM in SC. Complaint against Ann Lewis, formerly Overfelt, for outgoing in marriage.

4th mo 1785: A certificate from Crooked Run MM was produced for Sarah Pancost, wife of David Pancost, and her daughter Elizabeth. Mary Janney, jointly with her husband Abel Janney and their children Amos, Richard, Lightfoot, and Sarah, and their niece Mary Gibson, request certificates to Crooked Run MM. Complaint against Elizabeth Dixon for outgoing in marriage with her first cousin.

5th mo 1785: A certificate from Buckingham MM was produced by Joseph Bealle and Hannah his wife, and children Thomas, Elizabeth, Samuel and Hannah. A certificate was produced for Mahlon Taylor and wife Mary, from Falls MM. Ruth Rattikin requests membership.

6th mo 1785: Mary Cadwallader requests a certificate to Crooked Run. Martha Brown, wife of Isaac Brown requests membership.

7th mo 1785: A paper of acknowledgement was presented by Jane Cunard condemning her consenting to the purchase of a Negro woman. Sarah Matthews to succeed Lydia Hough as clerk. Deborah Lewellen and 6 children in their minority: Masheck, Deborah, Mary, Hannah, Shadrack, and Sarah; also daughters Ann and Margaret, who are of age, request certificates [no location]. A certificate to Cane Creek or Centre in NC, was requested by Ann Clark, jointly with her husband John Clark and their minor children Ann and Sarah, also for their daughter Rebecca, she being of age.

8th mo 1785: Complaints against Mary Ball, formerly Hutton, also Ann Connard, now Neare, for outgoing in marriage. Complaint against Elizabeth Vickars for dancing and keeping company in a disorderly manner with a man not in profession with us.

10th mo 1785: A certificate was produced from Hopewell for Ruth, wife of Aquilla Janney. Dorothy Schooley requests membership. Elizabeth Moore appointed overseer.

11th mo 1785: Testimony against Elizabeth Hart, formerly Vickers, for marriage out of unity. Certificate was requested for Sarah Hutton, with her husband Joseph, and children Abel, Sarah, Elizabeth, Amos, John, and Asael to Westland MM. Complaint against Hannah Reader for fornication and dancing. Complaint against Rebeckah Clawson formerly Clark, for outgoing in marriage.

12th mo 1785: Unable to deliver testimony to Mary Ball, she being removed some distance. Complaint against Lydia Tribbee for dancing. Friends at Leesburg ask to be indulged with a meeting during the winter season.

1st mo 1786: Edith Smith offered paper condemning her misconduct.

5th mo 1786: Certificate produced by Esther Schooley, wife of Reuben Schooly, from Gunpowder MM.

6th mo 1786: Certificate was produced by Joseph Talbot and wife Anna with children Samuel, Joseph, Sarah, Mary, Rachel, Elisha, Jessee, and Anna from Pipe Creek.

7th mo 1786: Lydia Tribby presented a paper of acknowledgement.

8th mo 1786: A certificate for Susannah Shrieve, wife of Benjamin Shrieve, was received from upper Springfield MM.

9th mo 1786: Susannah Rattikin with her husband, requests that remainder of their children {Jane, Samuel, Sarah} be taken under care of Friends (are not now in membership).

10th mo 1786: Rachel Hatfield, formerly Lewellin, condemned her breach of chastity. Complaint against Sarah Scott, formerly Randal for breach of chastity before marriage.

11th mo 1786: Ruth Steere requested a certificate to join with husband at Goose Creek. Phebe, wife of James Moore, produced a certificate from Crooked Run MM.

12th mo 1786: A certificate to Crooked Run MM was requested by Dinah Walters, with her husband and children.

1st mo 1787: Rachel Smith produced a certificate from Wrightstown MM. Elizabeth Oliphant condemned her breach of discipline. Hannah Poole, now Williams, has married out.

2nd mo 1787: Edith Smith produced a paper of acknowledgment which was accepted.

3rd mo 1787: Sarah Hutton requests a certificate for herself and son Jonah to South River MM.

4th mo 1787: Jemima Hollingsworth, with her husband John, and children Judith and John, produced a certificate from Kennett MM. Jonas and Ruth Janney presented a paper condemning their breach of order in marriage.

5th mo 1787: Jane Irvin presented a certificate from Gunpowder MM.

6th mo 1787: Sarah Burgess, with her husband Joseph Burgess and children Moses and Lydia, produced certificates from Falls MM. Mary Wharton, wife of John Wharton, with their children Joyce, Abner, Sarah, Mahlon, Phebe, John, and Margery produced a certificate from Haverford MM.

8th mo 1787: Complaint against Rebekah Mitchener, now Martin, for outgoing in marriage.

9th mo 1787: Complaint against Ann Mead, now Mason, for outgoing in marriage. Letitia Wildman presented a paper condemning her breach of discipline in marriage.

11th mo 1787: A certificate was produced by James Erwin and Mary his wife, with children Magdalen and Susannah, from Gunpowder MM. Friends at the Gap of the Short Hill request to hold a meeting for worship.

12th mo 1787: A certificate for Mary Davis, wife of Samuel Davis, was produced from Philadelphia MM. Complaint against Sarah Mason, formerly Hough, for outgoing in marriage.

1st mo 1788: Complaint against Rachel Fulton, formerly Smith, for outgoing in marriage. Letitia Wildman presented a paper condemning her misconduct for which she was disowned. She wishes to be restored to religious fellowship with South River MM.

3rd mo 1788: Amey Taylor and daughter Rachel presented a certificate from Goose Creek. Elizabeth Oliphant has resided at South River MM for some time. Therefore, it will be necessary to write to them respecting her request {to be received into membership}.

4th mo 1788: Elizabeth Everitt, daughter of Joseph Everitt produced a certificate from Pipe Creek MM.

5th mo 1788: Esther, wife of Thomas Lacy, produced a certificate from Gunpowder MM.

7th mo 1788: A certificate was received from Hopewell MM for Rebekah Curl, wife of Joseph Curl, and children Hannah, Amey, Charles, Rebekah, and Susannah.

8th mo 1788: Lydia Tribbee continues to dance. Complaint against Anne McCormick, formerly Moore, for outgoing in marriage, also for being guilty of unchastity before marriage.

10th mo 1788: Complaint against Lydia Green, formerly Hewes, for outgoing in marriage.

12th mo 1788: Mary Backhouse produced a certificate from Kennett MM.

1st mo 1789: Complaint against Sarah Miller, formerly Conrad {Connard}, for marrying out and unchastity before marriage.

2nd mo 1789: Jemima Hollingsworth appointed overseer at the Gap meeting.

4th mo 1789: Susannah Rattikin appointed overseer. Ruth Gregg, now Tribbee, married contrary to order.

5th mo 1789: A complaint was lodged by men against William Mitchenor for not complying with his contracts. Some care may be necessary towards his wife Esther Mitchenor.

6th mo 1789: Ann Stroud presented a certificate from Hopewell MM. Abigail Wood and daughters Mary and Abigail request membership. Hester Connard read a paper condemning her marriage by a hireling with a man once removed from a first cousin.

8th mo 1789: Complaint against Sarah Eblin for being present at the marriage of a friend accomplished contrary to the rules of our discipline.

10th mo 1789: Sarah Eblin condemned her breach of discipline. Margaret Dunkin condemned her marriage with a man not a member. A certificate for Elizabeth McPherson from Haverford MM was read. Also one for Deborah Stabler from Cedar Creek.

11th mo 1789: Elizabeth Baugham {Banghan} requests a certificate to South River MM.

2nd mo 1790: Complaint against Sarah Thompson, daughter of Isaac Thomson, for non-attendance of meetings, also for breach of chastity.

3rd mo 1790: Mary and Naomi Wood, daughters of Joseph and Abigail Wood, are received into membership.

4th mo 1790: Hannah Beale, wife of Joseph Beale is appointed overseer at Gap Meeting.

5th mo 1790: Complaint against Martha Humphreys, late Williams, for marriage before an hireling. Her mother, Ann Williams, by her conduct, appears to be consenting thereto.

6th mo 1790: Complaint against Elizabeth Stokes, late Smith, for outgoing in marriage.

7th mo 1790: Lydia Green made satisfaction and is returned to membership. Sarah and Rachel Hartshorn produced a certificate from Middletown MM.

8th mo 1790: Complaint against Rebeckah Neel {Nutt}, now Ashford, who hath accomplished her marriage with a man not in membership with us.

10th mo 1790: Grace Beale produced a certificate from Buckingham MM. Sarah Homes requests a certificate to South River MM. Richard Richardson and Thos. Taylor Jr. and their families, have requested certificates to Pipe Creek MM.

11th mo 1790: Sarah Dunkin's paper was received as satisfaction and she was received into membership again.

1st mo 1791: Martha McPherson's certificate from Hopewell MM was read.

2nd mo 1791: Sarah and Elizabeth Love, daughters of {Hannah and} James Love, presented certificates from Goose Creek MM. A certificate from Goose Creek in behalf of Samuel and Sarah Gover, and children

Moses, Jacob Janney, Mary, Elizabeth, Anthony, Sarah, and Robert was read.

4th mo 1791: Sarah Gore, formerly Hague offered a paper of acknowledgement to this meeting.

6th mo 1791: A certificate was sent here for Mary Tucker from Gun Powder MM, but it appears that she is not settled to satisfaction.

7th mo 1791: Joseph Kirkbride and Mary his wife, and infant daughter Frances Maria, produced a certificate from Chesterfield MM.

8th mo 1791: A certificate was read in behalf of Sarah Bently from Indian Spring. A paper of acknowledgement has been received from Esther Connard, and directed to Hopewell. A certificate was read in behalf of Mary Tucker from Gunpowder MM.

10th mo 1791: Complaint against Sarah Mitchener, who has been guilty of unchastity.

11th mo 1791: Sarah Gore is received into membership.

12th mo 1791: Mary Brooke, a minister from Indian Spring MM, comes to visit Warrenton and Fairfax Quarterly Meetings.

1st mo 1792: The clerk has for sometime had a certificate for Sarah Morgan, wife of William Morgan, who is now removed from among us.

2nd mo 1792: Sarah Morgan's certificate was from Gunpowder MM, held at Baltimore, with an endorsement from this meeting to Indian Spring where she now resides. Complaint against Rachel Wilkinson, formerly Hanks, who married out of unity {to a man with whom she has lived in a disreputable manner for a considerable time before marriage}. Peter Blaker has resided some time within the limits of this meeting with his family, who say they have a certificate, but neglected to give it in though they have been advised thereto.

3rd mo 1792: Ann Neil condemned her outgoing in marriage with her first cousin.

4th mo 1792: Sarah Bently, wife of Caleb Bently, requests a certificate jointly with her husband to Indian Spring MM. Complaint against Sarah Lewis, formerly Overfelt {Overfield} for marrying a man not in membership with us.

6th mo 1792: Solomon Nickols and Hannah his wife presented a paper condemning their marriage.

9th mo 1792: The case of Elizabeth Wear being revived, and nothing appearing to obstruct, this meeting agrees with the judgement of men Friends to endorse her certificate sent from Wrightstown MM, and forward to Goose Creek MM.

10th mo 1792: A certificate from Kennett MM was produced by Levi Hollingsworth for himself, Mary his wife, and children Thomas and David. Complaint against Sarah Chapman, formerly Eblin; and Elizabeth Matlock, formerly Ball, for outgoing in marriage.

11th mo 1792: Testimony against Abigail Pettit, formerly Wood, for marrying out of unity.

12th mo 1792: A certificate was produced by Sarah Thompson from Buckingham MM. Sarah Blaker presented a certificate from Warrenton MM.

2nd mo 1793: Rebeckah Talbert, wife of Joseph Talbert produced a certificate from Goose Creek MM.

5th mo 1793: It is thought proper to send a certificate after Mary Harris, she having removed a considerable time past to South River MM.

6th mo 1793: Hannah Beale is appointed clerk, in room of Sarah Matthews.

7th mo 1793: Sarah Moore, wife of Asa Moore produced a certificate from Hopewell MM. Complaint against Ann Fisher for persisting in her public appearance in meetings after being tenderly and repeatedly dealt with by Friends in a private way.

9th mo 1793: Martha Mendenhall, wife of William Mendenhall produced a certificate from New Garden MM. A certificate was produced for Sarah Smith wife of William Smith from Goose Creek MM.

10th mo 1793: Phebe Yates produced a paper condemning her outgoing in marriage, and requests to be received into membership again. Sarah Taylor requests a certificate with her husband and children to Pipe Creek MM.

4th mo 1794: Meeting at Leesburg should be discontinued. Ruth Taylor {wife of Jesse} received into membership. Complaint against Susannah Harrison, formerly Nutt, for marrying out of society.

8th mo 1794: Testimony prepared against Ann Gregg.

9th mo 1794: Mary Warton requests a certificate for herself and children Abner, Sarah, Mahlon, Phebe, John, Margery and Jonathan, and likewise her eldest daughter Joice, to Redstone MM.

10th mo 1794: Phebe Clevinger produced a certificate from Crooked Run MM. Alexandria Friends are granted the privilege of holding a preparative meeting.

11th mo 1794: Elizabeth Hirst, formerly Brown, hath accomplished her marriage out of unity.

12th mo 1794: Ann Barber requests membership.

2nd mo 1795: Complaint against Elizabeth Campbell, formerly Beson, for marriage out of unity. Hannah James, formerly Smith, hath been disowned many years ago for being guilty of fornication, which she condemns. Friends receive her into membership again, and conclude to send her a certificate to Westland MM. Men Friends to pay Rebeckah Nutt {wife of Joseph, children James, Elizabeth, Thomas, Rebecca} a visit as her certificate has lain some considerable time in meeting and she does not attend.

4th mo 1795: Complaint against Ann Southerland, formerly Taylor, for accomplishing her marriage out of unity.

5th mo 1795: Ruth Miller produced a certificate from Uwchlan MM. Elizabeth Stokes appeared at this meeting with a paper condemning her out going in marriage. Friends think best to appoint someone to visit her. A certificate from Buckingham MM was produced for William and Rachel Beal, with children Mercy, Phillip, Sarah, Joseph, William, and Hannah.

6th mo 1795: Rebeckah Talbert and Anne Steer appointed overseers.

7th mo 1795: Ann Coates produced a certificate from Baltimore MM. A certificate was produced by Mary Stabler, wife of Edward Stabler, from Sider [Cedar] Creek MM. Elizabeth Brown requests a certificate to Crooked Run MM {but it is not likely she can attend there}.

8th mo 1795: A certificate from Crooked Run MM was produced for Mary Woodrow and daughters Mary and Lydia; also one for Grace Woodrow.

9th mo 1795: Elizabeth Stokes is received into membership again. A certificate from Goose Creek was produced for Mary Jenney, wife of Elisha Jenney, also for their daughter Sarah Jenney. A certificate from Goose Creek was produced for Sarah Mires, wife of Jacob Mires. Joseph Kirkbride requests a certificate for himself, wife Mary, and children Frances, Maria, John, Paul, and Mary Ann, to Northern District in Philadelphia.

10th mo 1795: Hannah Bradfield sent a paper condemning her former conduct for which she was justly disowned.

11th mo 1795: Elizabeth Stokes requests a certificate to Westland MM. A certificate from Goose Creek was produced for Elizabeth Ware and children Sarah, William, Elizabeth and Jane. Complaint against Sarah Ware for being guilty of fornication, which appears by the birth brought forth.

12th mo 1795: Ann Griffith condemned her marriage.

1st mo 1796: Sarah Moore is appointed overseer.

2nd mo 1796: Rachel Beal requests a certificate with her husband William and small children Phillip, Sarah, Joseph, William and Hannah, also daughter Mercy to Hopewell MM. Tacy Nichols sent a paper condemning her out going in marriage which Friends take so much notice of as to write to Friends at South River.

3rd mo 1796: Complaint against Phebe Horner, formerly Clevinger for being guilty of unchastity and also has married her mother's brother.

4th mo 1796: Sarah Paxton and Elizabeth Scott are to have oversight of the youth and try to put an end to their irreverent behaviour.

5th mo 1796: A certificate from Bradford MM was produced for Elizabeth Fisher, wife of Thomas Fisher, and children Elizabeth, Rebeckah, and Mary.

6th mo 1796: A certificate from Bradford MM was produced by Rachel Miller. Complaint against Ann Thompson {Griffith, late Thompson} for frequenting places of diversions and likewise accomplishing her marriage out of unity.

7th mo 1796: A certificate from Upper Springfield was produced for Mary Shreve with her husband Ruben Shreve. A certificate from Nottingham, held at Little Britten, was produced for Catharine Pugh, with her husband Jesse Pugh and their son Isaac. Complaint against Ann Acres?, formerly Gregg, for marriage out of unity. Ann Hurst requests a certificate to Goose Creek. Complaint against Hannah Siddel (Sidwel) for unchaste conversation and she is delivered of a child in an unmarried state. Sarah Paxton and Elizabeth Scott request to be released from having the oversight of the youth, which the meeting grants. Sarah Scott brought a paper condemning her former conduct.

9th mo 1796: A certificate from Purchase MM in New York was produced for Elizabeth Browne, wife of Matthew Franklin Browne, and children William, Sidney, and Josiah. Case of Soloman Nichols and wife has been attended to and men Friends inform us they have concluded to give them a certificate.

10th mo 1796: Elizabeth Griffith, formerly Thompson married out of unity. Ruth Hague is guilty of fornication.

11th mo 1796: Martha Parker produced a certificate from Goose Creek. Elizabeth Janny, wife of John Janney, produced a certificate from Indian Spring MM. Sarah Milburn appeared at this meeting and produced a paper condemning her former conduct. A certificate from Goose Creek was produced for Elizabeth Parker with her children {Joseph, Eliza, Samuel, Silas, and Ann}.

12th mo 1796: A certificate from South River MM was produced for Rachel Wright with her husband Robert Wright.

1st mo 1797: Charity Cook and Susannah Hollingsworth visited from Bush River in SC.

2nd mo 1797: Joseph and Ruth Trebe produced a paper condemning their outgoing in marriage. A certificate from Pipe Creek MM was produced by Elizabeth Plummer with husband Moses Plummer and children Ann and Sarah. [note about Mary Fisher who resides in Alexandria].

4th mo 1797: Ann Schooly and husband produced a certificate from Redstone MM. Joseph Trebe and Ruth his wife, request that their children may have a right of membership, which this meeting grants.

5th mo 1797: Sarah and Ann Cunard produced certificates from Goose Creek MM. A certificate was sent after Sarah Mires who went with her husband to Goose Creek MM.

6th mo 1797: A certificate from Goose Creek was produced by Judith Cunard for herself and children Edward, Permelia, John, Henry, and Jarret. Elizabeth Bowne requests a certificate for herself and children to Purchase MM in NY. Margaret Elger and Sarah Farquer visited from Pipe Creek.

10th mo 1797: A certificate from Gunpowder MM was produced by Ann Taylor wife of Henry Taylor. A certificate was sent to Redstone MM for Sarah Plummer who removed with her husband Moses Plummer.

11th mo 1797: A certificate from New Garden MM was produced by Hanah Williams.

2nd mo 1798: Alexandria preparative meeting informs that Grace Woodrow has gone out in marriage with Israel Musgrove.

4th mo 1798: Complaint against Sarah Caveing [Cavin] formerly Baker for marrying out of unity. A certificate will be sent to Westland MM for Mary Gregg and her children (Elizabeth, Thomas, George, Martha, William, Levi, Samuel)

5th mo 1798: A certificate from Goose Creek was produced by James Moore, Phebe his wife, and children Joseph, Thomas, Sarah, Elizabeth, and James. Complaint against Sarah Williams, formerly Roach, for marrying out of unity.

6th mo 1798: A certificate from Goose Creek in Bedford Co., VA was produced by Mary Harris.

7th mo 1798: A certificate from Indian Spring was produced by Elizabeth Ellicott, with her husband Nathaniel Ellicott, and children John, Hannah, Nathaniel, and Cassandria. A certificate from Buckingham MM was produced by Tacy McPherson, wife of Isaac McPherson. Sarah Scott some time ago brought a paper to condemn her former conduct. Friends have now decided she is sincere and can be accepted into membership.

9th mo 1798: Rachel James, formerly Hough, hath been guilty of unchaste company.

10th mo 1798: Elizabeth Cole visited from Deer Creek MM, likewise Hannah Jackson from New Garden in PA. Lydia Green requests a certificate to Baltimore MM. A certificate will be sent to Goose Creek for Pleasant Hague who now resides there.[pages missing, skips from 181 to 184] Sarah Cavins presented a paper condemning her former conduct.

5th mo 1799: A certificate from Gunpowder MM was produced for Miriam Richardson, wife of Fielder. Testimony was produced against Rebecca Lloyd.

6th mo 1799: Ruth Smith, wife of David Smith, produced a certificate from Hopewell MM.

9th mo 1799: Complaint against Sarah Combs, formerly Richardson for out going in marriage.

10th mo 1799: Mary Suayne [Swain] visited from Nottingham MM.

12th mo 1799: A certificate from Pipe Creek MM was produced by Rebecca Kenworthy with her husband William Kenworthy.

1st mo 1800: Catharine Pugh proposed as overseer of Alexandria preparative meeting. Tacy McCann condemned her outgoing in marriage.

4th mo 1800: Dorothy Scooly requests a certificate to Resdstone? MM.

9th mo 1800: A certificate from Hopewell MM was produced by Perminus Lamburn and Hannah his wife.

10th mo 1800: Abraham Davis requests a certificate for himself, wife, and children. Likewise one for his daughter Tacy McCann, both to Redstone MM.

11th mo 1800: James and Dinah Young forwarded a paper condemning their outgoing in marriage, with a recommendation from Westland MM. A paper of acknowledgment was forwarded for Rebecca Clawson, formerly Clark, condemning her outgoing in marriage, from Cane Creek MM.

12th mo 1800: A certificate from Hopewell MM was produced for Aquilla Janney, Ruth his wife, and children Isaac, Hannah, Daniel, Rebecca, Aquilla, William, and Israel. Hannah and Merab Scott request a certificate to Pipe Creek MM.

GOOSE CREEK MONTHLY MEETING MARRIAGE CERTIFICATES

Joel Lewis, son of John and Alice, married Sarah Daniel, daughter of William and Esther, 9th day of 3rd mo 1786. Wit: William Daniel, Esther Daniel, Alice Lewis, Mary Smith, Esther Daniel, Anna Steer, Benjamin Steer, Thomas Cadwalader, Jane Cadwalader, Jesse Lewis, Martha Daniel, David Smith, Hannah Janney Junr., Thomas Gregg, Rebekah Gregg, Benjamin Daniel, ___ Lewis, Hannah Lewis, George Lewis, Evan Lewis, Israel Janney, Thomas Hatcher, Isaac Nicholls, Anna Janney, Ruth Gregg, Agness Dillon, Moses Cadwalader, Isaac Nicholls, Thomas Smith, John Hirst, Stephen Gregg, James Hatcher, Ann Gregg, John Smith, William Smith, Anne Smith, Elizabeth Howel, Deborah Howell.

David Hoge, {married 4th mo 1786 Ruth Gregg, per men's minutes}

Joseph Rhodes, of Bedford Co. VA, son of Moses Rhodes, {married Martha Daniel, per women's minutes, 5th mo 1786}.

James Trahern {married Dinah Gregg, per women's minutes, 5th mo 1786}

Robert Whitacre of Alexandria, son of John Whitacre, dec'd and Naomi his wife, married Hannah Janney, daughter of Jacob Janney, dec'd, and __ [10 mo 1786, per women's minutes]. Wit: Hannah Janney, Naomi Whitacre, Blackstone Janney, Benja Whitacre, Thomas Gregg, Israel Janney, Rebekah Gregg, Anna Janney, Phels Whitacre, Joseph Whitacre, Joshua Whitacre, Alice Whitacre, Esther Whitacre, Mary Janney, William Janney, Eliza. Janney, [others too faint to read].

Amos Hibbs, son of William Hibbs {married Mary Pool, 10th mo 1786, per women's minutes}.

Abijah Richards, son of Rowland Richards of Frederick Co. VA, and his wife Mary, dec'd; married Esther Daniel, daughter of William and Esther Daniel, 9th day of 3rd mo 1787. Wit: William Daniel, Esther Daniel, Rowland Richard, Thomas Gregg, Rebekah Gregg, ___ Richards, Elizabeth Richards, Susanna Richards, Joseph Daniel, Mary Smith, Mary Smith Junr., Elizabeth Howel, Deborah Howel, Jane Howel, Elizabeth Smith, Ann Smith, Hannah Smith, George Smith, William Paxon, Ruth Cadwalader, James Hatcher, ..., Thomas Hatcher, Rebekah Hatcher, ..., Wm.

Kenworthy, William Smith, Nathan Spencer, Hannah Spencer, Alice Smith, ... [illegible name].

Thomas Smith, son of John Smith and Ann his wife, of Frederick Co., VA; married Phebe Sinkler, daughter of James Sinkler and Mary his wife, at South Fork, 10th day of 10th mo 1787. Wit: John Smith, James Sinkler, Mary Sinkler, Robert Haines, Joshua Swayne, Isaac Gibson, James McNabb, Rachel Gibson, Esther Gibson, Archibald ..., Wm Barnside, Jacob Gregg, Samuel Gregg, Ann Gregg, James Sinkler Jr, Rebekah Trahern, Dinah Trahern, Susanna Smith, Miriam Gibson, Lettice McVicker, Thomas Hamilton, Isaac Taylor, Francis Peyton, James Trahern, Isaac Brown, Martha Brown, Anna Lemert, Ann Gibson, Esther Gibson, Euphamy Lacy, Ann Peyton, Moses Gibson, Rebekah Wilks, Mary Burson, Rebekah Burson, Mary Wilks, Elizabeth Russell, Ann Votaw, Alice Gibson, Tacey Lacey, John Preston, Rebekah Preston, Hannah Sweat, William Bronaugh, Charles Dulin, William Paxson, Jasper Seybold, James Burson, Jonathan Burson, William Trahern, Joseph Gibson, John Gibson, Sarah Gibson.

Solomon Dixon married Ann Lemard at South Fork, 3rd day of 12th mo 1788. Wit: Isaac Votaw, Benjamin Burson, Hannah Burson, Rebekah Preston, Mary Cleton, John Moore, Zachariah Ellyson, Daniel Eaches, Mary Votaw, John Preston, William Jones, Thomas Fred, Joshua Fred, Moses Gibson, John Gibson, William Reynolds, Jacob Lemard, Mary Lemard, Mary Climan, Esther Gibson, Samuel Dixon, Philip Clunard, Lydia Hayzel, Phebe Gibson, William Kinnan, Isaac Brown, Martha Brown, James Burson, Edward Pues, Jonathan Burson, Joseph Gregg, James Sinkler, Mary Sinkler, Joseph Burson, John Dyer, Deborah Drake, Mary Mason Bronaugh, Ann Cummings, Thomas Brown, Ann Dillon, Elizabeth Russell, George Burson.

William Hatcher, son of John and Sarah Hatcher, married Mary Smith Jr., daughter of Thomas and Rachel Smith, at meeting house near gap of Short Hill, 30th day of 4th mo 1789. Wit: John Hatcher, Sarah Hatcher, Thomas Smith, Rachel Smith, Elizabeth Russell, Elizabeth Smith, James Love, William Russell, Nicholas Snicker, James Love Jr., Bobby White, Natha Hough, Thomas Pue, Abram Lodge, Isabella Lodge, Thomas Smith, Martha Smith, Elisha Jenney, Joshua Hatcher, Jane Hatcher, John Stokes, Stephen Gregg, Joseph Beal, Thomas Janney, Thomas Gregg, Stacy Taylor, Fanney Taylor, John Russell, Samuel Gregg, Noah Hatcher,

David Smith, Hannah Smith, Sarah Smith, Sarah Love, Ann Smith, Elizabeth Love, Susanna Gregg, William Smith, William Daniel, William Smith, Esther Daniel, Martha White, Thomas White, Ann Fisher, Betty Fisher, Joseph Fisher, James Roach, John Hollingwsorth, Josabed Lodge, John Potts, McCabe.

James Curl married Ruth Randal, daughter of Joseph and Rachel Randal, at Goose Creek Meeting house, 2nd day of 7th mo 1789. Wit: Joseph Curl, Rebekah Curl, Sarah Scott, Isaac Hatcher, John Bland, Hannah Curl, Hannah Bland, Rebekah Dillon, Elizabeth Haines, Elizabeth Williams, Ann Gregg, Mary Smith, Hannah Pool, Ann Hirst, Edith Hatcher, Mary Hatcher, Ann Hatcher, Mary Randal, William Nickols, William Kenworthy, Moses Dillon, Aldon Dillon, Joseph Randal, William Brown, Rebecca Dillon, Elizabeth Brown, James Hatcher, Benjamin Mead, John Hirst, Stephen Gregg, Israel Janney, Sarah Smith, John Brown, Jacob Harriss, Rebekah Nickols, Rebekah Hatcher, Thomas Hatcher.

Nathan Spencer married Ann Smith at Goose Creek 29th day of 4th mo 1790. Wit: Nathan Spencer, Hannah Spencer, William Smith, Ann Smith, Margaret Spencer, Samuel Spencer, Alice Spencer, John Spencer, Lydia Spencer, Elizabeth Smith, Mary Smith, Hannah Spencer, William Spencer, Thomas Janney, Rachel Spencer, Sarah Spencer, Amy Greeg, Rebekah Gregg, Thomas Gregg, Jane Smith, Mercy Smith, Rachel Daniel, Edith Smith, John Gregg, Mary Hirst, Sarah Smith, Mary Janney, Ann Mead, Hannah Pool, Samuel Howell, Jane Howell, Esther Daniel, Joseph Daniel, Jacob Gregg, Benjamin Mead, James Hatcher, Blackstone Janney, William Daniel, John Hirst, Stephen Gregg, Israel Janney, Isaac Nickols, Joseph Pool, Samuel Gregg, Ann Gregg.

Joseph Burson married Abigale Conard, 12th day of 1st mo 1791, at South Fork. Wit: James Burson, Mary Burson, Jane Conard, Edward Conard, Jonathan Burson, Rebekah Burson, Lydia Burson, Ann Harriss, Elizabeth Bronaugh, ... Bronaugh, Edward Marton, Rachel Patterson, Henry ..., Tamer Burson, Jehue Burson, Jeremiah Wm. Bronaugh, ..., Rebekah Preston, Sarah Conard, Margaret Mead, Christian Mead, Catharine Davis, Amy ..., Thomas Brown, Ann Brown, Rachel Lane, ... Gibson, Isaac Burson, Martha Brown[Burson], James Trahern, William Reeder, Mary Reeder, John Bradfield, Hannah Bradfield, Edward Connard Jr., Joseph Shields, Isaac Votaw, Edward Mead, Thomas Gore, Benjamin ..., [5 names too faint to read] Joel ..., Sarah Fred.

James Dillon married Mary Smith, 27th day of 1st mo 1791 at Goose Creek. Wit: William Daniel, Esther Daniel, ... [many too faint to read], John Hirst, Mary Hirst, John Gregg, Ruth Gregg, Sarah Smith, Martha Smith, William Smith, Thomas Smith, Aldon Dillon, Hannah Dillon, Martha ..., John Randle, Mary Taylor, Fanny Taylor, James Hatcher.

Isaac White married Jane Smith, 31st day of 3rd mo 1791. Wit: Thomas White, Ann White, William Smith, Ann Smith, Levy Luken, Marcy Smith, Elizabeth Moore, Jane Janney, Jane Howell, Amy Gregg, Ann White, Asa Moore, Samuel Howell, Thomas Gregg, William Daniel, Thomas Gregg, Rebekah Gregg, Nathan Spencer, Hannah Spencer, Ruth Gregg, Jonathan Taylor, Hannah Pool, Esther Daniel, Samuel Smith, Rachel Smith, James Hatcher, Solomon Hoge, John Hirst, Stephen Gregg, James Moore, Phebe Moore, Rebekah Hirst, Sarah Smith, Ann Hirst, Christian Mead, Edith Hatcher, Ann Hatcher, Sarah Hatcher, Benjamin Mead, Israel Janney, Hannah Janney, Mary Hatcher, Mary Hirst, Catherine Hatcher, Ann Gibson, Edith Nickols, William Hatcher, John Sinkler, Thomas Gregg, Jacob Gregg.

William Kenworthy, son of William and Mary Kenworthy of Frederick Co., MD; married Rebekah Hoge, daughter of Solomon Hoge, and Ann his wife, dec'd, 28th day of 4th mo 1791. Wit: William Kenworthy, Mary Kenworthy, Solomon Hoge, Mary Hoge, Sarah Gore, Benjamin Steer, Ann Steer, Joshua Gore, David Hoge, George Nichols, Sarah Gregg, Sarah Nickols, Samuel Nickols, William Nickols, William Hoge, Catherine Hatcher, Isaac Nickols, Blackstone Janney, Thomas Conard, Ann Gore, Hannah Williams, John Hirst, Mary Hirst, Thomas Gregg, Rebekah Gregg, William Smith, Jane White, Rachel Spencer, Hannah Janney, James Hatcher, Anna Canby, Israel Janney, Jonas Janney, Benjamin Mead, Ann Mead, Isaac Nickols, John Gregg, John Brown, Jacob Gregg, Daniel Stone, James More, Jonathan Taylor, John Williams, Margaret Mead, Christian Mead, Samuel Hatcher, Elisha Janney, Ruth Janney, Edith Nickols, Mary Nickols, Margery Hatcher, Hannah Brown.

John Brown, son of William and Elizabeth Brown, married Ann Hirst, daughter of John and Mary Hisrt, 5th day of 5th mo 1791. Wit: John Hirst, Mary Hirst, Elizabeth Brown, Richard Brown, Rebecca Hirst, John Brown, Betsy Brown, Sarah Brown, Jesse Hirst, Phineas Newton, Daniel Hirst, William Brown, James Hatcher, Catharine Hatcher, Hannah Janney, Anna Janney, Margaret Ingleden, Margaret Indleden, Sarah

Slocome, Sarah Conard, Thomas Siddall, Edward Conard, Eliza Fairhirst, Richard Tavenner, Sarah Hatcher, Jacob Harriss, Samuel Gregg, Elizabeth Pool, George Fairsurst, Thomas Hatcher, Ann Hatcher, Edith Hatcher, Mary Hatcher, Edith Nickols, Margery Hatcher, David Casson, Judith Conard, Martha Hirst, Solomon Hoge, Mary Hoge, Esther Daniel, Rebekah Gregg, Ann Mead, Israel Janney, James Moore, Sarah Gregg, Jane White, Jane Janney, Barnerd Taylor, Benjamin Mead, William Daniel.

Israel Pool, son of Benjamin and Rebekah Pool, married Jane Howel, daughter of Timothy and Rebekah Howell, married 29th day of 12th mo 1791. Wit: Timothy Howel, Rebekah Howel, Israel Janney, Elizabeth Pool, Jacob Irey, Jane Janney, Samuel Howell, Nancy Thompson, Deborah Howel, Hannah Janney, James Gregg, William Smith, William Daniel, Mary Wilson, Amy Gregg, Jane Best, Ruth Hague, Elizabeth Parker, Isaac Schooley, Abijah Janney, Solomon Hoge, James Hatcher, Bleakstone Janey, Jonas Janney, Thomas Hatcher, Elisha Janney, Stephen Gregg, Sarah Smith, Joseph Holmes, Joseph Gore, Martha Best, Jacob Gregg, Joseph Daniel, Rachel Daniel.

John Smith, son of John Smith of Frederick Co., married Esther Gibson, daughter of Joseph Gibson, 7th day of 3rd mo 1792. Wit: Joseph Gibson, Phebe Gibson, Ann Smith, James Gibson, Mary Sinkler, Alice Gibson, Thos Smith, Cornelious Romine, James Sinkler, Moses Gibson, Sarah Gibson, Rachel Gibson, James Sinkler, James Sinkler, Amos Gibson, Miner Gibson, Rebekah Gibson, Mary Gibson, William Gibson, Esther Sinkler, Moses Gibson Jr., Thomas Vickers, Isaac Brown, Martha Brown, William Reeder, Edward Rees, John Haines, Benjamin Myres, Mary Reeder, Sarah Evens, John Glasscock, Stephen McPherson, Sarah Pancoast, Benjamin Fulkerson, James McPherson, James Hamilton, Thomas Evans, George Dulin, James Burson, James Trahern, Rebekah Preston, Rebekah Burson, Amy Vickers, Sarah Brown, Joseph Burson, Levi Lukens, Jacob Myers, Elizabeth Fry, Charles Glascock, James Lewis, Jacob Lewis, Lewis Lemert.

Jacob Gregg, son of Thomas and Rebekah Gregg, married Mary Sinkler Jr., daughter of James and Mary Sinkler, 30th day of 6th mo 1792. Wit: Thomas Gregg, Rebekah Gregg, James Sinkler, Mary Sinkler, Thomas Smith, Samuel Gregg, John Sinkler, Israel Gregg, James Sinkler, Solomon Nickols, Hannah Nickols, Abner Gibson, George Sinkler, Jane Sinkler,

Aney Gregg, Phebe Gibson, Isaac Brown, Martha Brown, Ruth Janney, Esther Gibson, Sarah Evans, Hannah Burson, Mary Burson, Isaac Gibson, Daniel Ferndn(sic), James Sinkler, Miram Gibson, Esther Sinkler, John Votaw, John Brown, George Burson, Jonathan Burson, James Dillon, Elizabeth McPherson, Phebe Yates, Lydia Gibson, Sarah Gibson, Sarah Skiner, Rebekah Gibson, Mary Reeder, Corns. Skinner Jr., Annie Burson, James Burson, Joseph Burson, James Burson, Simon Hains, Elisabeth Hains, Sarah Brown, Rebekah Burson, Thomas Beaford, Aaron Burson, Abraham Brown, Pownsend Peyton, Benjamin Mead, William Reeder, Benjamin Yates, Alice Gibson, Christian Mead, Margaret Mead, Elisha Janney, Benjamin Myres, James Trahern, Joseph Gibson, Phebe Gibson.

Joseph Talbott married Rebekah Hirst, 1st day of 11th mo 1792. Wit: John Hirst, Mary Hirst, Jesse Hirst, David Hirst, Samuel Talbott, Mary Talbott, Thomas Hirst, Ann Brown, Sarah Talbott, Sarah Smith, Mahlon Janney, Edward Conard, Sarah Janney, John Brown, Usala Plummer, Judith Plummer, Israel Janney, Talbott, Phineahas Heston, William Heston, Sarah Smith, Ann Cunard, Elizabeth Talbott, Mary Hoge, Hannah Janney, Mary Hatcher, William Hatcher, Joseph Talbott, Sarah Cunard, Sarah Smith, Bernard Taylor, Ann Smith, Rachel Smith, Ann Hinds, Benjamin Mead, Hannah Spencer, Edith Nickols, Jonathan Taylor, Hannah M., James Moore, Phebe Moore, William Smith, John Gregg, Thomas Gregg, Rebekah Gregg, Hannah Spencer Jr., John Hirst Jr., Blackstone Janney, Rachel Spencer, William Daniel, Nathan Spencer.

William Smith, son of Henry Smith dec'd, married Sarah Gregg, daughter of John Gregg, 7th day of 12th mo 1792. Wit: John Gregg, Ruth Gregg, Alice Smith, Stephen Gregg, Thomas Smith, Ann Smith, David Smith, Solomon Hoge, Hannah Janney, Sarah Janney, Israel Janney, Mary Baker, Mary Hirst, Sarah Smith, Mary Dillon, Rebekah Gregg, Ann Janney, Mary Hoge, Aaron Smith, James Moore, William Daniel, Phebe Moore, Sarah Thomas, Thomas Gore, Ruth Hauge, Stephen Gregg, Caleb Gregg, Ruth Hoge, Esther Daniel, Bernard Taylor, Sarah Taylor, Elizabeth Thompson, Hannah Smith, Ann Smith, John Stokes, Elizabeth Stokes, Abraham Smith, James Heaton, Martha Best, Mercey Smith, Benjamin Mead, Jonathan Taylor, Ann Mead, Mahlon Taylor, Mary Taylor, Isaac Hoge, John Sinclair, William Smith, Timothy Howel, Jane Janney.

John Votaw, son of Isaac and Ann Votaw, married Rebekah Burson, daughter of James and Mary Burson, 9th day of 1st mo 1793 at South Fork. Wit: James Burson, Mary Burson, Aaron Burson, Henry Plaster, Lydia Burson, Samuel Dunkin, Anna Dunkin, James Burson, Mary Ellyson, Solomon Burson, John Bradfield, Ann Burson, John Brown, Hannah Bradfield, Moses Burson, Joseph Burson, James Trahorn, Dinah Trahern, William Reeder, Mary Reeder.

Isaac Schooley, son of William and Ann Schooley, of Fayette Co., PA, married Sarah Slocum, daughter of of Robert Slocum, dec'd, and Abigail his wife, late of Loudoun Co., 3rd day of 10th mo 1793. Wit: John Schooley Jr., Timothy Howell, Rebekah Howell, Israel Janney, Anna Janney, William Hatcher, Mary Hatcher, Joseph Cavin, Thomas Slocum, Elizabeth Parker, Rebekah Gregg, Sarah Conard, Ann Conard, Peggy Mead, Mary Hirst, Mary Janney, Martha Hirst, Phebe Howell, Jane Pool, Hannah Janney, Ann Hisrt ?, William Daniel, James Moore, William White, Patterson Ingledue, Thomas Smith, George Fairhurst, Bleackstone Janney, John Hirst, David Hirst, John McClun, Samuel Smith, Bernard Taylor, Benjamin Mead, Thomas Gregg, James Dillon, Jonathan Taylor, Mahlon Taylor, Thomas Gore, John Sinclair, John Hirst Jr., Samuel Howell, Margaret Ingledeu, Jesse Hirst, Elizab. Fairhurst.

Noah Hatcher, son of John and Sarah Hatcher married Rachel Beanes, daughter of William and Hannah Beanes, 7th day 11th mo 1793. Wit: John Hatcher, William Beans, Sarah Hatcher, Isaac Hough, William Hatcher, Timothy Beans, David Gosden, Rebekah Nickols, Sarah Nickols, Ruth Beans, Edith Hatcher, Edith Nickols, Margery Hatcher, Sarah Fisher, Jane Beans, Matthew Beans, Job Cooper, An Dillon, Hannah Janney, Israel Janney, Solomon Hoge, Mary Hatcher, Stephen Gregg, Margaret Mead, Sarah Harry [Harris?], Asenath Mead, Hannah Mellon, Amos Paxson, Samuel Hatcher, Samuel Smith, Rachel Smith, James Dillon Jr., Samuel Russel, Sarah Russel, John Hirst, James Moore, James Dillon, Mary Dillon, William Nickols, Joshua Hatcher, James Hatcher, Mary Hatcher Jr., Fanny Taylor, Thomas Hatcher.

Jacob Myers, son of Benjamin Myers and Rachel his former wife, dec'd, married Sarah Pancoast, daughter of Adin and Abigail Pancoast, 15th day of 5th mo 1794. Wit: Elizabeth Myers, Benjamin Myers, John Pancoast, Walter Elgin, Margery Nickols, Isaac Myers, John Gibson, James Gibson, Isaac Nickols, Moses ? Gibson, Nancy Yours, Hannah Spencer, Alice

Gibson, Miriam Gibson, Thomas Hatcher, John Hirst, Mary Hatcher, Jonathan Taylor, Ann Taylor, Benjamin Mead, James Nickols, Rebekah Ewers, Samuel Howell, Levi Lukens, Elizabeth Lukens, Thomas Gregg, Bernard Taylor, Sarah Taylor, Sarah Cunard, Rebekah Gregg, Sarah Smith, Asenath Mead, Ann Cunard, Margery Hatcher, Jonathan Ewer, James Martin, James Moore, Phebe Moore, William Hatcher, William Smith, William Daniel, Jonas Janney, Elizabeth Fryer, Isaac Nickols, Margaret Mead.

Elisha Janney, of Alexandria, son of Jacob and Hannah Janney of Loudoun, married Mary Gibson, daughter of John and Ruth Gibson, 4th day of 3rd mo 1795 at South Fork. Wit: Hannah Janney, Sarah Gibson, Rachel Gibson, Mary Gibson, Amos Gibson, Meriam Gibson, James Trahern, William Reeder, Joseph Gibson, John Gibson, George Gibson, Jonathan Gibson, William Gibson, Samuel Gibson, James Gibson, Jonas Gore, William Elgin, Mary Reeder, James Burson, David Hoge, Mary Hatcher, Jonathan Taylor, Ann Taylor, Jonathan Fouin?, Joseph Burson, James Dillon, Thomas Gibson, Benjamin Yates, Phebe Yates, Dinah Trahern, Elizabeth Wilkinson, Jonathan Lovett, Ann Dillon.

Jonathan Lovett, son of Daniel and Sarah Lovett, married Ann Gore, daughter of Joshua and Sarah Gore, 5th day of 3rd mo 1795 . Wit: Joshua Gore, William Gore, Solomon Hoge, Mary Hoge, George Nickols, William Hoge, Elias Lovett, Benjamin Mead, Solomon Gore, Jonas Gore, Ruth Lumm, Lydia Lovett, Richard Vanpelt, Eliza Fairhurst, Thomas Whiteacre?, Thomas Hutson, Isaac Nickols, Margery Nickols, Israel Janney, Bernard Taylor, Jonas Janney, Isaac Hoge, Solomon Hoge, Joseph Gore, David Hoge, Lydia Janney, Hannah Mellon, Ann Mead, John Hirst, Mary Hirst, Thomas Gregg, Sarah Smith, James Heaton, Lydia Heaton, Samuel Smith, James Moore, Phebe Moore, Anne Janney, John Sinclair, Daniel Eacher, Ruth Hoge, Elizabeth Hoge.

Asa Holloway of Stafford, VA, son of George and Ruth Holloway, his wife, dec'd; married Elizabeth Pool, daughter of Benjamin Pool and Rebekah, his wife, dec'd, 28th day of 4th mo 1796. Wit: Joseph Pool, Elizabeth Pool, Hannah Janney, Rebekah Howel, Asenath Mead, Jane Janney, Hannah Pool, Hannah Williams, Rebekah Branson?, Aaron Holloway, Israel Pool, David Hirst, Sarah Iry, Solomen Hoge, William Smith, Samuel Howell, Joseph Daniel, Rebekah Gregg, Samuel Smith, Rachel Smith, Mary ___, Mary Nickols, Mary Janney, Abigail? Nickols, James Moore, Phebe Moore,

Bernard Taylor, Sarah Taylor, Benjamin Bradfield, ... [two names illegible], Lydia Heaton, Jonathan Taylor, Hannah Spencer, William Hatcher, Benjamin Mead, ..., Rebekah Janney, ..., Jesse Hirst, Mary Hirst, Martha Hirst, Mary Hatcher, James Hatcher.

William Ewers, son of John and Sarah Ewers, married Amy Gregg, daughter of Thomas and Rebekah Gregg, 2nd day of 11th mo 1797. Wit: John Ewers, Thomas Gregg, Rebekah Gregg, Hannah Janney, Sarah Gardner, Lydia Janney, Thomas Sharp, Israel Janney, James Dillon, Susanna Gregg, Nathan Spencer, E. Ewers, Ann Spencer, James Trahern, Dinah Trahern, Phebe Howell, Mary Hatcher, John Gregg, Jonas Janney, Bleackstone Janney, William Daniel, James Moore, Phebe Moore, Bernard Taylor, Sarah Taylor, Ann Mead, William Gore, John Hirst, Mary Hirst, Isaac Nickols, Solomon Hoge, Mary Dillon, Christian Mead.

William Piggott, son of John and Phebe Piggott, married Mary Nickols, daughter of William and Sarah Nickols, 30th day of 11 mo 1797. Wit: John Piggott, William Nickols, Sarah Nickols, Phebe Piggott, Ruth Janney, Levi Tate, Rebekah Hatcher, Samuel Piggott, Ezekiel Smith, Edith Tate, Mary McCullah, Mahlon Taylor, Mary Taylor, Sarah Smith, Ebenezar Piggott, Solomon Hoge, Isaac Nickols Sr., James Hatcher, Hannah Beanes, Isaac Nickols, Nathan Spencer, Hannah Spencer, William Daniel, Margery Nickols, Ann Spencer, Isaac Nickols, Catharine Hatcher, Swithin Nickols, Mary Taylor, Lydia Heaton, Elizabeth Hatcher, Mary Hatcher, Bernard Taylor, Mary Hollingsworth, Esther Daniel, Ruth Beanes, Rebekah Hatcher, Samuel Nickols, Nathan Spencer, William Nickols, Anna Mason.

Swithin Nickols, son of Jacob and Tacey Nickols of Campbell Co., married Rebekah Hatcher, daughter of James and Catharine Hatcher, 29th day of 11th mo 1798. Wit: James Hatcher, Catherine Hatcher, James Nickols, Margery Nickols, Thomas Hatcher, George Hatcher, Isaac Nickols Jr., Elizabeth Hatcher, Edith Hatcher, Mary Hatcher, Margery Hatcher Jr., William Spencer, Sarah Spencer, Richard Tavenner, Ann Tavenner, James Hatcher Jr., Isaac Hatcher, Rachel Hatcher, James Tavenner, John Hatcher, Judith Walters, Solomon Gibson, Eli Janney, Noah Hatcher, Rachel Hatcher, Sarah Tavenner, Jonas Tavener, Esther Janney, Mary Janney, John Hatcher Senr., Lydia Hoge, Ann Pancoast, Lydia Pancoast, Margery Hatcher Senr., Lydia Janney, Samuel Nichols Jr., William Hoge, Eliza Fairhurst, Ann Nichols, Rachel Fairhurst, William Nickols Jr.,

Samuel Hatcher, Samuel Russel, Sarah Russel, James Walters, Benjamin Bradfield, Jonas Janney, Israel Jannney, Sarah Smith, William Hatcher, Mary Hatcher, Rachel Smith, William Nickols Senr., Sarah Nickols, Solomon Hoge, Mary Hoge, William Daniel, Esther Daniel, Bernard Taylor, Levi Tate, Edith Tate, James Gibson, Mary McCullah, Margaret Nickols, Elizabeth Marsh.

Samuel Nickols, son of William and Sarah Nickols married Mary Janney, daughter of Bleackstone and Mary Janney, 6th day of 12th mo 1798. Wit: William Nickols, Sarah Nickols, Bleackstone Janney, Margery Nickols, Israel Nickols, Levi Tate, Edith Tate, Isaac Nickols, Ruth Janney, William Nickols, James Hatcher, Edith Hatcher, Jonas Janey, Swithin Nickols, Abel Janney, Rebekah Nickols, Ann Mead, Cosmelia Janney, Lydia Janney, Lydia Nickols, James Mead, Thomas Janney, Margaret Mead, Solomon Hoge, Elizabeth Hatcher, Mary Hatcher, Sally Gore, Phin Janney, William Hoge, Bernard Taylor, Sarah Taylor, Jesse Hirst, Hannah Spencer Jr., Sarah Spencer, Willliam Hatcher, Mary Hatcher, Nathan Spencer, Hannah Spencer, Isaac Hatcher, Joshua Gore, George Janney, Eliza Fairhurst, Red___ Fisher, Thomas Clowes, Isaac Nickols, Abijah Janney, James Janney, Judith Waller, Asenath Mead.

Joshua Gregg, son of John and Ruth Gregg, married Lydia Hoge, daughter of Solomon and Mary Hoge, 1st day of 5th mo 1800. Wit: John Gregg, Mary Hoge, Ruth Gregg, David Hoge, Ruth Hoge, Rebekah Kenworthy, Isaac Nickols, Margery Hoge, Margery Nickols, William Smith, Sarah Smith, Caleb Gregg, Hannah Gregg, Isaac Hoge, Mahlon Gregg, Joshua Gore, John Gregg, Solomon Gore, Joshua Hoge, Lydia Gregg, William Hoge, John Hirst, Benjamin Bradfield, James Trahern, Thomas Hatcher, William Nickols, Elisha Janney, Bernard Taylor, Sarah Taylor, John Donohoe, Sarah Donohoe, Sarah Smith, Rebecca Gregg, Mary Dillon, Mary Kirst, Hannah Janney, Mary Smith, Samuel Smith, Rachel Smith, William Smith, Thomas Janney, Ruth Janney, James Hatcher.

Jacob Brown, son of William and Elizabeth Brown, married Judith Walters, daughter of George and Dinah Walters, 4th day of 12th mo 1800. Wit: George Walters, Dinah Walters, William Brown, John Brown, Ann Brown, David Hirst, Ann Hirst, William Nickols Jr., Margery Nickols, Lydia Heaton, Mary Hirst, Sarah Smith, Israel Janney, Rebekah Gregg, James Dillon, Mary Dillon, Solomon Hoge, Mahlon Taylor, Mary Taylor,

Mary Nickols, Benjamin Mead, Bernard Taylor, Lightfoot Janney, Levi Hollingsworth, John Hirst, Samuel Meade, Jonas Janney, Samuel Nickols, Bleackston Janney, Israel Nickols, Lydia Janney, Joshua Hoge.

BURIALS OF FRIENDS IN GOOSE CREEK GRAVEYARD THAT ARE NOT PROPERLY RECORDED SINCE THE SPRING OF THE YEAR 1781.

[Dates are burials, not deaths]

Margaret Philips, wife of Edmund, 9th of 4th mo 1781.
Isaac Piggott, son of John, 11th of 7th mo 1781.
Susannah Smith, daughter of Samuel, 10th of 8th mo 1781.
William & Jonathan Hutton, sons of Samuel, 1st of 9th mo 1781. Sarah Hutton, daughter of Samuel, 12th of 9th mo 1781.
Elizabeth Gore, wife of Joshua, 27th of 1st mo 1782.
Jacob Janney, son of Jacob, 3rd of 4th mo 1782.
Mary Hutton, wife of Samuel, 26th of 4th mo 1782.
John Nickols, 1st of 8th mo 1782.
Mercy Philips, daughter of Edmund, 4th of 10th mo 1782.
Elizabeth Nichols, wife of James, 7th of 2nd mo 1784.
Samuel Smith, 25th of 8th mo 1784.
Thomas Clowes, 9th of 5th mo 1784.
Martha Brown, wife of John, 28th of 6th mo 1784.
Shadraach Luellen, 10th of 2nd mo 1785.
William Webster, 30th of 4th mo 1785.
George Whitacre, 13th of 6th mo 1785.
William Dillon, 30th of 3rd mo 1788.
William Dillon, son of William, 27th of 9th mo 1788.
Grace Beel, daughter of of Joseph, 10th of 5th mo 1789.
John Taylor, 14th of 9th mo 1786.
Samuel Hutton, 13th of 10th mo 1786.
John Smith, 14th of 11th mo 1786.
Ruth Pancoast, 23rd of 1st mo 1787.
Jacob Jannes [Janney], son of Jonas, 13th of 4th mo 1787.
Hannah Whitacre, wife of Robert, 31st of 5th mo 1787.
Rebekah Randal, daughter of of Abraham, 30th of 9th mo 1787.
Hannah Smith, son of Thos Smith Jr., 28th of 6th mo 1789.

William Hoge, 5th of 7th mo 1789.
Rebekah Dillon, wife of James, 7th of 9th mo 1789.
Ann Dillon Sr., 23rd of 3rd mo 1790.
Hannah Dillon, 14th of 4th mo 1791.
Rebekah Poole, 26th of 4th mo 1791.
Mary Finnikin, 4th of 5th mo 1791.
Ruth Steer, 19th of 7th mo 1792.
Absolom Beens, 23rd of 7th mo 1793.
Samuel Pool, son of Israel, 2nd of 8th mo 1793.
Grace Beel Sr., 3rd of 10th mo 1793.
___ Hoge, daughter of of Isaac, 9th of 10th mo 1793.
Joseph Parker, 23rd of 11th mo 1793.
Rachel Taylor, daughter of Bernard, 8th of 2nd mo 1794.
Timothy Howel, 11th of 2nd mo 1794.
Margaret Ingledue, 5th of 3rd mo 1794.
George Smith, 29th of 3rd mo 1794.
Keziah Smith, daughter of Samuel, 17th of 7th mo 1794.
Rebekah & Jesse Gregg, children of Thomas, 19th of 1st mo 1794.
Jacob Janney, son of Blackston, 11th of 8th mo 1794.
Phebe Janney, 17th of 8th mo 1794.
Blackston Janney, 21st of 8th mo 1794.
Rebekah Janney, daughter of Jonas, 3rd of 9th mo 1794.
Benjamin Bradfield's child, 22nd of 3rd mo 1801.
Alice Gibson, age 89, 11th of 4th mo 1790.
Benjamin Burson, age 52, 22nd of 12th mo 1790.
Ann McPherson, age 35, 27th of 8th mo [no year, prob. 1790]

REGISTERS OF BIRTHS AND BURIALS {ORGANIZED BY FAMILIES}

Jacob Janney, buried 5th of 9th mo 1786, married Hannah Ingledue, issue: Rebekah, Bleakston, Jonas, Joseph.

Solomon Hoge Senr. married ____, issue: Sarah, b. 8th of 11th mo 1752;; Joseph, b. 1st of 4th mo 1754, d. about 14 mo; David, b. 3rd of 11th mo 1755, d. about 14 mos; Solomon, b. 30th of 10th mo 1757; David, b. 21st of 3rd mo 1759; Ann, b. 20th of 2nd mo 1761; Isaac, b. 30th of 4th mo 1763; Mary, b. 7th of 3rd mo 1765; Hannah, b. 7th of 3rd mo 1767, d.

18th of 6th mo 1769; Tamar, b. 22nd of 4th mo 1769, d. 9 mos 4 days old; Rebekah, b. 11th of 12th mo 1770.

Solomon Hoge Sr. married Mary Nickols. Their issue: Lydia b. 26th of 9th mo 1774; William b. 23rd of 11th mo 1776; Joshua b. 8th of 2nd mo 1779; George b. 23rd of 5th mo 1781, d. 1782; Margery b. 28th of 12th mo 1783; Jesse b. 2nd of 4th mo 1785; Amy b. 21st of 3rd mo 1788, d. 11th of 7th mo 1794.

Edward Rees, married Sarah Smith, issue: Rachel, b. 1st of 3rd mo 1789; Mary b. 9th ____ ; Sarah, b. 3rd of 1st mo 1794, d. 18th of 6th mo 1796.

James Hatcher, b. 7th of 3rd mo 1732, married Catharine Nickols, b. 8th of 5th mo 1748, issue: Mary b. 3rd of 1st mo 1768; Isaac b. 10th of 8th mo 1769; Edith b. 14th of 8th mo 1772, d. 15th of 6th mo 1842; Ann b. 30th of 3rd mo 1774; Sarah b. 15th of 9th mo 1776; Rebekah b. 22nd of 10th mo 1779; Elisabeth b. 8th of 12th mo 1782; James b. 1st of 10th mo 1784; Margery b. 12th of 10th mo 1787; Catharine b. 20th of 7th mo 1792, d. 17th of 6th mo 1793.

Benjamin Burson married Hannah Young, issue: Sarah, b. 29th of 10th mo 1772; George b. 11th of 4th mo 1774; Esther b. 13th of 6th mo 1778; Silas b. 22nd of 4th mo 1785.
Benjamin Burson buried 22nd of 12th mo 1790.

Samuel Carey married ____, issue: Rachel, b. 2nd of 11th mo 1754; Cynthia b. 11th of 1st mo 1777; Sarah b. 7th of 7th mo 1778; Jonathan b. 28th of 2nd mo 1781; John b. 22nd of 6th mo 1783; Samuel b. 2nd of 12th mo 1785; Rachel b. 10th of 12 mo 1787; Elizabeth b. 19th of 9th mo 1789. d. 14th of 2nd mo 1790.

Joseph Gibson married Phebe, issue: Esther, b. 27th of 5th mo 1765; Alice b. 26th of 7th mo 1767, 18th of 11th mo 1784; John b. 13th of 1st mo 1770; Miriam b. 22nd of 7th mo 1772, d. 26th of 10th mo 1817; George b. 1st of 11th mo 1774; Mary, b. 16th of 4th mo 1777; Hannah b. 4th of 1st mo 1779; Phebe b. 29th of 6th mo 1782; Rebekah b. 11th of 10th mo 1785.

Thomas Hatcher, b. 15th of 1st mo 1750 married Rebecah Nichols, b. 14th of 9th mo 1749 (Both deceased at time register was written). Issue: Margery, b. 28th of 3rd mo 1774, d. 28th of 2nd mo 1812; Samuel b. 18th of 2nd mo 1776; Ruth b. 15th of 7th mo 1778, d. 12th of 8th mo 1794; Joseph b 6th of 7th mo 1780, dec'd; Thomas b. 1st of 8th mo 1782, d. 17th of 3rd mo 1816; Rebecah b. 1st of 7th mo 1784, d. 10th of 8th mo 1794; Isaac b. 3rd of 3rd mo 1788, d. 11th of 1st mo 1792; Jonah b. 22nd of 5th mo 1791, d. 10th of 8th mo 1794.

Swithin Nichols, b. 24th of 4th mo 1769 [damaged film] married Rebekah Hatcher, b. 22nd of 10th mo, prob. 1779 ?. Issue: Mary, b. 28th of 10th mo 1799; Tacy b. 25th of 8th mo 1801; Elizabeth b. 6th of 10th mo 1804; Sarah b. 1st of 1st mo 1806; Isaac b. 6th of 10th mo 1808; Samuel b. 22nd of 2nd mo 1811; James b. 10th of 3rd mo 1813, d. 14th of 9th mo 1826; Jacob b. 29th of 3rd mo 1815, removed; Rebeckah b. 10th of 10th mo 1817; Edith H. b. 25th of 1nd mo 1820; Lusannia, b. 23rd of 10th mo 1822, d. 2nd of 2nd mo 1823; Daniel b. 25th of 7th mo 1824, d. 1867.

Isaac Hatcher, b. 10th of 8th mo 1769, married Rachel Randel, b. 7th of 11th mo 1766. Issue: Joseph b. 25th of 1st mo 1788, d. 31st of 4th mo 1790; James b. 16th of 7th mo 1789; William b. 22nd of 5th mo 1791; Lydia b. 17th of 12th mo 1792, d. 19th of 5th mo 1794; Mary b. 19th of 12th mo 1794; Elizabeth b. 26th of 10th mo 1796; Samuel b. 27th of 5th mo 1798; Isaac b. 23rd of 9th mo 1801.

Bernard Taylor married Sarah Smith. Issue: Rachel b. 28th of 6th mo 1793, d. 8th of 2nd mo 1794; Yardley b. 12th of 12th mo 1794; Jonathan, b. 13th of 2nd mo 1797; Henry Smith b. 21st of 5th mo 1799; dau born dead 28th of 3rd mo 1802; Bernard b. 4th of 3rd mo 1803; William Field b. 23rd of 8th mo 1805, d. 26th of 1st mo 1815; Nancy b. 30th of 8th mo 1807, d. 23rd of 8th mo 1850; Sarah Alice b. 10th of 1st mo 1809; Maria Wilson b. 23rd of 9th mo 1813.

Amos Gibson, b. 14th of 6th mo 1779, married Hannah Millar, b. 26th of 4th mo 1787.

Samuel Hatcher married Sarah Reader. [*Issue born post 1800.*]

Abijah Janney, married Jane McPherson? [*Issue born after 1801.*]

Benjamin Bradfield married Rachel Smith. Issue: Thomas b. 3rd of 2nd mo 1790, d. 17th of 10th mo 1811; John b. 29th of 11th mo 1791, removed; Hannah b. 27th of 1st mo 1796, d. 14th of 10th mo 1815;

Jonathan b. 24th of 5th mo 1798, disowned; Sidney b. 7th of 9th mo 1800, d. 19th of 3rd mo 1801; Alice, (Urce) b. 7th of 9th mo 1800, d. 11th of 10th mo 1823; Anna, b. 6th of 8th mo 1805, removed.

Isaac Nichols b. 6th of 2nd mo 1773, d. 27th of 1st mo 1848, married Lydia Walters (dec'd Hopewell MM). Issue: Elizabeth b. 6th of 10th mo 1798; Thomas b. 30th of 3rd mo 1802, married Mary Gibson b. 16th of 4th mo 1777, d. 18th of 8th mo 1851.

Jesse Hirst, son of John & Mary Hirst, b. 18th of 12th mo 1766, married Mary Pierpoint, daughter of Obed & Hester Pierpoint, b. 7th of 2nd mo 1777, d. 7th of 11th mo 1864. [*Issue born post 1800.*]

Stephen Wilson married Martha Scott. [*Issue all born after 1800.*]

John Birdsall b. 9th of 6th mo 1791, d. 28th of 9th mo 1830, married Mary Brown b. 26th of 8th mo 1793, d. 12th of 3rd mo 1857. Issue all born after 1800.

Yardley Taylor, b. 12th of 12th mo 1794, married Hannah Brown, b. 5th mo 1792. Issue all born after 1800.

William Piggott, son of John & Phebe, b. 8th of 12 mo 1774, d. 26th of 9th mo 1846, married Phebe Nickols, daughter of William & Sarah, b. 5th of 7th mo 1776. Issue: Sarah b. 13th of 12th mo 1798; John b. 6th of 1st mo 1801; Isaac b. 4th of 10th mo 1802; Burr b. 8th of 9th mo 1805; Elizabeth b. 26th of 12th mo 1806; Phebe b. 12th of 9th mo 1810, d.22nd of 9th mo 1860; Jesse b. 25th of 8th mo 1812, disowned; William b. 28th of 12 mo 1815, dec'd; Mary b. 23rd of 5th mo 1818.

Daniel Janney, son of Israel, b. 18th of 4th mo 1757, d. 21st of 10th mo 1859; married Elizabeth, daughter of Nathan Haines, b. 30th of 12th mo 1800, d. 28th of 8th mo 1840.

William Wilson b. 20th of 8th mo 1795, d. 19th of 12th mo 1871, married Elizabeth Nichols, b. 6th of 10th mo 1798.

William C. Brown, son of Richard & Sarah, b. 30th of 5th mo 1788, d. 10th of 9th mo 1851, married Sarah Piggott, daughter of William & Sarah, b. 13th of 12th mo 1798.

Elisha Janney, b. 1st of 8th mo 1794, married Lydia Smith, b. 1st of 3rd mo 1799.

John Gregg, b. 10th of 8th mo 1786, d. 25th of 11th mo 1852, married Phebe Gibson, b. 29th of 1st mo 1782, d. 5th of 11th mo 1861.

Levi Tate, b. 7th of 4th mo 1766, d. 13th of 2nd mo 1846, married Edith Nichols, b. 16th of 4th mo 1771, d. 9th of 7th mo 1840. Issue: William b. 20th of 1st mo 1796; Jesse, b. 8th of 7th mo 1799, d. 31st of 1st mo 1806; Sarah b. 5th of 11 mo 1801; Ann b. 31st of 12th mo 1803; Edith b. 8th of 1st mo 1807; Mary b. 2nd of 3rd mo 1809; Elizabeth b. 5th of 7th mo 1811.

Richard Brown, b. 29th of 12th mo 1798, married Elizabeth Piggott.

David Burson, b. 21st of 1st mo 1798, married Elliza Frame, b. 12th of 10th mo 1804.

Jonas Smith, b. 17th of 2nd mo 1794, married Miriam Russell, b. 27th of 3rd mo 1808.

Eli Pierpoint b. 18th of 11th mo 1791, married Hannah Love.

William Holmes, b. 28th of 11th mo 1763.

List of Births & Burials:
[*All burials were after 1800 and are not included here.*]
Mary J. Nichols, b. 9th of 4th mo 1777.
Gourly Reeder, b. 7th of 12th mo 1787.
Sarah L. Brown, b. 22nd of 2nd mo 1800.
Rachel Birdsall, b. 1760.
Elizabeth Birdsall, b. 1789.
Hannah Birdsall, b. 1800.
Albenah Craven, b. 12th of 1st mo 1789.
William Smith, b. 8th of 3rd mo 1765.
Aquila Mead b. 2nd of 8th mo 1787.
Ann Brown, b. 8th of 12th mo1787.
Ann Dillon, b. 8th of 5th mo 1782.
Sarah Brown, b. 7th of 6th mo 1763.
John Smith, b. 15th of 2nd mo 1797, married Ruth Hannah Janney.

William Holmes, b. 28th of 11th mo 1763.
David Smith, b. 17th of 3rd mo 1767.
Hannah Gregg, b. 12th of 12th mo 1779.
Mary Howell b. 8th of 8th mo 1785.
Lydia Janney, b. 19th of 9th mo 1770.
Rebecca Gregg, b. 25th of 11th mo 1791, disowned.
Thomas Hughes, b. 3rd of 10th mo 1782, married Martha Canby, b. 22nd of 10th mo 1781. [*Issue born post 1800.*]
Fin? Taylor, b. 13th of 2nd mo 1797, d. 1st of 9th mo 1846, married Lydia Brown. Issue born post 1800.
Joseph Gibson, b. 19th of 12th mo 1796, married Rachel Shoemaker, b. 13th of 8th mo 1808. [*Issue born post 1800.*]

GOOSE CREEK MONTHLY MEETING CERTIFICATES OF REMOVAL

30th of 1st mo 1786: John Long, wife Mary, children Ann and John, were given a certificate to Cane Creek MM in NC.

24th of 4th mo 1786: Joel Lewis and Sarah his wife were given a certificate to South River MM. Also Thomas Cadwalader, Jane his wife, and child Elizabeth.

26th of 6th mo 1786: Martha, wife of Joseph Rhodes, was given a certificate to South River MM.

26th of 11th mo 1786: Hannah, wife of Robert Whitacre was given a certificate to Fairfax MM.

29th of 1st mo 1787: Aaron Plummer, having resided amongst us during his apprenticeship, was given a certificate to Pipe Creek MM.

26th of 3rd mo 1787: Evan Lewis and George Lewis were given certificates to South River MM in Campbell County.

30th of 4th mo 1787: Alice Lewis, wife of Jehu Lewis, and Ann Lewis, were given certificates to South River MM. Moses Cadwalader Senior, and his son Jesse, were given certificates to Pipe Creek MM. The children of William Harris Jr., deceased, namely Mary, Hannah, Levi, and Jonas were given certificates to South River MM, having removed with parents ___ and Elizabeth Clapham. Ruth Cadwalader was given a certificate to South River MM.

28th of 5th mo 1787: David [Daniel?] Smith was given a certificate to Hopewell MM.

24th of 9th mo 1787: Jesse Lewis and Esther, wife of Abijah Richards, were given certificates to South River MM.

26th of 11th mo 1787: Stephen Willson was given a certificate to Fairfax MM. Phebe the wife of Thomas Smith, was given a certificate to Crooked Run MM.

28th of 1st mo 1788: Thomas Neal, Rachel Neal his wife, and children George, Henry, William, Benjamin, James and Mahlon, were given certificates to Cane Creek MM. Amy Taylor, and her daughter Rachel were given certificates to Fairfax MM.

28th of 4th mo 1788: Daniel Clark was given a certificate to Cedar Creek MM.

29th of 12th mo 1788: Abner Gregg, Sarah his wife, and children Ann, Nathaniel, Ruth, William, Stephen and Albinah were given certificates to South River MM, Campbell Co.

25th of 5th mo 1789: Thomas Vickers, an approved minister, was given a certificate to Bradford MM in Chester Co.

25th of 1st mo 1790: Robert Whitacre was given a certificate to Crooked Run MM.

24th of 5th mo 1790: Thomas Gregg, made application for his son, Israel Gregg, whom he hath put apprentice to Goldsmith Chandlee a member of Crooked Run MM. Israel was given a certificate to Crooked Run.

27th of 9th mo 1790: Benjamin Scholfield was given a certificate to South River MM.

27th of 12th mo 1790: Hannah Love, wife of James Love and minor children Jan, Samuel and Hannah; along with James Love's daughters Sarah and Elizabeth were given certificates to Fairfax MM.

24th of 1st mo 1791: Samuel Gover and Sarah his wife, with their seven minor children Moses, Jacob Janney, Mary, Elizabeth, Anthony, Sarah, and Robert, were given certificates to Fairfax MM.

25th of 4th mo 1791: John Hirst requested certificate for his son Thomas [James?], he being placed as an apprentice among Friends at Crooked Run.Thomas Love was given a certificate to Fairfax MM. John Dixon was given a certificate to Wright's Town MM in Georgia.

30th of 5th mo 1791: Joseph Randal, Rachel his wife, and two younger daughters Jane and Charity were given certificates to Fairfax MM. Samuel Cary, Rachel his wife, and children Cynthia, Sarah, Jonathan, John, Samuel, Rachel, and Thomas; along with James Curl, Ruth his wife, and their son Joseph were given certificates to South River MM.

26th of 9th mo 1791: Joseph Pool, Hannah his wife, and child Naomiah were given certificates to Crooked Run MM. William Kenworthy and

Rebekah his wife were given certificates to Pipe Creek MM. Joseph Gregg was given a certificate to Westland MM.

24th of 10th mo 1791: Eli Dixon was given a certificate to Wrightstown MM. Solomon Dixon and Ann his wife, with children Henry, Joseph, Solomon and Stephen were given certificates to Wrightstown MM.

11th mo 1791: Mary Hannah, late Marsh, was given a certificate to New Garden MM in NC.

26th of 12th mo 1791: John Heston was given a certificate to Wrights Town MM. James Daniel, Hannah his wife, and four of their minor children, namely Rebekah, William, Jesper, and Hannah were given certificates to South River MM.

26th of 3rd mo 1792: Amy Vickers was given a certificate to Buckingham MM.

30th of 4th mo 1792: Esther Smith, late Gibson, was given a certificate to Crooked Run MM.

28th of 5th mo 1792: John Seybold, with Hannah his wife, and 2 children Sarah and Rebekah were given certificates to Wrightstown MM. Application made by John Gregg for his son Joshua whom he hath placed as an apprentice with Friends at Crooked Run MM.

30th of 7th mo 1792: David Hirst was given a certificate to York MM. John Preston, Rebekah his wife, and their eight minor children, Zenes?, John, Amos, Moses, Sarah, Peter, Ann, and William were given certificates to South River MM.

29th of 10th mo 1792: Isaac Hatcher, Rachel his wife, and two children James and William were given certificates to South River MM. Rachel Vickers was given a certificate to Bradford MM.

26th of 11th mo 1792: Isaac Votaw, Ann his wife, and six children Moses, Isaac, Joseph, Thomas, Daniel and Samuel were given certificates to Westland MM.

24th of 12th mo 1792: Rebekah Talbott, wife of Joseph Talbott, was given a certificate to Fairfax MM.

28th of 1st mo 1793: Mary White, wife of Jesse White, and the six minor children Uriah, Elizabeth, Jane, James, Rachel and Jesse were given certificates to Hopewell MM.

25th of 2nd mo 1793: Ann Gibson was given a certificate to Crooked Run MM. William Schooley, Hannah his wife, and their 7 children Richard, Reuben, Henry, Elizabeth, John, Aaron and Amos were given certificates to Fairfax MM. Thomas Reeder, Druscilla his wife, and their 5 minor children Joseph, Thomas, William, Elizabeth and Druscilla were given certificates to South River MM. Rachel Scholfield, wife of David

Scholfield and 2 children Aaron and David were given certificates to Crooked Run MM. Jane Scholfield, daughter of Rachel Scholfield has removed with her parents and was given a certificate to Crooked Run MM.

27th of 5th mo 1793: Elisha Janney was given a certificate to Fairfax MM.

26th of 8th mo 1793: Sarah Smith, wife of Wm. Smith was given a certificate to Fairfax MM.

30th of 9th mo 1793: Aquilla Janney, Ruth his wife, and their three children Isaac, Hannah, and Daniel were given certificates to Hopewell MM.

20th of 10th mo 1793: William Heston, his wife Mercy [Mary?}, and their three minor children Phinileas, Mary, and Amos were given certificates to Redstone MM.

30th of 12th mo 1793: Mary Randal was given a certificate to South River MM. Isaac Schooley and Sarah his wife were given certificates to Indian Spring MM.

26th of 5th mo 1794: Levi Lukens, and Elizabeth his wife, were given certificates to Hopewell MM. Edmund Phillips, son of Edmund Phillips, still in a state of childhood, was given a certificate to Cane Creek MM.

2nd of 3rd mo 1795: Ezra Plummer was given a certificate to Fairfax MM.Thomas Moore and Mary his wife, with their daughter Mary were given certificates to Indian Spring MM.

30th of 3rd mo 1795: Benjamin Myers and Elizabeth his wife; along with Jacob Myers and Sarah his wife, were given certificates to Fairfax MM.

25th of 5th mo 1795: Samuel Talbott and Rachel his wife were given certificates to Hopewell MM.

29th of 6th mo 1795: Mary Janney, wife of Elisha; Abner Gibson, and Elizabeth Wear, with her four children Sarah, William, Elizabeth and Jane, were given certificates to Fairfax MM.

27th of 7th mo 1795: Elisha Janney requested a certificate for his young daughter Sarah to Fairfax MM.

30th of 11th mo 1795: Amos Smith, son of Samuel Smith, who is placed as an apprentice in the verge of your meeting was given a certificate to Baltimore MM. Benjamin Yates, Phebe his wife, and seven of their children, Sarah, Phebe, James, Ruth, Mary, Jamima, and Benjamin were given certificates to Westland MM.

28th of 12th mo 1795: Abraham Vickers was given a certificate to Monthly Meeting for the Northern district of Philadelphia.

25th of 1st mo 1796: John Piggott, Jr., was given a certificate to Hopewell MM.

28th of 3rd mo 1796: John Votaw, Rebekah his wife, and their 2 small children Ann and Mary were given certificates to Westland MM. Mary Smith, wife of George Smith, was given a certificate to Crooked Run MM.

30th of 5th mo 1796: Mary Headen (we have concluded to accept the paper of acknowledgement offered by her) was given a certificate to Goose Creek MM, Bedford County, Virginia.

27th of 6th mo 1796: Elizabeth Holloway, wife of Asa Holloway, was given a certificate to Crooked Run MM.

26th of 9th mo 1796: Zachariah Ellyson, Mary his wife, and their 4 children Isaac, Gidien, Zachariah, and Robert were given certificates to Westland MM. Eliza Parker, with her 5 younger children, Joseph, Eliza, Samuel, Silas, and Ann were given certificates to Fairfax MM. Martha Parker was given a certificate to Fairfax MM.

30th of 1st mo 1797: Edward Whitacre was given a certificate to Westland MM.

27th of 3rd mo 1797: Sarah Smith was given a certificate to Buckingham MM. Judith Cunard and her 5 children, Edward, Pamela, John, Henry and Jerret were given certificates to Fairfax MM. Ann Cunard and Sarah Cunard who are about to remove with their parents, were given certificates to Fairfax MM.

24th of 4th mo 1797: Jonathan Taylor, Ann his wife, and daughter Rebekah were given certificates to Crooked Run MM. James Moore made application for his son Abner, who is placed as an apprentice at Indian Spring MM. Jonathan Lovett, Ann his wife, and their 2 children Nancy and Sarah were given certificates to Crooked Run MM. Mary Smith, who lately removed with her mother, was given a certificate to Buckingham MM.

29th of 5th mo 1797: Israel Gregg was given a certificate to Redstone MM.

30th of 10th mo 1797: Samuel Gregg, Ann his wife, and 6 children, Mary, Abel, Phebe, Eli, Gulielma, and Jesse were given certificates to Redstone MM.

27th of 11th mo 1797: Sarah Cogle, wife of Isaac Cople [Cowgill] was given a certificate to Westland MM. William Hatcher, Mary his wife, and their children Nancy, Rachel, Sarah, Thomas and John were given certificates to Westland MM.

26th of 3rd mo 1798: Abraham Randle, Jane his wife, and children Hannah, Sarah, Abraham, and Isaac were given certificates to Westland MM.

30th of 4th mo 1798: James Moore and Phebe his wife, with their 5 children, Joseph, Thomas, Sarah, Elizabeth and Tamar were given certificates to Fairfax MM.

26th of 11th mo 1798: Jesse White was given a certificate to Westland MM.

29th of 4th mo 1799: Samuel Sharp, Martha his wife, and their 5 minor children, Abigail, George, Jephthia, Sarah and Jesse were given certificates to South Land MM. Isaiah Williams, his wife Dinah, and 7 children, Benjamin, Mary, Tacy, Martha, Abraham, Susannah, and Ann were given certificates to West Land MM.

30th of 9th mo 1799: Joshua Hatcher, Jane his wife, and 5 small children, John, Mahlon, William, Sarah and Mary were given certificates to Westland MM.

28th of 10th mo 1799: Israel French Jr., who left a considerable time past in a state of minority, was given a certificate to Baltimore MM. Pleasant Hague was given a certificate to South Land MM.

30th of 12th mo 1799: Hannah Burson and her son Silas were given certificates to West Land MM.

27th of 1st mo 1800: Phineas Janney was given a certificate to Fairfax MM.

28th of 7th mo 1800: Redwood Fisher was given a certificate to the Monthly Meeting of Friends for the Southern District Philadelphia.

25th of 8th mo 1800: Hugh Hunter and Elizabeth his wife were given certificates to Westland MM.

MEN'S MINUTES OF GOOSE CREEK MONTHLY MEETING

26th of 12th mo 1786: South Fork complains against Thomas Russell for marrying a non-member.

27th of 2nd mo 1786: ___ Janney requests a certificate to Kennet MM, PA, in order to marry Mariah? Gregg. Robert Sybold charged with fornication, he denys the same.

27th of 3rd mo 1786: Zachariah Ellyson produced a certificate from White Oak Swamp, Henrico Co., VA. Thomas Cadwalader admits taking an over portion of strong drink and asserts he is sorry. This is accepted as satisfaction, whereupon a certificate for him, his wife Jane, and daughter Elizabeth was produced. Robert Sybold has left these parts, so friends have not had opportunity of treating with him.

4th mo 1786: Isaac Brown and ___ requested that two of their youngest children be received into membership [names unreadable]. Mary Wildman Parker has married a non-member.

29th of 5th mo 1786: Thomas Vickers produced a certificate from Bradford MM, PA.

6th mo 1786: Mary Tomlinson, wife of William, produced a certificate from Wrightstown MM, PA. It had been endorsed by Fairfax MM and directed to this meeting. Thomas Hatcher, Jr. made satisfaction for his misconduct. Phoebe Russel, married by assistance of a hireling.

7th mo 1786: Thomas Smith, Jr. requests certificate to Hopewell MM in order to marry Martha Ridgeway, a member of that meeting.

28th of 8th mo 1786: Albinah, wife of Elisha Janney, produced a certificate from Kennett MM, PA.

9th mo 1786: John Taylor spent some time at Solomon Hoge's, then was removed to Isaac Nicholl's, and after a short stay, departed this life.

30th of 10th mo 1786: Jesse White produced a certificate from Goshen MM, Chester Co., PA, endorsed at Hopewell, for self, wife Mary, and children Uriah, Elizabeth, Jane, James and Rachel.

27th of 11th mo 1786: A few lines from Uwchlan MM, informed that William Kirk offered a paper of acknowledgement for an offence for which he was disowned several years ago. James Beans married a non-member.

25th of 12 mo 1786: Martha, wife of Thomas Smith, produced a certificate from Hopewell. ___ Hoge guilty of fornication with her that is now his wife.

26th of 2nd mo 1787: [many references unreadable]. Evan and George Davis request a certificate to join South River MM. Complaint against

Isaac and Rachel Hatcher for being guilty of fornication and accomplishing their marriage by the assistance of a hireling. Complaint against Mercy Heston, late Vickers, for marrying a non-member.

3rd mo 1787: Samuel Gover produced a certificate for himself, Sarah his wife, and children Moses and Jacob Janney, also Elizabeth and Mary Gover.

30th of 4th mo 1787: Complaint against James Nicholls for marrying a non-member.

28th of 5th mo 1787: Complaint against Ruth McPherson, formerly Fred, for marrying a man not a member of our Society.

25th of 6th mo 1787: Discussion of the boundary between Goose Creek and Fairfax Monthly Meetings. Complaint against Ann Daniel, formerly Russell, being guilty of fornication and for marrying a non-member.

30th of 7th mo 1787: Amos Beans accomplished his marriage with a woman not a member of the Society with the assistance of a hireling.

27th of 8th mo 1787: Jane Hatcher, and her husband, request that their two small children, John and Mahlon be received into membership. Hannah Whitacre, wife of Robert, was taken by death before her certificate of transfer to Fairfax MM could be produced. Complaint against Joshua ____ for quarreling and fighting.

24th of 9th mo 1787: Joshua Hunt produced a certificate from Concord MM, PA. He has lived here, but intends to return to PA. William Kirk produced a certificate from Uwchland MM, PA. He requested membership for his wife and 5 small children Caleb, Betty, Sarah, William and Timothy. Complaint against Mary Lemart for having an illegitimate child.

29th of 10th mo 1787: A certificate for Abijah Richards from Hopewell MM was produced and read. He has removed to limits of South River MM. Testimony against Joshua Holmes was read, recorded, and signed.

24th of 12th mo 1787: Certificate requested for Amy Taylor, wife of Evan Taylor and child Rachel, to Fairfax MM. Complaint against Joseph Gibson Jr. for quarreling, fighting, and using profane language, he confessing most part of the charge.

25th of 2nd mo 1788: Thomas Reeder and Priscilla, and their 4 minor children, Joseph, Thomas, William and Elizabeth, request membership among Friends. Minute from Concord MM informs that Joshua Mercer, some time ago obtained a certificate to become a member, but did not give it in to be received. That, as well as other misconduct, particularly fornication with the woman to whom he is now married, requires attention to his case.

24th of 3rd mo 1788: John Preston not giving any reason for his absence at last meeting, he is desired to render one to next. Joshua Mercer does not deny charges against him. Complaint against John Dillon for being guilty of fornication.

28th of 4th mo 1788: A minute from Bucks Quarterly meeting informs that William Reeder, a resident of Goose Creek, married his first cousin, and of late has applied to the MM of which he was formerly a member in order for restoration of a right among Friends. William Kirk request a certificate for himself and children, Caleb, Betty, Sarah, William and Timothy to Westland MM, PA.

26th of 5th mo 1788: Complaint against Sarah Eirey, formerly Pool for marrying a man not a member of our Society, with the assistance of a hireling. Complaint against Josiah Dillon for fighting. Complaint against Samuel Wilson for accompanying his sister in her outgoing marriage, and who has also been accused with clandestinely taking a horse shoe at a smith shop which was not his own. He denys the latter charge.

30th of 6th mo 1788: Aaron Plummer was some time past granted a certificate to Pipe Creek MM. He has now returned and settled near Leesburg. [Later reported that he has no fixed residence].

25th of 7th mo 1788: A certificate was produced for Jonas Janney and Ruth his wife, from Fairfax MM.

26th of 8th mo 1788: Jonas Janney and wife Ruth request their children be received in membership, viz, Abel, Rebecah, George, Sarah, Hannah, and Ruth. Complaint against Israel Williams for being guilty of fornication.

29th of 9th mo 1788: David Smith produced a certificate from Hopewell MM. Aaron Plummer's certificate has been endorsed and forwarded to Pipe Creek MM as directed. Complaint against Anne Burson for having an illegitimate child.

27th of 10th mo 1788: Thomas Gregg produced a certificate from Hopewell MM for himself, wife Sarah and their child Uriah. Jesse White's acknowledgment was published and returned. A certificate for Esther, wife of John Matthews, was produced from Uwchlan MM, PA. He being in difficult circumstances, men appointed to enquire as to the situation of her care and report. Complaint against Abraham Vickers for being guilty of fornication, he does not deny the charge ... and having lately left these parts in a disreputable manner.

24th of 11th mo 1788: William Heston produced a certificate from Wrights town for himself, Mercy his wife, and three of their children, viz, Phineahas, Mercy, and Amos. Josiah Dillon's paper of acknowledgment was published and returned.Esther Matthews found to be so difficultly circumstanced as to believe it would be best to return her certificate to the MM from whence it came, with our full reason for so doing. Abraham Vickers left these parts without paying his just debts on several instances, and as he has removed out of reach of Friends treating with him. Testimony will be produced against him. Complaint against Mary Vickers, for being guilty of fornication.

26th of 1st mo 1789: Elizabeth Myers produced a certificate from Crooked Run MM. Complaint against Joseph Holmes for marrying a non-member. Simeon Haines produced a certificate from Fairfax MM for himself, wife Elizabeth and two children, Daniel and Joseph. Robert Whitacre produced a certificate from Fairfax MM for himself, and child Jonas. Complaint against Mary Smith, late Hibbs, for marrying a non-member. Joseph Elgar produced a minute from Menallen MM, about visiting within this meeting. Joseph Pool requests a certificate to Crooked Run MM in order to marry Hannah Hereford, a member thereof. Benjamin Whitacre and wife request that their three eldest children, still minors, viz, Thomas, Hannah, and Naomi, be received into membership.

30th of 3rd mo 1789: Ann Smith produced a certificate from Crooked Run MM, which was read and accepted. Complaint against Hannah Bland, late Randal, for marrying a non-member. Joseph Randal requests a certificate for himself, wife and four of their children to Fairfax MM.

27th of 4th mo 1789: Complaint against Jesse White for drinking so freely of spirituous liquors as to become intoxicated thereby. Complaint against Zechariah Ellyson and Mary Ellyson, late Votaw, for being guilty of fornication, thereby making it necessary to deviate from good order and accomplish their marriage by the assistance of an hireling.

29th of 6th mo 1789: Benjamin Scott produced a certificate from Fairfax MM. Samuel Cary produced a certificate from Fairfax MM for himself, Rachel his wife, and their children: Jonathan, John, Samuel, Cinthia, Sarah, and Rachel.

27th of 7th mo 1789: Jonathan Taylor produced a certificate from Falls MM in PA. Ann Taylor, wife of Jonathan, produced a certificate from Buckingham MM in PA. Both were read and accepted. Hannah Pool, wife of Joseph, produced a certificate from Crooked Run MM.

24th of 8th mo 1789: Joseph Holmes' acknowledgment was published. Testimony against Mary Smith was published and returned. James Sinkler asks to be released from being overseer at South Fork. Thomas Brown was appointed to the service.

9th of 9th mo 1789: It appears that Esther Matthews was married to another woman's husband and acknowledged that she had heard he was married before, though he endeavoured to make her believe otherwise. Robert Whitacre requests a certificate to Crooked Run MM in order to marry Patience McKay, a member of that meeting.

26th of 10th mo 1789: This meeting receives information from Bucks Quarterly and Wrightstown MM about Mary Reeder, [something about marrying a cousin, not clear].

30th of 11th mo 1789: A certificate for William Reeder Jr. from Buckingham MM, PA, was read and received.

28th of 12th mo 1789: Certificate produced for Aron and David, children of David Scholl, from Pipe Creek MM. Hester Matthews intends to appeal the judgment of meeting. Robert Whitacre requests certificate for himself and son Jonas to Crooked Run MM. Complaint against John Gibson Jr. for quarreling and fighting. Thomas Smith plans to remove with his family to West Land MM.

26th of 1st mo 1790: Rachel Randle intends to appeal the judgment of this meeting.

12th of 2nd mo 1790: Complaint against Sarah Votaw for having an illegitimate child. Thomas Love requests to be taken into membership. Complaint against Enoch Scholfield for neglecting attendance at meetings and joining himself in society with the Methodists.

29th 3rd mo 1790: Solomon Hoge reports that committee met with Thomas Love, his mother, and sisters, and will continue to watch over them. South Fork representatives inform that Benjamin Myres and six minor children have been under the care of their meeting.

26th 4th mo 1790: John Heston produced certificate from Wrights town MM in PA. John Gibson Jr. presented his paper of acknowledgment.

24th 5th mo 1790: Testimony against Sarah Votaw was published. She declines to appeal. Mary Reeder produced certificate from Wrights Town MM in PA. Enoch Scholfield is satisfied with membership with the Methodists. He is therefore dismissed from being a member of this society. Complaint against Agness Martin, formerly Dillon, for marrying a non-member. Certificate for Israel Gregg was produced and recorded. South Fork preparative meeting informs that William Reeder requests his four children, Ann, Sarah, Hanah, and Gourly, be taken into membership, they being in their minority.

28th of 6th mo 1790: Enoch Sholfield declines to appeal. Thomas Love, Hannah Love his mother, and two sisters Sarah and Elizabeth are received into membership. The parents requesting the three younger children, Jane, Samuel, and Hanah, minors, be likewise received.

26th of 7th mo 1790: Paper of acknowledgment by John Gibson Jr. is now returned. Agnes Votaw signified a desire to retain her right in the Society. Benjamin Myers received into membership with his seven minor children, Israel, Elisabeth, Benjamin, Susanah, Hannah, Thomas and John George, the latter being born after application made for the other six.

30th of 8th mo 1790: South Fork preparative requests a certificate for Benjamin Scholfield at the desire of his mother to South River MM.

27th of 9th mo 1790: James Moore produced a certificate for himself and Phebe his wife and their five small children, namely Abner, Thomas, Joseph, Sarah, and Elizabeth from Fairfax MM. Testimony against Agnes Martin was read and approved.

25th of 10th mo 1790: Certificate for James Curl was read and received. Complaint against Joseph Randle Jr. for clandestinely taking wheat out of a mill that was not his own, in the night. He hath acknowledged being convicted of the crime.

29th of 11th mo 1790: Complaint against Edith Smith for being guilty of fornication. Complaint against Moses Gibson Senr. for quarreling and fighting. Jacob Myers desires to be received into membership.

27th of 12th mo 1790: Isaiah Williams produced certificate for himself, Dinah his wife, and three children Benjamin, Mary, and Tacy, from Buckingham MM in PA. John Hirst hath returned from visiting South River MM. Complaint is brought from South Fork preparative against Joshua Fred for striking a man in anger, which he doth not deny.

24th of 1st mo 1791: Joseph Gibson is not desirous of condemning his misconduct and hath lately been guilty of using profane language also quarreling and fighting.

28th of 2nd mo 1791: Lott Trip produced an extract of a minute from Creek MM in New York. Stephen McPherson Jr. requests to be received in to membership. South Fork complains against Israel Lacey for purchasing two Negro Boys in their minority, and doesn't appear willing to secure their freedom at a proper age; also for marrying a non-member. Samuel Carey proposed to remove with his family to South River MM. James Curle requests advice of Friends on his prospects of removing to South River MM. South Fork Preparative proposed James Trehorn to serve in the station of an overseer in the place of Benjamin Burson, dec'd.

28th of 3rd mo 1791. Certificate produced for John Belt, from Indian Spring MM. Joshua Fred appeared sensible of his misconduct and desires that friends might receive his paper as satisfaction. Complaint forwarded by Goose Creek preparative against Thos. Williams for accomplishing his marriage contrary to the rules of our society with a woman not in membership with us, and as it is not likely any opportunity can be had with him any time soon, he having removed to Kentucky and signified he should leave friends at liberty to act therein as they thought best. It is therefore judged expedient to issue a testimony against him. Solomon Dixson requests the advice and sympathy of friends on his prospect of removing within the limits of Wrights Town MM in Georgia. Benjamin Myers requests advice in respect to his removing. Joseph Poole is about to remove, asks to be released from publishing papers for Goose Creek particular meeting. William Kenworthy appointed to serve in his stead.

25th of 4th mo 1791. Stephen McPherson Jr. is received into membership with his 2 young children Mary and Lydia being present.

30th of 5th mo 1791: Bernard Taylor produced a certificate from Falls MM. Daniel Vernon produced a certificate from Bradford MM. Marriage of John Brown and Ann Hirst was orderly accomplished. Prudence Hatcher refuses to make satisfaction for her offence. Fairfax MM forwarded a few lines informing that Sarah Gore had offered a paper condemning her outgoing in marriage. Complaint against William Spencer for spreading a scandalous report injurious to the character and reputation of a young woman.

27th of 6th mo 1791: Elizabeth Holmes was received into membership. Isaac Nickols appointed to publish papers at Goose Creek in the room of Wm. Kenworthy who does not now expect to settle within this meeting.

25th of 7th mo 1791: Jacob Myers was received into membership.

29th of 8th mo 1791: Certificate was produced by John Brown from Fairfax MM. Complaint against Timothy Beans Jr. for being guilty of fornication and clandestinely leaving these parts. Complaint against Joseph Daniel for dancing. Complaint against Stephen McPherson Jr. for accomplishing his marriage by the assistance of an hireling with Sarah Hibbs, a woman in membership with us. Complaint against Hannah Spencer Jr. for spreading an evil report injurious to the reputation of a member of this meeting, and also for not keeping to the truth in expressing herself on some occasions. Jane and Deborah Howell request to be received into membership.

26th of 9th mo 1791: Joseph Daniel made satisfaction for his offense. Hannah Spencer Jr. is willing to condemn her misconduct. Moses Gibson Jr. is sensible of his error, and desires being continued as a member. Thos. Janney joined light company in dancing.

24th of 10th mo 1791: Timothy Howell was received into membership with his 4 minor children, Phebe, Mahlon, Thomas and Ann, also his grandson, Henry Nickols. Levi Lukens produced a certificate from Gwynett MM in PA.

28th of 11th mo 1791: Sarah Smith and two daughters Mary and Prudence produced a certificate from Buckingham MM, but Prudence was not received because she is not attending here. A voluntary paper of acknowledgement from Mary Dillon condemning her misconduct in keeping company before her late marriage with a man not in membership with us was forwarded to this meeting. Moses Gibson Jr.'s paper of acknowledgment was published and returned. Joseph Daniel's paper of condemnation was published and returned. Mary and Nancy Wilson's paper of acknowledgment was published and returned.

26th of 12th mo 1791: Prudence Smith married her first cousin, and married out of the unity of friends. Mary Moore, wife of Thos. Moore Jr. produced a certificate from Indian Spring MM. Certificate was produced for Jas. Daniel, Hannah his wife, and 4 children in their minority.

30th of 1st mo 1792: John Smith Jr. and Esther Gibson intend to marry. John is not a member of this meeting, therefore, must produce a certificate from Crooked Run MM. Wm. Spencer's paper of acknowledgement was published and returned. Jane Silcot, wife of Jesse Silcot, produced a certificate from Richland MM in Bucks Co., PA. Thos. Brown requests to be release from serving as overseer at South Fork. Acquilla Janney appointed to serve in his stead.

27th of 2nd mo 1792: Joshua Gore was received into membership with his 5 children, William, Ann, Solomon, Thomas and Sarah Gore. James Moore appointed to serve as clerk for the ensuing year.

26th of 3rd mo 1792: Certificate was produced for Thomas Moore Jr. from Fairfax MM. Complaint against James Nichols for marrying a non-member. Paper was submitted by Isaac Hatcher and wife condemning their misconduct for which they were disowned.

30th of 4th mo 1792: Levi Tate produced a certificate from Kennett MM. Sarah Gore was reinstated into membership, based on letter from Fairfax. Complaint against Elias Lacy for being charged by a young woman with being the father of her illegitimate child. Complaint against Solomon Burson for marrying a non-member.

28th of 5th mo 1792: James Trehorn requests to be released from publishing papers at South Fork, and they have proposed Thomas Moore Jr. in his room.

26 of 6th mo 1792: Complaint against Ann Tavener, late Hatcher, for marrying a non-member. Complaint against Josiah Dillon and George Sinkler for marrying non-members.

30th of 7th mo 1792: South Fork informs that Samuel Scholfield has removed and settled within the compass of South River MM considerable time past. South Fork complains against Lewis Leonard for marrying a non-member. Testimony against Charity Randle produced and signed. She declines appeal. Levi Luken requests a certificate for himself and wife to Hopewell MM. Benjn. Yates and wife request their seven youngest children be received into membership. All are in a state of minority. Children accepted were Sarah, Phebe, James, Ruth, Mary, James, and Benjamin. Complaint against Rachel Johnson, late Spencer, for marrying a non-member. Our part of the expense for keeping Charles Pierpoint in the Pennsylvania ... last year being ... .

27th of 8th mo 1792: Certificate was produced for Joseph Randle and Rachel his wife from Fairfax MM. Testimony against Elias Lacey having been published is returned. The is an obstruction to preparing a certificate for Samuel Scholfield. Therefore it is referred back to the Overseer of South Fork meeting. Bernard Taylor requests certificate to join in marriage with Sarah Smith, a member of Fairfax MM.

24th of 9th mo 1792: Joseph Talbott and Rebeckah Hirst intend to marry. Joseph is a member of Fairfax MM, therefore, must produce a certificate. South Fork complains against Samuel Scholfield for neglecting the attendance of our religious meeting, keeping libertine company, using profane language, and gaming.

29th of 10th mo 1792. Certificate for Ezra Plummer, from Pipe Creek MM. Ann Tavener was furnished a copy of the testimony against her. She not inclining to appeal, it was published and returned.

24th of 12th mo 1792: Certificate was produced for Isaac Schooley, from Westland MM. Samuel Smith produced certificate from Buckingham MM. Josiah Dillon refuses to give in and declines endeavoring to make satisfaction for his offence. Testimony is ordered against him.

28th of 1st mo 1793: Women friends have a certificate for Elizabeth Wear, wife of Robert Wear, but there is a problem so it has not been received at the present.

25th of 2nd mo 1793: Sarah Taylor, wife of Bernard Taylor produced a certificate from Fairfax MM. Complaint against John Brown for marrying a non-member.

25th of 3rd mo 1793: Israel Janney reports that John Brown is not suitably disposed to condemn his marriage. Therefore, it is necessary to issue a testimony against him. Sarah Slocomb is received into membership.

29th of 4th mo 1793: Edward Whitacre is received into membership. Complaint against Nathan Nickols for marrying a non-member. Likewise a complaint against Isaac Hoge and wife for accompanying Nathan Nickols in the accomplishment of his marriage. South Fork complains against Isaac Gibson Jr. for wrestling by appointment for a wager, quarreling, fighting, and keeping libertine company.

27th of 5th mo 1793: Jonathan Ellyson produced a certificate from Henrico MM. Levi Hollingsworth gave in a certificate for himself, Mary his wife, and their 2 children Thos and David, dated at Fairfax MM. The committee on the case of Elizabeth Wears report that she appeared willing to condemn her misconduct and has produced a paper for that purpose. The meeting is not fully satisfied. The committee on the case of Isaac Gibson Jr. report they have had full opportunity with him and believe he was in a good degree sensible of his deviation from the order of truth, expressed his sorrow for the same, and has now produced a paper of condemnation in order to be reconciled with friends, but from the nature of the complaints against him the meeting judges it not safe to rest his case.

24th of 6th mo 1793: Nathan Nickols appeared; desires of retaining his right of membership. His case is continued under the care of same friends. Elizabeth Russell, late Randle, has married a non-member. South Fork informs that Levi Lukens plans to marry Elizabeth Cleavour, a member of Hopewell MM. Complaint against Mary Whitacre, late Wilson, for consummating her marriage with a man not a member of our society.

29th of 7th mo 1793: Isaac Hoge and wife, not attending this meeting, gave in a paper of condemnation for their offence. It was accepted as satisfaction.Complaint against Bernard Taylor for being guilty of fornication before marriage with her that is now his wife which he does not deny. Complaint against Mary Gore, late Smith, for marrying a non-member.

26th of 8th mo 1793: Bernard Taylor and wife appeared in a good degree sincerely sorry for their misconduct and were desirous of making satisfaction. South Fork informs that Acquilla Janney requests to be released from serving as an overseer and they have proposed Benjamin Yates in his room.

30th of 9th mo 1793: Certificate was produced for John Buchannon from Crooked Run MM. Testimony against Elizabeth Russell, Isaac Gibson Jr., and also Mary Whitacre, was published and returned.

28th of 10th mo 1793: David Hirst gave in a certificate from York MM. Nathan Nichols has been served with a copy of the testimony against him. He is not inclined to appeal. Complaint against William Spencer for being guilty of fornication with her that is now his wife.

25th 11th mo 1793: Elizabeth Wear, after much consideration, now received on certificate. Sarah Brown produced a copy of minute dated at Hopewell MM. She is encouraged to attend Fairfax MM. Likewise Sarah Lupton.

30th of 12th mo 1793: Certificate produced for Joseph Gregg and Martha his wife from Redstone MM. Bernard Taylor and wife are sincerely sorry for their misconduct and are desirous of making satisfaction to Friends. Certificate produced for Elizabeth Lukens, wife of Levi Lukens, from Hopewell MM. Wm. Spencer and wife do not appear disposed to make any offering to this meeting for their offence. Testimony will be issued against them. Complaint against Rebeckah Dillon and Charity Randle for being guilty of fornication.

27th of 1st mo 1794: Rebeckah Dillon is sensible of her reproachful conduct and is willing to make satisfaction. Complaint against Sarah Frazier, late Evans, for marrying a non-member. South Fork complains against John Belt for being guilty of fornication which he does not deny. Complaint against John Buchannan for marrying a non-member. South Fork informs that Jonathan Lovett requests membership. Sarah Pancoast, daughter of Eden Pancoast, requests to become a member of this meeting, she having had a birthright among friends, but her parents having removed from New Jersey and obtained a certificate from a MM in that province directed to Fairfax or Indian Spring MM sometime before her birth. For some reason their certificate was never gave in, consequently she is not a member of any particular meeting, although she has an undoubted right in society ... it is concluded to now accept her as a member.

24th of 2nd mo 1794: Complaint against Thomas Gregg Jr. for being guilty of fornication which he does not deny. Complaint against Ezer Dillon for marrying a non-member. South Fork complains against John Brown for being guilty of fornication with Lydia Burson, a member of this society, which they do not deny. They have also accomplished their marriage by the assistance of an hireling. Complaint against Ruth Beans for having an illegitimate child.

24th of 3rd mo 1794: Jacob Myers and Sarah Pancoast intend to marry. They have consent of his parents and her uncle with whom she has lived for some years past and who was by her parents desire to act as guardian for her, they having removed when she was in her minority. Jonathan Lovett received into membership, along with his daughter Nancy, who is in a state of minority. Testimony against Rebeckah Dillon was published and returned. Ezar Dillon did not express a desire to retain his right [membership] but he did appear suitably disposed to condemn his misconduct. Ruth Beans objected to Friends taking an opportunity with her by keeping out of their way and desires friends omit paying her any further visit. Complaint against Rebeckah Eblen, late Parker, for marrying a non-member.

28th of 4th mo 1794: Benjn. Bradfield produced a certificate for himself, Rachel his wife, and 2 children, Thomas and John, from Buckingham MM. Testimony against William Spencer and wife was published and returned. Certificate was produced for Phebe Yates, wife of Benjamin, dated at Fairfax MM. Rebeckah Eblen is willing to submit her case to the judgment of the meeting.

The microfilm copy is very bad from this point until 8th mo 1794. In some instances names can be read, but not the entries or complaints. This is the condition on pages 185-192.

25th of 8th mo 1794: [still poor quality] Cases are continued for Simeon Haines, Stephen McPherson and wife, and Zachariah Ellyson and wife. Testimony against Lewis Lemard ... considering his situation and occupation. Complaint against Stephen Gregg Jr., father of an illegitimate child. He denys the charge. He is also charged with accompanying his cousin in the accomplishment of his marriage by an hireling.

29th of 9th mo 1794: Complaint against Daniel Votaw [Vernon?] for being guilty of fornication with her who is now his wife, and for accomplishing his marriage by the assistance of an hireling with a woman not a member. Zachariah Ellyson and wife, not attending here again received into membership, together with their three small children, Isaac, Gideon and Zachariah.

24th of 11th mo 1794: John Vernon produced a certificate for self and wife and children, James, Mary, and Elizabeth from Bradford MM, PA. Hugh Hunter produced a certificate for self, and Elizabeth his wife, from London Grove MM.

29th of 12th mo 1794: William Lodge's certificate from Fairfax MM was read and accepted.

26th of 1st mo 1795: Testimony was produced against Alice Harrison. Complaint against John Gibson for fornication with her that is now his wife, and accomplishing marriage by the assistance of an hireling with one not a member. Complaint against Moses Gibson for quarreling, fighting and using profane language. Likewise a complaint against John and George Gibson, sons of Joseph, for quarreling and fighting.

2nd of 3rd mo 1795: Mary Gibson produced a certificate from Crooked Run MM. A certificate was brought forward by Daniel Frency, Jr. [French] from Pipe Creek MM. Testimony against Daniel and Rebeccah Vernon was read. Complaint against Levi Tate, for marrying a near relative, Edith Tate, a member of the society, by the assistance of an hireling. Complaint against Hannah Hockley, late Dillon, for marrying a non-member. Benjamin Myers requests certificate for self, wife and 8 children, Isaac, Elizabeth, Benjamin, Susannah, Hannah, Thomas, John George and Sarah to Fairfax MM.

30th of 3rd mo 1795: Marriages of Jonathan Lovett to Ann Gore, and Elisha Janney to Mary Gibson were orderly accomplished. John Gregg requests to be released from serving as overseer. Jonas Janney appointed in his place.

4th mo 1795: Abraham Vickers, son of Thomas Vickers presented a paper to condemn his behavior.

25th of 5th mo 1795: Complaint against Jonathan Sinkler for being guilty of fornication with her that is now his wife, also for card playing, and marrying a non-member. Two daughters of Edmond Phillips removed with their father many years past, but no certificate was sent for them. Complaint against Ann Randle for being guilty of fornication.

29th of 6th mo 1795: Complaint against Aby [Abijah] and Phineas Janney for giving way to a disposition of lightness and vanity. Complaint against James Sinkler Jr. for being guilty of fornication, which he does not deny.

27th of 7th mo 1795: Paper of acknowledgement given in by Abijah and Phineas Janney was published but not returned.

24th of 8th mo 1795: Paper of acknowledgement was signed by Mary Smith, formerly Hibbs. Complaint against Mary, daughter of Thomas Smith. [rest is unreadable].

28th of 9th mo 1795: Stephen McPherson and wife were again received into membership. Isaac Nickols, son of William, requests a certificate to Crooked Run MM in order to marry Lydia Walter, a member of that meeting.

30th of 11th mo 1795: Testimony against Aaron Smith was read. Paper of condemnation was signed by Mary Headon, formerly Lemard. She lives within the verge of Goose Creek MM, Bedford Co., VA. Complaint against Joseph Daniel for being guilty of fornication with her that is now his wife, and marrying a non-member.

25th of 1st mo 1796: Complaint against Caleb Gregg for marrying a non-member. Money for defraying the last year's expense of keeping Charles Pierpoint in the hospital at Philadelphia is due.

29th of 2nd mo 1796: The money for the use of Charles Pierpoint, not being all ready, South Fork Friends are deferred to pay their part to Jonathan Taylor, who is appointed to receive Goose Creek's quota and forward the whole to Asa Moore at Fairfax. David Hirst is cleared to marry Ann Smith. Her father, Thomas Smith, having been for a considerable time from home, and is now about to remove to the western country. Complaint against John Parker for fighting.

28th of 3rd mo 1796: Thomas Hatcher proposed as new clerk.

25th of 4th mo 1796: Samuel Sharp produced a certificate for himself, wife Martha, and children Abigail, George, Jepthah, and Sarah from Kennett MM. Lydia, wife of Isaac Nichols, produced a certificate from Crooked Run MM. Peter Blaker, Sarah his wife, and children Amos and David, produced a certificate from Fairfax MM.

27th of 6th mo 1796: Israel Gregg produced a certificate from Crooked Run MM. South Fork informs that George Burson married a non-member. Thomas Russell Jr. accomplished his marriage by the assistance of an hireling.

25th of 7th mo 1796: Paper of acknowledgment given by John Parker. Testimony was produced against Mary Trehern.

29th of 8th mo 1796: Elizabeth Myers, formerly Parker, accomplished her marriage with a non-member. Complaint against Elizabeth Lemard, formerly Haines, for marrying a non-member. Complaint against Solomon Gibson and Nathan Gregg for joining in light company and dancing at a gathering.

24th of 10th mo 1796: Joshua Gregg produced a certificate from Crooked Run MM. A paper of condemnation from Jesse White, who resides within Westland MM, was forwarded here. Complaint against Samuel Gregg, son of Stephen, for being at a frolick and dancing.

28th of 11th mo 1796: A certificate was produced from Crooked Run MM for George Walters, Dinah his wife, and 4 children, Judith, Isaac, Mahlon and Ann. Ann, wife of David Hirst, produced a certificate from Fairfax MM. Sarah Walters produced a certificate from Crooked Run

MM. Complaint against Abraham Brown for marrying a non-member. Complaint against Hannah Beans Jr. for being guilty of fornication.

26th of 12th mo 1796: John Sinclair produced a certificate from Menallen MM. James Walters produced a certificate from Crooked Run MM. Complaint against Nathan Piggott for accomplishing his marriage contrary to the rules of Friends, with a young woman a member of Society, and he now lives a considerable distance, and does not appear desirous of Friends taking further trouble with him.

30th of 1st mo 1797: Ann Gibson produced a certificate from Crooked Run MM.

24th of 2nd mo 1797: Solomon Nickols produced a certificate for self and wife Hannah, from Fairfax MM. They also requested membership for their children Thomas, James, Elizabeth, John and Hannah. Acknowledgement given by Solomon Gibson was published and returned. Complaints against Thomas Gregg Jr. for fighting, and against Wm. Russel for quarreling, using profane language, and dancing.

24th of 4th mo 1797: South Fork proposes Isaac Brown to the position of overseer in the room of Jonathan Lovett.

26th of 6th mo 1797: Complaint against John Burson for marrying a non-member.

24th of 7th mo 1797: William Ewers is received into membership. Esteemed Friend, Ann Jessop attended this meeting and produced a certificate from New Garden MM in NC. She was in the company of Lydia Hiatt and Joel Willis, her companions.

28th of 8th mo 1797: A paper was forwarded to this meeting from Sarah Cogel, condemning her misconduct for which she stands disowned.

30th of 10th mo 1797: Certificate produced for Samuel Gregg, Jr., wife and family, to Redstone MM, PA. Certificate was produced for James Dillon and family to Westland MM. Jesse Hirst requests a certificate to Fairfax MM in order to marry Mary Peirpoint, a member of that meeting.

27th of 11th mo 1797: Complaint against Solomon Nickols for taking spiritus liquor to excess which occasioned him to quarrel and fight. Complaint against Jonathan Ellyson for gaming at cards.

25th of 12th mo 1797: Beloved Friend David Brooks, from Deep River MM, NC, attended this meeting. He was accompanied by John Clark. Complaint forwarded against Joshua Gregg for dancing, which he doth not deny, but has laid a paper on the table condemning the same. Likewise a complaint against Ebenezer Piggott for joining with light company and attempting to dance. He too, brought a paper of acknowledgement. Complaint against Hannah Spencer Jr. for dancing. Likewise a complaint against Nancy Willson for joining with light company in dancing. Complaint against Cynthia Carter for joining in marriage with her first cousin, a man not in membership with us.

29th of 1st mo 1798: Complaint against John Hatcher Jr. for riding horse races that run for wagers.

26th of 2nd mo 1798: Complaint against Benjamin Daniel for fornication. Also a complaint against Samuel Daniel for dancing.

26th of 3rd mo 1798: Isaac Hatcher produced a certificate from South River MM, for self, wife Rachel, and 4 children, James, William, Mary, and Elizabeth. Papers of acknowledgement were given in by Hannah Spencer Jr., Joshua Gregg, and Ebeneezer Piggott. John Sinclair requests a certificate to Menallen MM in order to marry a young woman who is a member of that meeting.

30th of 4th mo 1798: Certificate from Hopewell MM for William Newland Senr, Margaret his wife, and 6 children, James, Deborah, Jesse, David, Sarah, and Elijah. Likewise, John Newland and Thamer Newland also produced certificates from Hopewell MM. Certificate was produced for John Sinclair, as directed.

28th of 5th mo 1798: Complaints against Sarah Pancost, formerly Phillips, and Elizabeth Tavener, formerly Janney, for marrying non-members. Jonas Janney requests to be released from service as overseer. Isaac Nickols appointed in his room.

25th of 6th mo 1798: Abijah Janney requests a certificate to Hopewell MM in order to marry Jane McPherson, a member of that meeting. William Reader requests to be released from place of an overseer at Southfork. Stephen McPherson appointed in his room.

30th of 7th mo 1798: Mary, wife of Jesse Hirst, produced a certificate from Fairfax MM. William Nickols having requested to be released from the place of an overseer. William Smith is appointed in his stead. Complaint against Jonathan Ellyson for horse racing for wagers and using profane language. Complaint against Joshua Lemert for marrying a non-member.

27th of 8th mo 1798: Abraham Blaker produced a certificate from Fairfax MM. Redwood Fisher produced a certificate from Philadelphia MM. Swithern Nickols was accepted into membership.

26th of 9th mo 1798: Complaint against William Vickers for going out in his marriage with his first cousin, who is also a member.

29th of 10th mo 1798: Joseph Gurly produced a certificate from Sadsbury MM, directed to Fairfax, and endorsed from there. Jane, wife of Abijah

Janney, produced a certificate from Hopewell MM. Complaint against Ann Vickers, formerly Reader, for joining in marriage with her first cousin.

26th of 11th mo 1798: Benjamin Scott (his wife uniting) requests that his children may have a right of membership, they being all born whilst she was not in unity. They being in their minority, the request is granted for Israel, Ann, Elizabeth, Joseph, and William Scott.

24th of 12th mo 1798: Marriage of Samuel Nickols and Mary Janney was orderly accomplished. Marriage of Swithern Nickols and Rebekah Hatcher was orderly accomplished.

24th of 1st mo 1799: Complaint against Amos Blaker for using profane language and offering to fight. Pleasant Hague produced a certificate from Fairfax MM. Rebeccah Sypold's situation requires the care and sympathy of friends. Elizabeth Purdom produced a certificate from Fairfax MM, wishing to visit here and at Southfork.

25th of 2nd mo 1799: Complaint against Israel Pool for quarreling and using profane language. Complaint against Thomas Whitacre for fighting. John Gregg requests that his two grandchildren who reside in his family, Betsy and Joshua Gregg, be raised into membership. They being in their minority, his request is granted.

27th of 5th mo 1799: Sarah, wife of Israel Schooly, produced a certificate for herself and son William from Indian Springs MM. Cosmelia Janney received as a member. Complaint against Aaron Burson for being guilty of fornication with her that is now his wife, she being his first cousin. This meeting requested by letter from Indian Springs MM to assist them with Israel Schooley on a matter that prevents his obtaining a certificate (non-payment of a debt).

29th of 7th mo 1799: The case of Jonathan Ellyson being now revived, he being long gone out of these parts that no opportunity has been had with him, this meeting believes it now right to appoint some friends to write to him informing him that if he doth not speedily return and make satisfaction for his misconduct, Friends will be under a necessity to disown him. Mary Hirst, a minister in good esteem, wishes to visit Warrington QM. Anna Janney, and Bernard Taylor will accompany her.

30th of 9th mo 1799: Isaac Schooley produced a certificate from Indian Springs MM. Phineas Janney requests certificate to Hopewell MM, in order to marry Ruth Sutton, a member of that meeting. Complaint against Ebenezer Piggot for being guilty of fornication. Complaint from South Fork against Joseph Burson for differing with a neighbor and using profane language.

28th of 10th mo 1799: Ruth Piggott produced a certificate from Hopewell MM. South Fork complains against John Parker for running a foot race for a wager, and likewise for dancing.

25th of 11th mo 1799: Complaint against Thomas Whitacre for quarreling and fighting. 30th of 12th mo 1799: Complaint against Abraham Brown for striking a man in anger.

27th of 1st mo 1800: Paper of acknowledgement given by Joseph Burson. Rachel Randal declines appealing so testimony against her is published at South Fork.

24th of 3rd mo 1800: Complaint from Southfork against John Newland for marrying a non-member.

28th of 4th mo 1800: John Newland appears to be in a good degree sensible of his errors. Complaint against John Whitacre for taking strong drink to excess and marrying a woman not a member. Complaint against William Newland Jr. for marrying a woman not a member. Esteemed friends Hannah Reeve and Hannah Trimble attended this meeting. They produced a certificate from Concord MM in Delaware county, PA.

6th of 5th mo 1800: Complaint against Mahlon Gregg for joining light company in dancing.

30th of 6th mo 1800. ____ Janney produced a certificate from White Oak Swamp MM, Henrico Co. Women friends report that Asenath Gregg, late Mead, married a man not a member. An additional complaint has been lodged against Thomas Whitacre for taking strong drink, which he does not deny.

28th of 7th mo 1800. Women friends report Eleanor Burson is guilty of fornication. Lydia Brown's offering is accepted from Westland MM. Complaint against Samuel Dillon for quarrelling and fighting, and he hath now offered a paper in order to condemn the same. Mary Dillon wants to visit the somewhat remote members of this meeting. Women friends will appoint a companion. This meeting appoints Isaac Nickols to bear them company. Complaint against Mahlon Howel for using profane language. Complaint against Isaiah Burson for fighting.

5th of 8th mo 1800: Lydia Brown's paper of acknowledgment having been published is returned and a certificate is being produced for her. Samuel Dillon appeared desirous of retaining his right of membership, and also in some measure sensible of his deviation. Complaint against Jonathan and Aaron Gibson for joining light company in dancing. Women inform that Ruth and Dinah Gibson joined light company in dancing. Stephen Wilson informs that he has thought of removing his habitation.

29th of 9th mo 1800: Jonathan Gibson made offering which was accepted. In the case of Dinah and Ruth Gibson, Dinah is in some degree sensible of her misconduct. She offered a paper to condemn the same.

2_ of 10th mo 1800. Certificate received for Jacob Brown from Fairfax MM. Complaint against Joseph Blaker for joining the military in training, using profane language, and he being out of the way of friends.

24th of 11th mo 1800: Jacob Brown and Judith Walter continue their intentions of marriage. William Brown and Hannah Janney intend to marry. William being a member of Fairfax MM, is directed to produce a certificate with respect to his clearness in engagements with others.

WOMEN'S MINUTES OF THE GOOSE CREEK MONTHLY MEETING

[*Begins with notes (Women's) regarding the organizing of a monthly meeting at Goose Creek.*] Signed by Ruth Holland, Rachel Hollingsworth, Marty Updegraff, Isaac Everitt, William Ballinger, James Steer, William Kersey, Herman Updegraff, Allan Farquer, Elisha Kirk, Jonah Hollingsworth, Nethaniel Whell [White] ... to attend the opening of [the meeting], which James Mendenhall, Richard Ridgeway, Joel Wright, Joseph Wright, Abel Walker, Goldsmith Chandler and Andrew M. Kay are appointed and Margaret Ridgeway, Abigail Steer, ... Fanly, Hannah Hollingsworth, Jane Hibberd and Susan Farquhar ... will report to next quarterly meeting.

12th mo 1785: Mary Hatcher appointed overseer in the room of Anna Janney. Mary Hirst, Mary Hatcher, Mary Hoge, Anna Janney, and Ruth Gregg to sit with men at the opening of first preparative meeting.

1st mo 1786: Certificate was produced for Mary Long and children.

4th mo 1786: Complaint against Mary Wilson, formerly Parker for marrying a non-member.

5th mo 1786: Rachel Smith, wife of Samuel Smith, produced a certificate to this meeting for herself and children, Jacob, Amos, Mary, James, and Rachel, from Buckingham MM in PA. Mercy Vickers and Rachel Vickers produced certificates from Bradford MM. Martha Rhodes requests certificate to South River MM.

6th mo 1786: Ruth Roos, formerly Philips married a non-member. Priscilla Reeder, wife of Thomas Reeder, requests membership.

8th mo 1786: Testimony produced against Mary Wildman.

10th mo 1786: Abigail Cunnard produced a certificate from Gunpowder MM.

11 mo 1786: Certificate was produced for Hannah Whitacre. Priscilla Reeder was received into membership.

12th mo 1786: Martha Smith, wife of Thomas, produced a certificate from Hopewell MM. Complaint against Ruth Hoge for marrying by hireling.

1st mo 1787: Susannah Gregg appointed assistant clerk.

2nd mo 1787: Complaint against Rachel Hatcher, formerly Randal, for marrying a non-member. She likewise confesses that she has been guilty of unchastity with him who is now her husband.

5th mo 1787: Jane Hatcher, wife of Joshua Hatcher, requests membership. Complaint against Ruth McPherson, formerly Fred, for marrying a non-member. [*negative copy of microfilm is very blurry for next 4 pages*]. Complaint against Ann Daniel, formerly Russel, for being guilty of fornication and marrying a non-member.

8th mo 1787: Jane Hatcher is received into membership. Certificate was granted for Hannah Whitacre wife of Robert Whitacre to Fairfax MM, but she being deceased before it was given in, it is returned.

26th of 11th mo 1787: Martha, wife of George Scott, produced a certificate from Uwchlan MM. Request was made by Friends living at and near the Gap of the Short Hill for the indulgence of a meeting for the winter season.

12th mo 1787: Edith Smith produced a certificate from Fairfax MM.

2nd mo 1788: Complaint against Rachel Whitacre, formerly Willson, for marrying a non-member. Certificate was produced for Phebe Evan and 9 children, Thomas, Sarah, Margaret, Mary, Catherine, Phebe, Evan, Wheelon, and Martha from Hopewell MM.

4th mo 1788: Sarah Gover is appointed assistant clerk. Rachel, wife of William Kirk, requested certificate to West Land MM.

5th mo 1788: Certificate was produced by Grace Beal, daughter of Joseph Beal, from Buckingham MM.

8th mo 1788: Certificate was produced for Ruth, wife of Jonas Janney, from Fairfax MM.

10th mo 1788: Sarah Gover is released from being assistant to the clerk as she is about to remove from here.

3rd mo 1789: Complaint against Mary Smith, formerly Hibbs, for marrying a non-member. Certificate from Fairfax MM was produced by Elizabeth Harris, husband and children.

3rd mo 1789: Request for certificate to Fairfax MM by Rachel Randal, husband and children.

6th mo 1789: Certificate was produced from Fairfax MM for Rachel Cary, her husband and children, Cynthia, Sarah, and Rachel.

8th mo 1789: Certificate to Fairfax MM requested by Sarah Gover, her husband, and children Moses, Jacob Janney, Mary Elizabeth, and Ann. Men Friends request women to join them to visit Esther Matthew, wife of John Matthew, to treat with her at the request of Uwchlan MM, for being married to a man that is said to have another wife. Esther says she was wrongfully charged, but men disagree.

3rd mo 1790: Hannah Love, wife of James Love, and her daughters Sarah and Elizabeth, request to be joined in membership. Complaints against Sarah Votaw and Charity Nichols for being guilty of fornication which they do not deny.

4th mo 1790: A certificate was produced from Wrightstown for Mary, wife of William Reeder. Complaint against Agness Martin, formerly Dillon, for marrying a non-member.

10th mo 1790: Mary Hoge appointed overseer.

12th mo 1790: Complaint against Ruth Dyer, formerly Burson, for marrying her first cousin.

3rd mo 1791: Complaint against Prudence Hatcher for giving way to lightness and dancing, which she doth not deny.

4th mo 1791: Elizabeth Holmes requests membership. Ruth Curl applied for certificate to South River, with her husband and one child, named Joseph.

8th mo 1791: Complaints against Ann and Elizabeth Randal, also Mary and Ann Willson for endeavoring to dance at a place of merriment. Complaint against Hannah Spencer Jr. for spreading a scandalous report of one that is a member.

10th mo 1791: Esther Penquite produced a certificate from Middletown MM. The meeting feels it necessary to forward certificates to New Garden MM in NC for Mary Marsh, Ruth Janney, and Phebe Moore.

12th mo 1791: Mary Moore produced a certificate from Indian Spring MM.

4th mo 1792: Mary Reeder is appointed overseer at South Fork in place of Rebekah Preston who desired to be released. Committee appointed to visit Isaac Hatcher and wife agree to accept their offering.

[Next pages are very faint, and difficult to read. Much information was omitted.]

4th mo 1793: Paper of acknowledgement was produced by Elizabeth Hoges? condemning her conduct in marriage. Complaint against Mercy Gore, formerly Smith, for marrying a non-member. Complaint against Sarah Taylor for being guilty of fornication with him that is now her husband.

10th mo 1793: Complaint against Sarah Spencer, formerly Hatcher, for being guilty of fornication with him that is now her husband. Mary Randal, daughter of Joseph Randal, requests certificate to visit Deep River MM. Sarah Schooley requests certificate to Indian Spring MM. Certificate from Wrightstown MM, was produced for Elizabeth Weers, wife of Robert Weers, directed to Fairfax MM. They having endorsed it, it is accepted.

4th mo 1794: Certificate for Rachel Bradfield. Certificate was produced by Phebe Yates from Fairfax MM. Complaint against Rachel Johnson, formerly Spencer, for marrying a non-member.

5th mo 1794: Paper of acknowledgement was produced by David and Ruth Hoge, condemning misconduct for which they were disowned. Sarah Smith appointed to serve as clerk.

6th mo 1794: Certificate was produced by Martha Wilson, joining with her husband, from Fairfax MM. Certificate was produced by Catharine Lodge from Fairfax MM. Testimony against Rachel Johnson was produced.

7th mo 1794: Paper of acknowledgment was forwarded by Zachariah and Mary Ellison condemning their conduct for which they were disowned. Stephen and Sarah McPherson forwarded a paper to this meeting, condemning their outgoing in marriage, for which they were disowned.

10th mo 1794: Case of Rebekah Vernon is continued.

11th mo 1794: Certificate was produced by Ruth Marsh and Elizabeth Hunter, with their husbands, from London Grove MM. A certificate was produced by Phebe Vernon, joined with her husband, from Bradford MM.

12th mo 1794: Complaint against Alice Harrison, formerly Seybold, for being guilty of fornication, with him that is now her husband. She has removed out of the reach of Friends.

1st mo 1795: Rachel Talbott produced a certificate from Hopewell MM.

3rd mo 1795: Mary Gibson produced a certificate from Crooked Run MM. Complaint against Edith Tate, formerly Nickols, for marrying a non-member. Complaint against Hannah .... Hannah Hawkley is not capable of making satisfaction at this time. Mary Janney is appointed overseer in the place of Esther Daniel.

4th mo 1795: Complaint against Hannah Hogue, formerly Brown, for marrying a non-member. Complaint against Margaret B [Beale?], formerly Evans, for marrying out with first cousin. She has removed out of the reach of Friends.

5th mo 1795: Complaint against Rachel Sinkler, formerly Daniel, for being guilty of fornication with him that is now her husband.

6th mo 1795: Complaint against Ann Vickers for being guilty of fornication.

7th mo 1795: Testimony was prepared against Deborah Best. Complaint against Mary Smith for being guilty of fornication.

9th mo 1795: Sarah McPherson, being present, her offering is accepted.

3rd mo 1796: Mary Hatcher appointed overseer.

4th mo 1796: A certificate was produced by Martha Sharp, joining with her husband and children, from Kennett MM. Complaint against Mary Treyhern, formerly Randal, for being guilty of fornication with him that is now her husband.

7th mo 1796: Testimony against Mary Prichard was produced.

8th mo 1796: [some too faint to read]. Complaint against Elizabeth Leonard, late Haines, for marrying a non-member. Mary Ellis, joining with her husband, requests a certificate to Westland MM. Martha Parker has removed and settled within the verge of Fairfax MM.

10th mo 1796: Complaint against Esther Powell, formerly Burson, for marrying a non-member. Complaint against Rachel Gibson, formerly Fred, for being guilty of fornication with him that is now her husband.

12th mo 1796: Committee appointed to treat with Hannah Beans report they endeavored to have an opportunity with her, which she refused. Complaint against Mary Evans, formerly Nickols for marrying a non-member.

2nd mo 1797: Certificate was produced for Hannah Nickols, joining with her husband from Fairfax MM. Mary Smith offered a paper to this meeting condemning her conduct for which she was disowned.

5th mo 1797: Complaint against Margery Nickols for charging Ann Connard with taking a coverlet from her secretly, which charge she is not likely to make good.

6th mo 1797: Friends Margaret Elgar and Sarah Farquahar visited from Pipe Creek MM.

8th mo 1797: Complaint against Sarah Hays, formerly Whiteacre, for marrying a non-member. Sarah Cogill offered a paper of acknowledgement.

9th mo 1797: Mary Hatcher and Ann Dillon, joining with their husbands, request certificates to Westland MM.

11th mo 1797: Complaint against Ann Ewers, formerly Gregg, for accomplishing her marriage contrary to the rules of our discipline.

12th mo 1797: Complaint against Lydia Potts, formerly Brown, for being guilty of fornication with him who is now her husband. Nancy Wilson does not appear capable of making satisfaction for her offense. Hannah Spencer offered a paper of acknowledgement which is accepted. Complaints against Alice Logan, formerly Gibson; also Cynthia Carter, formerly Parker, for marrying non-members.

2nd mo 1798: Complaint against Alice Smith Junr. for joining with light company and dancing. She offered a paper of acknowledgement. Complaint against Sarah Vickers for dancing. Complaint against Rachel Randal for joining with light company and dancing.

3rd mo 1798: Complaint against Hannah Russell for being guilty of fornication. Sarah Vickers denys the charges against her.

4th mo 1798: Complaint against Margery [Nancy?] Hatcher for being guilty of fornication.

7th mo 1798: Alice Smith being present, her offering is accepted.

8th mo 1798: Testimony was produced against Elizabeth Tavener. Nancy Wilson being present, her offering is accepted. Lydia Brown offered a paper of acknowledgment condemning her conduct for which she was disowned.

9th mo 1798: Sarah Pancoast's offering is accepted. Sarah Scott, wife of Benjamin Scott produced a certificate from Fairfax MM.

10th mo 1798: Complaint against Nancy Wilson for being guilty of fornication.

11th mo 1798: Dinah Williams, joining with her husband and children, requests certificate to Westland MM.

1st mo 1799: Pleasant Hague [Hoge] produced a certificate from Fairfax MM.

6th mo 1799: Complaint against Hannah Gregg, formerly Brown, for marrying a non-member.

10th mo 1799: Mary Swaine visited from Nottingham MM. Ruth Pickett produced a certificate from Hopewell MM.

12th mo 1799: Complaint against Sarah Shore, formerly Burson, for marrying a non-member. She has removed without the limits of this meeting.

11th mo 1799: William Beavers [Brown] and Hannah Janney intend to marry.

12th mo 1800: Complaint against Elizabeth Young, formerly Hatcher, for marrying a non-member. Ruth Piggott applied for a certificate to Hopewell MM.

BAPTISMS, NEW JERUSALEM LUTHERAN CHURCH
From the Pastor's Register
1784 - 1800

Philip, b. 3 Dec 1783, bapt. 18 June 1784, of ... and wife Angelia.

Johan Henrich, bapt. 18 June 1784, of Henrich Keim and wife Catharina. Sponsors: Antoni Amend and Magdalina.

Leonhard, b. 14 May 1784, bapt. 18 June 1784, of Geo Hardmann and wife Magda. Sponsors: Leonhard Anzel and wife Catharina.

Thomas, b. 4 Apr 1784, bapt. 18 June 1784, of Thomas Davis and wife Esther. Sponsors: Peter Heckmann, Christina Weinsbergin.

Magdalena, b. 31 Mar 1784, bapt. 18 June 1784, of Friderich Boger and wife Regina. Sponsors: Michael Boger, Magda. Moll.

Magdalena, of Henrich Wolf and wife Magdalena. Sponsors: David Kunz, Magda. Wolf.

Philip, bapt. 20 June 1784, of Richard ... ... , bapt. 11 Aug. 1784, of Johannes Alt and wife Maria Barbara. Sponsors: Michael Palmer and wife Barbara.

Anna Elisabetha, of Justus Arnold and wife Ca[tharina]. Sponsors: Johann Philip Ott, and Elisabeth...

Eva, bapt. 11 Aug 1784, of Adam Putscher. Sponsor: Jacob Eberhard.

Johannes Peter, of Peter Steinbrenner and wife Susanna. Sponsor: Johannes Camper.

..., b. 3 August, bapt. October, of ... and wife Catharina. Sponsors: ... and wife Sophia.

..., b. 11 Aug., bapt. 12 Oct, of ... Oehler, and wife Dorothea. Sponsors: ...nes Frey, Magd. Hough.

..., b. 2 Aug. bapt. 12 Oct, of ... Schlotz, and wife Margaret. Sponsors: ... Roller and wife Rosina.

..., b. 26 Aug, of ...auer and wife Barbara. Sponsors: ... Wentzel, Barbara.

... Shapley, b. 27 June 1774, bapt. 30 Oct, of ... Wyett and wife Debora. Sponsors: ... Martin and wife Louisa.

..., b. June, bapt. 31 Oct, of Jacob Land and wife Barbara. Sponsors: Haushalter and wife Catharina.

..., b. 19 Sept, bapt. 31 Oct, of ... Schneider and wife Margaretha.

Simon, of Georg Schumacher. Sponsors: Johannes Sch... and Margreth.

Susanna, b. 3 Aug, of Wilhelm Roesle... . Sponsors: Johannes Junkin and wife Catharina.

Johannes, b. 23 Sept, bapt. 31 Oct, of Johannes Stier and wife Margretha. Sponsors: George Schack and wife Margretha.

Maria Magd. b. 20 Sept 1783, bapt. 15 Dec, of Christoph Holtzman and wife Magd. Sponsor: Margareth Bauer.

Maria Catharina, b. 27 Oct 1784, bapt. 15 Dec 1784, of Isaac Miller and Maria. Sponsors: Isaac Ritsche, Maria Catharina.

Johann Philip, b. 19 Oct 1784, bapt. 15 Dec 1784, of Adam Wolff and Catharina. Sponsors: Parents.

Andreas, b. 11 Jan 1785, bapt. 2 Mar 1785, of Fredrich Steinbrenner and Julianna. Sponsors: Andreas Spring, Anna Maria.

Barbara, of Johannes Torch.

Peter, b. 11 Mar 1785, of ... and Susanna. Sponsors: Peter Jacob and Elisabeth.

Charlotta, b. 7 Mar 1785, bapt. 13 Apr 1785, of Christoph Holtzmann and Magdalena. Sponsor: Charlotta Eberhardt.

Christoph, b. 6 Mar 1785, bapt. 13 Apr 1785, of George Ebel and Catharina. Sponsors: Christoph Bornhaus, Rosina.

Johan Adam, b. 27 Feb 1785, bapt. 13 Apr 1785, of Fredrich Spring and Barbara. Sponsors: Joh. Adam Wolff, Margreth Steinbrenner.

Michael, b. 28 Feb 1785, bapt. 13 Apr 1785, of Joh Philip Frey and Anna Dorothea. Sponsors: Michael Boger, Elisabeth Brenner.

Catharina, b. 15 Dec 1784, bapt. 13 Apr 1785, of Jacob Schmid and Salome. Sponsors: Catharina, wife of Henrich Kuntz.

Adam, b. 22 Feb 1785, bapt. 13 Apr 1785, of Caspar Mahler and Elisabeth. Sponsors: Adam Schober, Magdalena.

Daniel, b. 17 Feb 1785, bapt. 13 Apr 1785, of Samuel Thiel and Margreth. Sponsors: Samuel Ritchie, Appellonia Heckmann.

Anna Maria, b. 16 Mar 1785, bapt. 13 Apr 1785, of Carl Gross and Elisabeth. Sponsors: Caspar Traut, Anna Maria Amend.

Catharina, b. 15 Nov 1784, bapt. 1 May 1785, of Melchor Strupp and Marianna. Sponsors: Catharina, daughter of Andreas Beltz.

Anna Susanna, b. 8 Mar 1785, bapt. 1 May 1785, of Johannes Battenfelt and Barbara. Sponsors: Luding Wentzel, Anna Susanna Hammanin.

Salome, b. 22 May 1784, bapt. 1 May 1785, of James But, Bale (sic) Roger. Sponsors: Jacob Eberhardt, Charlotta Baurin.

Anthoni, b. 10 Apr 1785, bapt. 1 June 1785, of Jacob Hoffman and Elisabeth. Sponsors: Anthoni Amend, Magdalena.

Georg Wentz and Maria Catharina [These are parents, no inormation about child or sponsors].

Elisabeth, of Fridrich Be... Sponsor: Susanna, wife of Johannes...

Jacob, b. 21 Mar 1785, of Peter Müller. Sponsor: Barbara, wife of Jacob Sch...

Anna Catharine, 28 ....., of Johan Adam Kadel. Sponsor: Catherine, wife of Jacob...

Anna Margreth, bapt. 1 June 1785, of Benjamin Dewall. Sponsors: Lorentz Ament, Clara.

Johannes, 21..., of Wilhelm Wenner. Sponsors: Nichlaus Bader, wife ...

Esther, b. 6 Apr 1785, of Jacob Biber and Catharina. Sponsors: Peter Wirtz, Ch[ristina].

Michael, b. 3 June 1785, of Michael Rus. Sponsors: Henrich Hartman and wife.

Margretha, 9 Jan 1785, of Johannes Schad and Magdalena. Sponsors: Gottlieb Geist and wife M[argretha].

Anna Eva, 18 June 1785, of Adam Reibsamen. Sponsors:Jacob Steinbrenner and wife.

Maria Elisabeth, bapt. 19 June 1785, of Carl Hoffman and Julianna. Sponsors: Michael Boger, Maria.

Mariagretha, b. 20 May 1785, of Gottlieb Pfingstag. Sponsors: Jacob Hoffman, Elisabetha.

Eva Salome, b. 22 June 1785, of Nicholas [Heck]man. Sponsors: Eva Salome, wife of Johannes.

Adam, b. 12 June 1785, of Jacob Emmerich and Ca... Sponsors: Adam Wentzel, Anna.

Carl Grimm, [no information about child. Last name of female sponsor was Hüterin].

...., b. 15 June 1785, bapt. 3 Aug 1785, of Elisabetha. Sponsors: Lorentz Amend.

....na, b. 10 June 1785, bapt. 3 Aug 1785 of ...[Tri]ttebach and Maria Magdalena. Sponsors: ...na Brennern, Michael Trittenbach.

... Margretha, b. 14 July 1784, of ... Benoton and Eva ... Sponsors: ... Haman, Magdalena.

Daniel, b. 20 July 1785, bapt. 14 Sept 1785, of ... Schumacher and Margretha. Sponsors: [Daniel] Schumacher.

Elisabeth, b. 3 June 1785, bapt. 14 Sept 1785, of ... Sanders and Anna Margreth. Sponsors: ... Schumacher and wife Eva Barbara.

..., b. 30 Apr 1785, bapt. Oct, of ... Gotthard and Elisabeth. Sponsors: Johannes Wust, Catharina.

..., b. 30 Aug 1785, bapt. 9 Oct 1785, of Christoph Bornhaus and Rosina. Sponsors: ... Ebel, Catharina.

Johannes, b. 9 Sept 1785, bapt. 9 Oct 1785, of Peter Heckmann and Regina. Sponsors: Johannes Wolf, Abigail Heckmann.

Anthoni, b. 26 Aug 1785, bapt. 9 Oct 1785, of Johann Goertner and Anna. Sponsors: Anthoni Sanders, Margreth.

Elisabeth, b. 11 Sept 1785, bapt. 9 Oct 1785, of ...tz Hautenschild and Susanna. Sponsors: Jacob Shaeffer, Maria Elisabeth.

Johannes, b. Sept 1785, bapt. 9 Oct 1785, of ... Jung and Christina. Sponsors: Johannes Wentzel, Barbara Strehm.

Daniel, b. 16 Oct 1785, bapt. 8 Nov 1785, of Michael Kiefer and Catharina. Sponsors: Daniel Schumacher, Elisabeth.

..., b. 16 Oct 1785, bapt. 8 Nov 1785, of... Corniss and Rachel. Sponsors not named.

Adam, b. 5 Sept 1785, bapt. 1785, of Andreas Belz and Ju... Sponsors: Adam Haushalter and wife.

Johann Jacob, b. 26 Sept 1785, bapt. 1785, of Andreas Koehler and Anna. Sponsors: Conrad Lang, Anna Maria Fuherin.

Christina Rahel, b. 23 Oct 1785, bapt. 8 Nov 1785, of William Harris and Magdalena. Sponsors: Christina, daughter of Jacob Weinsberg.

Henirich, b. 19 Oct 1785, bapt. 2 Feb 1786, of Isaac Ritsche and Catharina. Sponsors: Henrich, son of Frantz Ritsche; Appolonia, daughter of Conrad Heckmann.

Elisabeth, b. 17 Oct 1785, bapt. 2 Feb 1786, of Fridrich Fuller and Catharina. Sponsors: Eva, wife of Johannes Krombacher.

Jacob, b. 27 Dec 1785, bapt. 2 Feb 1786, of Adam Faeber and Susanna. Sponsors: Jacob Derri, Catharina.

Susanna, b. 28 Nov 1785, bapt. 2 Feb 1786, of Adam Wentzel and Anna Maria. Sponsors: Johannes, son of Adam Wentzel, Susanna, daughter of Georg Hamann.

Georg, b. 28 Dec 1785, bapt. 2 Feb 1786, of Peter Jacob and Maria Elisabeth. Sponsors: Georg Hamann and wife Maria.

Johann Philipp, b. 7 Feb 1786, bapt. 9 Mar 1786, of Henrich Hartmann and Elisabeth. Sponsors: Ludewig Kentzel, Catharina Schumacher.

Susanna Catharina, b. 6 Feb 1786, bapt. 9 Mar 1786, of Phillipp Gross and Barbara. Sponsor: Catharina, daughter of Jacob Frey.

Conrad, b. 7 Feb 1786, bapt. 23 Apr 1786, of Conrad Roller and Elisabeth. Sponsors: Parents.

Solomon Bernhard, b. 17 Apr 1786, bapt. 23 Apr 1786, of Philipp Noff and Rosina. Sponsors: Johann George Bernhardt, Catharina.

Adam, b. 22 Jan 1786, bapt. 23 Apr 1786, of Justus Arnold and Catharina. Sponsors: Adam Riebsamen, Dorothea.

Matthis Naphzinger and Anna, parents. [No information about child or sponsors.]

Catharina, b. 24 Feb 1786, bapt. 23 Apr 1786, of Johannes Schumacher and Susanna. Sponsor: Catharina, wife of Fridrich Beltz.

Johannes, b. 22 Feb 1786, bapt. 23 Apr 1786, of Johannes Hemt and Susanna. Sponsors: Johannes, son of Johannes Schaeffer.

Michael, b. 28 Jan 1786, bapt. 21 Apr 1786, of Christian Rus and Anna Catharina. Sponsors: Parents.

George, b. 5 June 1773, bapt. 17 May 1786, of Christoph Schneider and Ruth. Sponsors: Christoph Schaeffer and Maria.

Magdalena, b. 20 Apr 1783, bapt. 17 May 1786, of Christoph Schneider and Ruth. Sponsors: Magdalena, daughter of Joh. Mich Schwenck, Georg Schaeffer.

Anna Maria Christina, b. 18 May 1786, bapt. 30 July 1786, of Andreas Spring and Anna Maria. Sponsors: Peter Frey, Christina.

Anna Maria, b. 1 July 1786, bapt. 30 July 1786, of Thomas Davis. Sponsors: Conrad Lang and wife Anna Maria.

Eva Barbara, b. 12 June 1786, bapt. 30 July 1786, of Georg Reiser. Sponsors: Michael Finfrock, Catharina Elisabeth.

Christina, b. 9 July 1786, bapt. 30 July 1786, of Conrad Wolf and Elisabeth. Sponsors: Conrad Bader, Christina Buschkirk.

Catharina, b. 14 May 1786, bapt. 30 July 1786, of Johannes Oechslein and Christina. Sponsors: Adam Haushalter, Catharina.

Dorothea, b. 25 May 1786, bapt. 30 July 1786, of Leonhard Ansel and Catharina. Sponsors: Johannes Stump, Dorothea.

Johann Christoph, b. 21 June 1786, bapt. 30 July 1786, of Christoph Bruhl and Margareth. Sponsors: Johannes Junghenn, Catharina.

Johann Michael, b. 25 June 1786, bapt. 30 July 1786, of Joseph Fenerstein and Catharina. Sponsors: Johannes Sieber, Magdalena.

..., b. April 1786, bapt. 30 July 1786, of ... Thomas and Elisabeth. Sponsors: not named.

Conrad, b. 14 ... 1786. Parents not named. Sponsors: Conrad Roller and wife.

Thomas, b. 24 May 1786, bapt. 1786, of James Tomson and wife. Sponsors: Georg Bader, Salome.

Betsy, 28 May 1786, bapt. 1786, of Thomas Tomson and wife. Sponsors: Fridrich Steinbrenner.

Philip, 15 Aug 1786, of Michael Boger and Elisabeth. Sponsors: Philip Brenner, Magdalena.

Melchior, b. 29 June 1786, of Geo. Hardmann and Magdalena. Sponsors: Parents.

Elisabeth, b. 6 July 1786, bapt. Sept 1786, of Isaac Miller and Anna. Sponsors: Nicolaus Bater and wife.

Elisabetha, b. 7 July 1786, of Jacob Waldmann and Margretha. Sponsors: Samuel Waldmann, Elisabetha.

Elisabetha, b. 16 Aug. 1786, bapt. 6 Sept 1786, of Johannes Frantz and Elisabetha. Sponsor: Elisabetha Usselmännin.

Elisabetha, b. 27 Aug 1786, bapt. Nov 1786, of Johannes Berger. Sponsors: Christian Bügly, Eva.

Julianna, b. 10 July 1786, bapt. Nov 1786 of Daniel Lang and Anna. Sponsors: Frid. Steinbrenner and wife.

Johannes Wilhelm, b. March 25 1786, 18 Nov 1786, of Wilhelm Slag.Sponsors: Geo. Däschner, Sophia.

Jac. b. 1 Oct 1786, of Henrich Wiesemer. [Sponsors not named].

..., bapt. Nov. 1786. Sponsors: ... Wirtz, Christina.

Johannes, b. 2 Nov 1786, bapt. 19 Nov 1786, of Nicolas Frey and Anna Margreth. Sponsors: ... Haller, Christina Magdalena.

Elisabeth, b. 16 Sept 1786, 19 Nov 1786, of Jacob Krug and Elisabetha. Sponsor: Elisabetha, widow of Martin Ulm.

Sophia, b. 26 Oct 1786, bapt. 19 Nov 19 1786, of Peter Steinbrenner and Susanna. Sponsors: Georg Doeschner, Sophia.

Magdalena, b. 17 Apr 1786, bapt. 19 Nov. 1786, of Matthis Riple and Barbara. Sponsors: ...ich Zollmann, Magdalena.

Anna Maria, b. 23 Sept 1786, bapt. 19 Nov 1786, of Peter Heckmann and Regina. Sponsor: Anna Maria, widow of David Wittemann.

Mon, b. 28 Oct 1786, bapt. 19 Nov 1786, of Johannes Mayer and Sarah. Sponsors: ... Amend, Magdalena.

Anna Margareth, b. 23 Sept 1786, of Michael Fünfrok [Sunnafrank ?] and Catharina Elisabetha. Sponsors: ... Reiser, Maria Magd.

Joseph, 25 Aug 1786, bapt. 19 Nov 1786, of Friederich Boger and Regina. Sponsors: ..., Catharina.

Eva, b. 8 Nov 1786, bapt. 19 Nov 1786, of Johannes Wentzel and Magdalena. Sponsors: Ludwig Wentzel, Eva Hamann.

Georg Friederich, bapt. 1 Feb 1787, of Philip ... and Dorothea. Sponsors: J. Geo. Bernhard, Catharina.

Susanna, b. 20 Feb 1787, bapt. 29 Mar 1787, of Peter Freu and Christina. Sponsors: Jacob Schloetzer, Susanna.

Johann Wilhelm, b. 17 Dec 1786, bapt. 29 Mar 1786, of Wilhelm Alt and Rahel.Sponsors: Parents.

Christina, b. 25 Feb. 1786, bapt. 29 Mar 1787, of Conrad Wirtz and Barbara. Sponsors: Peter Wirtz, Christina.

Margretha, b. 2 Feb 1787, bapt. 29 Mar 1787, of Christoph Bornhaus and Rosina. Sponsors: Fridrich Schloetz, Margretha.

Christina, b. 25 Dec 1786, bapt. 29 Mar 1787, of Fridrich Schloetz and Margretha. Sponsors: Conrad Roller, Elisabeth.

Michael, b. Nov 3, 1786, bapt. 29 Mar 1787, of Simon Rickert and Susanna. Sponsors: Abraham Stedler, Elisabeth.

Salome, b. 5 Mar 1786, bapt. 29 Mar 1787, of Justus Arnold and Catharina. Sponsors: Adam Battenfeld, Elisabetha.

Anna Maria, b. 8 Jan 1787, bapt. 29 Mar 1787, of Fridrich Bettz and Catharina. Sponsors: Catharina, daughter of Johann Herchelroth.

Georg, b. 17 Apr 1787, bapt. 6 May 1787, of Johannes Siebert and Magdalena. Sponsors: Georg Schwenk, ...

Johann Adam, b. 14 Mar 1787, bapt. 6 May 1787, of ...am Lang and Anna Maria. Sponsors: Adam Lang, Anna Maria.

Gottlieb, b. 1 Dec 1786, bapt. 6 May 1787, of Jacob Steinbrenner and Barbara. Sponsors: ... Steinbrenner, Anna Eva.

Philip, b. 26 Mar 1787, bapt. 6 May 1787, of Fried. Steinbrenner and Juliana. Sponsors: Johannes Campfer, Catharina.

Johannes, b. 14 Apr 1787, bapt. 6 May 1787, of Geo. Flotzer and Margaretha. Sponsors: Adam Strãm, Anna Maria.

Fried., b. 11 Mar 1787, bapt. 6 May 1787, of Fried. Funck and Catharina. Sponsors: Fried. Füller and Catharina.

Avon, b. 17 Feb 1787, bapt. 6 May 1787, of Peter Miller and Catharina. Sponsors: Parents.

Johann Georg, b. 21 Feb 1787, bapt. 6 May 1787, of Jacob Schafer and Elisabetha. Sponsors: Carl Bugly, Catharina.

Magdalena, b. 4 May 1787, bapt. 17 July 1787, of Mattis Sorg and Christina. Sponsors: Adam Schober, Magdalena.

Johann Philipp, b. 20 May 1787, bapt. 17 July 1787, of Daniel Thomas and Elisabeth. Sponsors: Philipp Frey, Dorothea.

Anna Elisabeth, b. 4 Oct 1786, bapt. 17 July 1787, of Wilhelm Roesler and Margreth. Sponsors: Henrich Ruff, Elisabeth.

Thomas, b. 30 Nov 1786, bapt. 17 July 1787, of Blayn... and Marsil... Sponsors: Parents.

Elisabetha, b. 15 Mar 1786, bapt. 18 Nov 1786, of Geo. Führer. Sponsors: Jacob Waldmann, Marg...

Elisabeth, b. 19 June 1786, of Georg Schumacher and Magdalena. Sponsors: Michael Schaeffer, Elisabeth Schwenck.

Christina, b. 15 May 1787, bapt. 17 May 1787, of Martin Gut and Christina. Sponsors: Philipp Gros, Anna Barbara.

Jacob, b. 22 June 1787, of Henrich Guthardt and E. Sponsors: Andreas Koehler, Barbara.

Catharina, b. 6 July 1787, of Johannes Phale and Marg. Sponsors:Anna Marai Phale.

Eva, b. 5 July 1787, of Nicolas Schuckmann and Susanna. Sponsors: Eva wife of Johannes Krombach.

Catharina, b. June, of Georg Wild and Susanna. Sponsors: Isaac Ritsche, Catharina.

Elisabeth, b. 15 March 1787, of Johannes Ziegefuss and Sarah. Sponsors: Christian Ruff, Elisabeth.

Barbara, b. 9 May 1787, bapt. ... 18, 1787, of Jacob Lang and Barbara.Sponsors: Johann Nicolas Bader and wife E...

Margreth, b. 7 May 1787, of Michael Russ and E... . Sponsors: Nicolas Franz, Mar... .

Johannes, b. 7 July 1787, bapt. 19 Aug 1787, of ... ...ler and Priscilla. Sponsors: Johannes Wenzel, Maria.

Catharina, b. 3 Apr 1787, bapt. 19 Aug 1787, of Johannes Schumacher and Anna Maria. Sponsors: Henrich Oechslein, Catharina.

Elisabeth, b. 4 June 1787, bapt. 19 Aug 1787, of Jacob Eberhardt and Charlotta. Sponsors: Anna Elisabeth, wife of Joh. Georg Eberhardt.

Elisabeth, b. 4 Sep 1787, bapt. 19 Sep 1787, of Michael Usselmann and Elisabeth. Sponsors: Johannes Georg, Elisabeth.

Catharina, b. 18 Aug 1787, bapt. 19 Sep 1787, of Johannes Jungken and Catharina. Sponsors: Jacob Jungken, Hannah.

Jacob, b. 2 Sep 1787, bapt. 19 Sep 1787, of Jacob Martin and Anna Magdalena. Sponsors: Johann Adam Faerber, Regina Susann.

Wilhelm, b. 2 Sep 1787, bapt. 19 Sep 1787, of Jacob Martin and Anna Magdalena. Sponsors: Wilhelm Roesler, Anna Margreth.

Johannes, b. 3 July 1787, bapt. 14 Oct 1787, of Georg Schultz and Elisabeth. Sponsors: Fridrich Beltz, Catharina.

Maria Magdalena, b. 20 July 1787, bapt. 14 Oct 1787, of Jacob Biber and Cathrina. Sponsors: Maria Magdalena, wife of Adam Schober.

..._, b. 10 July 1787, bapt. 14 Oct 1787, of Carl Grimm and Catharina. Sponsors: Parents.

Michael, b. 7 Oct 1787, bapt. 28 Nov. 1787, of Peter Heckmann and Regina. Sponsors: Michael Boger, Elisabeth.

Regina, b. 30 Oct 1787, bapt. 28 Nov 1787, of Christian Rus and Anna Catharina. Sponsors: Parents.

Maria Sara, b.20 ___, bapt. 6 Feb 1788, of Conrad Dritten. Sponsor: Maria Sara Prielin.

Catharina, b. 29 Dec 1787, bapt. 2 Apr 1788, of Conrad Roller. Sponsors: Catharina Herchlr...

Fridrich, b. 17 Feb 1788, bapt. 1788, of Geor Ebel and Catharina. Sponsors: Fridrich Schloetz and wife.

Fridrich, b. 10 Mar 1788, bapt. 2 Apr 1788, of Fridrich Lüneburg. Sponsors: Dieterich Loher, Anna Maria Weber.

Andreas, b. 5 Dec 1787, bapt. 2 Apr 1788, of Andreas Koehler and Anna Barbara. Sponsors: Georg Reser, Magdalena.

Elisabeth, b. 31 Dec 1787, bapt. 2 Apr 1788, of Johann Ruff and Margreth. Sponsors: Margreth, wife of Bernhardt Bauer.

Jacob, b. 16 Jan 1788, bapt. 2 Apr 1788, of Johannes Scholetzer and Catharina. Sponsors: Jacob Scholetzer, Susanna.

Johannes, b. 17 Mar 1788, bapt. 2 Apr 1788, of Philipp Gros and Barbara. Sponsors: Johannes Phale, Eva Margretha.

Juliana, b. 24 Nov 1787, bapt. 2 Apr 1788, of Conrad Wismann and Catharina, daughter of Isaac Muller? Sponsors: Christoph Bornhaus, Rosina.

Johannes, b. 14 Mar 1788, bapt. 2 Apr 1788, of Joh Adam Kadel and Elisabeth. Sponsors: Conrad Trittebach, Maria Mag... .

Anna Maria Catharina, b. 29 Jan 1788, bapt. 2 Apr 1788, of Jacob Walther and Anna M... Sponsors: Adam Schober, Maria Magdalena.

Adam, b. 3 Nov 1787, bapt. 11 Apr 1788, of Jacob Schneider and Margeretha. Sponsors: Parents.

..., b. 10 Feb 1788, bapt. 27 Apr 1788, of Adam Wensel and Anna Maria. Sponsors: Martin Stifel.

Johannes, b. 6 Feb 1788, bapt. 27 Apr 1788, of Johannes Battenfeld and Barbara. Sponsors: Martin Heckendorn, Catharine.

Christina, b. 9 Mar 1788, bapt. 27 Apr 1788, of Jac. Henrich and Catharina. Sponsors: Ludwig Wentzel, Christina Henrich.

Barbara, b. 6 Nov 1788, bapt. 27 Nov 1788, of Martin Heckendon and Catharina. Sponsors: Johannes Battenfeld, Barbara.

Anna Magd. b. 27 Dec 1777 (sic), bapt. 27 Apr 1788, of Johannes Hemd and Susanna. Sponsors: Michael Schaefer, Mari Lang.

Johannes, b. 2 May 1788, bapt. 4 June 1788, of Johannes Wüst and Catharina. Sponsors: Johannes Schaefer, Clara Mann.

Philip Henrich, b. 30 Mar 1788, bapt. 4 June 1788, of Johannes Ockslein and Christina. Sponsors: Philip Henrich, Catharina.

Johannes, b. 2 Dec 1787, bapt. 4 June 1788, of Adam Michler and Catharina. Sponsors: Johannes Ruf, Margaretha.

Maria Magd., b. 9 May 1788, bapt. 4 June 1788, of Michael Boger and Maria. Sponsor: Magdalena Brenner.

Johannes, b. 4 Mar 1788, bapt. 4 June 1788, of ... Sponsors: Philip Frey, Dorothea.

Caspar, b. 16 Apr 1788, bapt. 4 June 1788, of Andreas Spring. Sponsors: Parents.

Elisabeth, b. 17 Apr 1788, bapt. 4 June 1788, of Johannes Wentsel. Sponsors: Philip Hof, Rosina.

Anna Maria, b. 27 Jan 1788, bapt. 4 June 1788, of Johannes Schmid and Sus[anna]. Sponsors: Anna Maria, widow of Johannes .... .

Johann Anthon, b. 7 July 1788, of Caspar Trout and Anna. Sponsors: Anthon Amend, Maria Mag... .

Magd., b. 26 June 1788, bapt. 27 Aug 1788, of Stophel Briel and Margareth. Sponsors: Conrad Trittenbach, Magd.

Martin, b. 29 Feb 1788, bapt. 27 Aug 1788, of Herman Knoshenhauer [?] and Elisabetha. Sponsors: Martin Jecky, Catharina.

Anna Maria, b. 11 ... , b. 27 Aug 1788, of Peter Ritshy and Elisabetha. Sponsors: Wilhelm Wenner, Anna.

Elisabetha, b. 20 June 1788, bapt. 27 Aug 1788, of Simon Richert and Susanna. Sponsors: Abraham Stetler, Elisabeth.

Michael, [no info on birth or parents]. Sponsors: Leonhard Antzel, Catharina.

Jacob, b. 13 Sept 1788, bapt. 28 Sept 1788, of Adam Wolf and Margaretha. Sponsor: Jacob Steinbrenner.

Hannah, b. 5 Aug 1788, bapt. 28 Sept 1788, of Georg Reiser and Magdalena. Sponsors: Andreas Koehler, Barbara.

Susanna, b. 30 Aug 1788, bapt. 28 Sept 1788, of Leonhard Antzel and Catharina. Sponsors: Melcher Hertzel, Margaretha.

Johann George, b. 27 Aug 1788, bapt. 28 Sept 1788, of Lorentz Amend and Anna Barbara. Sponsors: Martin Bauer, Barbara.

Johann Adam, b. 16 Sept 1788, bapt. 29 Oct 1788, of Wilhelm Alt and Rachel. Sponsors: Parents.

Eva Catharina, b. 18 Sept 1788, bapt. 29 Oct 1788, of Johannes Siebert and Maria Magdalena. Sponsors: Mich. Schwenck, Eva Catharina Schwenck.

Anna Maria, b. 8 Oct 1788, bapt. 29 Oct 1788, of Johannes Phale and Eva Margreth. Sponsors: Johannes Phale, Anna Maria.

Elisabeth, b. 9 Aug 1788, bapt. 29 Oct 1788, of Christoph Daenges and Catharina. Sponsors: Maria, daughter of Fridrich Lampert.

Elisab., b. 26 Jan 1789, bapt. 4 Mar 1789, of Fried, Beltz and Catharina. Sponsors: Christoph Shafer, Elisabetha.

Catharina, b. 18 Nov 1789, bapt. 4 Mar 1789, of Henrich Segel and Tercky [sic]. Sponsors: ... Catharina.

Friederich, b. 1 Feb 1789, bapt. 4 Mar 1789, of Friederich Funck and Catharina. Sponsors: Friederich Füller, Catharina.

Catharina, b. 15 Oct. 1788, bapt. 4 Mar 1789, of Jacob Steinbrenner and Barbara. Sponsors: Johannes Campfer, Catharina.

Anna Maria, b. 11 Jan 1789, bapt. 4 Mar 1789, of Philip Freu and Dorothea. Sponsor: Anna Maria Wittemaen.

Susanna, b. 17 Dec 1788, bapt. 4 Mar 1789, of Georg Wild and Susanna. Sponsors: Jacob Waldmann, Margaretha.

Christina Margaretha, b. 28 Feb 1789, bapt. 4 Mar 1789, of Martin Bauer and Barbara. Sponsors: Fried. Bauer, Christina Bernhard.

Carl, b. 17 Jan 1789, bapt. 4 Mar 1789, of John Pasken and Magdalena. Sponsors: Peter Haller, Magdalena.

Johannes, b. 30 Oct 1782, bapt. 4 Mar 1789, of Levi Printz and Anna Elisabeth. Sponsors: Jacob Schloetzer, Susanna.

Mathaeus, b. 21 Feb 1784, bapt. 4 Mar 1789, of Levi Printz and Anna Elisabeth. Sponsors: Andreas Spring, Anna Maria.

Nathan, b. 21 Jan 1786, bapt. 4 Mar 1789, of Levi Printz and Anna Elisabetha. Sponsors: Georg Schaefer.

Isaac, b. 10 Sept 1788, bapt. 4 Mar 1789, of Levi Printz, and Anna Elisabetha,. Sponsors: Johannes Schaefer, Margareth.

Georg, b. 21 Feb 1789, bapt. 19 Apr 1789, of Conrad Lang and Magdalena. Sponsors: Georg Reiser, Magdalena.

Johannes, b. 29 Jan 1789, bapt. 19 Apr 1789, of Christoph Bornhaus and Rosina. Sponsors: Johannes Herchelroth, Barbara.

Anna Maria, b. 4 Feb 1789, bapt. 19 Apr 1789, of Christian Krumrein and Elisabeth. Sponsor: Anna Maria, daughter of Andreas Beltz.

Elisabeth, b. 28 Mar 1789, bapt. 19 Apr 1789, of Fridrich Samuel Waldmann and Elisabeth. Sponsor: Magdalena, daughter of Peter Bekener.

Elisabeth, b. 2 Dec 1788, bapt. 19 Apr 1789, of Jacob Philipps and Magdalena. Sponsors: Johannes Davis and Elisabeth.

Eva Margareth, b. 21 Dec 1788, bapt. 19 Apr 1789, of Johannes Stier and Margareth. Sponsors: Georg Schaka, Eva Margreth.

Elisabeth Barbara, b. 23 Sept 1788, bapt. 19 Apr 1789, of Roberts Steward and Maria Magdalena. Sponsors: Martin Bauer, Anna Barbara.

Louisa Christina, b 21 Apr 1788, bapt. 19 Apr 1789, of Georg Brand and Rosina. Sponsors: Christian Bugle, Eva.

Peter, b. 23 Feb 1789, bapt. 19 Apr 1789, of Fridrich Boger and Regina. Sponsors: Peter Heckmann, Regina.

Georg, b. 21 Feb 1789, bapt. 19 Apr 1789, of Wilhelm Adams and Barbara. Sponsors: Georg Mayer, Barbara.

Abraham, b. 6 Apr 1789, of Johannes Wü.... Sponsors: Abraham Stettler and Elisabeth.

Elisabetha, b. 21 Jan 1789, bapt. June 1789, of Georg Floetzer and Marar. Sponsors: Elisabetha Ullmer.

Maria Margaretha, b. 15 May 1789, bapt. 7 June 1789, of Johannes Hepler and Catharina. Sponsors: Peter Schumacher, Margaretha.

Georg, b. 23 Mar 1789, bapt. 7 June 1789, of Johannes Stump and Dorothea. Sponsors: Leonhard Antzel, Catharina.

Maria Magd., b. 7 May 1789, bapt. 7 June 1789, of Michael Rus and Elisabetha. Sponsors: Georg Schumacher, Maria M. Frontz.

Barbara, b. 27 Feb 1789, bapt. 7 June 1789, of Geo. Wentz and Catharina. Sponsors: Geo. Mayer, Barbara.

Maria Margaretha, b. 7 ___ 1789, bapt. 7 June 1789, of Peter Beltz and Magd. Sponsors: Deobald Moll, Eva Margretha.

Elisabetha, b. 18 June 1789, bapt. 4 Aug 1789, of Henrich Straehm and Magd. Sponsors: Maria Margaretha Straehm.

Jacob, b. 30 May 1789, bapt. 9 Aug 1789, of Peter Freu and Christina. Sponsors: Jacob Schloezer, Susanna.

Jacob, b. 15 June 1789, bapt. 9 Aug 1789, of Simon Schumacher and Carlotta. Sponsors: Georg Schumacher, Magd.

Samuel, b. 17 July 1789, bapt. 9 Aug 1789, of Conrad Drittenbach.

... , b. 24 June 1789, bapt. 9 Aug 1789, of ... Schmitt and Christina. Sponsors: Jacob Waldmann, Margaretha.

Margaretha, b. 29 Apr 1789, bapt. 9 Aug 1789, of Geo. Maul and Rosina. Sponsors: Philip Hof, Rosina.

Catharina, b. 22 Aug 1789, bapt. 9 Sept 1789, of Nicolaus Freu and Margaretha. Sponsors: Parents.

John, b. 5 June 1789, bapt. 9 Sept 1789, of John Pirsen and Peggy Bright. Sponsor: Mother.

Margaretha, b. 25 Dec 1788, bapt. 25 Oct 1789, of [Adam] Hofmann and Chrisina. Sponsors: Geo. Daeschner, Margaretha.

Johannes, b. 2 Oct 1789, bapt. 25 Oct 1789, of Samuel Melon and Maria. Sponsors: Johannes Wuertz, Elisabetha.

Georg, b. 20 May 1789, bapt. 25 Oct 1789, of Willhelm Stacks and Catharina. Sponsors: Johannes Campfer, Catharina.

Antony, b. 21 Oct 1789, bapt. 3 Dec 1789, of Johannes Schloeter and Catharina. Sponsors: Antony Sauter, Margaretha.

Susanna, b. 26 Oct 1789, bapt. 3 Dec 1789, of Jacob Schloetzer and Catha. Sponsors: Jac. Schloetzer, Susanna.

Anna Maria, b. 9 Oct 1789, bapt. 3 Dec 1789, of Adam Kurz and Elisabeth. Sponsor: Barbara Schmitt.

Samuel, b. 10 Nov 1788, bapt. 3 Feb 1790, of Thomas Davis and Esther. Sponsors: Carl Hoffmann, Julianna.

Georg, b. 7 Nov 1789, bapt. 21 Feb 1790, of Fridrich Steinbrenner and Juliana. Sponsors: Jacob Schloetzer, Susanna.

Johannes, b. 19 Feb 1790, 21 Feb 1790, of Adam Wolf and Margareth. Sponsors: Johannes Kamper, Catharina.

Peter, b. 16 Jan 1790, bapt. 21 Feb 1790, of Peter Steinbrenner and Susanna. Sponsors: Johannes Kamper, Catharina.

Maria Magd., b. 6 Feb 1790, bapt. 17 Mar 1790, of Christian Rus and Anna Catharina. Sponsors: Parents.

Elisabetha, b. 15 Jan 1790, bapt. 17 Mar 1790, of Johannes Frey and Susanna. Sponsors: Henrich Guthard, Elisabetha.

Adam, b. 17 Feb 1790, bapt. 17 Mar 1790, of Johannes Wentz and Magd. Sponsors: Adam Wentzel, Anna Maria.

Jacob, b. 24 Feb 1790, bapt. 17 Mar 1790, of Joh. Ullm and Elisabetha. Sponsors: Jacob Schloetzer, Susanna.

Eleonora, b. 16 Oct 1789, bapt. 17 Mar 1790, of Georg Hartman and Magdalena. Sponsors: Adam Schober, Magdalena.

Georg, b 31 Jan 1790, bapt. 17 Mar 1790, of Peter Bader and Susanna. Sponsors: Georg Hartmann and Magdalena.

Rahel, b. 1 May 1786, bapt. 11 Apr 1790, of Johannes Alt and Magdalena. Sponsors: Michael Palmer, Maria Barbara.

Georg Adam, b. 16 Dec 1789, bapt. 11 Apr 1790, of Martin Heckedorn and Catharina. Sponsors: Adam Battefeld, Eva Margaret.

Maria Magdalena, b. 20 Nov 1789, bapt. 11 Apr 1790, of Johannes Battefeld and Barbara. Sponsors: Parents.

Maria Magdalena, b. 10 Feb 1790, bapt. 11 Apr 1790, of Peter Schumacher and Anna Maria Margareth. Sponsors: Abigail, daughter of Daniel Schumacher.

Johannes, b. 18 Nov 1789, bapt. 11 Apr 1790, of Henrich Strehm and Magdalena. Sponsors: Henrich Strehm, Sr., Maria Margreth.

Friederich, b. 17 Feb 1790, bapt. 5 May 1790, of Conrad Roller and Elisabetha. Sponsors: Friederich Schloetz, Anna Marga.

Catharina, b. 28 May 1790, bapt. 1 July 1790, of Michael Boger and Elisabeth. Sponsors: Philipp Frey, Dorothea.

Georg, b. 27 Apr 1790, bapt. 1 July 1790, of Johannes Schaeffer and Margreth. Sponsors: Siegried Schaeffer, Margreth Schwenck.

Samuel, b. 31 Mar 1790, bapt. 1 July 1790, of Matthis Naphzinger and Anna. Sponsors: Fridrich Boger, Regina.

Sarah, b. 21 May 1790, bapt. 11 Aug 1790, of Adam Wentzel and Anna Maria. Sponsors: Jacob Waldman, Margareth.

Christina, b. 9 Aug 1789, bapt. 11 Aug 1790, of Carl Grimm and Catharina. Sponsors: Philipp Frey, Dorothea.

Anna Elisabeth, b. 23 ..., bapt. 11 Aug 1790, of Melchor Strupp and Ma... Sponsors: Samuel Waldman, Elisabeth.

Philipp, b 20 Mar 1790, bapt. 19 Sept 1790, of Andreas Koehler and Barbara. Sponsors: Ludewig Brenner, son of Philip; Elisabeth, daughter of Georg Reiser.

Johann Fridrich, b. 18 Aug 1790, bapt. 19 Sept 1790, of Gottlieb Pfingsttag and Maria Magdalena. Sponsors: Johannes Stump, Dorothea.

Philippina, b 27 Aug 1790, bapt. 19 Sept 1790, of Fridrich Füller and Catharina. Sponsors: Elisabeth, daughter of Nicolas Bader.

Elisabeth, b 6 June 1790, bapt. 19 Sept 1790, of Ludewig Wentzel and Christina. Sponsors: Elisabeth, wife of Andrew Thomson [?]

Wilhelm, b. 27 Aug 1790, bapt. 19 Sept 1790, of Johannes Martin and Catharina. Sponsors: Lorentz Amend, Barbara.

Andreas, b. 9 Sept 1790, bapt. 20 Oct 1790, of Andreas Springer and Anna Maria. Sponsors: Jacob Schloetzer, Susanna.

Elisabeth, b. 13 Sept 1790, bapt. 20 Oct 1790, of Johanes Wirtz and Elizabeth. Sponsors: Elisabeth, daughter of Conrad Wirtz.

Georg Jacob, b. 17 July 1790, bapt. 20 Oct 1790, of Adam Sorg and Catharina. Sponsors: Parents.

Catharina, b. 18 Sept 1790, bapt. 20 Oct 1790, of Jacob Hemmerich and Catharina. Sponsor: Johann Georg Bernhardt.

Jacob, b. 15 Sept 1790, bapt. 31 Dec 1790, of Georg Mann and Hanna. Sponsors: Wilhelm Becker, E...

Jacob, b. 21 Sept 1790, bapt. 31 Dec 1790, of Georg Wild and Susanna. Sponsors: Johannes Dorsch, Christina.

Elisabetha, b. 19 Oct 1790, bapt. 31 Dec 1790, of Friedrich Schloetz and Anna Margareth. Sponsors: [not named].

Maria Christina, b. 11 Oct 1790, bapt. 30 Jan 1791, of Georg Reiser and Maria Magdalena. Sponsors: Georg Hartmann, Magdalena.

Catharina, b. 17 Oct 1790, bapt. 30 Jan 1791, of Christoph Brühl and Margaretha. Sponsors: Conrad Trittebapt.ch, Magdalena.

Catharina, b. 12 Jan 1790, bapt. 23 Jan 1790, of Peter Stock and Elisabeth. Sponsors: Philip Frantz, Cathrina.

Maria, b. 9 Jan 1791, bapt. 3 Apr 1791, of Wilhelm Alt and Rahel. Sponsors: Michael Palmer, Barbara.

Michael, b. 6 Sept 1790, bapt. 3 Apr 1791, of Jost Arnold and Catharina. Sponsors: Michael Schaeffer, Anna Elisabeth.

Johann Michael, b. 27 Sept 1790, bapt. 3 Apr 1791, of Johannes Hemp and Susanna. Sponsors: Johann Michael Schwenck, Catharina.

Catharina, b. 26 Jan 1791, bapt. 3 Apr 1791, of Michael Schaeffer and Anna Elisabeth. Sponsors: Margareth, Johannes Schaeffer.

Simon, b. 2 June 1790, bapt. 3 Apr 1791, of Simon Rickert and Susanna. Sponsors: Parents.

Barbara, b. 26 Feb 1791, bapt. 3 Apr 1791, of Jacob Steinbrenner and Barbara. Sponsors: Jacob Steinbrenner, Anna Eva.

Johannes, b. 25 Jan 1791, bapt. 3 Apr 1791, of Heinrich Hoff, son of Philip Hoff and Elisabeth, daughter of Johann Michael Schwenck. Sponsors: Johanna Georg Schwenck, Margreth.

Johannes, b. 5 Mar 1791, bapt. 3 Apr 1791, of Leonardt Ansel and Catharina. Sponsors: Johannes Stump, Dorothea.

Anna Margareth, [no birth info], bapt. 3 Apr 1791, of Johannes Stump. Sponsors: Anna Margareth, daughter of Leonhardt.

Elisabeth, b. 31 Jan 1791, bapt. 3 Apr 1791, of Johannes Brühl and Anna Maria. Sponsors: Margreth, wife of Christoph Brühl.

Georg Jacob, b. 27 Mar 1791, bapt. 8 May 1791, of Samuel Waldmann and Elisabeth. Sponsors: Jacob Waldmann, Margreth.

Johann Philipp, b. 26 Mar 1791, bapt. 8 May 1791, of Conrad Lang and Maria Magdalena. Sponsors: Georg Hartmann, Anna Maria.

Johannes, b. 16 Dec 1790, bapt. 8 May 1791, of Henrich Neuschwanger and Ca... Sponsors: Parents.

Johann, b. 2 Apr 1791, bapt. 8 May 1791, of John Majer and Sahra. Sponsors: John Wentzel, Maria.

Sarah, b. 20 Dec 1790, bapt. 8 May 1791, of George Floetzer and Margaret. Sponsors: Jacob Kadel, Catharina.

Catharina, b. 16 Apr 1791, bapt. 8 May 1791, of Johann Gottlieb Dorsch and Christina. Sponsors: Frantz Ritsche, Catharina.

Conrad, b. 6 June 1791, bapt. 17 July 1791, of Peter Wirtz and Christina. Sponsors: Conrad Wirtz, Barbara.

Sara, b. 10 Apr 1791, bapt. 17 July 1791, of Johannes Seiffert and Catharina. Sponsors: Johannes Campher, Catarina.

Johannes, b. 13 May 1791, bapt. 17 July 1791, of Friederich Boger and Regina. Sponsor: Johannes Shaffer.

Juliana, b. 24 Apr 1791, bapt. 17 July 1791, Christoph Bornhause and Rosina. Sponsors: Johannes Stear, Margareth.

Philip, b. 27 May 1791, bapt. 17 July 1791. Sponsors: [not named].

Johannes, b. 2 June 1791, bapt. 17 Aug 1791, of Johannes Schloetzer and Catharina. Sponsors: Johannes Kamp, [Campher] Cath.

Georg, b. 24 Oct 1790, bapt. 17 Aug 1791, of Georg Herschelmann and Elisabeth. Sponsors: Adam Lang, Anna Maria.

Anna Catharina, b. 9 Aug 1791, bapt. 18 Sept 1791, of Andreas Maurer and Anna Margaretha. Sponsors: Fridrich Funck, Anna Catharina.

Philipp, b. 14 Sept 1791, bapt. 18 Sept 1791, of Adam Wolf and Anna Margreth. Sponsors: Johannes Kamper, Catharina.

Anna Elisabeth, b. 3 Feb 1791, bapt. 8 Oct 1791, of Levi Printz and Anna Elisabeth. Sponsors: Jacob Kadel, Catharina.

Christina, b. 2 Mar 1791, bapt. 8 Oct 1791, of Wilhelm Wirtz and Christina Biber. Sponsors: Johanna Gottlieb Dursch, Christina.

Wilhelm, b. 11 June 1783, bapt. 9 Oct 1791, of James Best and Maria Elisabeth. Sponsor: Jacob Waldemann.

Johannes, b. 9 Apr 1785, bapt. 9 Oct 1791, of James Best and Maria Elisabeth. Sponsor: Jacob Schumacher.

Henrich, b. 4 Nov 1787, bapt. 9 Oct 1791, of James Best and Maria Elisabeth. Sponsor: Philipp Frey.

Anna Maria, b. 24 Apr 1791, bapt. 9 Oct 1791, of Fridrich Weber and Elisabeth. Sponsors: Jacob Kadel, Catharina.

Andreas, b. 20 Oct 1791, bapt. 23 Oct 1791, of Peter Frey and Christina. Sponsors: Andreas Spring, Maria.

Elisabeth, b. 9 Oct 1791, bapt. 9 Nov 1791, of Jacob Slötzer and Catharina. Sponsor: Cathar. Schlötzer.

Johann Peter, b. 26 Sept 1791, of Fridrich Spring. Sponsors: Johann Peter Steinbrenner, Suanna.

Elisabeth, b. 1 Oct 1791, of Johannes Ulm and Elisabeth. Sponsor: Elisabeth, widow of Martin ... .

Catharina, b. 10 Oct 1791, bapt. 11 Dec 1791, of Georg Mann and Hanna. Sponsors: Samuel Becker and wife Clara.

George, b. 11 Nov 1791, bapt. 11 Dec 1791, of George Schwenck and Margareth. Sponsors: Georg Meyer, Barbara.

Elisabeth, b. 4 Nov 1791, bapt. 11 Dec 1791, of Michael Rus and Maria. Sponsors: Nathanael Tomplison, Elisabeth.

Johannes, b. 26 Oct 1791, bapt. 25 Dec 1791, of John Axlein and Christina. Sponsors: Adam Rohrbach, Hannah.

Johannes, b. 8 Dec 1792, bapt. 28 Mar 1792, of Johannes Mack and Margretha. Sponsors: Johannes Hüter, Christina.

Johannes, b. 3 Jan 1792, bapt. 28 Mar 1792, of Johannes Wentzel and Maria Magdalena. Sponsors: Johannes Phale, Eva Margaretha.

Susanna, b. 24 Jan 1792, bapt. 28 Mar 1792, of Peter Stock and Elisabetha. Sponsor: Susanna, daughter of Philipp Hoff.

Anna Maria, b. 25 Feb 1792, bapt. 28 Mar 1792, of Andrew Thompson and Elisabeth. Sponsor: Anna Maria, wife of Adam Wentzel.

Johannes, b. 27 Oct 1791, bapt. 28 Mar 1792, of Johannes Schneider and Maria Magdalena. Sponsors: Johannes Stautzenberger and wife.

Marg. b. 3 June 1790, bapt. 28 Mar 1792, of William Chambers and Marg. Sponsors: Jacob Waldmann, Margretha.

Adam, b. 16 Feb 1792, of Carl Grimm and Catharina. Sponsors: [not named].

... , b. 19 Mar 1792, bapt. 28 Apr 1792, of ... Wentzel and Catharina. Sponsor: ... Demig.

[Elisa]beth, b. 1 Sept 1791, bapt. 29 Apr 1792, of Abraham Bernhardt and Catharina. Sponsor: Susanna, daughter of Philipp Hoff.

Elisabeth, b. 14 Nov 1791, 29 Apr 1792, of Johannes Stier and Margreth. Sponsors: Jacob Battefeld, Elisabeth Georg.

Peter, b. 17 Dec 1791, bapt. 29 Apr 1792, of Johannes Schaeffer and Anna Margreth. Sponsor: Daniel Haller.

Wilhelm Fridrich, b. 5 Mar 1792, bapt. 29 Apr 1792, of Fridrich Schmid and Christina. Sponsors: Wilhelm Wenner, Jr., Anna Maria.

Maria Agatha, b. 5 Mar 1792, bapt. 29 Apr 1792, of Fridrich Schmid and Christina. Sponsors: Jacob Sonnefrank, Maria Agatha.

Henrich, b. 28 Jan 1792, bapt. 29 Apr 1792, of Thomas Davis and Esther. Sponsors: Henrich Horn, Elisabeth.

Johann Jacob, b. 30 Apr 1791, bapt. 29 Apr 1792, of Edward Row and Anna Maria. Sponsors: Johanna Jacob Kadel, Catharina.

Fridrich Adam, b. 22 Jan 1792, bapt. 29 Apr 1792, of Georg Hartmann and Magdalena. Sponsors: Adam Schober, Magdalena.

Catharina, b. 30 Sept 1791, bapt. 29 Apr 1792, of Christian Neuschwanger and Ruth. Sponsor: Dorothea, daughter of Johann Schmitz.

Andreas, b. 29 May 1790, bapt. 30 Apr 1792, of Peter Beltz and Magdalena. Sponsors: Andreas Beltz, wife Juliana, daughter Anna Maria.

Maria Magdalena, 20 Oct 1791, bapt. 30 Apr 1792, of Peter Beltz and Magdalena. Sponsors: Andreas Beltz, wife Juliana, daughter Anna Maria.

Johannes, b. 4 Dec ..., bapt. 30 Apr 1792, of Peter Temmeries [?], Sponsors: Georg Schaed, Julianna Wolf.

Elisabetha, b. ... Mar 1791, bapt. 30 Apr 1792, parents not named, Sponsors: Georg Schaed, Julianna Wolf.

Georg, b. 5 Oct 1791, bapt. 30 Apr 1792, of Henrich Kuntz and Barbara. Sponsor: Georg Schaed.

Susanna, b. 15 Nov 1791, bapt. 30 Apr 1792, of Thomas Bradley and Elisabeth. Sponsors: Parents.

Abraham, b. 26 Mar 1792, bapt. 1 June 1792, of Christian Russ and Catharina. Sponsors: Parents.

Daniel, b. 29 Apr 1792, bapt. 24 June 1792, of Peter Steinbrenner and Susanna. Sponsors: Jacob Steinbrenner, Eva.

Margreth, b. 26 Apr 1792, bapt. 24 June 1791, of Mattheis Feuerstein and Anna Maria. Sponsors: Margreth, daughter of Joseph Feuerstein.

John, b. 2 Aug 1787, [prob. bapt. 24 June 1792]. of James Booth and Phrene. Sponsors: Christian Eberhardt, Sibilla.

Eleonora, b. 6 Aug 1789, [prob. bapt. 24 June 1792]. of James Booth and Phrene. Sponsors: Christian Eberhardt, Sibilla.

Aaron, b. 18 Nov 1791, [prob. bapt. 24 June 1792], of James Booth and Phrene. Sponsors: Jacob Eberhardt, Charlotta; Johannes Georg, Elisabeth.

Adam, b 12 May 1792, bapt. 24 June 1792, of Adam Seyfort and Susanna. Sponsors: Christian Eberhardt, Sibilla.

Johannes, b. 29 June 1792, bapt. 7 Aug 1792, of Samuel Becker and Catharina. Sponsor: Johannes Mann, son of Georg Mann.

Margreth, b. 5 Apr 1792, bapt. 7 Aug 1792, of Johannes Schmid and Susanna. Sponsor: Jacob Waldmann.

Anna Maria, b. 3 June 1792, bapt. 7 Aug 1792, of Georg Stamm and Maria Clara. Sponsors: Adam Rohrbach, Hannah.

Henrich, b. 11 July 1792, bapt. 29 Aug 1792, of Peter Heckmann and Regina. Sponsors: Henrich Frey, Christina Engelbrecht.

Johan Georg, b. 6 Aug 1792, bapt. 29 Aug 1792, of Friedrich Kieffer and Maria Magdalena. Sponsors: Johan Georg Kieffer, Anna Maria Comper.

Anna, b. 20 Mar 1792, bapt. 3 Sept 1792, of Mathis Naphzinger and Anna. Sponsors: Parents.

Fridrich, b. 26 June 1792, bapt. 26 Sept 1792, of Fridrich Schloetz and Margreth. Sponsors: Conrad Roller, Elisabeth.

Jonathan, b. 26 Aug 1792, bapt. 26 Sept 1792, of Conrad Roller and Elisabeth. Sponsors: Fridrich Schloetz, Margreth.

Catharina, b. 8 July 1792, bapt. 14 Oct 1792, of Johannes Würtz and Elisabetha. Sponsor: Catharina Ritsche, [Single].

Christina, b. 16 Sept 1792, bapt. 15 Oct 1792, of Georg Wild and Susanna. Sponsors: Johannes Dorsch, Christina.

Johann Georg, b. 12 Apr 1792, bapt. 14 Oct 1792, of Michael Fünfrock and Elisabeth. Sponsors: Georg Wild, Susanna.

Christina, b. 6 Oct 1792, bapt. 25 Nov 1792, of Johannes Fahle and Margreth. Sponsors: Peter Frey, Christina.

Michael, b. 1 Dec 1792, bapt. 24 Mar 1793, of Michael ... . Sponsors: Philipp Brenner.

Johannes, b. 20 Oct 1792, bapt. 24 Mar 1793, of Wilhelm Alt and Regina. Sponsors: Parents.

Catharina, b. 20 Dec 1792, bapt. 24 Mar 1793, of Jacob Fahle and Barbara. Sponsor: Anna Maria Fahle.

Maria Elisabeth, b. 14 Jan 1793, bapt. 24 Mar 1792, of Andreas Koehler and Barbara. Sponsors: Johannes Schaefer, Maria Elisabeth ... .

Johann Jacob, b. 10 Oct 1792, bapt. [24 Mar] 1793, of Georg Reiser and Maria M... Sponsors: Jacob Wladmann, Margreth.

Michael, b. 28 Feb 1793, bapt. 21 Apr 1793, of Andreas Spring and Anna. Sponsors: Michael Boger, Maria Elisabeth.

Anna Catharina, b. 19 Dec 1792, bapt. 21 Apr 1793, of Johannes Brühl and Anna. Sponsor: Anna Catharina, wife of Christoph Ding ... .

Catharina, b. 17 Oct 1792, bapt. 21 Apr 1793, of Henrich Neuschwanger. Sponsors: Parents.

Adam, b. 13 Jan 1793, bapt. 21 Apr 1793, of Christoph Bornhaus and Rosina. Sponsors: Jost Arnold, Catharina.

Jacob, b. 10 Mar 1793, bapt. 15 May 1793, of Jacob Steinbrenner and Barbara. Sponsor: Daniel Steinbrenner, widower.

Johann Michael, b. 7 Apr 1793, bapt. 15 May 1793, of Johann Georg Schwenck and wife. Sponsors: Johann Michael Schwenck and wife.

Fridrich, b. 26 Mar 1793, bapt. 15 May 1793, of Fridrich Steinbrenner and Juliana. Sponsors: Jacob Schloetzer and Susanna.

Barbara, b. 7 Apr 1793, bapt. 15 May 1793, of Johannes Hempt and Susanna. Sponsor: Maria Barbara, widow of Joh. Ge.....

Peter, b. 27 Apr 1793, of Peter Beltz and Maria. Sponsors: Parents.

Elisabeth, b. 14 Oct 1792, bapt. 11 June 1793, of ... Andreas and Elisabeth. Sponsors: Parents.

Catharina, b. 28 Oct 1792, bapt. 16 June 1793, of Johannes Stedler and Priscilla. Sponsors: Catharina, Henrich Ritchie.

Jacob, b. 5 June 1793, bapt. 14 July 1793, of Peter Wirtz and Christina. Sponsor: Jacob Wirtz.

Christina, b. 17 May 1793, bapt. 14 July 1793, of Philipp Frey and Dorothea. Sponsors: Parents.

Rahel, b. 19 July 1790, bapt. 22 July 1793, of Jacob Schaefer and Mary Elisabeth. Sponsors: Parents.

Margareth, b. 19 Nov 1792, bapt. 13 Aug 1793, of Christian Neuschwanger and Ruth. Sponsors: Lorentz Amend, Barbara.

Johannes, b. 6 May 1791, bapt. 18 Sept 1793, of Georg Mohn and Ruth. Sponsors: Parents.

Jacob, b. 22 Apr 1793, bapt. 18 Sept 1793, of Georg Mohn and Ruth. Sponsors: Parents.

Margretha, b. 5 Aug 1793, bapt. 6 Oct 1793, of Peter Wacker and Maria Eva. Sponsors: Gottlieb Geist, Margretha.

Michael, b. 8 Aug 1793, bapt. 6 Oct 1793, of Peter Steinbrenner and Susanna. Sponsors: Jacob Steinbrenner, Eva.

[Jac]ob, b. 6 Sept 1793, bapt. 6 Oct 1793, of Jacob Waldman and Margretha. Sponsors: Jacob Waldmann, Margreth.

..., b. 28 July 1793, bapt. 6 Oct 1793, of Johannes Ulm and Elisabeth.

Anna Magdalena, b. 9 ... 1793, bapt. 27 Oct 1793, of Johann Ruff and Mar... . Sponsor: Anna Maria Beltz, daughter of ... .

Anna Maria, b. 18 Sept 1793, bapt. 27 Oct 1793, of Johannes Schlötzer and Catharina. Sponsors: Andreas Spring, Anna Maria.

Herich, b. 1 Oct 1793, bapt. 27 Oct 1793, of Christian Russ and Anna Catharina. Sponsors: Parents.

Samuel, b. 1 Oct 1793, bapt. 27 Oct 1793, of Johan Adam Catel and Elisabeth. Sponsors: Johannes Emig, Anna Maria Bruhl.

Magdalena, b. 18 Sept 1793, bapt. 27 Oct 1793, of Johannes Schafer and Margreth. Sponsors: Georg Schaffer, Catharina.

Susanna Catharina, b. 3 Sept 1793, bapt. 27 Oct 1793, of Susanna Rickert, widow. Sponsors: Adam Houshalder, Catharina.

Cathrina, b. 25 Oct 1793, bapt. 1 Jan 1794, of Conrad Drittenbach and Maria Magdalena. Sponsors: Carl Hoffman, Juliana.

Christian, b. 16 Nov 1793, bapt. 12 Jan 1794, of Georg Stamm and Maria Clara. Sponsors: Christian Reynold, Mary.

Johann Henrich, b. 23 Mar 1794, bapt. 13 Apr 1794, of Daniel Steinbrenner and Anna Maria. Sponsors: Johannes Fahly and Anna Maria.

Johann Jacob, b. 13 Mar 1794, of Fridrich Kiefer and Maria Magdalena.

Maria Catharina, b. 16 Feb 1794, bapt. 13 Apr 1794, of Johannes Mann and Magdalena. Sponsors: Johannes Ka..., Catharina.

Anna, b. 22 Jan 1794, bapt. 13 Apr 1794, of Christoph Brühl and Margaretha. Sponsor: Magdalena, daughter of Dorsheimer.

Elisabeth, b. 3 Oct 1792, bapt. 13 Apr 1794, of Henrich Adam Strehm and Appelonia. Sponsor: Maria Barbara M..., widow of Georg.

Maria, b. 16 Sep 1793, bapt. 13 Apr 1794, of Christian Ruff and Elisabeth. Sponsors: Philipp Frey, Dorothea.

Johann George, b. 7 Oct 1793, bapt. 13 Apr 1794, of Adam Wolf and Margareth. Sponsors: Jacob Steinbrenner, Eva.

Anna, b. 30 Jan 1794, bapt. 13 Apr 1794, of Michael Russ and Maria Elisabeth. Sponsors: Parents.

Dewald, b. 18 Mar 1794, bapt. 17 May 1794, of Johann George Mohll and Catharina. Sponsors: Dewald Mohll.

Abraham, b. 17 Apr 1794, bapt. 18 May 1794, of Thomas Davis and Esther. Sponsors: Georg Harmann, wife... .

Margreth, b. 20 Mar 1794, bapt. 18 May 1794, of Georg Wild and Susanna. Sponsors: Jacob Wellman, Marg...

Anna Maria, b. 28 Mar 1794, bapt. 18 May 1794, of Johannes Davis and Anna. Sponsors: Johannes Schaeffer, Anna Maria.

Catharina Magdalena, b. 16 Apr 1794, bapt. 18 May 1794, of Georg Fichter and Catharina. Sponsors: Conrad Trittebach, Maria Magdalena.

Sarah, b. 25 May [1793?], bapt. 22 May 1794, of Isaac Müller and Catharina. Sponsor: Barbara Muller.

Elisabeth, b. 31 Jan 1794, bapt. 22 May 1794, of Matthis Naphzinger and Anna. Sponsor: Madgalena, wife of Conrad Trittebach.

Daniel, b. 27 Jan 1794, bapt. 22 May 1794, of Carl Grimm and Catharina. Sponsors: Parents.

Anna Maria, b. 29 June 1794, bapt. 3 Aug 1794, of Jacob Phale and Barbara. Sponsors: Johannes Phale, Anna Maria.

Catharina, b. 8 July 1794, bapt. 3 Aug 1794, of Jacob Schloetzer and Catharina. Sponsors: Johannes Schloetzer, Catharina.

Georg Fridrich, b. 9 June 1794, bapt. 3 Aug 1794, of Georg Hartmann and Magdalena. Sponsor: Fridrich Bauer.

Juliana, b. 21 Apr 1794, bapt. 3 Aug 1794, of Peter Beltz and Maria Magdalena. Sponsors: Andreas Beltz, Juliana.

Eleonora, b. 12 Apr 1794, bapt. 3 Aug 1794, of Christian Neuschwanger and Ruthi. Sponsors: Catharina, daughter of Anthoni Amend.

David, b. 9 Mar 1794, bapt. 11 Sept 1794, of David Moll and Magdalena. Sponsors: David Moll, Margareth.

Elisabeth, b. 4 June 1794, bapt. 11 Sept 1794, of Peter Stock and Elisabeth. Sponsors: Jacob Schloetzer and wife Elisabeth.

Maria Magdalena, b. 4 June 1794, bapt. 11 Sept 1794, of Peter Stock and Elisabeth. Sponsors: Johannes Wentzel and wife Maria Magdalena.

Anna Catharina, b. 8 Aug 1794, bapt. 11 Sept 1794, of Peter Ansel and Elisabeth. Sponsors: Anna Catharina, wife of Leonardt Ansel.

Anna Magdalena, b. 8 Aug 1794, bapt. 11 Sept 1794, of Peter Tauberman and Elisabeth. Sponsors: Conrad Wirtz, Barbara.

Anna Maria, b. 2 Dec 1793, bapt. 5 Oct 1794, of Johann Fridrich Spring and Barbara. Sponsors: Johannes Mann, Anna Maria.

Adam, b. 23 Aug 1794, bapt. 5 Oct 1794, of Fridrich Steinbrenner and Juliana. Sponsors: Adam Wolf, Margretha.

Jacob, b. 27 Apr 1794, bapt. 5 Oct 1794, of Jacob Lentz and Juliana. Sponsors: Jacob Sonnefranck, Agatha.

Johann Fridrich, b. 11 Sept 1794, bapt. 5 Oct 1794, of Jacob Eberle and Magdalena. Sponsors: Michael Schaeffer, Elisabeth.

Johannes, b. 26 Aug 1794, bapt. 5 Oct 1794, of George Wentzel and Catharina. Sponsors: Johannes Oeh [Axline]..., Magdalena.

Christian, b. 18 Sept 1794, bapt. 5 Nov 1794, of Conrad Roller and Elisabeth. Sponsors: Friedrich Schlötz, Margreth.

Johan Carl, b. 16 Oct 1794, bapt. 16 Nov 1794, of Peter Steinbrenner and Susanna. Sponsors: Carl Gros, Elisabeth Catharina.

Maria Margaret, b. 4 Jan 1795, bapt. 11 Jan 1795, of George Ham and Maria Clara. Sponsors: Adam Rohrbach, Hannah.

Jacob, b. 25 Dec 1794, bapt. 29 Mar 1795, of Johann Georg Schwenck and Margareth. Sponsors: Georg Jacob Walt[man], Marg.

Henrich Adam, b. 15 Feb 1795, bapt. 29 Mar 1795, of Friedrich Schmid and Ludimagister. Sponsors: Henrich Adam Roh..., Margareth Roh..., widow.

Johann Philipp, b. 23 Dec 1794, bapt. 29 Mar 1795, of Henrich Joseph Frey and Christina. Sponsor: Philipp Frey.

Anna Maria, b. 31 Dec 1794, bapt. 29 Mar 1795, of Michael Boger and Maria Elisabeth. Sponsors: Anna Maria Wiltemaen, widow.

Sarah, b. 2 Feb 1795, bapt. 18 Apr 1795, of Johannes Berg and Catharina. Sponsors: Anna Maria..., Jacob Eberardt.

Michael, b. 1 Jan 1795, bapt. 19 Apr 1795, of Nicholas Frey and Anna Margreth. Sponsors: Leonhardt An..., Catharina.

Johann Henrich, b. 5 Jan 1795, bapt. 19 Apr 1795, of Adam Riebsaamen and Dorothea. Sponsors: Johanna Adam..., Margretha.

Anna Maria Christine, b. 6 Jan 1795, bapt. 13 Apr 1795, of Johannes Hergert and Margareth. Sponsors: Henrich Joseph..., Christina.

David, b. 13 Mar 1795, bapt. 19 Apr 1795, of Michael Müler and Catharina. Sponsors: David Oe...

Hillem, b. 18 Jan 1794, bapt. 19 Apr 1795, of James Dunnin and Zinna. Sponsors: Parents.

Johannes, b. 6 Apr 1795, bapt. 14 May 1795, of Adreas Spring and Anna Maria. Sponsors: Johannes Schloetzer, Catharina.

Jacob, b. 9 Feb 1795, bapt. 14 May 1795, of Christoph Bornhaus and Rosina. Sponsors: Jacob Bornhaus, Elisabeth.

Joseph, b. 24 Nov 1794, bapt. 14 May 1795, of Wendel Wentz and Elisabeth. Sponsors: Conrad Trittebach, Maria M...

Johannes, b. 5 May 1795, bapt. 28 June 1795, of Johannes Schaeffer and Anna Margreth. Sponsors: Johannes Schaeffer, Anna Maria.

Philipp, b. 24 Jan 1795, bapt. 28 June 1795, of Hiob Marcker and Anna Margreth. Sponsors: Johannes Schaeffer, Anna Maria.

Catharina, b. 12 May 1795, bapt. 28 June 1795, of Peter Müller and Catharina. Sponsors: Joseph Schmidt, Margreth.

Jacob, b. 6 May 1795, bapt. 28 June 1795, of Johannes Phale and Margreth. Sponsors: Jacob Phale, Barbara.

Wilhelm, b. 23 Dec 1792, bapt. 28 June 1795, of Michael Wirtz and Catharina. Sponsors: Parents.

Elisabeth, b. 6 Apr 1794, bapt. 28 June 1795, of Michael Wirtz and Cathrina. Sponsors: Adam Kiel, Elisabeth.

Juliana, b. 7 Apr 1795, bapt. 28 June 1795, of Henrich Neuschwanger and Catharina. Sponsors: Parents.

Anna Maria Magdalena, b. 2 Apr 1795, bapt. 28 June 1795, of Christian Krumrein and Maria Catharina. Sponsors: Peter Beltz, Maria Magdalena.

Henrich, b. 26 Feb 1795, bapt. 28 June 1795, of Henrich Strehm and Appellonia. Sponsors: Lorentz Amend, Barbara.

Georg, b. 21 May 1795, bapt. 28 June 1795, of Michael Schaeffer and Elisabeth. Sponsors: Georg Schu..., Mag... .

Maria Eva, b. 26 Feb 1795, bapt. 28 June 1795, of Henrich Kuntz and Barbara. Sponsors: Peter Beltz, Maria Magdalena.

Sibylla, b. 13 June 1795, bapt. 9 Aug 1795, of Peter Wirtz and Christina. Sponsors: Margareth ... .

Anthoni, b. 15 June 1795, bapt. 9 Aug 1795, of Georg Moll and Catharina. Sponsors: Peter ..., Maria Magdalena.

Michael, b. 7 Feb 1795, bapt. 9 Aug 1795, of Georg Berger and Catharina. Sponsors: Michael Rei... .

Georg Ludewig, b. 5 Mar 1795, bapt. 1 Sept 1795, of Adam Seyfort and Susanna. Sponsors: Georg Ludewig, Catharina.

Maria Magdalena, b. 15 Aug 1795, bapt. 1 Sept 1795, of Michael Meyer and Maria Elisabeth. Sponsors: Adam Schober, Maria M...

Maria Catharina, b. 15 Aug 1795, bapt. 11 Oct 1795, of Friderick Kieffer and Maria Magdalena. Sponsors: Johannes Campher, Catharina.

Elisabeth, b. 8 Oct 1795, bapt. 27 Oct 1795, of Johannes Stautzenberger and Maria Margaretha. Sponsor: Catharina, wife of Frantz...

Jacob, b. 24 Sept 1795, bapt. 1 Nov 1795, of Wilhelm Wirtz and Barbara. Sponsors: Jacob Miller.

Johann George, b. 2 Sept 1795, bapt. 30 Oct 1795, of Johannes Schloetzer and Catharina.

Fridrich, [no further information].

Carl Philipp, b. 6 Oct 1795, bapt. 1 Nov 1795, of ...ounken and Catharina. Sponsors: Carl Dorshimer, Catharina.

Daniel, b. 19 Aug 1795, bapt. 1 Nov 1795, of Philipp Eberhard and Charlot. Sponsors: Johannes Kline, Christina.

Johann Jacob, b. 1 Oct 1795, bapt. 1 Nov 1795, of Johannes Mann and Anna Maria. Sponsors: Fridrich Kieffer, Magdalena.

Anna Maria, b. 10 Sept 1795, bapt. 1 Nov 1795, of Jacob Becker and Catharina. Sponsors: Andreas Spring, Anna Maria.

Daniel, b. 17 Oct 1795, bapt. 13 Dec 1795, of William Baker and Eva. Sponsor: George Mann.

Elisabeth, b. 19 Nov 1795, bapt. 13 Dec 1795, of Daniel Steinbrenner and Anna Maria. Sponsor: Elisabeth Fahley.

Catharina, b. 5 July 1794, bapt. 13 Dec 1795, of ... Gorver [Gover?] and Maria Elisabeth. Sponsors: John Yunken, Catharina.

Friedrick, b. 4 Nov 1795, bapt. 13 Dec 1795, of Christian Truse? and Anna Catharina. Sponsors: Parents.

Susanna, b. 28 Nov 1795, bapt. 13 Dec 1795, of Johann Adam Wolf and Margaretha. Sponsor: Susanna Steinbrenner, Jacob Steinbrenner's single daughter.

Christina, b. 23 Mar 1796, bapt. 22 May 1796, of Jacob Lenz and Juliana. Sponsors: Friederick Smith, wife Christina; and Agatha Sunefrank.

Catharine, b. 28 Apr 1796, bapt. 19 June 1796, of ... Waroker and Eva. Sponsors: Andreas Beltz, Juliana.

Margareth, b. 18 Jan 1796, bapt. 19 June 1796, of ... Tritenbach and Margaretha. Sponsors: Christian Biegel, Eva.

Adam, b. 30 Apr 1796, bapt. 19 June 1796, of Friedrich Sletzer and Margareth. Sponsors: Adam Wolf, Susanna.

Anna Maria, b. 27 Feb 1796, bapt. 17 July 1796, of ... Axline and Christina. Sponsors: Daniel Householder, Catharina.

Christina, b. 8 Aug 1796, bapt. 9 Aug 1796, of ... and Anna Maria. Sponsors: Christina Wirtz, daughter of Peter Wirtz's son.

Christian, b. 11 June 1796, bapt. 14 Aug 1796, of ... Fry and Christ. Sponsors: John Philipp Fry, Dorothea.

Abraham, b. 16 Jan 1796, bapt. 14 Aug 1796, of ... Stettler and Priscilla. Sponsors: Solomon Shoemaker, Elisabeth.

Lydia, b. 30 Mar 1796, of ... Jacoby and Anna. Sponsor: Julianna Beltz, Andreas Beltz's wife.

Magdalena, b. 20 June 1796, bapt. 14 Aug 1796, of ... Trittebach and Susanna. Sponsor: Margaretha Swenk, wife of Michael Swenk.

Catharina, b. 14 May 1796, bapt. 14 Aug 1796, of ... Huff? and Catharina. Sponsors: Conrad Trittebach, Maria Magdalena.

David, b. 30 Aug 1796, bapt. 9 Oct 1796, of Conrad Roller and Elisabeth. Sponsors: Johannes Hercher, Magareth.

Johannes, b. 27 Aug 1796, bapt. 9 Oct 1796, of ...ter Tauberman and Elisabeth. Sponsors: Philip Fry Jr., Catharine.

Elisabeth, b. 1 Sept 1796, bapt. 9 Oct 1796, of Anthony Fahly and Catharina. Sponsor: Elisabeth Fahly, Johannes Fahly's single daughter.

Daniel, b. 9 Sept 1796, bapt. 9 Oct 1796, of ... and Eva. Sponsor: Adam Householder.

Jacob, b. 29 Aug 1796, bapt. 6 Nov 1796, of Peter Whip and Elisabeth. Sponsors: [not named].

Magdalena, b. 22 Sept 1796, bapt. 6 Nov 1796, of John Arnietz? and Magadalena. Sponsor: Maria ... .

Magdalena, b. 12 Mar 1796, bapt. 6 Nov 1796, of Jacob Slelzer?, Jr. and Catharina. Sponsor: Peter Fry.

Elisabeth, b. 16 Sept 1795, bapt. 6 Nov 1796, of George Mann, Jr. and Hannah. Sponsor: Juliana ... .

Elisabetha, b. 16 Oct 1796, bapt. 4 Dec 1796, of Jacob Fally and Barbara. Sponsors: John Fahly.

Sarah, b. 9 Sept 1796, bapt. 1 Jan 1797, of Christian Ruff and Elisabeth. Sponsor: David Axline.

Michael, b. 25 Nov 1796, bapt. 1 Jan 1797, of Jacob Cooper and Barbara. Sponsor: Michael Ruse.

Anna Margaretha, b. 20 Jan 1797, bapt. 26 Feb 1797, of John Adam Kadel. Sponsor: Johann Stouseberger.

Margareth, b. 21 Dec 1796, bapt. 26 Feb 1797, of Conrad Trittebach and Maria Magdalena. Sponsor: John. George Schwenck.

Catharina, b. 14 Jan 1797, bapt. 26 Feb 1797, of Johann George Schwenck and Margaretha. Sponsor: Catharina, ...'s daughter.

Catharina, b. 30 Nov 1796, bapt. 26 Nov 1797, of Philipp Frey and Dorothea. Sponsor: Peter Heckmann.

Wilhelm, b. 15 Dec 1796, bapt. 26 Feb 1797, of Friederich Lampert and Anna Maria. Sponsor: Wilhelm Schäffer.

Daniel, b. 31 Ja 1796, bapt. 26 Mar 1797, of Johannes Schäffer and Margaretha. Sponsor: Georg Schuma[cher].

Sarah, b. 10 Feb 1797, bapt. 26 Mar 1797, of Philipp Frey and Catharina. Sponsor: Anna Mar... .

Jonathan, b. 12 Feb 1797, bapt. 26 Mar 1797, of Daniel Haushalter and Catharina. Sponsor: David Axline.

Susanna, b. 10 Nov 1795, bapt. 26 Mar 1797, of Christian Neuschwanger and Ruth. Sponsors: Jacob ... .

Henrich, b. 25 July 1796, bapt. 26 Mar 1797, of Henrich Neuschwanger and Catharina. Sponsor: Henrich ... .

Hannah, b. 31 Dec 1796, bapt. 26 Mar 1797, of Michael Meyer and Elisabeth. Sponsor: Adam R... .

Salomon, b. 20 Feb 1797, bapt. 23 Apr 1797, of Jacob Filler and Anna Barbara. Sponsor: Eva ... .

Christina, b. 20 Apr 1797, bapt. 21 May 1797, of Friederich Schmidt and Christina. Sponsor: Peter Wirtz ... .

Elisabetha, b. 28 Feb 1797, bapt. 21 May 1797, of Johannes Schletzer and Catharina. Sponsor: William ... .

Maria Catharina, b. 29 Mar 1797, bapt. 21 May 1797, of Georg Keisser and Maria Magdalena. Sponsor: Mich... .

Elisabetha, b. 15 Mar 1797, bapt. 21 May 1797, of Johannes Mann and Anna Maria. Sponsor: Samuel ... .

Catharina, b. 8 Apr 1797, bapt. 21 May 1797. Sponsors: Friederick Smith, Christina. [*Parents non-readable*].

Margaretha, b. 27 Sept 1797, bapt. 21 May 1797, of ... and Catharina. Sponsors: Johannes Stautzenberger, Anna Margaretha.

Johannes, b. 3 Dec 1796, bapt. 31 May 1797, of ... and Catharina. Sponsors: Philip Fry, Dorothea.

Margaretha Elisabetha, b. 1 Apr 1796, bapt. 11 June 1797. Sponsors: Parents.

Elisabetha, b. 29 Mar 1797, bapt. 16 June 1797, of ... Spring. Sponsors: Friederich Steinbrenner, Julianna.

Elisabetha, b. 13 June 1797, bapt. 2 July 1797, of ... Eberhard. Sponsors: Christian Eberhard, Sybilla.

Georg, b. 27 July 1797. bapt. 13 Aug 1797, of ... Schäfer. Sponsors: Georg Schumacher.

Christina, b. 3 Mar 1797, bapt. 13 Aug 1797, of ... and Elisabeth. Sponsors: Parents.

Anna Barbara, b. 10 June 1797, bapt. 13 Aug 1797, of ... Krumrein and Catharina. Sponsor: Margaretha Moll.

For the following, the parents' names were completely eradicated.

Johannes, b. 1 July 1797, bapt. 2 Sept 1797. Sponsors: Peter Heilmann, Regina.

Michael, b. 13 May 1797, bapt. 2 Sept 1797. Sponsors: Philipp Eberhard, Charlotta.

Anna Maria Yuliana, b. 24 July 1797, bapt. 2 Sept 1797. Sponsors: Friederich Steinbrenner, Yuliana.

Michael, b. 22 July 1797, bapt. 3 Sept 1797. Sponsors: Michael Wirtz, Catharina.

Johannes, b. 1 Aug 1797, bapt. 3 Sept 1797. Sponsors: Simon Schumacher, Charlotta.

Catharina, b. 27 July 1797, bapt. 3 Sept 1797. Sponsors: Melchor Strupp, Maria Anna.

Daniel, B. 5 Auig 1797,. bapt. 3 Sept 1797, of [Stei]nbrenner. Sponsors: John Adam Wolf, Susanna.

Sarah, b. 20 Aug 1796, bapt. 8 Oct 1797, of ...widow. Sponsors: Jacob Lärck, Margaretha.

Johannes, b. 25 Aug 1797, bapt. 8 Oct 1797. Sponsors: Conrad Wirtz, Barbara.

Anna, b. 24 Aug 1797, bapt. 8 Oct 1797. Sponsor: Sussanna Schmidt, Jacob Schmidt's single daughter.

Wilhelm, b. 14 May 1797, bapt. 8 Oct 1797, of Gerlach Stigler and Elisabetha. Sponsor: Wilhelm Wirtz.

Anna Margaretha, b. 27 Aug 1797, bapt. 8 Oct 1797, of Niclaus Frëy and Anna Margretha. Sponsors: Peter Frey, Ch...

Magdalena, b. 11 Aug 1797, bapt. 8 Oct 1797, of Georg Wentzel and Catharina. Sponsor: Maria Striffler.

Christian, b. 15 Sept 1797, bapt. 25 Dec 1797, of Jacob Steinbrenner and Barbara. Sponsors: Friderich Spring and wife.

Ann Maria, b. 15 Oct 1797, bapt. 3 Dec 1797, of Henrich Joseph Frey and Christina. Sponsor: Anna Maria ..., widow.

Michael, b. 10 Oct 1797, bapt. 3 Dec 1797, of Jacob Lang and Eva. Sponsors: Friederich Schep, Margaretha.

Maria Magdalena, b. 7 Nov 1797, bapt. 3 Dec 1797, of Johannes Lang and Barbara. Sponsor: Anna Maria Sauther, widow.

Michael, b. 9 Nov 1797, bapt. 3 Dec 1797, of Michael Ansel and Catharina. Sponsors: Georg Keisser, Catharina Ansel.

Anna Catharina, b. 18 Dec 1797, bapt. 25 Dec 1797, of Christoph Bornhauss and Rosina. Sponsor: Anna Stegers, wife of Adam Stegers.

David, b. 6 Sept 1797, bapt. 25 Feb 1798, of Jacob Käffer and Barbara. Sponsors: Johannes Schäffer, Margaretha.

Jacob, b. 24 Dec 1797, bapt. 25 Feb 1798, of John Thomas and Catharina. Sponsors: Jacob Wertz and wife.

Salomon, b. 1 Jan 1797, bapt. 25 Mar 1798, of Christian Ruse and Anna Catharina. Sponsors: Parents.

Samuel, b. 19 Jan 1798, bapt. 25 Mar 1798, of John Fassa, single man, and Elisabeth Trittebaugh, daughter of Conrad Trittebaugh, single. Sponsors: John Trittebaugh and wife.

Elisabetha, b. 8 Feb 1798, bapt. 22 Apr 1798, of George Fahley and Magdalena. Sponsors: Henrich Strehm, Margaretha.

Sally, b. 6 Oct 1797, bapt. 22 Apr 1798, of Philip Heater and Elisabeth. Sponsors: Eva Crumbacher, widow.

Peter, b. 31 Jan 1798, bapt. 22 Apr 1798, of Peter Reberick and Catharine. Sponsors: Conrad Trittebaugh and wife.

Catharina, b. 2 Apr 1798, bapt. 20 May 1798, of John Wencil and Magdalen. Sponsor: Frederick Smith.

Christina, b. 2 Nov 1797, bapt. 20 May 1798, of Jacob Seteer [Sletcer?] and Catharina. Sponsors: Peter Fry and wife.

Jacob, b. 1 Oct 1797, bapt. 20 May 1798, of Adam Syfet and Sussana. Sponsors: Philip Everhart.

Wilhelm, bapt. 20 May 1798, of Christian Newschwanger and wife.

Samuel, b. 22 May 1798, bapt. 6 June 1798, of ... Bark and wife. Sponsors: Parents.

Michael, b. 25 Apr 1798, bapt. 17 July 1798, of John Trittebach and Susanna. Sponsors: Johann Georg Schwenck, Margaretha.

John Melchior, b. 11 May 1798, bapt. 17 July 1798, of Samuel Waltman and Elisabeth. Sponsors: Melchior Strup, Mary Ann.

Carl, b. 15 May 1798, bapt. 15 July 1798, of Jacob Jacoby and Anna. Sponsors: Parents.

Benjamin, b. 19 May 1798, bapt. 15 July 1798, of Margaretha, Johann Michael Schwenck's single daughter. Sponsors: John Trittebach, Sussana.

Maria Magdalena, b. 20 May 1798, bapt. 15 July 1798, of Michael Trittebach, Conrad Trittebach's single son and Catharina Schwenck, Johann Michael Schwenck's single daughter. Sponsor: Eva Catharina Schwenck, wife of Johan Michael Schwenck.

John Jacob, b. 2 May 1798, bapt. 12 Aug 1798, of John Stouseberger and Margaret. Sponsors: Jacob Waltman, Margaretha.

Christian Adam, b. 12 Mar 1798, of Augustus Fridericus Wilhelmus Vogel and Elisabeth. Sponsors: Henry Adam Rohrbach, Hannah.

Johannes, b. 8 Aug 1798, bapt. 9 Sept 1798, of Peter Fry and Christina. Sponsors: Johannes Fahly, Eva Margaretha.

Daniel, b. 18 Aug 1798, bapt. 7 Oct 1798, of Conrad Roller and Elisabeth. Sponsors: Frederick Sletz, Anne Margareth.

Emannuel, b. 18 July 1798, bapt. 7 Oct 1798, of David Axline and Eva. Sponsors: John Axline, Christine.

Frederick, b. 4 Sept 1798, bapt. 7 Oct 1798, of Ludwig Draer and Anna Maria. Sponsor: Frederick Belz, son of Andrew Belz.

David, b. 21 Aug 1798, bapt. 7 Oct 1798, of Philip Everhard and Charlotta. Sponsors: David Axline, Eva.

Salomon, b. 19 Sept 1798, bapt. 7 Oct 1798, of Michael Ruse and Maria Elisabetha. Sponsors: Salomon Schumacher, Elisabetha.

Cornelius, b. 20 Aug 1798, bapt. 7 Oct 1798, of Leonard Crove and Catharine. Sponsors: Simon Shoemaker, Charlotta.

Michael, b. 17 Sept 1798, bapt. 7 Oct 1798, of John Adam Wolf and Sussana. Sponsors: George Fawley, Magdalene.

Johannes, b. 23 Sept 1798, bapt. 4 Nov 1798 of Frederick Cooper and Maria Magdalen. Sponsors: Peter Camper, son of Johannes Camper.

Anna Barbara, b. 23 Sept 1798, bapt. 4 Nov 1798, of ... Tauberman and Elizabeth. Sponsors: Conrad Wirtz, Barbara.

Elisabeth, b. 26 Aug 1798, bapt. 4 Nov 1798, of ... Wenk and Margaretha. Sponsors: Johannes Trittebach, Sussana.

Jacob, b. 18 Nov 1798, bapt. 27 Jan 1799. [*Parents' names non-readable*]. Sponsors: Jacob Fahly, Barbara.

Michael, b. 26 Nov 1798, bapt. 23 Mar 1799, of ... Kieffer and Anna Maria. Sponsor: Michael Kieffer.

Peter, b. 9 Oct 1798, bapt. 24 Mar 1799, of Nicolaus Fry and Margaretha. Sponsor: Peter Fry.

Maria Magdalena, b. 7 Feb 1799, bapt. 24 Mar 1799, of Michael Ansel and Catharina. Sponsors: Magdalena Rifer, George ... .

Carl, b. 6 Nov 1798, bapt. 24 Mar 1799, of John Shaffer and Anna Margareth. Sponsors: Michael Kieffer and wife.

Susana, b. 5 Mar 1799, bapt. 21 Apr 1799, of Daniel Steinbrenner and Anna Maria. Sponsors: Johannes Fahly, Sr. and wife.

Magdalena, b. 24 Jan 1799, bapt. 21 Apr 1799, of Georg Wensel and Catharina. Sponsors: Maria Stiffler, daughter of John Stiffler.

Jacob, b. 10 Feb 1799, bapt. 21 Apr 1799, of Michael Boger and Maria Elisabeth. Sponsors: Philip Souder and Susanna.

Johannes, b. 2 Jan 1799, bapt. 21 Apr 1799, of John Gowff and Catharina. Sponsors: Jacob Waltmann, Margretha.

Margaret, b. 21 Apr 1799, bapt. 19 May 1799, of Frederick Smith and Christina. Sponsors: Jacob Waltman and wife.

Sally, b. 14 Feb 1799, bapt. 19 May 1799, of Philip Kist and Nancy. Sponsors: Gotlieb Kist, Mary.

Thomas, b. 9 Jan 1797, bapt. 19 May 1799, of Philip Kist and Nancy. Sponsors: Philip Kist.

Peter, b. 25 Nov 1798, bapt. 19 May 1799, of Eva Wauker, widow. Sponsors: George Adam Steger and wife.

Henrich, b. 11 Apr 1799, bapt. 19 May 1799, of Christian Crumrine and Catharina. Sponsors: Parents.

Susana, b. 25 Nov 1798, bapt. 19 May 1799, of Henry Newsanger and Catharina. Sponsors: Parents.

Henrich, b. 17 Mar 1799, bapt. 19 May 1799, of Michael Miller and Catharina. Sponsor: Henrich Dee, a single man.

Johannes, b. 21 Apr 1799, bapt. 19 May 1799, of Michael Mier and Elisabeth. Sponsors: John Stouseberger, Margaret.

Adam and Eva (twins), b. 21 Jan 1799, bapt. 19 May 1799, of Henry Beltz and Susanna. Sponsors: Parents.

Nicholas, b. 6 Dec 1798, bapt. 16 June 1799, of Adam Kile and Elisabeth. Sponsors: Jacob Dury, Catharine.

Magdalena, b. 5 Apr 1799, bapt. 16 June 1799, of Peter Hickman and Regina. Sponsors: Johannes Shaffer, Anna.

Julianna, b. 14 May 1799, bapt. 16 June 1799, of Jacob Stinebrener, Jr. and Margaretha. Sponsors: Frederick Stinebrenner, Elisabeth.

Margaretha, b. 13 July 1799, bapt. 11 Aug 1799, of Lawrence Mink and Rachel. Sponsors: Margaretha Moll, widow.

Magdalena, b. 2 [?] June 1799, of ... Fahly and Barbara. [Sponsors not named.]

John George, b. 28 July 1799, bapt. 8 Sept 1799, of [Jaco]b Durry and Catharina. Sponsors: George Shever, Elisabeth.

Elizabeth, b. 25 Apr 1799, bapt. 8 Sept 1799, of ... Goos [Gross?] and Catharina. Sponsors: John Stouseberger, Margaretha.

Susanna, b. 4 Feb 1799, bapt. 21 Apr 1799, of ... Householder and Sussannah. Sponsors: Parents.

Anna Elisabetha, b. 2 Aug 1799, bapt. 3 Nov 1799, of ... Virts and Christina. Sponsors: Wilhelm Virtz, Barbara.

Samuel, b. 8 Oct 1799, bapt. 3 Nov 1799, of ... Kieffer and Anna Eva Barbara. Sponsors: Michael Kiefer, Catharina.

Jonathan, b. 30 Sept 1799, bapt. 3 Nov 1799, of ... Ruse and Susanna. Sponsor: Jacob Axline, single.

Charlotta, b. 15 Sept 1799, bapt. 1 Dec 1799, of ... Sletser, Jr. and Catha. Sponsors: Johannes Fahly, Eva Margaretha.

Catharina, b. 2 Nov 1799, bapt. 1 Dec 1799, of ... Shaffer and Anna Maria. Sponsors: Michael Wirts, Catharina.

Johannes, b. 4 May 1799, bapt. 1 Dec 1799, of ...tin and Margareth. Sponsors: John Shaffer, son of John, Anna Maria.

Sybilla, b. 12 Nov 1797, bapt. 26 Jan 1800, of ... Fry and Dorothy. Sponsors: Henry Joseph Fry, Christina.

Child of Samuel Brill, [no further information].

Thomas, b. 9 Dec 1799, bapt. 2 Mar 1800, of ... Martin and Lydia. Sponsors: Parents.

Susanna, b. 26 Nov 1798, bapt. 11 Apr 1800, of ... Sletzer and Catharina. Sponsors: Peter Fry, Christina.

Hanna, b. 5 Dec 1798, bapt. 11 Apr 1800, of ... Fry and Margaret. Sponsor: Catharine Ansel, Leonard Ansel's single daughter.

Christina, b. 8 Feb 1800, bapt. 11 Apr 1800, of George Sunafrank and Elizabeth. Sponsors: Frederick Smith, Christina.

Magdalena Elizabeth, b. 3 Mar 1800, bapt. 11 Apr 1800, of George Fahly and Magdalena. Sponsors: Michael Boger, Elizabeth.

Johannes, b. 24 Dec 1798, bapt. 11 Apr 1800, of Frederic Stoneburner and Elizabeth. Sponsors: John Stouseberger, Margaretha.

Elizabeth, b. 11 Feb 1800, bapt. 11 Apr 1800, of ... Adam Wolf and Maria Elizabeth. Sponsors: Jacob Derry, Catharina.

Benjamin, b. 13 Feb 1800, bapt. 11 Apr 1800, of ... and Catharina. Sponsors: John Stouseberger, Margaretha.

Elizabeth, b. 5 Jan 1800, bapt. 11 Apr 1800, of William Davis and Bally. Sponsors: Elizabeth Davis.

Maria Magdalena, b. 1 Mar 1800, bapt. 11 Apr 1800, of Conrad Shaffer and Anna Maria. Sponsors: George Reiser, Maria Magdalena.

Simon, b. 26 Jan 1800, bapt. 20 Apr 1800, of Henrich Frey and Catarin. Sponsor: Philipp Frey.

Paul, b. 11 Dec 1799, bapt. 20 Apr 1800, of Chaspar Traut and Anmari. Sponsors: Wilhelm, Elisabeth.

Joseph, b. 24 Feb 1800, bapt. 20 Apr 1800, of Jacob Waldman, Margareth. Sponsor: Joh. Wa[ldmann], Jr.

Joh. b. 18 Feb 1800, bapt. 20 Apr 1800, of Jacob Miller and Maria. Sponsors: Wilhelm, Barbara.

Sara, b. 25 Feb 1800, bapt. 20 Apr 1800, of Michael Chenne? and Elisab. Sponsor: Julianna ...

Susana, b. 3 May 1800, bapt. 18 May 1800, of Jacob Steinbrenner and Ana Barbara. Sponsor: Thorida?

Joh., b. 4 Sept 1799, bapt. 18 May 1800, of Jacob Hoffman and Chatarin. Sponsors: Joh. S. ...

Jacob, b. 13 Jan 1800, bapt. 15 June 1800, of Christia. Neushwanger and Ruthe. Sponsors: Melisa... .

Georg, b. 18 Oct 1799, bapt. 15 June 1800, of Joh. Miller and Rebek[ah]. Sponsors: George... and wife Chat... .

Joh., b. 12 June 1800, bapt. 13 July 1800, of Joh. Drittibach and Sussana.

Friedrich, b. 8 Jan 1799, bapt. 13 July 1800, of ... Beck [?] and Maria Magdalena. Sponsors: Parents.

Wilhelm, b. 7 July 1800, bapt. 7 Sept 1800, of ... Keist and Anna. Sponsors: Gottlieb Geist, wife.

Elisabeth, b. 15 May 1800, bapt. 7 Sept 1800, of ... Lang and Barbara. Sponsor: Sofia Wister.

Henirich, b. 18 July 1800, bapt. 7 Sept 1800, of ... Sheffer and Annamaria. Sponsors: Jacob Waltmann, wife.

Elisabeth, b. 12 Aug 1800, bapt. 7 Sept 1800, of ... Klein and Eva. Sponsors: Parents.

Samuel, b. 15 Aug 1800, bapt. 7 Sept 1800, of Elisabeth Wèldmann, widow. Sponsors: Adam Household[er], Sussanna.

Elisabeth, b. 14 [Mar ?] 1800, bapt. 7 Sept 1800, of ... Fichter. Sponsors: Lennerd Anzel, Catharina.

Johannes, b. 21 Oct 1800, bapt. 23 Oct 1800, of ... Mann and Anna. Sponsors: Parents.

Sara, b. 19 Sept 1800, bapt. 2 Nov 1800, of ... Alt. Sponsors: Parents.

Philipp, b. 1 Sept 1899, bapt. 2 Nov 1800, of ... Swanck and Margareth. Sponsor: Philipp Swanck.

Siegfriedrich. b. 21 Sept 1800, bapt. 2 Nov 1800. [Parents not named]. Sponsors: Georg Shefer, Catarin.

Marcareth, b. 1 Mar 1798, bapt. 2 Nov 1800, of Wilhelm Orffer and Margareth. Sponsor: Anna Barbara Steinbrenner.

Hannah, b. 9 Sept 1800, bapt. 4 Nov 1800, of Johann Garlach Stigler and Elisabetha. Sponsor: Hanna Dehin [Dey].

Salmon, b. 12 Oct 1800, bapt. 30 Nov 1800, of Heinrich Joseph Fræy and Christina. Sponsors: Joh. Wittemann.

Anamari, b. 24 Aug 1800, bapt. 30 Nov 1800, of Joh. Wentzel and Mari Magdalen. Sponsors: Caspar Traut, Anamari.

Heinrich, b. 17 Oct 1800, bapt. 30 Nov 1800, of Peter Daubeman and Elisabeth. Sponsors: Georg Steger, Hana.

Prissila, b. 25 Oct 1800, bapt. 30 Nov 1800, of Conrath Roller and Elisabeth. Sponsors: Parents.

Peter, b. 4 Dec 1800, bapt. 25 Jan 1801, of Peter Frey and Christina.Sponsors: Peter Fahly, Sussanna.

Gideon, b. 5 Nov 1800, bapt. 25 Jan 1801, of Adam Hausshalter, Sr. and Sussanna. Sponsors: Parents.

Margaretha, b. 12 Dec 1800, bapt. 22 Mar 1801, of Philipp Frey and Catharina. Sponsors: Peter Wirtz, Christina.

Jacob, b. 23 Dec 1800, bapt. 17 May 1801, of Samuel Brill and Catharina. Sponsors: Conrad Trittebach, Jr., Maria Magdalena.

David, b. 20 July 1800, bapt. 15 Aug 1802, of David Watson and Mary Magdalene. Sponsors: Parents.

Samuel, b. 3 Jan 1792, bapt. 7 Jan 1802, of Isaac Shunk and wife. Sponsors: Parents.

MARRIAGES OF NEW JERUSALEM LUTHERAN CHURCH

Wilhelm Wenner, Wilhelm Wenner's son married Priscilla Schumacher, George Schumacher's daughter, 20 June 1784.

Christoph Bornhaus married Rosina Roller, 11 Aug 1784.

Adam Muschler married Catharina Derri, Baltaser Derri's daughter, 12 Oct 1784.

Christian Bügly married Maria Eva Reutenbach, Friederich Reutenbach's surviving widow, 15 Dec 1784.

Peter Heckmann, Conrad Heckmann's single son married Regina Boger, the late Joseph Boger's legitimate single daughter, 15 Dec 1784.

Geo Ebel married Catharina Roller, Joh. Roller's daughter, 3 Jan 1785.

Michael Boger married Elisabetha Brenner, Philip Brenner's daughter,13 Apr 1785.

Henrich Oeckslein married Catharina Beck, Philip Beck's first daughter, 19 June 1785.

Henrich Segel married Tercky Gämmel, 3 Aug 1785.

Peter Warner married Judith Schumacher, 14 Sept 1785.

Simon Schober married Charlotta Eberhardt, 8 Nov 1785.

Philipp Lang married Christina Meile, 9 Mar 1786.

Johannes Frey married Susanna Kehler, 8 May 1786.

Jacob Eberhardt married Charlotta Baur, 17 May 1786.

Michael Usselmann married Elisabetha Palmer, 17 May 1786.

Conrad Lang married Anna Maria Führer, 30 May 1786.

Johannes Siebert married Maria Magdalena Schwenck, 27 June 1786.

Johannes Wentzel married Magdalena Hoff, 24 July 1786.

Georg Wild married Susanna Biber, 19 Nov 1786.

Georg Warner married Sarah Schumacher, 29 Mar 1787.

Johann Georg Schaeffer married Anna Catharina Marckert, by license, 4 May 1787.

Jacob Schumacher married Elisabeth Cloninger, by license, 2 Apr 1788.

Johannes Wirtz married Elisabeth Stedler, by license, 25 Sept 1788.

Wilhelm Wenner, Reformed schoolmaster, married Elisabeth Buschkirk, both widowed, proclaimed, 28 Sept 1788.

Georg Schumacher, Daniel Schumacher's son married Magdalena Frantzin, Nicolaus Frantzen's daughter, 7 June 1789.

Georg Herschelmann married Elisabeth Landers, 3 Dec 1789.

Adam Battefeld, Adam Battefeld's legitimate single son married Eva Margareth Schaka, Georg Schaka's legitimate single daughter, 11 Apr 1790.

Michael Schaefer married Maria Elisabetha Eberly, Fried. Eberly's legitimate single daughter, 11 Aug 1790.

Fridrich Kiefer, Michael Kiefer's legitimate son married Maria Kemper, Johannes Kamper's legitimate daughter, by license, 11 Dec 1791.

Jacob Fahly, Johannes Fahly's legitimate son married Barbara Neis, Dewald Nies's legitimate daughter, by license, 28 Mar 1792.

William Oldom married Magdalena Ziegenfuss, by license, 29 Apr 1792.

Peter Ansel, Leonhard Ansel's son married Elisabeth Frey, Nicolaus Frey's legitimate daughter, by license, 13 Aug 1793.

Joseph Henrich Frey, widow Willemanin's legitimate son married Christina Cooper, Engelbrecht's step-daughter, by proclamation, 27 Oct 1793.

Christian Repold, Georg Repold's legitimate single son married Maria Margreta Rohrbach, Adam Rohrbach's legitimate single daughter, by license and proclamation, 12 Nov 1793.

Jacob Wirtz, Peter Wirtz' legitimate son married Elisabeth George, Johannes Georg's legitimate daughter, by license, 21 Apr 1795.

Friederick Bügel, David Bügel's legitimate son married Maria Kittelmeyer, Martin Kittelmeyer's legitimate daughter, by license, 1 Nov 1795.

Thomas Davis married Lea Ball, Earl ... Ball's daughter, by license, 6 Jan 1796.

Georg Küffer married Anna Maria Edelmann, by license, 11 Oct 1796.

Ludwig Dreher, Michael Dreher's son married Anna Maria Belz, Andreas Beltz' legitimate daughter, by license, 5 Dec 1798.

BURIALS RECORDED BY PASTORS
NEW JERUSALEM LUTHERAN CHURCH

Jacob Freu, buried 9 Oct 1785, 74y, 2m, 4d.
Georg Schlötzer, Jacob Schlötzer's son, buried 13 Nov 1785, 19y, 8m, 13d.
Jacob Martin, buried 18 Dec 1785, about 66y.
Henrich Leinenweber, buried 22 Dec 1785, 22y, 3m, 3w, 1day.
Margaretha Philips, buried 11 Jan 1785, aged 64y.
Adam Fahly, son of Johannes Fahly, b 18 Jan 1786, 16y, 8m, 14 d.
Peter Hoff, son of Philip Hoff, buried 3 Mar 1786, 3y, buried 17 Mar 1783.
Anna Magdelena Schäfer, Geo. Schèfer's wife, buried 20 Mar 1786, 55y, 9m.
Johann Adam Amend, buried 31 Aug 1786, 24y.
Georg Schuckmann, buried 8 Oct 1786, 15y, 1m, 3d.
Gottlieb Geist's son, buried 16 July 1787, 6y, 11m, 4d.
Johann Jacob Walter, buried 24 Oct 1787, 40y.
Carl Hofmann's son Carl, buried 1 Dec 1787, 4y, 7m, 2w, 3d.
Carl Hofmann's daughter Maria Elisabetha, buried 13 Dec 1787, 2y, 6m, 17d.
Conrad Drittenbach's daughter Maria Magdalena, buried 29 Jan 1788, 2y, 7m, 13d.
Conrad Drittenbach's daughter Maria Sara, buried 20 Feb 1787, 29d.
Johannes Oechalein's son Daniel, buried Oct 22 1788.
Nicolaus Freu's daughter Magdalena, buried 2 Nov 1788, 11y, 4d.
Jacob Waldman's daughter Anna Margaretha, buried 27 Jan 1789, 17y, 6m, 8d.
Friederich Bels' daughter Elisabetha, buried 2 Jan 1789, 4y, 2m, 20d.
Peter Steinbrenner's son Georg, buried 2 Feb 1789, 2m, 6d.
Peter Steinbrenner's son Peter, buried 12 Feb 1789, 4y, 7m, 10d.
Martin Heckendorn's daughter Barbara, bur. 24 Feb 1789, 1y, 3m, less one day.
Friederich Boger's son Joseph, buried 4 May 1789, 2y, 8m, 3w, 1d.
Henrich Strohm's daughter Elisabetha, buried Aug 1789, 1y, 1m, 3w, 1d.
Sibilla Barbara Freund, buried 19 Nov 1789, 70y, 10m, 13d.
Thomas Davis' son George, buried 23 Jan 1790, 8y, 10m, 13d.
Thomas Davis' daughter Anna Maria, buried 31 Jan 1790, 3y, 6m, 29d.
Friederich Boger' son Peter, buried 21 Feb 1790, 1y, less 4 days.
Johannes Wentzel's daughter Elisabetha, buried 29 Apr 1790, 2y, 10d.
Johann Joseph Feuerstein, buried 11 Aug 1790, 53y, 3m, 2d.

Friedrich Schlöetzer's daughter Elisabeth, buried 1 Nov 1790, 11d.
Levi Printz' son Isaac, buried 20 Nov 1790, 2y, 2m, 1w, 1d.
Friedrich Spring's son Daniel, buried 16 Dec 1790, 10m.
Maria Shober, buried 22 Jan 1791, 81y, 3w, 5d.
John Ulm's son Jacob, buried 23 Jan 1791, 10m, 2w, 6d.
John Shade, buried 14 Feb 1790, 69y, 10m, 2w.
... Hardmämnin, buried 7 Mar 1791, 78y, 9m, 2w.
Georg Wentzel's son Johannes, buried 17 Mar 1791, 13d.
Martin Brill, buried 1 May 1791, 81y.
Daniel Tammelson's daughter Maria, buried 31 May 1791, 7m, less 2d.
Peter Ziegenfus, buried 8 Aug 1791, 26y, 6m.
John Martin's son William, buried 10 Aug 1791, 11m, 1w, 5d.
Abraham, son of John Jacob Walter, dec'd, buried 30 Sept 1791, 11y, 10m, 2w, 5d.
Jacobus Besh, buried 4 Oct 1791, 36y, 6m.
Levi Printz' son Johannes, buried 8 Oct 1791, 8y, 11m, 1w.
Friederich Boger, buried 16 Oct 1791, 39y, 2m, 2w, 4d.
Peter Steinbrenner's daughter Sophia, buried 18 Oct 1791, 4y, 11m, 2w, 6d.
Friedrich Beltz' son Johannes, buried 23 Nov. 1791, 10m, 2w, 6d.
Catarina Würts, buried 31 Dec 1791, 85y, 8m, less 2days.
Martin Wishard's wife Catharina, buried 13 Mar 1792, 43y.
Georg Mann's wife, Maria Catharina Mann, buried 24 May 1792, 67y, 8m.
Christina Russ' son Abraham, buried 5 June 1792, 2m, 1w.
Thomas Davis' son Henrich, buried 26 June 1792, 5m, less 3days.
Peter Steinbrenner's son Daniel, buried 5 July 1792, 2m, 5d.
Margaretha, daughter of Margareta Schmidt, widow, buried 12 July 1792, 24y, 8m, 2w.
Doctor Fichler's son, buried 2 Sept 1792, 3y, 11m.
Georg Brand's daughter, buried 3 Sept 1792, 4y, 4m, 2w.
Michael Bönly, buried 30 Sept 1792, 87y.
Conrad Drittenbach's son Samuel, buried 11 Oct 1792, 3y, 2m, 3w.
Christian Krummrein's wife Maria Elisabeth, buried 17 Nov 1792, 28y, 2m.
Anna Long, Daniel Long's wife, buried 18 Jan 1793, 45y, 5m, 1d.
Simon Rickert, buried 11 Feb 1793, 40y.
Georg Mëyer, buried 7 Mar 1793, 66y.
Peter Beltz' son Peter, buried 18 June 1793, 1m, 3w, 2d.
Georg Hardman's son Friederich Adam, [no date], 1y, 5m, 2w, 5d.
Christian Meyer, buried 24 July 1793, 46y.

Johannes Kalbfleisch's son Johannes, buried 28 July 1793, 1y, 3m, 3w, 2d.
Christoph Prühl's son Christoph, buried 30 Aug 1793, 7y, 2m, 1w, 1d.
Christian Krummrein's wife Margaretha, buried 18 Sept 1793, 26y.
George Wild, buried 29 Sept 1793, 27y, 7m, 3d.
Johannes Schmidt, buried 22 Oct 1793, 36y, 10 m.
Johannes Geuer's wife buried 15 July 1793, 36y.
Christoph Münder's daughter Rosina, buried 24 Jan 1794, 28y.
Rosina Roller, Johan Andreas Davis Roller's wife, bur. 30 Jan 1794, 69y, 3m.
Samuel Andereas' son Georg, buried 11 Feb 1794, 19y, 7m, 3w, 2d.
Johan Andonius Lambach, buried 2 Mar 1794, 69y, 7m, 7d.
Johannes Ruff, buried 2 Apr 1794, 43y, 8m, 5d.
Leonhart Ansel's daughter Magdalena, [no date], 12y, 2m, 6d.
Jacob Stamm's daughter Maria Magdalena, buried 6 June 1794, 2y, 3m, 3d.
Johannes Schäfer's son George, buried 22 June 1794, 4y, 2m, less 6d.
Mary Marshal, buried 3 July 1794, 74 y.
Johannes Schäfer's son Per, buried 5 July 1794, 2y, 6m, 2w, 2d.
Margaret Ruff, Johannes Ruff's surviving widow's daughter Anna Magdalena, buried 1 July 1794, 11m, less 3d.
William Alt's daughter Maria, buried 9 July 1794, 3y, 6m.
Christian Repold, buried 11 July 1794, 30y, 5m, 1w, 5d.
John Martin's wife Louisa, buried 14 July 1794, 75 y.
Johannes Schäfer's daughter [no given name] bur. 14 July 1794, 9m, 3w, 4d.
Sarah, daughter of Justus Arnold, deceased, bur. 3 Aug 1794, 6y, 8 m less 8d.
Christoph Minder's daughter's child, buried 3 Aug 1794, 1y 6 m.
Adam Haushalter's wife Catharina, buried 10 Sept 1794, 44y, 6m, less 7d.
Peter Beltz' daughter Maria Magdalena, buried 8 Nov 1794, 6m, 2w, 3d.
Christoph Minder's son Lucas, buried 18 Oct 1794.
George Ham's daughter Maria Margaretha, buried 13 Jan 1795, 8d.
Christina Elisabetha Lambach, widow of Johann Anthony Lambach, deceased, buried 28 May 1795, 74y, 5m, and some days.
Johannes Selzer's son Johann Georg, buried 22 July 1795, 6m, 1w, 2d.
Thomas Davis' wife, buried 23 Sept 1795, 45y, 1m.
Heinrich Neuschwanger's daughter Juliana, buried 3 Oct 1795, 5m, 3w, 1d.
George Barker's son, buried 25 Oct 1795, 8m, 2w, 2d.
Michael Dreher's son Jacob, buried 16 Nov 1795, 12y, 2m, less 1d.

Johann Adam Wolff's wife Margretha, buried 10 Dec 1795, 27y.
Peter Gauer's daughter Catharina, buried 15 Dec 1795, 1y, 5m, 8d.
Jacob Steinbrenner Sr.'s wife Anna Eva, buried 10 Jan 1796, 65y.
Friederic Smith's son Jacob, buried 23 Feb 1796, 6y, 8m, less 2d.
Anna Maria Söhnlein, widow of Michael Söhnlein, deceased, buried 3 Mar 1796, 80y, 6 m less 1d.
Philipp Hoff, buried 9 Mar 1796, 53y, 3m.
William Alt's child, buried 12 Mar1796, 1y, less 5d.
Friederich Biegel, buried 18 May 1796, 27y, 11m, 3d.
Jacob Lenz' child Christina, buried 29 May 1796, 2m, 3d.
Daniel Lang's daughter Maria Magdalena, buried 26 June 1796, 7y, 8m, 13d.
Peter Steinbrenner's son Wilhelm, buried 6 July 1796, 6m, 3w, 4d.
Johannes Wust's son Johanna Adam, buried 12 July 1796, 4y, 7m, 3w, 5d.
Anna Buhmer's daughter Clara, buried 1 Aug 1796, 5y, 9m, 5d.
Johannes Wüst's son Peter, buried 2 Aug 1796, 2y, 5m, 3w, 5d.
Michael Russ' daughter buried 8 Aug 1796, 6d.
Johannes Schäffer's daughter Christina, buried 10 Aug 1796, 1d.
Wilhelm Stacks, buried 21 Aug 1796, 44y, 7m.
Maria Barbara Eberlin, widow of Friederich Eberlein, deceaased, buried 14 Oct 1796, 56y, 9m, 15d.
Christian Müller, buried 14 Jan 1797, 73y, 2w, 5d.
William Schmidt, buried 1 Apr 1797, 28y, 11m, 3w, 3d.
Johann Jacob Steinbrenner, buried 24 May 1797, 67y, 2m, 16d.
Peter Wipp's son [no given name] buried 27 May 1797, 8m, 3w, 4d.
Conrad Roller's son Christian, buried 18 June 1797, 2y, 7 m less 1d.
Anna Maria Kohin's daughter Magdalena, buried 31 July 1797, 10m, 67d.
Johann Peter Taubermann's wife Magdalena, buried 20 Sept 1797, 58y.
Peter Frey's son Johannes, buried 25 Sept 1797, 1y, 5m, 14d.
Maria Schmidt, Johannes Schmidt's surviving widow, bur. 4 Apr 1797, 72y.
Georg Wenzel's daughter Magdalena, buried 6 April 1798, 8m, less 6 days.
Sarah Mëyer, Peter Mæyer's wife, buried 1 May 1798, 88y.
Philip Peter Wirtz, Sr. buried 23 May 1798, 60y, 11m, 9d.
Charlotta Lähn buried 24 May 1798, 57y.
Paul Weens, buried 14 June 1798, 22y, 6m, 22d.
Peter Stock's daughter Margaretha, buried 16 July 1798, 2y, 3m, 2w, 5d.
Peter Stock's daughter Magdalena, buried 17 July 1798, 4y, 1m, 12d.
Henrich Adam Strehm's daughter Elisabetha, buried 18 July 1798, 5y, 9m, 13d.

Elisabetha Schwenck's son Johannes Hoff, buried 30 July 1798, 7y, 6m, 3d.

John Evans' son William, buried 26 July 1798, 2y, 5m, 2w, 4d.

Georg Fahly's daughter Magdalena, buried 10 Aug 1798, 2y, 7m, 3w, 5d.

Catharina Cadel, Jacob Cadal's widow, buried 9 Aug 1798, 73y, 1m, 3d.

Maria Bèrcker, buried 19 Aug 1798, 73 y.

Johannes Schäffer's son Georg, buried 22 Aug 1798, 1y, 9w, 2d.

Johannes Schäffer, buried 14 Sept 1798, 67y, 5m, 3w, 5d.

Jacob Schleser's daughter Christina, buried 11 Dec 1798, 1y, 1m, 5d.

Friederich Steinbrenner's wife Juliana, buried 2 Mar 1799, 38y, 11m, 3w, 4d.

John McBride, buried 30 March 1799, 71y, 10 m.

Georg Friederich Samuel Waltman, buried 17 Feb 1800, 38y, 11 m.

Widow Arnold's son, Simon Arnold, buried 24 Apr 1800, 7y, 14d.

Conrad Trittebach's daughter Elisabeth, buried 4 July 1800, 21y, 2w, 4d.

Widow Eva Wackern's son, buried 11 Aug 1800, 1y, 8m, 16d.

Levi Printz' wife Anna Elisabeth, buried 23 Sept 1800, 43y.

Anna Maria Cruysin, buried 2 Nov 1800, 80y, 8m, less 6 days.

Johannes Johns Jr.'s wife Sarah, buried 8 Nov 1800, 34y.

MINUTES OF SHELBURNE PARISH VESTRY

Vestry met at Leesburg for Shelburne, April 10th 1771, Present: William Smith, Josias Clapham, Thomas Lewis, Lèven Powell, James Hamilton, John Lewis, Francis Peyton, Thomas Owsley, Craven Peyton, Thomas Shore. Ordered that Oliver Price act as Clerk to the Vestry. Ordered that John Lewis and Thomas Shore are appropriately Elected and Chosen Church Wardens for the Present Year. Ordered that the Church Wardens employ some Men to Preform Devine Services in the Parish once every three months during the present year that the ... be given to [the Revd.] Mr. Scott. Ordered that the Minister employed by the Parish at Leesburg and the other Chapel in the Parish is also at some convenivent place near the Gap of the Short Hill to be fixed on by the Church Wardens. Ordered that if any Minister do offer himself to perform divine service on the Sabbath that the Church Warden do employ him accordingly and that the other Minister be discharged.

At a Vestry held at Leesburg for Shelburne Parish, June 27th 1771. Present: William Smith, James Hamilton, Thompson Mason, John Lewis, Craven Peyton, Thomas Lewis, Francis Peyton, Thomas Owsley, Leven Powell, Thomas Shore. The Revd. Mr. Archibald Owen in consequence of a converstation with some of the Gentlemen of the Vestry and with the Church Warden having moved himself and Family into this Parish and claiming three months salary he submitted his Pretentions to this Vestry but it appearing that he had Notice from the Church Warden before he removed his Family that they would not receive him it is the unanimous opinion of this Vestry that the said Archibald Owens is not entitled to receive anything from the Parish. Ordered that the Church Wardens Advertize in the Virginia Gazette that the Parish of Shelburne at present is vacant and that any Minister of the Church of England who come well recommended and whose preaching shall be approved by the Vestry will meet with encouragements.

At a Vestry held at Leesburg for Shelburne Parish, August 11th 1771: Mr William Leigh, a student of William and Mary College, having been warmly recommended to this Vestry by the Present Masters and Proffesors of the said College as a Young Gentlemen of sound learning umpinged piety and unexceptionable morals we do hereby undertake and agree to receive the said William Leigh as Minister of this Parish provided the Parish should continue vacant till he returns from Great Britain in holy orders unless he should by some misconduct forfeit the good opinion we at Present entertain of him.

At a Vestry held at Leesburg for Shelburne Parish [Nov]ember 25th 1771. The Vestry proceeds this day to lay the Levy as follows (pounds of tobacco):

To the Revd Mr James Scott as P Acct	5312
To John Heryford, Sexton at Leesburg	400
To John Harris, Sexton at the Mountain Chapel	400
To Oliver Price, Clerk of the Vestry	500
To Josias Clapham as P Acct	160
To Thomas Owsley P Acct	104
To Joseph Stephens as assigned for Timothy Russel as P Acct	480
To Robert Popkins as P Acct due for Services done in the Year 1770 being omitted last Fall	100
To James Sanders for keeping Rhody Welton 1 year	960
To James Poston as P Acct	400
To Levin Powell as P Acct	428
To John Lewis as P Acct	540
To Leanah Ward as P Acct	56
To James Abbett for nursing a Child one month	240
To William Nelson as P Acct	2184
To Joseph Cox as P Acct	1080
To Samuel Canby as P Acct	617
To William Head for Boarding of Mary Robinson 1 Month	204
To William Douglass as P Acct	1912
~~To Doctor Jacob Coutsman as P. Acct~~	
To Joseph Wildman for Boarding Charles Griffith for One year	600
To John Hough as P Acct	
To Oliver Price for a Minute Book	20

Ordered that Josias Clapham and Leven Powell, Gent. are appointed Church Wardens for the Present year having taken the Oaths according to Law. Ordered that the Church Wardens do get the Land (on which the Mountain Chapel stands) laid off and Deeds for the same. Ordered that the Church Wardens for the Parish do Settle with the Church Wardens of Cameron Parish for their Proportion of Tobacco levyed in this Parish. Ordered that the church wardens collect of each tithable 25 lb. of tobacco per pole (1871 tithables). Ordered that the church wardens do inquire and report a convenient place for a Glebe and also a convenient place for building a chapel near the Short Hill.

At a vestry held at Leesburg for Shelburne Parish, December 23rd 1771. Ordered that the Revd. Mr. David Griffith is received as minister of this parish and he be presented by the unanimous opinion of the vestry to the governor to be inducted into this Parish. Ordered that the Revd. Mr. David Griffith do receive from this Parish the quantity of 5000 lb tobacco per annum in lieu of a glebe until he the R. Mr. Griffith is furnished with a Glebe.

To Samuel Gregg, for boarding Jesse Wilson, 1 yr and 2 wks ... 1440
To Samuel Rich for boarding, lodging and washing for Patrick Poe 1120
To Docter Cogswell for sundry mediums for Jesse Willson, furnished him before January last 120
To John Quin for the support of Eliz Powderel and Thomas Byrem 2400

Ordered that the Parish Collector do pay to the above claimers according to the above account and that the same be allowed out of the tobacco leveyed for the use of the Parish.

At a vestry held at Leesburg for Shelburne Parish ... the 15th 1772. Ordered that the church wardens do endeavour to agree with Francis Hague and Joseph Coombes for a certain tract of land in the North Fork of Goose Creek containing four hundred and sixty five acres for a Glebe for the Minister of this Parish upon the best terms they can and enter into articles of agreement for the same. Orderd that church wardens agree with workmen to build a dwelling house for the minister on the most convenient part of the said lands, either of brick or stone, 48 ft long x 20 ft wide [continues with description of house]. Ordered that Craven Peyton, James Hamilton, and Thos. Lewis & Stephen Donaldson advertize and agree with workmen to build a chapel on the most convenient place on the Short Hill to be by them agreed on and that they contract with the undertaker to have the money remaining in the church wardens hands towards paying for the said building.

March 9, 1772. Ordered that a former order of the vestry, made Feb. 15, 1772 empowering Craven Peyton, James Hamilton, Thomas Lewis, and Stephen Donaldson to empower workmen to build a chappel near the

Short Hill be revoked and that the aforesaid gentlement do not act in the said matter until further orders of the vestry.

June 15, 1772. Ordered that a church be built on the land of the Honorable John Tayloe, Esqr. near the dwelling house of Ralph Martin, of the following dimensions .... Ordered that the Church Wardens agree for two acres of land on which the said church is to be built and to advertize and agree with workmen to build the same. Ordered that the minister do perform devine service every 3 weeks, at or near the place where the above said church is to be built. Ordered that the Church Wardens pay the Rev. Mr. David Griffith the 5000 pounds tobacco formerly ordered to be paid to him in lieu of a Glebe out of the tobacco that was leveyed for the use of this parish.

August 7th 1772. Present: Revd. David Griffith, rector; Stephen Donaldson, Thomas Lewis, Thomson Mason, Craven Peyton, John Lewis, Thomas Ousley, Thomas Shore. Rev. David Griffith may set the buildings on the glebe at any place he doth choose. As it is inconvenient for church wardens to go to Hon. John Tyloe, [Tayloe] Esqr. for two acres of land whereon a church was ordered to be built at the last vestry, then Thomson Mason, Gent., to agree with Tayloe for the same. Ordered that Stephen Donaldson, Thos Lewis and John Lewis, Gent, or any two of them, agree with workmen to build the said church, and purchase from the tenent his right to the said two acres.

August 25th 1772. Vestry is in doubt whether under the laws now in force they are to pay the minister's salary in tobacco at the rate of 12 shillings and six pence per hundred or whether they are obliged to pay the said minister's salary in tobacco in order to avoid the expense of litigation. Ordered that George With Esqr. be employed to support the rights and interest of the parish. Order to build church on land of John Tayloe, near house of Ralph Martin be revoked and ordered that the church be built on the land of Honble. George William Fairfax, near the dwelling house of James French, of the following dimensions .... Ordered that Stephen Donaldson, Thomas Lewis, and John Lewis, Gent, or any two of them agree with workmen to build the said church and purchase 2 acres from landlord and tenant, and get deeds for same. All glass in Glebe building to be 8' by 10' instead of 7' by 9' and the undertaker be allowed the difference... .

Sept 29th 1772, present: The Revd. David Griffith, rector, Leven Powell, Josias Clapham, Church Wardens; Thomas Lewis, Thomas Ousley, Thompson Mason, Thomas Shore, James Hamilton, John Lewis, Francis Peyton, Craven Peyton, Stephen Donaldson. Absent at their own request: Francis Peyton, Thomas Lewis, Stephen Donaldson, Craven Peyton. A motion was made that this vestry come to a resolution that two churches will be sufficient in this parish, which being seconded, the aforesaid men desired to be entered as absent. Annulled order to build church on land near James French. Resolved that a church shall be built near the forks of the roads, the one leading to Nolands Ferry and the other to William Kirks Mill.

Nov 30, 1772, The vestry proceeds this day to lay the levy as follows:

To The Revd. David Griffith, Rector	17120
Thomas Lewis, clerk for Mountain Chapple, Leesburg, & the Short Hill	2400
John Heryford, sexton at Leesburg	400
John Harris, sexton at the Mountain Chapple	400
Oliver Price, clerk of the vestry	500
To John Pursel for the use of his house as a church	650
To Samuel Butcher per order of church wardens	160
To Joseph Janney, assn. of John Queen	1532
To Samuel Canby, as per acct	248
To John Hough, as per acct	892
To Appolles Cooper, for drawing a plan for the Glebe House	400
To Powell & Harrison, as per acct	1041
To Levin Powell. as per acct	1749
To Josias Clapham, as per acct.	1098
To John Collings for burying Jno. Hite's waggoner	400
To John Lewis, as per acct.	3764
To Joseph Cox, as per acct.	726
To James Sanders for the support of an orphan, one year	960
To Isaac Jacob Wright, as per acct.	360
To Joshua Gore, as per acct.	420
To Shadrach Lewellen for supporting Rachel Miller, 3 months?	425
To Craven Peyton, as per acct.	80
To William Auton, as per acct.	832
To Francis Peyton, as per acct.	2240
To Stephen Jones for balance of burying Ann Miller	155
To Thomas Goram, assn. of Corngiver, as per acct.	872
To Powell & Harris, assn. of Wm. Hutchinson	240

To Mary Chamberlin, as per acct. 230
To Joseph Claige, as per acct. 320
To Doctor Jacob Coutsman, as per acct. 2212
To Hezekiah Boon, as per acct. 304
To Isaac Sands, as per acct. 1200
To John Taylor for two bushels wheat 64
To Reuben Doughty for keeping Jesse Wilson 440
To Dr. Joseph Cogswell 348
To Joseph Wildman for boarding Charles Griffith one year 600
To Rev. David Griffith, rector, in lieu of his Glebe for a year 6400
To Josias Clapham in part pay for Glebe building 46240
To William Ellzey, as per acct. 250
To William Douglass, per order of church wardens 101
To Jonathan Monkhouse for burying Dan'l Burkitt 1851

Tithables.
Ordered that the Church Wardens collect from each tithable 72 lbs. of Tobacco.
Rev. Mr. David Griffith giving up to the vestry the disposal of the Glebe Lands until the first of October next. Whereas Josias Clapham has rented some of the land.

Revoked the order to build a church on the forks of the road. Ordered to build a church on the lands of the Honble. Geo. William Fairfax Esqr., some where near the Ketockton on the Road leading from Leesburg to Pursley's on the particular spot to be fixed on by Leven Powell, James Hamilton, Thomas Ousley, Gent, who are appointed to purchase the land on which it is to stand [followed by dimensions]. Ordered that the church wardens provide benches to accommodate the persons who come to attend devine services at the court house in Leesburg. Ordered that a vestry house be built near the dwelling house of Thomas Gore, of the following dimensions ... . To be built of wood according to direction of Thomas Lewis, and Thomas Ousley, Gent, who are appointed to purchase land and let the building of the same.

November 16th 1773: The vestry proceeds this day to lay the levy as follows:

To The Revd. David Griffith, Rector 200
Thomas Lewis, clerk, Mountain Chapple, Leesburg, & Short Hill 2400
John Heryford, sexton at Leesburg 400
John Harris, sexton at the Mountain Chapple 400

Oliver Price, clerk of the vestry 500
Thomas Mongommory, assn. of Wm Grayson
per Joseph Coombs 3200
Cuthbert Bullet per order of Joseph Coombs 3200
Joseph Coombs, his balance of Glebe Land 62650
George Johnston as per acct. 320
Simon Triplet assignee of Val Corngiver 1072
Thomas Strickland assn. of Isaac Jacob Wright 1400
Robert Adam and Co. as per acct. 746
Craven Peyton per acct. 80
Stephen Donaldson per acct. 154
John Queen for support of Eliz. Powderal 1624
Thomas Shore for indemnfying the parish from any further
trouble with Henry Pursley Fitzgerald 1600
Thomas Goram per acct. 712
John Thomas per acct. 3.20
Henry Ousley, assn. of Thomas Ousley, for building a
vestry house 6400
John Pursel 9.20
Joshua Gore, assnd. to Leven Powell 2312
Leven Powell for a set of deeds for church land 80
Powell and Harrison 8.7.6
Thomas Lewis 5.8.0
Appolles Cooper for a plan of a church 400
Samuel Butcher 485
Richard Williams 1000
Docter Humphrey Fullerton 33.6.2
Docter Jacob Coutsman 17.6.4
Leven Powell assn of William Hutchinson 17.48
Josias Clapham for Balance of the Glebe buildings 46.240
William Metheeney for the support of his daughter
Elizabeth, 1 year 1600
Samuel Adams for his support 1600
Samuel Coombs 7.0
Francis Peyton for the support of an orphan, 1 year 128.0
To Joseph Wildman for the support of Charles Griffith,
1 year 9.6.0
William Baker for being over listed in the year 1772 .... 7.2
Rev. David Griffith in lieu of the Glebe, six months 3.7.6

Church wardens pay Joseph Coombes 40000 lbs tobacco.

Stephen Donaldson and Leven Powell, Gent, appointed wardens for ensuing year. Church wardens to collect from each tithable 100 lb of tobacco; pay Joshua Gore Junior 218 lb tobacco for land on which the vestry house is built; furnish Evan Davis and Eleonar his wife with all necessary food and clothing; agree with physician to attend the sick, poor for coming year for a sum not to exceed 20 pounds; receive collected tobacco from the sheriff and sell to the best advantage for cash.

Dec 20, 1774: Vestry proceeds to lay the levy as follows (in pounds of tobacco):

David Griffith, rector, ... 17120
Thomas Lewis, clerk of Mountn. Chapple, Leesburg, and
Short Hill 2400
John Heryford, sexton at Leesburg 400
John Davis, sexton at Mountn. Chapple 400
Oliver Price, clerk of the vestry 500
John Queen, per acct. 2400
John Ward, per acct, Wm Donaldson, assgn. 960
Cornelius Holdren per acct, and wife, assgned to
Wm. Douglass 24
Richard Williams per acct. 800
Hezekiah Boone per acct. assigned to Wm Douglass 1012
Thomas Ousley per acct George Chilton, assn.
Valintine Corngiver 1280
Valentin Corngiver shoes and cloaths made for Thos Byram 150
Joshua Gore Senr. as per acct. 864
Thomas Roper per acct. 684
Isaac Nichols per acct. 110
John Pursel per acct. 400
Piter Eblin for making church benches 9.6
Wm. and Hugh Nelson per acct. 300
William Nelson per acct. 518
William Douglass per acct. 1132
James Cummins for boarding Wm. Yelding to this date 960
Saml Potts per acct. 328
Joseph Claige, assigned to Wm Douglass 1192
Jonah Moffett, as per acct of Doctr Budd 1880
Doctr Geo Budd as per balance of acct. 432
Doctr Jacob Coutsman per acct of Doctr Budd 173

Doctr Kirby as per acct of Doctr Budd 532
Joseph Janney assn. of Eliz. Sorrell 420
Joseph Wildman as per acct, ... 1280
Craven Peyton as per acct. 160
George Rine as per acct. 408
Shadrach Lleuellin as per acct. 1304
Thos Lewis as per acct. 1200
Farling Ball as per acct. 332
Joseph Janney assn. of Henry Oxley per acct. 710
Joseph Janney as per acct. 421
Joseph Janney as per acct. 2058
Israel Thompson as per acct. 3256
Josias Clapham as per acct. 3600
Rev. David Griffith, assn. of John Sparhawk 4880
Joseph Gore, as per acct. 240
Leven Powell and Harrison as per acct. 1314
James Leith for crying the letting of a church 48
Leven Powell for a book chest for the church 176
Jonathan Monkhouse for Hannah Shute for 3 months and
9 days 260
Joseph Coombes for balance of building
Ketockton Church 48000
John Ebling for being overlist in the year 1773 100

Craven Peyton resigned as vestry man from this parrish. William Bronaugh elected in his place. Ordered that the churchwardens have a hen house built on the Glebe land, that the vestry house be received as sufficient for the purpose intended, that there be a church built at or near the place where the chapple now stands at Stephen Rozels and that it be 50 ft. by 40 ft. To be built of brick or stone. Ordered that the wardens receive from Ralph Murray the balance of last year's diposition, Out of which they are to pay John Schooly and Lewis Ries 20/ per acre for the land on which the Ketocktin church stands. Ordered that the wardens employ a physician to attend the sick poor. May 22 1776: Rev. David Griffith, rector, William Smith, Stephen Donaldson, Thomas Lewis, Thomson Mason, Leven Powell, John Lewis, Thomas Shore.

To Rev. David Griffith 17120
John Heryford, sexton at Leesburg 400
John Harris, sexton at Mountain Chapple 400
Oliver Price, clk of vestry 500

Doctr Jacob Coutsman for adm. medicine to the poor 3040
Elexander Cooper as per acct. 544
William Baker for being overlisted in the year
Thomas Roper as per acct. 173
Leonard Warner as per acct 40
Adam Gough for boarding Mary Robinson 960
Craven Peyton as per acct. 720
Thomas Lewis as per acct. 1200
James Sanders for Burying --- Fox 400
Docter Coutsman per Thos Lewis 64
Joseph Gore for tending the vestry house 240

June 10, 1776: The vestry continued the parish levy.
Rev. David Griffith assn of Geo. Muirhead 1680
Geo. Muirhead, bal of his acct. 976
Henry Warner as per acct 640
Saml Potts as per acct. 4056
ditto 998
George Wilson for keeping and supporting John Davis 960
ditto 144
Israel Thompson as per acct. 3189
Eliza Sorrell as per acct. 760
Jacob Jocobs for keeping and supporting Honor McKinsey 960
James Sanders as per acct. 732
Henry Harris as per acct. 350
Wm Smith, Gt. assn of Henry Harris 350
Thos Lewis, Gt. for officiating as clerk, 3 months at
all churches 600
Joseph Janney as per acct. 1846

James Hamilton, Gt., dec'd, and Thos Ousley have resigned.
George West and Joshua Gore, Gent, chosen to replace them.
Ordered that Evan Davie [Davis] deliver all his property to the church.

April 27, 1779: Ralph Murray appointed clerk of the vestry.
Josias Clapham and Willm Bronaugh, Gent. appointed church wardens for the present year.

Simon Triplett, Gent, appointed vestryman in the room of Thompson Mason, Esqr.

Jno Alexander, Gent, appointed vestryman in the room of Stephen Donaldson.

James Respass, Gent, appointed vestryman in the room of Willm. Smith.

Ordered that Major Alexander be paid for keeping and returning the said glebe in good repair.

Levy, amount brought forward 44042
Doctor Jacob Coutsman as per acct. 2840
    do for administering medicine, 2 years 6080
Catharine Wilson as per acct. 1400
Richd Stephens as per acct. 880
Thomas Lewis as per acct. 120
Israel Thompson as per acct. 64000

John Minor, Gt., appointed collector for this parish levey.

April 11, 1780: Col. Josias Clapham, Col. Wm Bronaugh, Thos Lewis, Geo West, Major John Alexander, Thos Shore, Thos Respess, and Joshua Gore.

Valentine Corngiver as per acct. 50
Michl Gohagan as per acct. 100
Val Corngiver as per acct. 342
Farlin Ball's acct in 1775, alld as much money as
    vestry think proper 7.6
Capt. Wm. Douglass as per acct 3.2
Farlin Ball as per acct. 8.6.9
William Bolton as per acct. 180
Capt. Alexander McMichen as per acct. 200
Robert Jameson as per acct. 48
Israel Thompson as per acct. 850
Colo. Josias Clapham as per acct. 89
John Oneal as per acct. 405
Joshua Gore Senr. as per acct. 150
Thos James assn of John Smith 274.5
Moses Furr as per acct. 83
Jas Wheelouk for keeping Thos Donohai [sic] to be
    pd 20 lb per mo 162
Joseph Wildman as per acct. 1300
Israel Thompson as per acct. 30.13.0
Joseph Baily as per petition 50
Ralph Murray, clerk of vestry 150

Major John Alexander and Joshua Gore be appointed chruchwardens for the ensuing year. Churchwardens should advertize for a minister for Shelburne Parish.

April 28 ..., Josias Clapham, Colo. William Bronaugh, Thos. Lewis, Colo. John Alexander, Joshua Gore, John Lewis, Thos Short, Thos Respass, Capt.

To Ralph Murray, clerk of vestry	300
Israel Thompson	2944
Capt. John Lucketts as per acct.	[ink blot]
Colo. Josias Clapham as per acct.	238
Richd Hopkins for keeping widow Phillips two months last part at 20 per month old way	240
Richd. Hopkins for cloathing widow Philips	260
James Davis as per acct.	960
John Delkin as per acct.	338
Luke Burd as per acct.	540
Colo. John Alexander as per acct.	63
Joshua Gore Senr. as per acct.	549
Saml Potts as per acct.	600
Christopher Costaloe as per acct.	100
Joseph Baily as per acct for his mother	1000
Doctr Wm. Smith Belt as per acct.	570
Catharine Norris as per acct.	450
Thos Shore as per acct.	6
[blot] Pines Owsley as per petition	200

Thomas Lewis and Thomas Respass, Gent, appointed churchwardens. Appointed John Luckett and Joseph Combs in the room of John Lewis who has resigned, and Simon Triplet who has refused to take the oath of vestryman.

13th of May 1782: Present, Josiah Clapham, Thos Lewis, Jno Alexander, Thos Respass, Joshua Gore, Thos Shore, Joseph Combs, Leven Powell.

Israel Thompson as per acct.	£32.14
Samuel Boyd as per acct.	10.7.0
James Whelock as per acct.	1.11.6
Thos Shore as per acct.	13.8.9
Ricd Hopkins as per petition	16.5.0

Joshua Taylor as per petition 6.0.0
Levin Powell as per acct. 2.6.9
Danl Losh for Boarding Mary Ashby, 7 weeks, and 2 days 1.16.0
Thos Respass as per acct. 2.0.0
Jno Lewis as per acct. 2.10.0
Joseph Baily for support his mother for one year and
one month 10.7.6
Thos. Lewis as per acct. 1.14.0
Stuffle Mendlor for supporting his son 6.0.0
Ann McNeal as per petition 3.0.0
Wm. Drish the same allowance that Danl Losh [had] for keeping
Mary Ashby 16.0
Jno. Delkin for boarding Thos Donohuy 2 mos and 13 days .. 211.0.0
Ralph Murray, clerk of vestry 3.2.6

Ordered that Colo. Simon Triplet be appointed vestry man in the room of Jno. Luckett who hath removed out of the Parish. Leven Powell and Thos Shore appointed church wardens. Ordered that Jno Alexander, Joshua Gore along with present church wardens, settle with former wardens and collectors.

25th Nov 1782: Present, William Bronaugh, Thos Lewis, Leven Powell, Thomas Respass, Thos Shore, Joshua Gore, Joseph Coombs. The vestry proceedeth to lay the levy as followeth:

Ralph Murray, clerk 500
Richard Hopkins for the support of Ann Phillips from
13th May 1782 1920
Catharine Morris as per petition 185
Israel Thompson as per acct. 2184
Abigail Corngiver for the support of Mary Lemmon, 6 mos. 1184
Abigail Corngiver for support of her grandchild from
4th day of July last 750
John Delkin for keeping Thos Donohou from 13th May 1782 1068
John King Senr. for supporting Levin Harle from Oct. 1780 1680
Jacob Reed for the support of Mary Hurst, 8 mos. 992
Jas Sinkler for support of Mary Hunt [Hurst?] from
March 10th last 1106
Thomas Kibby for the support of Richd Caster 512
Jno Brown for burying Elizh Washington 560
Catharine Morris for support of a child, 6 weeks 360

Thomas Shore as per acct. 3120
Noble Leonard for burying Mary Shively 960
Joseph Baily for the support of his mother from 13 May 1782 .. 928
William Drish per acct. 576
Joshua Taylor per petition 960
Stuffle Mendlor as per do 960
Jno Johnston as per acct. 720
Revd. David Griffith for the balance of his salary levied in 1776 and not collected to July 1779 when the depreciation was 21 [blank] and not rec'd by him 16305
Ditto for another claim as assignee of Geo Muirhead circumstanced as above 1596
Anthony Forrest as per petition 800
Ann McNeal as per petition 480
Thos Gore for furnishing the vestry with fire and water 250

2200 Tithables. Thos Lewis, Gent, appointed parish collector the the ensuing year, and he to collect 20 pounds of tobacco from each Tithable.

Ralph Murray who took the collection in 1775, moved to be relieved, attesting that the commencement of the war with Great Britain made it impractical to complete the same. Moved that Ralph Murray be accordingly discharged upon his rending to the church wardens a fair and exact acct. Thos Lewis, Gent, agreeing to finish the said collection ordered that he do the same. Ordered that he enter into bond. Ordered that Joshua O'Daniel be chosen a vestryman in the room of Josias Clapham, who resigned his seat. Leven Powell and Thos Shore continued as church wardens for present year. Ordered that church wardens make proper application to Thompson Mason and Francis Payton late Ch. W. for the money Ralph Murray paid them in 1774.

To John Brown for burying Eliza. Worthenton 560

7 Nov 1783. Present Colo. Fras Peyton, Levin Powell, Thos Lewis, Gt., Colo William Bronaugh, Joshua Gore, Gt., Colo. Simon Triplett, Joseph Combs, Gt., Thos. Shore, Gt.

Colo. Francis Peyton as per act. 752
Colo. Leven Powell assnee of Joshua Gore who is assnee of Stuffle Mendler, by petition 960
Joshua Taylor by petition 1440

John Delkin in part for keeping Thos Donohoe and
making clothes 516
Joseph Janney 1440
John Osburn for keeping Anthony Forest until 10 of Jan 1784 . 1120
James Sinkler by petiton for keeping Mary Hurst to this day . 1600
John Bond for keeping Ann Thornton from 10th of Aug last 416
Israel Thompson as per acct. 4104
William Jenkins as per acct. 368
Abigail Corngiver as per acct. 1334
Doctr. John Neilson as per acct. 1624
William Whitely for boarding, medicine and attending Robt. Snipe an inhabitant of Leeds Parrish in the Co. of Prince Wiliam & Fauquier 1613
Thos Shore 6 days boarding said Snipe and expenses for removing him to said parrish of Leeds 220
John Henry Senr. for boarding Jno Wamsly 400
Capt. Thos Shore as per acct. 4560
Joseph Baily as per petition 1600
Do for future suppor of his mother 1280
Doctor Willm Smith Belt for visit and taping Robert Snipe of Leeds 272
Do per acct for medicine and attendance on sundry parishoners 3412
John Reeder for the support of his father 960
Ralph Murray, clerk of the vestry 500

Ordered that Colo. Simon Triplet and Josa. Daniel, Gent, be appointed Clerk for present year. Mason French appointed parrish collector for third battalion, John Binns for first battalion and both enter into bond according to law. Parish collectors to collect from each tithable person in this parish the sum of sixteen pounds of tobacco and pay off the several claimers and acct to the next vestry. Wardens with Colo. Leven Powell make arrangements with respect to the application of 30 pounds parish money put into the hands of Geo. Johnston, Dec'd, by Colo. Thos Peyton in the year 1775, and recover the same. Present clerks with Colo. Leven Powell settle with Thompson Mason Esqr., late church warden. Present C.W. make application to vestry of Leeds Parish to be reimbursed the money expended on Robert Snipe and his removal. Joseph Combs, Gent, have leave to resign and Thos Kennon be appointed a vestryman in his room. Pay Joshua Gore Jr. 31 sh. 3 pence. Thos Shore, Gent., late C.W.

produced an acct. to the vestry showing how he had disposed of 1007 lb. crop tobo. rec'd of W. C. Harrison, the same is approved of.

15 Dec 1784. Present, Levin Powell, Simon Triplett, Joshua Gore, Thos Respess, Joshua Daniel, Thos Shore, Thos Kinnen, Thos. Lewis, Jno Alexander.

Israel Thompson as per acct.	2480
Leven Powell as per acct.	240
Thos Shore as per acct.	1920
Francis Triplett as per acct.	2000
William Tomkins as per acct.	1100
William Smith Belt as per acct.	2968
Alexander McMakin as per acct.	596
Stuffle Mendlor as per petition	960
Samuel Murray as per acct.	160
John Osburn as per acct.	280
Joseph Caldwell as per acct.	978
Benjamin Benly as per acct.	704
William Cavins as per acct.	150
James Davis as per acct.	104
John Bond for keeping Ann Thornton	1600
John Delkin as per acct.	1920
Samuel Hough as per acct.	88
William Roads as per acct.	160
Joshua Daniel as per acct.	696
John Neilson as per acct.	2352
Richard Stephens as per acct.	408
Peter Greyham as per acct.	1016
Alexander McMackin as per acct.	280
Henry Eaton as per acct.	272
John Morriss as per acct.	352
Colo. Simon Triplett	104

Colo. John Alexander and Capt. Thos Kinnon appointed Church wardens for ensuing year. The collectors pay Ralph Murray the sum of 3.2.0 out of the depositors. Glebe lands and buildings be rented out on the following conditions, viz: The tenent to hold it 7 years, to put under timely and proper order... .

Jan 28th 1792. Not enough members to constitue a quorum. It was thought advisable by the members, viz: Wm. H. Powell, Chas. Bennet, Abraham M. Mason, and Jospeh Lane, to proceed to let the said glebe to farm for one year upon the best terms they can procure, as the time of the last tenant hath expired., and the said members being of opinion that it would be much to the damage of Glebe to be left vacant. Therefore, they proceeded to let it to the highest bidder under the following terms ... Ordered that Ricd Davis have the Glebe for one year, to expire on the 1st day of Jany 1793, for eighteen pounds excluding of repairs. He complying above and given bond with approved security to the C. wardens.

18 Aug. 1796. Vestry met at Glebe House. Present, The Rev. Alexr. McFarlane, J. T. Mason, W.C. Seldon, Levin Powell, William Bronaugh, Senr., Joseph Lane, John Alexander, Matthew Rust, William Jones, and Benja. Grayson. Ordered that Benjamin Grayson officiate as clerk for the present meeting. Alexr. McFarlan inducted into the Parish. William Jones, Gent. to assist William Bronaugh Jr, and Thomas Fouch in superintending the repairs of the Glebe. The collector pay to Wm Fowlk, admr. of Rev. D. Fowke, dec'd, £12.11.8 for an [act?] of Boarding the Revd. Mr. Edwd Jones during his residence in this parish, provided there shall be as much due the said Jones for his services as minister. Teste. Ben Grayson, Wm Bronaugh, Jos Lane, Jo Alexander, Levin Powell, Matthew Rust, Wilson C. Selden.

25th Nov. 1782. Ralph Murray took the collection for the parish in 1775, moved to be released from the position, alledging that the coming war with Great Britain made it impractable to complete the same. Thomas Lewis, Gent, agreed to furnish the said collection. Levin Powell and Thos Shore, Gent, continue as church wardens for the present year.

2 Oct. 1786. Francis Peyton, William Bronaugh, John Taylor, Thomas Kennah, Joseph Lane, John Alexander, Charles Bennett, Thomas Lewis, Stev. Thom. Mason, and Benja Grayson. Ordered that church wardens insitute a suit against Joseph Combs and his securities, upon their bond for building the upper church in this parish. William Bronaugh and Jos. Lane to settle the accounts of the differnt collectors for this parish prior to the appointment of the present vestryman and report. Thos Kennan, Charles Bennett, clerks.

17 Sept 1794. ... Ordered that the church wardens furnish the collector and lay before the vestry at their next meeting an accurate account of the time the Glebe has been rented to what persons the same has been rented, what has been the annual rent, and what is the sum due from each tenant. Mr. Jones to preach during the said year one Sunday at the Church at Rozells and the next at Leesburg.

4 Nov. 1795. Thos. Lewis, William Bronaugh, Joseph Lane, A.B. Mason, Benjamin Grayson, Wm Bronaugh Jr., Wm H. Powell, and Leven Powell. The Revd. Alexander McFarlan having professed his services to the parish as minister, the vestry consent to receive him for one year and agree to allow him as a compensation for his services the sum of fifty six pounds current money to be paid quartely, provided the said McFarlan will accept the same. Ordered that the said McFarlan [preach] once a fortnight at Leesburg and once a fortnight at Pot House and Middleburg alternately. Ordered that Colo. Jos. Lane ascertain the bounds of the Glebe Lands by survey and make return thereof.

28 March 1796. William Bronaugh, Leven Powell, Ben Grayson, Jos Lane, Wm Bronaugh Jr., William Jones, Thos Fouch, Matthew Rust, John Alexander, Stes Thom Mason, Wilso Cary Selden. Ordered that Williams Bronaugh Jr. officiate as clerk for the present meeting. Thomas Fouch and William Bronaugh Jr. were elected church wardens. William Bronaugh Jr. and Benjamin Grayson collectors are continued in their respective appointments. Wilson Cary Selden appointed as lay deputy to attend with Revd. Alex. McFarland the convention in Richmond on the first Tuesday in May next. Ordered that the roof of the Glebe House and underpennings of the room that Mr. McFarlan occupies be repaired. Ordered that Mr. McFarlan preach one in three weeks at Leesburg, Middleburg, and the Pot House the following at Leesburg and the next at Middleburg and so in rotation the whole year.

17 Apr 1797. Alex. Mc Farland, Revd., Joseph Lane, Benjamin Grayson, Thomas Fouch, William Bronaugh Jr., Wilson Cary Selden, William Jones, Leven Powell, and William Bronaugh. Revd. Alexander McFarlan is appointed to represent the Parish in the state convention to be held in Richmond on the first Tuesday in May next. Collectors to furnish Mr. McFarlan with thirty dollars towards defraying his expenses to the convention. Ordered that Wilson Cary Selden attend as lay deputy with the Revd. Alex McFarlan and bring in his account. The collectors to pay

Jos Lane $3.91 agreeably to the said Lane's acct. Collectors to pay Mr. McFarlan fourteen pounds for his last quarterly payment. Wm Bronaugh Jr., Thos Fouch, Church Wardens.

13 Nov. 1797. Vestry meeting held at house of Mr. McCabe in Leesburg. Francis Peyton Esqr, appointed lay deputy for the parish to represent the same in the Convention of the Protestant Episcopal Church in Virginia. Revd. Alexander McFarland also to attend.

[Next minutes are dated 20 June 1801].

BIRTHS AND BAPTISMS
REFORMED CHURCH OF LOUDOUN COUNTY

Children of Frantz Ritschy: Samuel Rithschy, "a son born to me." 11 July 1764. Sponsors: Samuel Diel and wife.
Henrich Ritschy, 20 June 1766
Michael Ritschy, 6 April 1768
Johannes Ritschy, 15 March 1771
Christina, 11 May 1773
Jacob Ritschy, 1 Aug 1774
Philip Ritschy, 20 April 1776
Isaac Ritschy, 20 June 1779
Abraham Ritschy, 22 June 1781

Joh. Jacob b. 28 Oct 1789, bapt. 25 Apr 1789 of Henrich Hembd (sic) and Catharina. Sponsors: Lorenz Amend and wife Barbara.

Maria Magdalena b. 12 Nov 1789, bapt. 25 Dec 1789, of Johannes Juncken and Catharina. Sponsors: Jacob Dorsheimer and wife Clara.

Johannes b. 17 Nov 1786 of Philipp Drumm and Magdalena. Sponsors: Isaac Ritshy and wife Catharina.

Johan Adam b. 17 Nov 1786 of Philipp Drumm and wife. Sponsors: Adam Schober and Magdalena.

Wilhelm b. 17 Nov 1786 of Phil. Drumm and Magdalena. Sponsors: Willhelm Wenner and Margaretha.

Barbara b. 25 Nov 1786 of Georg Schober and wife Catharina. Sponsors: Barbara Schober, widow.

Johan Conrad b. 6 Dec 1786 of Andreas Maurer and wife Margaretha. Sponsors: Martin Bauer and wife Barbara.

Catharina b. 29 June 1787 of Joh. Adam Reibsam and wife Dorothea. Sponsors: Johann Gamfer and wife Catharina.

Margaretha b. 14 Jan 1787 of Friedr. Spring and wife Barabara. Sponsor: Margaretha Steinbrenner.

Maria Magdalena b. 5 Jan 1787 of Peter Jacob and wife Eva. Sponsors: Joh. Schober and wife Maria Magdalena.

Elisabetha b. 15 Dec 1786 of Christian Ruf and wife Elis. Sponsors: Jacob Walther and wife Maria.

Christina b. 7 Nov 1786 of Peter Werner and wife Judith. Sponsors: Adam Wentzel and wife Maria.

Andreas b. 5 Dec 1786 of Michael Ballmer [Palmer] and wife Catharina. Sponsors: Andreas Beltz and wife Juliana.

Catharina b. 14 March 1787 of Peter Maurer and Sarah. Sponsors: Henrich Oechslein and wife Catharina.

Sara b. 2 Feb 1787 of Martin Bauer and wife Barbara. Sponsors: Friederich and wife Catharina.

Georg Friederich b. 13 Jan 1787 of Philipp Frey and Dorethea. Sponsors: Georg Bernhard and wife Catharina.

Catharina b. 14 Oct 1787, bapt. 4 ... 1787 of Conrad Bader and wife Elisab. Sponsors: Friederich Fuller and wife Catharina.

Christina b. 19 Jan 1789 of Johann Schumacher and wife Anna Maria. Sponsors: Magdalena Becker.

Peter b. 28 June 1789, bapt. 16 Aug 1789, of Peter Heckmann and Regina. Sponsors: Peter Maurer and wife Sara.

Maria Catharina b. 29 Aug 1789 of Christian Ruf and wife Elisabetha, bapt. 4 Nov 1789. Sponsors: Adam Haushalter and wife Maria Catharina.

Johannes b. 10 Sep 1789, bapt. 4 Oct 1789 of Conrad Basler and wife Elisabetha. Sponsors: Willhelm Wenner and wife Elisabetha.

Johannes b. 26 Oct 1789 of Andreas Thomson and wife Elisabetha. Sponsor: Johannes Stèdtler.

Elisabetha b. 31 Dec 1789 of Daniel May and Elisabetha, bapt. 3 Jan 1790. Sponsors: Jacob Dorscheimer and wife Clara.

Johannes b. 13 Feb 1790, bapt. 7 March 1790 of Henrich Rittschy and Catharina. Sponsors: Joh. Gottlieb Dorsch and wife Christina.

Daniel b. 14 Feb 1790, bapt. 7 March 1790 of Friederich Steinbrenner and Barbara. Sponsors: Jacob Steinbrenner and wife Eva.

Magdalena b. 4 Feb 1790, bapt. 7 March 1790 of Jacob Heckmann and wife Sara. Sponsor: Magdalena Wien, single.

Elisabetha b. 31 Dec 1789 of Daniel May and wife Elisabetha, bapt. 3 Jan 1790. Sponsors: Jacob Dorscheimer and wife Clara.

Johannes b. 13 Feb 1790, bapt. 7 March 1790 of Henrich Rittschy and wife Catharina. Sponsors: Joh. Gottlieb Dorsch and wife Christina.

Daniel b. 14 Feb 1790, bapt. 7 March 1790, of Friederich Steinbrenner and wife Barbara. Sponsors: Jacob Steinbrenner and wife Eva.

Magdalena b. 4 Feb 1790, bapt. 7 March 1790, of Jacob Heckmann and wife Sara. Sponsor: Magdalena Wien, single.

Additions to 1786 & 1789

Catharina b. 25 Jan 1786, bapt. 23 Nov, of Gimes Buth [James Booth] and Serena. Sponsor: Matthias Jacobi's wife.

Elisabetha b. 17 Feb 1786, bapt. 23 Nov of Thomas Wenz and Magdalena. Sponsor: Clara Maurer.

Christina b. 22 Oct 1786 of Jacob Sautor and Maria Catharina. Sponsor: Wife of Johannes Hüther.

Adam b. 21 Sep 1786 of Henrich Eplein and Catharina. Sponsor: Adam Eplein.

Jacob b. 22 Oct 1789, bapt. 23 May 1789, of Christoph Winter and Margaretha. Sponsors: Jacob Sonnenfranck and his wife.

Sussanna b. 5 Jan 1790, bapt. 23 May 1790, of Georg Ebel and Cathar. Sponsors: Simon Rickart and wife Susanna.

Maria Sophia b. 8 March 1790, of Johannes May and Maria Sophia, bapt. 25 April 1790. Sponsors: Henrich Eplein and wife Catharina.

Elisabetha b. 11 May 1790, of Johann Städler and wife Priscilla, bapt. 8 Aug 1790. Sponsors: Abraham Städler and Elisab.

Susanna Catharina b. August 1790 of Peter Heckmann, bapt. 1 Oct. Sponsors: Conrath Heckmann and his wife.

Levi Printz, born a Jew, bapt. on 21 Nov 1790 and promised to behave himself as a good Christian.

Jacob b. 2 Nov 1790 of Jacob Adams, bapt. 25 Dec. Sponsors: Jacob Dorscheimer and wife.

Magdalena b. 17 Oct 1790 of Samuel Becker, bapt. 25 Dec. Sponsor: Magdalena Becker.

Catharina b. 18 Nov 1790 of Henrich Guthhard, bapt. 25 Dec 1790. Sponsors: Johannes Wust and wife.

Johannes b. 10 Dec 1790 of Adam Rübsam, bapt. 25 Dec. Sponsors: Johannes Gambert and wife.

Valentin b. 19 April 1785 of Pastor Henrich Giese. Sponsors: Christian Miller and wife.

Elizabeth b. 23 June 1790 of Adam Zehnbaur, bapt. 20 Feb 1791. Sponsors: Adam Schower and wife.

Maria Christina b. 18 Jan of Philip Gross, bapt. 20 March. Sponsors: Johannes Fahl (Eichler) and wife.

George b. 4 Oct 1790 of George Schultz, bapt. 20 March 1791. Sponsors: George Schumacher and wife.

Johannes b. 5 Feb 1791 of Adam Maurer, bapt. 20 March. Sponsor: Joh. Maurer.

Sophia Elisabeth b. 4 Jan 1791 of Freiderick Lohr, bapt. 20 March. Sponsors: Georg Detchers and wife.

Johannes b. 1 Dec 1790 of Daniel Schumacher, bapt. 24 April. Sponsors: Joh. Reimer and wife.

Catharine b. 7 March 1791 of Jacob Stetler, bapt. 24 April. Sponsor: Prisilla Städtler.

Elisabeth b. 18 Feb 1791 of Henry Hein, bapt. 24 April. Sponsors: Georg Schweny and wife.

Maria Magdalena b. 3 March 1789 of Philip Drom, bapt. 24 April. Sponsors: Adam Schober and wife.

Nency b. 10 July 1790 of Christian Neuschwanger, bapt. 22 May 1791. Sponsors: Jacob Dorscheimer and wife.

Adam Christ: b. 30 Nov 1790 of Ludwig Löwe, bapt. 22 May. Sponsors: Adam Schober and wife.

Eve Elisabeth b. 23 April 1791 of Conrad Bader, bapt. 22 May. Sponsors: Joh. Filler and wife.

Catharina b. 19 Nov 1786 of Pastor Giese.

Anna Maria b. 14 Nov 1791 of Pastor Henrich Giese. Sponsors: Johannes Oechslein and wife.

Catharina b. 15 April 1791 of George Schumacher, bapt. July 1791. Sponsors: Friederich Beltz and wife.

Daniel b. 16 May 1791 of Henrich Eplein, bapt. Aug 1791. Sponsors: Daniel Schumacher and wife.

Joh. Adam b. 13 Nov 1791 of Johannes Wiess, bapt. 22 Nov. Sponsors: Henrich Guthard and wife.

Jacob b. 5 Oct 1791 of Henrich Segell, bapt. 22 Nov 1791. Sponsors: Samuel Ritschy and wife.

Elisabeth b. 12 Oct 1791 of Jacob Heckmann, bapt. 27 Nov 1791. Sponsors: Wilhelm Wenner and wife.

Johann George b. 31 Oct 1791 of Nicolaus Sender, bapt. 25 Dec. Sponsors: Jacob Schumacher and wife.

Johann Wilhelm b. 2 Nov 1791 of Wilhelm Wenner, bapt. 8 Jan. Sponsors: Father Wilhelm and wife.

Jacob b. 7 Nov 1791 of Peter Warnert, bapt. 11 May. Sponsors: Jacob Schumacher, Sr. and wife.

Johann Jacob b. 1792 of Isaac Miller, bapt. 27 June 1792. Sponsors: Johannes Oechslein and wife.

Peter b. 14th day before Christmas 1791 of Siemon Schober, bapt. 27 May. Sponsors: Peter Wertz and wife.

Benjamin b. 25 March 1792 of Jacob Eberhardt, bapt. 27 May. Sponsors: Jacob Waldtmann and wife.

Christina b. 21 Nov 1791 of Johannes Battenfeld, bapt. 27 May. Sponsors: George Hamann and wife.

Catharina b. 23 Feb 1792 of George Stull, bapt. 27 May 1792.

Elisabeth b. 20 March 1792 of Pastor Henrich Giese, bapt. 27 May. Sponsors: Adam Schober and wife.

Elisabeth b. 17 March 1792 of Samuel Rithschi, bapt. 27 May. Sponsor: Elisabeth Gergen.

Maria Magdalena b. 14 March 1792 of Adam Senbaur, bapt. 8 July 1792. Sponsors: Adam Schober and wife.

Elisabeth b. 28 June 1792 of Jacob Adams, bapt. 8 July 1792. Sponsors: Magdalena Dorschheymer.

Barbara b. 22 June 1792 of Jacob Eberle, bapt. 19 Aug. Sponsors: Barbara Becker.

Michaell b. 29 Sep 1792 of George Schultz, bapt. 25 Dec 1792. Sponsors: Siemon Schumacher and wife.

Siemon b. 2 Sep 1792 of Joh. Arnold, bapt. 25 Dec 1792. Sponsors: Siemon Richert and wife.

Michael b. 29 Sep 1792 of George Schultz, bapt. 25 Dec 1792. Sponsors: Siemon Schumacher and wife.

Susanna, b. 17 Dec. 1792, of Adam Riebesam, bapt. 11 Jan 1793. Sponsor: Susanna Steinbrenner.

Johannes b. 23 Sep 1792 of Johannes Becker.

Philip b. Dec 1792 of Henrich Oechslein, bapt. 10 March. Sponsors: Philip Becker and wife.

Jacob, b. 19 Nov. 1792, to Abraham Winn, bapt. 10 March. Sponsors: Jacob Berg and wife.

Jacob b. 8 Nov 1792 of Johannes Schuester, bapt. 10 March. Sponsors: Jacob Eberle and wife.

___ a daughter, b. 14 March 1793 of Jacob Bornhauss, bapt. 19 June 1793. Sponsors: Friederich Doerflinger and wife.

Sara, b. 1 March 1793 of Conrath Bader, bapt. 19 Jun 1793. Sponsors: Jacob Heckmann and wife.

George b. 5 May 1793 of Jacob Schumacher, Junr., bapt. 30 June 1793. Sponsors: George Schumacher, Jr. and wife.

___ b. 1793 of Henrich Sengall.___ 1793 ___

In ... 1793 a ... was born to Henrich Sengall.

In ... 1793 a ... was born to ... Leberich.

Salome b. 11 June 1793 of Johannes Stautzenberger, bapt. 29 Sep 1793. Sponsors: Conrath Schuester and wife Salome.

David b. 26 April 1793 of Wilhelm Wenner, bapt. 1 Dec. Sponsors: Jacob Berg and wife.

George b. 10 Oct 1793 of Joh. Juncker, bapt. 26 Dec 1793. Sponsors: Jacob Adams and wife.

Susanna b. 11 Nov 1793 of Joh. Wentzell, bapt. 5 Jan 1793 [sic]. Sponsor: Susanna Hoff.

Peter b. 5 Jan 1794 of Joh. Wiess, bapt. 2 March 1794. Sponsors: Peter Frey and wife.

Henrietta b. 4 Dec 1793 of Pastor Giese, bapt. 2 March 1794. Sponsor: Elisabeth Juergen.

Jonathan b. 22 Oct 1793 of Barbara Kast. She confessed that Joh. Dorschheimer was the father. After confessing that she had erred, and was sorry, the child was baptised on 2 March. Sponsors: Carl Dorschheimer and wife.

Magdalena b. 9 Jan 1790 of Siemon Schober. Sponsors: Adam Schober and wife.

Isaac b. 21 Dec 1793 of Jacob Berg, bapt. 30 March. Sponsors: Isaac Ritschi and wife.

Hanna b. 4 May 1793 of Peter Warner, bapt. 1794. Sponsor: Elisabeth Schumacher.

Maria Elisabeth b. 16 Jan 1794 of Henrich Gudhard, bapt. 1794. Sponsors: Johan Anthon Lange and wife.

Jacob b. 6 March 1794 of George Schumacher, Jr., bapt. 27 April 1794. Sponsors: Siemon Schumacher and wife.

Isaac b. 26 Dec 1793 of Abraham Wien, bapt. 27 April 1794. Sponsors: Isaac Ritschy and wife.

Catharina b. 15 March 1794 of Carl Dorschheimer, bapt. 27 April 1794. Sponsor: Magdalena Dorschheimer.

Daniel b. 19 Aug 1794 of Daniel Schumacher, bapt. 10 Sep 1794.

Magdalena b. 1794 of Levi Printz and bapt. {crossed out by Giese}

Siemon b. 12 April 1776 of Daniel Schumacher. Sponsors: Siemon Schumacher and wife.

Adam b. 25 Dec 1779 (sic) of Daniel Schumacher. Sponsors: Adam Oechslein and wife.

Johannes b. 20 Feb 1793 of Johannes Lange, bapt. 22 March. Sponsors: Johannes Wiess and wife.

Catharina Elizabeth b. 8 Oct 1794 of Georg Schultz, bapt. 5 April 1795. Sponsors: Jacob Schumacher and wife.

Maria Elisabeth b. 11 July 1794 of Johannes Becker, bapt. 2 Dec. Sponsor: Maria Elizabeth Crumbacher.

George b. 22 Oct 1794 of Samuel Baker (Becker) , bapt. Christmas day. Sponsors: George Mann.

Anna Maria b. 20 Oct 1794 of John Adams, bapt. 26 Dec 1794. Sponsor: Anna Maria Scheutz.

Catharina b. 1 April 1795 of Oswald Hahn and Anna Maria. Sponsor: Jacob Schletzer.

Sussanna b. 10 Nov 1795, bapt. 7 Feb 1796, of Johannes Ulm and Elisabeth. Sponsor: Elisabetha Schletzer.

Antonius b. 1 Aug 1795, bapt. 7 Feb 1796, of Carl Lang and Catharina. Sponsors: Antonius Lang and Barbara.

Johann Adam b. 14 Jan 1795, bapt. 6 March, of Jacob Berg and Margaretha. Sponsors: Johann Adam Schober and wife Magdalena.

Elisabeth b. 10 Dec 1795, bapt. 6 March, of Jacob Bornhaus and Elisabeth. Sponsors: Jacob Wuertz and wife Elisabeth.

Eve Margar: b. 13 Nov 1795, bapt. 28 March, of Samuel Ritches and Anna Maria. Sponsor: Margaret Rebold.

Christine b. 12 Dec 1795, bapt. 28 March, of Georg Euell and Catharina. Sponsors: Christoph Bornhaus and wife Rosina.

Jacob b. 3 Feb, bapt. 28 March, of Jacob Eberhard and Marianna. Sponsors: Geo. Jac. Waldmann and wife Anna Margaret.

Catrina b. 7 Feb, bapt. 28 March of Henr. Lambert and Elisabet. Sponsors: Hannes Stèdtler and Christine.

Christina b. 15 Dec 1795, bapt. 28 March 1796, of Jacob Lang and Eva. Sponsors: Christian Eberhart and wife Sybilla.

Maria b. 15 Dec 1796, bapt. 1 May 1796, of Johannes Eske and Elizabeth. Sponsor: Maria Steer.

Joseph b. 10 Dec 1796, bapt. 1 May 1796, of Johannes Feinstein and Catharina. Sponsors: Johannes Stautsenberger and wife Margaretha.

Maria b. 3 Oct 1793 (5), bapt. 1 May 1796, of Levy Printz and Elisabeth. Sponsors: Joh. Emich and Maria.

Salomon b. 1 May 1796 of Elizabeth Heckmann (illegitimate). She gave the father's name as Michael Hallebart.

Christian b. 25 Dec 1795, bapt. 29 May 1796, of Philip Doerry and Barbara. Sponsors: Christ. Eberhardt and wife Sybilla.

Johannes b. 5 April, bapt. 29 May 1796, of Peter Frey and Christina. Sponsors: Joh. Fally and Eva Marg.

Wilhelm b. 7 Dec 1795, bapt. 29 May 1796, of Peter Steinbrenner and Susanna. Sponsors: Joh. Stantzenberger and Margaretha.

Elizabeth b. 30 April, bapt. 29 May 1796, of Johannes Wentzel and Maria Magdalena. Sponsor: Elisab. Crumbach.

Josias Clapham b. 4 May of Benjamin Price and Sarah, bapt. 26 June 1796.

Georg b. 4 June of Wilhelm Wenner and Anna Maria, bapt. 26 June 1796. Sponsors: Georg Schober and wife Catharina.

Elisabeth b. 2 March of David Mohl and Magdalena, bapt. 26 June 1796. Sponsors: Georg Schultz and Elizabeth.

Johannes b. 16 March of Isaac Miller and Catharina, bapt. 26 June 1796. Sponsors: Johannes Georg and Elisabeth.

Magdalena b. 13 May of Johannes Becker and Maria Dorothea, bapt. 26 June 1796. Sponsors: Joh. Kramer and Magdalena.

Margaretha b. 18 Oct 1795 of Johannes Hemb and Susanna Cath., bapt. 26 June 1796. Sponsor: Margaretha Schafer.

Anna b. 8 March of Johannes Filler and Elisabeth, bapt. 26 June 1796. Sponsor: Eva Crumbach.

Maria Magdalena b. 4 Feb of Wilhelm Olden and Magdalena,bapt. 26 June 1796. Sponsors: Geo. Schober and Catharina.

Johannes b. 27 Dec 1795 of Leonard Groh and Catharina, bapt. 26 June 1796. Sponsors: Jacob Berg and Margaretha.

Johannes b. 14 May of Georg Ungefehr and Catharina, bapt. 26 June 1796. Sponsors: Salomòn Schumacher and Elisabeth.

Margaretha b. 25 March of Peter Stockman and Elisabeth, bapt. 26 June 1796. Sponsor: Sussanna Maurer.

Daniel b. 21 May of Daniel Rankins and Elendor, bapt. 26 June 1796.

Philip b. 13 Sep 1795 of Philip Locker and Margareth.

Joh. Philip b. 5 Aug, bapt. 4 Sep 1796, of Samuel Becker and Catharina. Sponsors: Wm. Becker and Eva.

Maria Elisabeth b. 11 April 1796, bapt. 31 Oct, of Adam Maurer and Magdalena. Sponsors: Abraham Wien and Maria Elisabeth.

Joh: Jacob [no date] of Michael Raimund and Elisabeth. Sponsors: Jacob Doerr and wife Catharina.

Sussanna b. 8 Sep, bapt. 6 Nov 1796 of Georg Schultze and Elizabeth.

Maria Cathar. b. 22 Sept, bapt. 6 Nov 1796, of Peter Ritchie and Elisabeth. Sponsor: Cathar. Ritshie.

Elisabeth b. 18 Dec 1796, bapt. 12 Feb 1797, of Peter Steinbrenner and Sussanna. Sponsors: Jacob Dorstheimer and Elisab.

Sally b. 12 Oct 1796, bapt. 12 Feb 1797, of Carl Dorstheimer and Catharina. Sponsors: Benj. Prill (Price) and wife Sally.

Elisabeth b. 1 Dec 1796, bapt. 12 Feb 1797, of Michael Miller and Catharina. Sponsors: Jacob Wuertz and Elisabeth.

John b. 26 Nov 1796, bapt. 12 Feb 1797, of Salomon Schumacher and Elisabeth. Sponsors: John Stettler and Priscilla.

Elisabeth b. 28 March 1796, bapt. 5 March 1797, of George Miller and Maria. Sponsor: Jacob Wuertz and Elisabeth.

Margaretha b. 30 Sep 1796, bapt. 25 March 1797, of Abrah. Wien and Elisabetha. Sponsors: Isaac Ritchie and wife Margaretha.

Johannes b. 4 Nov 1796, bapt. 14 April 1797 of Geo. Schumacher and Magdalena. Sponsors: Joh: Schaefer and Anna Maria.

Johann Peter b. 13 March, bapt. 17 April 1797, of Joh. Ad. Riebsam and Dorothea. Sponsor: Peter Kamper.

Wilhelm b. 5 Dec 1796, bapt. 17 April 1797, of Catharina Schmidt, widow. Sponsors: Christian Bornhaus and wife Rosina.

Rahel b. 16 June 1796, bapt. 17 April 1797, of Peter Warner and Judith. Sponsors: Salom. Schumacher and wife Elisab.

Sibilla b. 18 June, bapt. 21 May 1797, of Caspar Eberhard. Sponsors: Christian Eberhard and wife Sibilla.

Jacob b. 14 Feb 1797, bapt. 21 May 1797, of Michael Strahm and Elisabeth. Sponsors: Jacob Dorstheimer and wife Elisabeth.

Adam b. 15 June 1797, bapt. 23 July 1797 of L. Minck and Rahel. Sponsors: Michael Palmer and wife Barbara.

John Peter Casper Wilhelm b. 28 June 1797, bapt. 23 July 1797, of John Eskin and Elisabeth. Sponsors: John Peter Eskin, Casper Eskin, Wilhelm Schaefer and wife Elisabeth.

Maria Magdalena b. 16/18 July 1797, bapt. 20 Aug 1797, of Samuel Brill and Catharina. Sponsors: Anthon Ament and wife Catharina.

Maria Magdalena b. 28 May 1797, bapt. 20 Aug 1797, of John Feurstein and Catharina. Sponsor: Eva Feuerstein.

Christina b. 17 May 1797, bapt. 20 Aug 1797, of Peter Wuertz and Sussanna. Sponsor: Christina Wuertz.

Samuel b. 16 July 1797, bapt. 20 Aug 1797, of Peter Canert [Cauert?] and Maria Elisabeth. Sponsors: Adam Haushalder and wife Suhsanna.

Leonhard(try) b. 13 May 1797, bapt. 20 Aug 1797, of Vilsen (P)asten (Bosten) and Mery. Sponsors: Vilsen Pasten and wife Mery [Mary].

Wilhelm b. 30 July 1796 of Peter Gamber and Maria. Sponsors: Wilhelm Dorschheimer and Elisabeth.

Adam b. 18 May 1797 of Peter Miller and Catharina. Sponsors: Adam Haushalter and wife Susanna.

Margaretha b. 18 June 1797, bapt. 9 Sep 1797, of Isaac Miller and Catharina. Sponsor: Margar. Schmidt.

Anna Christina b. 7 Sep 1797, bapt. 15 Oct 1797, of Jacob Eberly and Magdalena. Sponsor: Anna Christina Becker.

Susanna Elisab. b. 25 June 1797, bapt. 15 Oct 1797, of Simeon Schober and Sharlota. Sponsors: Conrad Heckman and wife Susanna.

Margareda b. 21/23 Sept 1797, bapt. 18 Nov 1797, of Christian Mack and Magdalena. Sponsor: Z. Dea Pachmanu.

___ b. 14 Aug 1797 of Jacob Schletzer and Catharina. Sponsors: Jacob Dorschheimer and wife Elisabeth.

___ b. 29 Sep 1797, bapt. 10 Dec 1797, of Johannes Ulm and Elisabeth. Sponsors: Jacob Dorschheimer and wife Elisabeth.

___ b. 7 Nov, bapt. 10 Dec 1797, of Johann Philip Doerry and Barbara. Sponsors: Johannes Joerg and wife Elisabeth.

Wilhelm b. 4 Oct 1797 of Ruben Beckly and Christina. Sponsors: Philip Eberhard and wife Charlotte.

Georg b. 22 Oct 1797 of Johannes Hemp and Sussanna. Sponsors: Georg Wentzel and wife Catharina.

Johannes b. (?) Dec 1797 of Theophilus Preh. and Elisabeth. Sponsor: Johann Stantzenberger.

Johannes b. 30 July 1797 of Dorothea Blackburn. The father, William Allen was gone. She showed repentance for her deviation. Sponsors: Henridi Strohm and wife Margaretha.

Johan b. 7 Jan 1798, bapt. 13 May 1798, of John Taly and Margaretha. Sponsors: Johannes Wuertz and wife Catharina.

Johannes b. 13 March 1798, bapt. 13 May 1798 of Caspar Trout and Anna Maria. Sponsors: Lorentz Ament and wife Barbara.

John b. 19 March, bapt. 13 May 1798, of Philip Schaefer and Deci. Sponsor: Conrat Schaefer.

George b. 19 Jan 1798, bapt. 13 May 1798, of Henrich Wolf (Walts) and Juty [Judy]. Sponsors: Georg Fahly and wife Magdalena.

John b. 22 Dec 1798, bapt. 13 May 1798, of Georg Moll and Catarina. Sponsors: John Schafer and Anna Maria.

Eva Margareta b. 1 April 1798, bapt. 13 May 1798, of David Moll and Magdalena. Sponsor: Eva Margareta, widow Moll.

Philip Emich b. 1 Jan 1798, bapt. 13 May 1798 of Milly Farmer, born outside the married state. She gave Michael Emich as the father.

Anna Catharina b. 29 April, bapt 28 May, of Jacob Bornhaus and Elisabeth. Sponsors: Peter Jacob and wife Elisabeth.

Solomon b. 4 March 1798, bapt. 28 May 1798, of Wilhelm Becker and Maria Sponsors: Samuel Becker and wife Clara Catharina.

Maria Catarina b. 2 April 1798, bapt. 27 June 1798, of John Becker and Dorothea. Sponsors: Joh. Kramer and wife Magdalena.

Salome b. 8 May 1798, bapt. 22 July 1798, of Henrich Segel and Lurcky [Tercky] Sponsor: Catharina Ruse.

Elizabeth b. 18 May, bapt. 22 July 1798, of Georg Ungefehr and Catharina. Sponsor: Elisabeth Edelmann.

Elisabeth b. 18 June, bapt. 16 Sep, of Jacob Wirtzer and Elisabetha. Sponsors: Johannes Georg and Elisabetha.

Catharina b. 19 July, bapt 16 Sep 1798, of Michael Reimund and Elisabetha. Sponsors: Michael Scheck and Catharina.

Maria Catharina b. 22 July, bapt. 16 Sep, of Abraham Wien and Elisabetha. Sponsor: Margaretha, daughter of Isaac Ritschy.

Wilhelm b. 21 July, bapt. 16 Sep 1798, of Michael Strehm and Magdalena. Sponsors: Henrich Strehm, Sr. and Margaretha.

Magdalena b. 6 Sep 1797, bapt. 16 Sep 1798, of Daniel Gammerich and Anna. Sponsors: Sussanna Steinbrenner, daughter of Peter Steinbrenner.

Ana Margreta b. 11 Sep 1798, bapt. 14 Oct, of Jorg Schumacher and Magdalena. Sponsor: Margreta Shaffer.

H. Salomon b. 12 Aug, bapt. 14 Oct 1798, of Georg Schultz and Elisabeth. Sponsors: Georg Schumacher and wife Magdalena.

Matilde b. 1 July, bapt. 14 Aug 1798, of John Adams and Dorothea. Sponsor: Sussana Shnutz.

Nicolaus and Sarah, b. 3 Aug, bapt 14 Oct 1798, of Henrich Hempt and Catharina. Sponsors: Henrich Strem, wife Margaretha, and Barbara Meier.

Clara b. 27 Sep, bapt. 18 Nov, of Carl Dorshheimer and Catharina. Sponsors: Lorentz Amen and wife Barbara.

Joh. Adam b. 11 Sep, bapt. 18 Nov, of Jacob Haeffner and Catharina. Sponsors: Joh. Adam Schober and wife Magdalena.

Maria Magdalena b. Oct, bapt. 18 Nov, of Saml. C. Brill and wife Catharina. Sponsors: Caspar Traut and wife Anna Maria.

Johannes b. 2 Nov, bapt. 3 March, of Johanes Dorstheimer. Sponsors: Jacob Dorsth. and Elisabeth.

Johann Jacob b. 3 July, bapt. 3 March, of Peter Mayer. Sponsors: Joh. Stautzenberg and Margareta.

Br__kt b. 22 Dec, bapt 3 March, of Wilhelm Strem and Anna Maria. Sponsors: John Georg and Elisabeth.

Sabilla [no date] of Willhelm Wenner. Sponsor: Peci Bachman.

Sussana b. 13 Feb, bapt. 3 March, of Friedrich Steinbrenner. Sponsors: Peter Steinbrenner and Susanna.

Johannes b. 2 Dec 1798, bapt. 25 March 1799, of Phillip Hueter and Elizabeth. Sponsor: Johannes Huter (Gueter).

Sussanna b. 28 Jan, bapt. 25 March 1799, of John Eskin and Elisabeth. Sponsor: Sussanna Schaeffer.

Samuel b. 2 Sep 1798, bapt. 31 March 1799, of Rudolph Juncken and Elisabet Sponsors: John Junken and wife Catarina.

Lorentz b. 2 Feb, bapt. 31 March, of Fredrich Lampert and Maria. Sponsors: Lorentz Ament and wife Barbara.

Ferdinant b. 7 Oct 1798, bapt 31 March 1799, of Peter Stock and Peci. Sponsor: Henrich Hoff.

Elisabeth b. 3 March 1799, bapt. 19 May 1799, of Peter Wirtz and Sussana. Sponsor: Elisabeth Stock.

Sara b. 28 March 1799, bapt. 19 May 1799, of Richard Schafer and Elisabeth. Sponsor: Catharina Arnold.

Georg b. 20 April 1799, bapt. 26 May 1799, of Georg Moll and Catharina. Sponsors: Georg Schumacher and Magdalena.

Friederich b. 20 April 1799, bapt. 26 May 1799, of George Moll and Catharina. Sponsor: David Boger.

George F. (Joseph) b. 26 April 1799, bapt. 26 May 1799, of Salomon Schumacher and Elizabeth. Sponsors: Simon Schumacher and wife Scharlot.

Margreda b. 9 April 1799, of Daniel Heckenthorn and Christina. Sponsors: Adam Wolff and wife Sussana.

John Adam b. 11 Aug 1799, bapt. 13 Oct 1799, of Abraham Wien and Elisabeth. Sponsors: John Adam Shober and wife Magdalena.

Johannes b. 27 Aug 1799, bapt. 13 Oct 1799, of Johannes Müeller and Barbara. Sponsors: Johannes Schaefer and wife Anna Maria.

Margareta b. 1799, bapt. 20 Nov 1799, of Michael Schuck and Catharina. Sponsors: Isaac Ritschie and wife Catharina.

Johannes b. 12 Oct, bapt 5 Jan 1800, of Willhelm Wolf and Anna Margareda. Sponsors: Johannes Wentzel and wife Magdalena.

Michael b. 7 Feb 1800, bapt. 1 May 1800, of Friedrich Lambert and Anna Maria. Sponsors: Caspar (Lothar) Traut and wife Anna Maria.

Wilhelm b. 27 Sep 1800 [sic], bapt. 1 May 1800, of Wilhelm Schaefer and Elisabeth. Sponsors: John Ellich and wife Rebecca.

Jacob b. Jan 1800, bapt. 1 May 1800, of Susanna Schafer. Sponsor: Jacob Dorschheimer.

Joseph b. 18 Oct 1799, of Isaac Miller and Catharina. Sponsor: Isaac Ritschie.

Michael b. 4 Dec 1799, of Philip Derre and Barbara. Sponsor: Michael Eberhard.

Joh. Michael b. 3 March 1800 and Elisabeth b. same day, of Henrich Segel and Dorcas. Sponsors: George Fahling, wife Magdalena and Christian Ruhs and wife Catharina.

Nancy b. 21 March 1800, of Michael Stroehm and Magdalena. Sponsors: George Schultz and wife Elisabeth.

Anna Maria b. 15 April 1800, of Johannes Becker and Dorothea. Sponsors: Wilhelm Wenner and wife Magdalena.

Johannes b. 31 March 1800, of Johannes Ulm and Elisabeth. Sponsor: Joh. Steinbrenner.

Catharina b. 14 Dec 1799, bapt. 8 June 1800, of David Saarbach and Anna. Sponsor: Susanna Schmidt.

Peter b. 28 Feb 1800, of Peter Ritschie and Elisabeth. Sponsor: Peter Meyer.

Georg b. 13 Feb 1800, bapt. 8 June 1800, of Georg Ebel and Catharina.

Elisabeth b. 26 April 1800, of John Conner and Maria. Sponsor: Anna Maria Schnutz.

___ , of Susanna Schnutz, bapt. 20 June, born outside the married state. She gave father as Peter Faley. Sponsors: Jacob Dorschheimer and wife.

Maria Magdalena b. 29 June 1800, bapt. 2 Aug 1800, of Jacob Spring and Beci. Sponsors: Jacob Dorstheimer and wife Elisabeth.

Magdalena b. 12 July 1800, bapt. 3 Aug 1800, of Peter Reidenbach and Pechi. Sponsors: Georg Schober and wife Peci.

Maria Magdalena b. 29 May 1800, bapt. 3 Aug 1800, of Jacob Haffner (Hastner) and Catharina. Sponsors: Adam Schober and wife Magdalena.

Johann Jacob b. 18 May 1800, bapt 3 Aug 1800, of Jacob Eberle and Magdalena. Sponsors: Samuel Becker and wife Clara.

Peter b. 12 July 1800 of Peter Myers and Amelia. Sponsors: William Wenner and wife Magdalena.

Magdalena b. 6 July 1800 of Jacob Gover and Maria. Sponsor: Catharina Berg.

Catharina b. 25 May 1800 of Wilhelm Becker and MariaEva. Sponsors: Daniel Haushalter and wife Catharina.

Jacob b. 2 Aug 1800 of Jacob Becker and Catharina. Sponsors: Jacob Schletzer and wife Susanna.

Adam b. 11 June 1800 of Simon Schober and Charlotte. Sponsors: Jacob Wertz and wife Elisabeth.

Peter b. 14 July 1800 of Christoph Bornhaus and Rosena. Sponsors: Peter Jacob and wife Elisabeth.

Isaac b. 18 Sep 1800 of Jacob Steinbrenner and Margaretha. Sponsors: Jacob Dorschheimer and Elisabeth.

David b. Sep 1799 of Henrich Lambert and Elisabeth. Sponsors: Adam Kadel and wife Elisab.

Margaretha b. Sep 1800 of Carl Dorschheimer and Catharina. Sponsors: Conrad Schaefer and wife Elisab.

Johan Adam b. 9 May 1800, bapt. 6 Sep, of Peter Jacob and Elisabeth. Sponsors: Peter Jacbob and Elisabeth.

Peter b. 16 Aug 1800, bapt 9 Sep 1800, of Henrich Wolff and Juliana. Sponsors: Adam Wolff and Sussana.

Anna Maria b. 6 Oct 1800, bapt 9 Nov 1800, of Isaac Ritschie and Margaretha. Sponsors: Michael Schuck and Catharina.

John Melchor b. 13 Sep 1800, bapt. 9 Nov 1800 of Philip Wentz and Maria Elisabeth. Sponsors: Melchor Strupp and Maria.

Joseph b. 21 Sep 1800, bapt. 7 Dec 1800, of Jacob Eberhardt and Maria Anna. Sponsors: Adam Schober and wife Magdalena.

Georg b. 7 Nov 1800, bapt. 1 March 1801, of Georg Schumacher and Magdalena. Sponsors: Georg Schultz and wife Elisabeth.

Salomon b. 13 Nov 1800, of Wilhem Wenner and Magdalena. Sponsors: Johannes Becker and wife Dorothea.

Elisabetha b. 9 Dec 1800, of Johannes Dorschheimer and Magdalena. Sponsor: Elisab. Post.

Lea b. 13 Dec 1800 of Jacob Wuertz and Elisabeth.

Johann Jacob b. 2 Jan 1800 [or 1801] of Peter Jecke and Sara. Sponsors: Jacob Dorscheimer and wife Elisabeth.

Joh. Adam b. 19 Feb 1800 [or 1801] of Christian Seger and Elisabeth. Sponsors: Adam Schober and wife Magdalena.

FRYING PAN BAPTIST CHURCH

[The tops of many of these pages are water spotted and impossible to read. The following notes were written on the first page of the record book.]

List of negroes:
___, belonging to Benj. Cockrill, dismist 1796___, belonging to Robt Thomas, excommunicated.
Bett, belonging to Stephen Lay, dismist 11 Mar 1801.
Dinah, belonging to Temple Smith, dismist.
Tom and Patt, belonging to Wm Lane, Jr.
Kate, belonging to Wm. Brown Carter, dismist 12 Jun 1802
Kate, belonging to Charles Brent.
_inia, belonging to Jeremiah Hutchison Jr.
Victory, belonging to Colo. Summers.
Winny, belonging to Mr. Washington.
Cezer and June, his wife rec'd March 14, 1798, Cezar dead.
Harry, belongs to Edward Washington, rec'd from Popeshead, 17 June 1801
Baptized George, the property of Ludwell Lee.
Baptized John, belonging to Edward Washington.
The fourth sabbath in June 1801:
Baptized a negro woman, the property of Edward Washington.
Harry and John belonging to Edward Washington both dismist July 1804.

At a meeting of Frying Pan Spring, the 13th of May 1791: Brother Major chose for our minister. Brother Coleman Brown chose for Elder, Brother Benjamin Cockerill chose for Deacon, Brother Moses Thomas chose for Clerk, Brother ___ Cockerill chose for clerk to sing, Brother D. M. Talbert dismist to Popeshead.

25 June 1791: Brother John Jenkins rec'd by dismission from Difficult. Allen Davis and Ann his wife, rec'd by dismission from Difficult. Brother Jackson and Brother Thomas appointed to go to Sister Blincoe and Enquire into the cause of her not attending meeting and make their report to the next meeting. Baptized Nathaniel Barker, Jonathan Cockerill, ___ Barker, Sarah Jenkins, Sarah Love.

23 July 1791: The church satisfyed with the report of Brother Thomas and Brother Jackson concerning sister Blincoe. Baptized Nancy Lay.

20 August 1791: It is unanimously agreed by us that every church has power to call and appoint their own ministers. Brothers Coleman Brown, Benjamin Cockrill, John Evans, Moses Thomas, appointed as messengers to the Ensuing Association.

21 September 1791: Brother John Evans permitted to carry on meeting and to exort among his brethren.

October 1791: Brothers Coleman Brown, Benj. Cockrill join with messengers of Bull Run to go to Little River to consult on business. Brother John ___, and wife, and Brother Leroy Vaughan to have letters of dismission.

21 December 1791: Thomas Harris excommunicated for repeatedly getting drunk, and ill behaviour. Church to pay Brother Cockerill fourteen shillings for his and Brother Evans expences at the Association.

24 February 1792: Brother Riley is dead. It is agreed that each member shall pay to the support of the minister and for other uses according to their ability.

23 March 1792: Moses Thomas' Judah is suspended from communion for telling an untruth. Brothers Coleman Brown and Moses Thomas apppointed messengers to Bull Run next meeting.

26th May 1792: Brother S. Lay chose for a Deacon. Brother John Evans restored as Elder, Sarah Love dismist to apply to the clerk.

22 June 1792: ... any person known and distinguished by the name of James Hutchisons ... Baptized Thompson Kitchen and Brother Lay's Will.

July 1792: Baptized Hepsiba Turley, ... , Mr. Summers' Victory. Appoint Brothers Brown, Evans and Moses Thomas to attend the Association. Brother Brown to write the letter. Our day of church business altered to Thursday before the third Sabbath in each month.

13 September 1792: Brother Cooney appointed to give Sister Gardner notice to attend our next day of business. Brother Robt. Jackson appointed to give Brother Charles Helm notice to attend our next day of business.

18 October 1792: It is ordered that Brother John Harris have a dismission when he applys for it. Brother John Evans and Brother Benj. Cockrill are directed to attend at Bull Run the next day of business.

15 November 1792: Brother Robt. Jackson is appointed to speak to Brother Helm to attend our next day of business. Sister Talbert is granted a dismission by applying to the clerk. Brother Cooney suspended from communion for fighting. Brother Brown, Brother Evans, and Brother Cockerill to meet at Brother Major's next Wednesday.

13 Dec 1792: Resolved that every male member that do not attend the day of business, shall give satisfaction to the church, or they shall not commune before they do so.

17 January 1793: Brother James Cooney is restored to fellowship. Brother Moses Thomas is to give Brother Helm notice to attend the next day of bussiness.

March 1793: Bayley, Hannah Harden, John Evans, and Benj. Cockrill to attend at Difficult's meeting house the Friday before the first Lord's day in April to endeavour to settle aggrevances in that church.

18 April 1793: After having examined into the accusation brought against Mr. Summers' Judah and finding her guilty of the crime laid to her charge which was having a base born child the church excommunicated her.

July 1793: We have examined into the matter between Moses Thomas and John Turley and the voice of the the church is that Moses Thomas should be admonished for some hard speeches he made against sd. Turley which he Rec'd in love. We excommunicated Charles Helm for marrying a second wife in his first wife's lifetime. We appoint Brother Brown, Brother Stephen Lay, and Brother Moses Thomas messengers to the insuing Association. Brother Brown appointed to write the association letter.

17 October 1793: Brother Nicholas and his wife applied for a dismission and was directed to the clerk for the same.

14th November 1793: Sister Turley applied for a dismission and was directed to the clerk for to get it. Brother Jackson entered a complaint against Brother Thomas respecting a difference between sd. Thomas and Turley and the church are agreed to let it lay over till next meeting.

January 1794: The church is satisfied with Brother Thomases acknowledgement.

17 April 1794: Brother John Evans to have a dismission and directed to Brother Brown to write it.

17 July 1794: Absent James Cooney, Daniel Dunbarr, John Kent, Thadius Dulen. Brother Coleman Brown appointed to write the Association letter. Brother Brown, Brother Thomas and Brother Cockrell appointed as mesengers to the Association. We appoint Robert Jackson and Moses Thomas to attend Brother Jonathan Cockrill and John Kent, and to endeavour to show them their fault.

17 September 1794: Brothers Benj. Cockrill and Stephen Lay to give Brother Jonathan Cockrill and John Kent notice to attend our next day of business. Mr. Temple Smith Gilson is excommunicated. Sister Athey dead. Brother James Cooney is to give Brother Dulen notice to attend our days of business.

16 October 1794: Negroe Judah restored, belonging to Brother Thomas. Sister Cockrill, Brother Thomas and Judah to have dismission. Brother Cockrill to write them. Brother Jonathan Cockrill dead.

18 December 1794: Brother James Cooney appointed Clerk to keep our church book. Mary Reid dismissed. Rec'd Negroe woman belonging to William Brown Carter by recommendation of Brother Fristor from his church.

15 January 1795: Resolved that this church pay our minister Richard Major the sum of fifteen pounds for the year of 1794 to be paid immediately.

12 March 1795: Paid Brother Richard Major eleven pounds three shillings. Received by dismission William McNeily and Sarah McNeily. Sister Whalley dismist.

14 May 1795: Paid seventeen shillings and one pound answered by to Mr. Major. Seventeen shillings deposited in Brother Brown's hands. Resolved that Brother Cockrill be paid two dollars for wine for communion. Resolved that Revd. Richard Majors be paid Twenty pounds for the year 1795 to be paid by our church meeting in Novr.

18 June 1795: Sister Burns is laid under suspension for unjustly accusing Sister Roach or family of changing some Linnon which sd. Roach had to make into a shirt for sd. Burns.

16th July 1795: Sister Burns restored.

17 September 1795: Brother Jackson and Sister Blincoe upon a controversy are not reconciled to one another upon which Sister Blincoe is suspended it being the opinion of the church that she is in the fault. Brother Cockrill is permitted to exhort among his Brethren he being conscientious that it is his duty.

12 November 1795: Sister Burns applyed for a dismission. Ordered that Brother Cockrill write her one. Received four shillings and three pence for Brother Majors which was deposited with the clerk.

17 March 1796: Brother Jackson cite Sister Widow Sally Lane to attend our next day of business to answer a complaint from certain Brethren of New Valley.

15 April 1796: Rec'd by the clerk three pounds twelve shillings which was sent by Brother Cockrill to Brother Majors. Sister Lane cited by Brother Jackson attended and gave general satisfaction. Resolved that Brother Cooney make it known to Brother Thrift that he may make it known to the Brethren of New Valley.

May 1796: Resolved that Sister Widow Lane come before the church respecting some unguarded expressions of hers. Resolved that Brother McNeily cite her to our next day of business. Resolved that we invite Brother Thrift to come as a transient minister and preach when he can make it convenient and that Brother Cooney give him the invitation in behalf of the church. Resolved that we invite Brother Moore to come as a transient minister and preach when he can make it convient and that Brother Brown give him the invitation.

30 July 1796: Resolved that Sister Harding, late Sister Blinco [to attend] to our next day of business or be dealt with. Brother Moore accepted our invitation. Brother Thrift accepted likewise. Brother Jackson appointed with Brother Cooney messengers to the Association. Resolved that Brother Thrift to be paid 12s per day for every day he will preach and has preached, and Brother Moore the same. Resolved that we pay or give Brother Majors 12 pounds for past services. Resolved that the Brethren pay unto the clerk the several quotas annexted to their names for the purpose of paying Brother Thrift and Moore occasionally.

15 September 1796: Sister Widow Sally Lane came forward and the church is satisfied with her acknowledgement respecting some unguarded expressions. Brother Cooney to cite Brother Thaddeus Dulin to attend our Church Meetings. The Brethren requested to cite Brother John Kent to our Church Meeting.

16 November 1796: Brother McNeily to cite sister Blinco to our next day of business or be dealt with. Paid for Brother Moore and Thrift, two pounds five shillings deposited with the clerk. Also two pounds nine and ten pence for Brother Majors deposited with Brother Cockrill.

29 Dec 1796: Resolved that Sister Blinco be publickly excommunicated for disorderly behavior and disobedience to the church. Resolved to call Brother Moore to be our minister.

12 Jan 1797: Brother Moore accepted the call of the church. Our stated day of preaching altered at his request to the first Lord's Day in each month. Resolved that our subscriptions for Brother Majors be put in Brother Cockrilll's hands.

6 Feb. 1797: Paid Brother Cockrill six pounds three shillings for the use of Brother Major. Church in debt to Brother Cooney 7/6 for expenses going to Association. Agreed that Brother Cockrill lay all the papers relating to the business of our meeting house before the church at next meeting so that the ballance due Mr. Weathers Smith for work done on

the same may be assertained. Agreed to receive Dozer Bennitt and Amey his wife by dismission from Upper Carter's Run.

13 April 1797: Brother Stephen Lay paid ___ by subscription. The Brethern agreed to pay the sum stated on the back of Weathers Smith acct. Agreed Brother Brown write to John Kent requesting him to [attend] next church meeting. Agreed that our Church meeting in future be held the Wednesday before the third Sabath in each month.

17 May 1797: Whereas we have received information that a difference now subsists between Dozer Bennit a member of this Church and William Bucher a member of the Church at Difficult. Agreed that Stephen Lay, Nathaniel Barker, and James Cooney be appointed to a committee to meet a delegation from the church at Difficult. Was rejected that Brother Moore sit with the committee. Whereas we have been informed that Sister Harden has lately been all night in ... [illegible] assembly. Agreed Brother Lay give her notice to attend the next church meeting.

15 June 1797: The Brethern appointed to settle the difference between Dozer Bennitt and William Bucher reports their progression that ... that the clerk furnish the Church at Difficult with a copy of their report. Brother Cooney reports that he had paid Brother Thrift the money put into his hands for that purpose. Brother Lay reported that he had spoke to sister Harden and she appeared confest her fault which was satisfactory. Three dollars deposited with the clerk to be by him pd. to Brother Thrift, conveyed through the hands of Brother Thaddeus Dulin to Brother Thrift. The Church appoints Brother Brown Leaor Dulin as messenger to the Association.

11 Octobert 1797: Brother Coleman Brown paid 5 pounds 1/2 his part money due Mr. Weathers Smith. Agreed that Brother John Kent have a dismission. Robert Jackson and Sarah ... [illegible] requests her [attendance] at their next Church meeting.

13 December 1797: Gave Brother Cockrill sixteen dollars and two shillings and a receipt of Mrs. Smith for twenty shillings.

14 March 1798: Agreed to receive Negroes Sezor and Jane his wife into our fellowship by dismition from the Church at Davenports Meeting house, Prince George County. Agreed Sarah Lane has been long under

dealing and no hope of her being reclaimed notwithstanding she has been repeatedly admonished. Agreed that she be excommunicated. Agreed that Brother Coleman Brown be our record clerk and take the book and papers accordingly. Agreed that the committeee appointed to settle the difference between William Bucher and Dozer Bennett enquire into the state of that business as we are informed a reconciliation has taken place.

16 May 1798: The committee appointed to hear the matter depending between Br. Dozer Bennitt and William Boocher reported that an consiliation does not appear likely to take place. Agreed that we invite ... [illegible] to come and be with us at our next meeting to assist in settling the aforesaid dispute.

22 June 1798: The committee appointed to Brother Bennit and Brother Butcher think that the acknowledgment of Brother Bennit is satisfactory and that he ought to be restored to his place. Agreed that Brother Bennit be restored accordingly. Agreed to received Andrew Lane by dismission from the church at Sennica in the state of Maryland subject to any dealings that may be against him the church aforesaid. Cassey Edmonds baptised June 24th.

21 July 1798: A letter prepared to send to the Association brought to the church read and approved of, and Andrew Lane, Dozer Bennit and Robert Jackson are appointed to bear the same.

12 September 1798: Brother Dozer Bennet reported he had advanced 13/6 at the Association which is to be repaid him. Brother Lay reported that the money put into his hands was all spent which was satisfactory.

17 October 1798: Agreed to receive Brother John Waugh by dismission from Bull Run, his wife Judith did in the same dismission to be rec'd when she comes forward. Brother Dooling applied for a dismission which was granted.

November 1798: Brother John Hunt brought a dismission from Bull Run which was rec'd. Brother Lay appointed to notify Brother Andrew Lane to attend our next church meeting to satisfy the church relative to some matters laid to his charge. Rec'd of Robt Jackson one pound ten shillings, Mr. Natl. Fitzhugh and forty shillings Captn. William Lane Senr. their subscription money to Mr. Moore which the clerk rec'd and paid Mr. Moore.

11 Dec 1798: Brother Andrew Lane attended meeting agreeable to request and gave his reason for not attending meeting which now thought reasonable. Agreed that the sum of twenty pounds be raised for the support of Mr. Moore and be paid by the church accordingly. Agreed to postpone meeting of business until the Wednesday before the third Lord's day in March 99.

3 April 1799: A letter from Backlick Creek Church was read and after some consultation had thereon, agreed to refer giving a direct answer thereto at present. Various reports respecting the conduct of Andrew Lane and his habitually neglecting to attend divine worship and the meetings of the Church for the purpose of keeping up and maintaining fellowship. Agreed that unless he appears at our next meeting if in health and give satisfaction for these things that he be excommunicated and that the clerk furnish him with a copy of this minute.

1 May 1799: The clerk gave Andrew Lane notice agreeable to order. Resolved that whereas the aforesaid Andrew Lane has been charged with various disorders, especially respecting drinking to excess, and failing to attend divine worship both for business and solemn worship, keeping a disorderly house, etc. It is agreed that he be publickly excommunicated. Brother Brown moved the consideration of Mrs. Donaldson's case when it was agreed to postpone the subject till our next term.

29 June [1799]: Brother Brown to write an ansr. to the Church at Back Lickrespecting the situation of Mrs. Donaldson. Agreed that Brothers Stephen Lay, Coleman Brown, Benjamin Cockrill, Robert Jackson or any two of them be our messengers to the Depending Association, and Brother Brown do write the letter. Agreed that Coleman Brown write to the Church at Occoquan respecting the situation of John Kent.

11 September 1799: We rec'd a letter from Occoquan Church in ansr to a letter we sent them respecting John Kent. They inform us that he has never offered to join them and that his life and conduct is not consistant with the gospel.

13 November 1799: Brother Cockrill informed the Church that he had given John Kent notice to attend which he failed to do. Agreed that he be excommunicated. Agreed that Brother Brown and Brother Cockrill give dismission to such persons who may be in good standing that may apply for that purpose. Agreed to adjourn till the Wednesday before the third Lord's day in March unless we meet by special call.

12 Mar 1800: Brother Brown informed the Church that he had given Eleanor Riddle, formerly Hutchison, a dismission agreeable to order and Brother Cockerill informed that he had given Sister Barbary Sands a dismission. Also it appears from papers now in hand that Brother Moore rec'd for the year 1797 the sum of fifteen pounds, eighteen shillings, and for the year 1798 the sum of eighteen pounds and two shillings.

16 April 1800: Agreed to pay the Deacons a/c which ... [illegible] Brethern to come prepared to pay the ... [illegible] of the next meeting.

14 May 1800: Sundry resolutions drawn up by the Difficult Church was presented by James Marshall, George Kilgore, and Jeremiah Moore their Minister, stating that the Church had resolved to unite with us agreeable to the statement contained in the resolutions aforesaid. After considering the circumstances it is agreed to receive them and that the resolutions together with the names of the members be recorded in this church book. Settled the Deacons a/c and find him indebt one shilling and nine pence half penny. It appears that our church covenant has never been recorded. Agreed that the clerk record it now in the front of our record book.

At a church meeting held at Difficult April 18, 1800: Whereas it appears that we have long been greatly on the decline as to our numbers and strength and divine providence having lately removed from us several of our respectable members so that we are now reduced to two male members beside our stated minister and several other reasons. Considering with the weakness of our number seems to justify the taking some measure in our present situation to promote the glory of GOD and the mutual comfort of ourselves that Remain. Resolved therefore that we unite with the Church of Fryingpan Spring, as the most eligible method to obtain the above valuable ends. But the union contemplated when carried into effect shall not operate against our withdrawing from the Church aforesaid as a body at any time when the same may be judged expedient, or any individuals from obtaining dismissions agreeable to the general rules adapted by the Baptist Society in this case made and provided. Resolved 2nd that while we remain united with the Church aforesaid we will submit to the covenants and discipline of the ... [illegible] that our names be enrolled in their church book for this purpose. Resolved that Brother George Kilgore and James Marshall, together with our Brother Jeremiah Moore present the resolutions to the Church aforesaid, and act in our behalf. Resolved that these resolutions be fully recorded in our Church book and also in the Church book of the aforesaid Church of Fryingpan Spring. Resolved that our Church Records be lodged in the hands of Brother George Kilgore till called for and in case of his Death, in the time of our continuing in Union with the Church aforesaid that in that case they be lodged in the hands of Jeremiah Moore or any where else as the members of the present church of Difficult or a majority of them which may at that time be in this part of the world shall direct.Names of the members come from Difficult Church: Jeremiah Moore, James Marshall, George Kilgore, Lydda Moore, Rennie Williams (dismist 9 March 1803) Mary Dowel, Keron Smith, Susanna Kidwel, Martha Dickey, Milley Howel, Betsey Foreman, Mary Gardner, Mary Money, Sarah Littimore, Martina Kilgore, Jerusha Barker, Elizabeth Cummings, Negroe Fillis, Jeremiah Moore, Rachel Smith (dismissed 9 March 1803), Elinor King Clark.

June 1800: Agreed Brother Cockerill and B. Thompson Kitchen speak to the trustees appointed to oversee the repairs of the meeting house and request them to push the undertakers to finish the work agreeable to contract. Agreed that Brothers Jermiah Moore, George Kilgore, Stephen Lay, and Coleman Brown be our messingers to the depending association and that Brother Moore write our letter.

17 September 1800: Brother James Fox, lately a member of Difficult Church having given the members of this church satisfaction is therefore admitted to membership with the other members of that church.

[*The following month's notes were too faint to read.*]

KETOCTIN BAPTIST CHURCH

Aug 3, 1776: Rev. John Marks; Elders, Deacons and Members present for the whole has concluded and ordered that William Moxley, James Loyd and his wife, Ruth Loyd, Ezebel Wilson, Ester Bexley, Mary Lewis, John Hail and his wife, have absented themselves unbecoming the Gospel of Christ from amongst us that they being discontinued as members of this church unless they return and make a suitable acknowledgment to the Church for the offense. Likewise ordered that Thos. Humphrey and Timothy Hickson are appointed to go to the yearly meeting.

Subscribers of the Covenant: Michael Summars, John Mark and wife, Henery Oxley, Timothy Hickson and his wife, Joseph Cothwell(?), Jenkin Philips and his wife, Rachel Ozben, Sarah Ozben, Rebeckony White, Morry Ozben, Thos. Humphrey and wife, Elias James and wife, Benjamin Davis, Robt. Maccoly and wife, Wm. Bor... and wife, Peter Romine and wife, George Levil(?) and wife, Sarah Russel, Abel Morgan, Thomas West, John Williams, Elizabeth Amos, Elizabeth Bartan, Pathia Milnor, John Summers and wife, Jemime Sumers, Samuel Hill, Hannah Morland, Joseph Powel, Elizabeth Carter, Martha James, Mary Keney.
Jemimah ... excommunicated.

June 2, 1777
Abel Morgan suspended. Received by letter, Cravin Payton and wife.

1778Anne James excommunicated. Letter of recommendation for Elizabeth Carter.

April 4, 1779
Letter of dismission for Samuel Hill and a letter for Rachel Orsburn. A difference has arisen between Elias James and Daniel James.
Letter of dismission for Pethia Milnor.

Aug 4, 1781
Abe Morgan received.

May 4, 1782
Subscribers of the covenant: John Marks, Peeter Romine, Jenken Phillips, George Lewis, Benjamin Davis, William Hutchison, Thomas Humphry, Joseph Drake, John Williams, Timothy Hixon, Joseph Caldwell, William

Borrum, Robert McColoch, Abel Morgan, John Sumers, Joseph Powel, Thomas West, David Thomas and Ruth his wife, joined this church.

May 5, 1798
[*Pages are torn around the edges*]
Joined this church - John Worford and Benjamin Hesket, Mary ..., Uriah ..., Sarah ..., Mary ..., Sarah R..., Deborah ..., Hester Ph..., Caterin Lewis, Rebecka White, Rachel Hixon, Ann Payton, Elizabeth Sumers, Mary McColoch, Elizabeth Am..., Elizabeth Barton, Abigail Romine, Martha James, Mary McKeney, Sarah Hutchison, Pethia Milnor, Elizabeth Carter, Sarah Roberts, Mary Worford, Caterin Hesket, Elizabeth Palm..., Ann Vickers.

Sep 3, 1784
Mrs. Ann Payton excommunicated.

Aug 6, 1786
Letter of dismission for Thomas West.

... 1789
Received Elenor Craven by letter.

1789
Wm. Skott received.

June 4, 1791
Received Charles Lee and Fanny Currell.
Baptized Ann Grant, Ava(?) Morehead, Jane Worner, Peter Levant, Martha Currey. Received Negro Cate.

July 1792
Agreed that Mary Humphrey was clear of any charge that Mr. Fox laid against her. To visit Alderson Weeks regarding his conduct.

Aug 1794
Letter for Sister Baldwin. Received Mary Lewis by baptism. Ann Vickers received.

July 1796. Received Sarah Roberts. Letter of dismission to Rachel Moffit.

Excommunicated Robert McColoch (for absence from meetings).

Nov 4, 1797
Received Mary Worford by baptism.

Feb 1798
Received John Worford.

June 2, 1798
Received by baptism Benjamin Hesket and wife Caterin, Elizabeth Hudon (Heedon?).
Letter of dismission to Sister Morehead.

May 3, 1800
John Hutchison received.

NORTH FORK PRIMITIVE BAPTIST CHURCH
1784 - 1800

13 Aug 1785. James Weeks and his wife (Elizabeth) received by letter. Black Jacob received by letter. Thomas Garrett to speak to Samuel Guy to attend meeting.

12 Nov 1785. John Garret to act as deacon, and James Weeks as elder on trial.

11 Feb 1786. Samuel Guy acknowledged his fault.

11 Aug 1786. Complaint against Margaret Ringo concerning a report against Benjamin Davis; she is censured.

12 May 1787. Thomas Garrett and Joseph Moxley to visit Margaret Ringo.

4 Aug 1787. Margaret Ringo is restored.

10 Nov 1787. Sister Mary Riddle and Sister Carngiver(?) request letters of dismission.

4 July 1788. Mary Guy [wife of Samuel Guy] gives satisfaction.

30 Jan 1789. Edward O'Neal and his wife Susan applied for a letter of dismission. Granted. Complaint against John Griffith for adultery.

28? Feb 1789. John Griffith excommunicated. Samuel Guy restored.

31 July 1789. An association letter to be written and Alderson Weeks and Thomas Garrett to bear it.

30 July 1790. Margaret Ringo is charged with bearing a false report respecting the character of Sister Kerick. Margaret Ringo excommunicated.

10 Aug 1792. Joseph Moxley is charged with departing from the faith.

June 1793. Josiah Harbert charged with killing a hog, property of Thomas Thomson, which he denies. Benjamin Davis and John Garrett to make inquiry. A meeting is scheduled at Peter Harbour's.

10 Aug 1793. Meeting regarding Harbert and Thomson is attended by Ritchard Mager and William Thrift. Hobert (Harbert) to be read out at the next meeting.

25 April 1795. Representatives from Little River and Buck Marsh for rehearing of Josiah Horbert's case.

26 March 1796. Joseph Moxley charged with being heretical in departing from faith. Excluded from amongst us.

23 April 1796. Charged against Honour Lefever.

21 May 1796. Sarah Moxley to be cut off and secluded from being a member.

23 July 1796. A letter to be written to the association. Samuel Guy and Able Garrett appointed as messengers.

25 March 1797. Joseph Longley presented a letter in order to join us by postponed.

6 or 8 June 1797. Mr. Burris gave his experience and was received.

22 June 1797. A dispute between Able Garrett and his brothers John and Joseph Garrett respecting a mill dam. It was the judgement of the church that he should drown no land in the possession of John or Joseph Garret without making all damages good. Able refusing to do so, the Church suspended him for the present.

23 Jun 1798. Sister Moxley restored.

24 Aug 1799. James Weeks and his wife Elizabeth applied for letters of dismission. Granted.

23 Nov 1799. John Garrett and his wife Mary dismissed; also Elloner McCar---; likewise Joseph Longly and John Hutcheson.

23 Aug 1800. Samuel Guy formerly a member of this church is excluded for disorderly walk; Black Jacob is excluded for absenting himself from church. Honour Lefever having given satisfaction is restored.

INDEX

-K-

-L-